FRANCE AGAINST HERSELF

HERBERT LUETHY

FRANCE AGAINST HERSELF

A Perceptive Study of France's Past, Her Politics, and Her Unending Crises

TRANSLATED BY
ERIC MOSBACHER

GREENWOOD PRESS, PUBLISHERS
WESTPORT, CONNECTICUT

Library of Congress Cataloging in Publication Data

Lüthy, Herbert, 1918-
   France against herself.

   Translation of Frankreichs Uhren gehen anders.
   Reprint of the ed. published by Praeger, New York.
   Includes index.
   1. France--Politics and government--1945-1958.
2. France--Economic conditions--1945-   I. Title.
DC401.L812   1974   320.9'44'082   74-20277
ISBN 0-8371-7854-1

First published as *FRANKREICHS UHREN GEHEN ANDERS* by Europa Verlag, Zurich

Copyright 1955 by Frederick A. Praeger, Inc.

All rights reserved

Originally published in 1955 by Frederick A. Praeger, New York

Reprinted with the permission of Praeger Publishers, Inc.

Reprinted in 1974 by Greenwood Press, a division of Williamhouse-Regency Inc.

Library of Congress Catalog Card Number 74-20277

ISBN 0-8371-7854-1

Printed in the United States of America

CONTENTS

PREFACE TO THE SECOND (SWISS) EDITION . . . ix

PART I

THE NATIONAL STRUCTURE 1
  2. THE STATE APPARATUS 5
  3. THE REPUBLIC 28
  4. HUMAN PROPORTION 49
  5. THE STRANGE DEFEAT 76

PART II

BACK TO THE THIRD REPUBLIC 95
  2. FROM "PEOPLE'S DEMOCRACY" TO RESTORATION . 105
  3. YEAR OF DECISION 130
  4. VICTORY OF THE SMALL TOWN 158
  5. ORTHODOXY V. SOCIAL CONSCIENCE . . . 170
  6. HOLIDAY FROM POLITICS 186

PART III

OVERSEAS FRANCE 203
  2. THE TWO FACES OF FRENCH COLONIAL HISTORY . 206
  3. A HUNDRED MILLION FRENCHMEN . . . 217
  4. CATASTROPHE IN THE DISTANCE 225
  5. NORTH AFRICAN BASTION 235
  6. THE ADMINISTRATION AND THE PROTECTORATES . 255

PART IV

THE FULCRUM 283
  2. DOUBLE BOOK-KEEPING 286
  3. ROCK OF SISYPHUS 316
  4. WAY TO EUROPE AND BACK 335
      Power Politics in a False Equilibrium . . 336
      Europe, Made in U.S.A. 352
      L'Europe Cordiale 359
      "Little Europe" 375
      Hesitation on the Brink 395
  5. *La France, la France seule* 424

EPILOGUE 449

INDEX 471

Ce n'est pas servir la France que de répéter à tort et à travers qu'elle se porte bien, qu'elle ne s'est jamais mieux portée. . . . Ah! des millions et des millions d'hommes se fichent absolument d'apprendre que nous désespérons pas de nous-mêmes; ce qu'ils souhaitent, c'est de savoir s'ils peuvent espérer en nous. Ils n'ont cure de notre optimisme. Notre optimisme ne les rassure nullement, bien au contraire. Notre optimisme leur fait froid dans le dos.

GEORGES BERNANOS
La liberté pour quoi faire?

PREFACE TO THE SECOND [SWISS] EDITION

EVERY BOOK, particularly of course every political book, bears the imprint of the time when it was written. This is not just because the chronicle of recorded events necessarily does not extend beyond that time, and because the facts and figures reflect the state of current knowledge and are necessarily always a few months in arrears. If this were a mere chronicle of events or a reference book, these things could be rectified. But a book which tries to give a total picture must either be rewritten every year or remain unaltered, with the truth that it possessed for the time when it was written and the truth which was of somewhat longer duration. The march of events continues, and with every step both the past and future look different. Signs of new beginnings which were present fade away, infirmities heal, new forces and new combinations of old forces come into play; yesterday's hopes or anxieties may now be certainties, and promises and threats that loomed on the horizon may have vanished and passed into oblivion. It is better to admit in advance that, in spite of all efforts at objectivity, emotions such as hope and anxiety, which can never be completely impartial, played a part in building up the picture; for the latter is a product, not of an impartial electronic brain, but of someone who was emotionally involved. There can be no contemporary history without such emotional involvement. Only the light of events, which daily transform a bit of open future into the irrevocable past, can show that the picture was neither a wish phantasy nor a caricature.

It is therefore important to date this book.

It was written in the spring and early summer of 1953, and was substantially finished when the great crisis of the summer of that year threw all France's internal and external problems simultaneously into an inextricable tangle and ended in the "great indecision" of the Government of M. Laniel. While the book was still in the press it was possible to insert some summary references to the events of the autumn of that year without retouching the picture as a whole; in any case, as it turned out, there would have been little to add.

This date has a double significance.

In the spring of 1953 France was still under the spell of the last inflationary wave which passed over her after the outbreak of the Korean war. The slightest breath of wind still seemed a threat to the artificial stability that she so painfully preserved, the franc was still in danger, and with the spring there came acute financial and treasury crises which shook Government and Parliament. A year later, after a period of stability and recovery, in the mild climate of a world of relaxed tension which was quietly setting about adapting itself to the uneasy peace of this post-war world and trying to shake off awareness of its danger together with anxiety about it, the French economy has attained an internal equilibrium; a still artificial and fragile equilibrium behind the shelter of protectionism, deficit financing, universal state aid, and foreign support in many open and concealed forms. Nevertheless the equilibrium has been durable enough to yield scope for the forces of recovery and to clear the way for a slow, almost painless, correction of inflationary distortions without interfering with the inherited economic and social structure. The fundamental problems remain, but they have lost their dramatic urgency, and the moment is favourable for bringing long-planned reform into operation under the most favourable conditions—or for enjoying the calm which will last until the next shock.

On the other hand the political crisis of France, her empire, and her world policy, the clouds of which gathered more and more thickly on the horizon in the course of 1953, at last broke out: disaster in Indo-China, unrest and the danger of civil war in North Africa, the crisis of the Atlantic alliance and the policy of European integration, and, indissolubly connected with all these, the crisis of the parliamentary system itself, which had no answer to all these problems other than refusing to commit itself about them. The tragedy of Dien Bien Phu, and the collapse of the desperate game of poker with which M. Bidault when Foreign Minister sought to divert the consequences of this defeat, were a brutal notification of the end of *immobilisme* and the "holiday from politics". The National Assembly, with its back to the wall, was compelled to act, or rather to permit action to be taken; and it greeted with a kind of delighted desperation the liquidator, the miracle man, who was ready to cut all the Gordian knots and rid it within three months of all the unsolved problems which had been accumulating round its neck for many years.

The liquidation is in progress, and its extent will perhaps not be clear for many years. It had long been obvious that it must come. But in the relief bordering upon rejoicing with which it was at first greeted there was not to be detected a new and youthful determination to look reality in the face, but rather something of "that relief which always comes from turning away from a creative task and falling back into the old ruts which still look good enough." Liquidation is a negative thing. Its positive value can appear only in the new beginning for which it opens the way.

This book describes the way that necessarily led to this crisis. During the year that passed after it was written the crisis ripened and eventually broke out, but fundamentally little was changed. There can be no question of correcting the picture then drawn in the light—or rather the twilight—of that crisis: that would be an undertaking with no beginning and no end, and at the same time it would be a falsification. It is for the reader to judge how the analysis of 1953 has stood up to events, and it is for him to put in the past a good deal that yesterday could be said in the present. Only a new epilogue will describe what in the meantime has come to an end and what has begun anew.

PART I

THE NATIONAL STRUCTURE

THIS BOOK is dedicated to contemporary France. But France can never be considered in isolation from the past, which is still the strongest of the forces at work within her. She is more than the sum-total of living Frenchmen, their thoughts, activities and possessions. She lives in her own time, in the rhythm of her own history, which does not quite keep time with the clocks of the twentieth century. The result is that she has got into the bad habit of keeping the world waiting, sometimes to the detriment of both, while she is engaged with things other than those which the world thinks vital. Between the eternal France to whom her poets and all too often her popular orators dedicate a cult and the contemporary, everyday France whose joys and sorrows, crises and moods are reported in the newspapers there lies the France that endures. Reformers and organisers from within and without, neighbours and treaty negotiators, have again and again discovered, often with impatience, the existence of a French personality which clings with the greatest cunning and tenacity to its habits, including its bad habits; and those who study this country more closely, whatever their angle of approach, find themselves continually confronted with this personality, just as in an old house every cupboard, every picture, every piece of furniture, even the shadows and smells, retain the imprint of the character of the generations who have lived in it and passed it on to succeeding generations.

La France est une personne. Michelet's meaningful and meaningless phrase has fascinated all who have sought to interpret her. Personifying nations and cataloguing national characteristics can lead to confusion, illusion, and often disaster, but Michelet's phrase contains a truth. There is an inherent tendency in any community which has attained self-awareness to aspire towards a higher form of itself which it is granted to only a few to attain. For Michelet it was one of France's privileges to be a *personne*; and he added that Germany was a people and England an empire; and once more we feel the attraction and the danger of a phrase which so pregnantly and so ambiguously sums up the historical characteristics of three countries that even after a century it has not become wholly devoid of meaning. What is the personality of France?

No "interpretation" or analysis is to be undertaken here. But some explanation seems to be called for if we too in the course of this essay are sometimes to talk of France, not just as a political or statistical unit, but as a thinking or acting, or even non-acting, unit. True, it is common practice to do so in dealing with other countries besides France. But in the French case we have to do with more than the political fiction which treats nations and countries *en bloc* and moves them about like pawns on a chessboard in diplomacy and war; and more than the dubious allegory of patriotic poets and orators. The French language itself keeps the myth alive. "France" is the name of a living being, a beloved, a queen, a person. *France, la douce France, la France glorieuse, la France meurtrie, la France douloureuse.* The personification which takes place in all national traditions is no poetical artifice, but an ordinary ingredient of everyday speech; the traditional virtuosity with which every French after-dinner speaker is able to play on this chord between the sweets and the coffee is familiar. *La France est une personne.* For every Frenchman France has a face, and always the same face, whether it be that of Jeanne, or Marianne, or the republic of the Arc de Triomphe, and it incorporates many myths; from Barrès's reactionary myth of the "cult of the earth and the dead" to the revolutionary myth, that of France as the revolutionary torchbearer of all mankind. But all these myths have the same name, France. History herself foreshadowed the greater France in the lesser, just as the man is foreshadowed in the child. She grew outwards from her tiny original home, the Île de France, in ever widening concentric circles until she became that greater France whose asymptote seemed to be all mankind; and greater France still bears the name of the area round Paris which gave birth nearly eight hundred years ago to the first and most amiable woman poet of the Middle Ages and gave her the name by which she is known in literary history:

Marie ai nom, si suis de France . . .

There is no question here of race, or of a collective soul. France, if she believes in a soul at all, does not believe in a collective soul, and she does not believe in race, which in this melting-pot of migratory peoples would be even more absurd than elsewhere; or rather she believes in both, but only as the result of history, a by no means blind but uncommonly clear and sensible history, the history of a self-realisation; *i.e.*, in the course of a thousand years she developed a soul and formed many races into a nation, the special, individual character of which is based exclusively on awareness of a common civilisation. As France has pondered, philosophised, and written about herself a great deal—perhaps too much and too exclusively—to say nothing of praising and blaming herself—this awareness of her historical personality is tremendously solid and alive. It was obvious that Michelet should think of his country as a person; every Frenchman does so. France lives in her own myth.

Abstractions can be exhaustively defined, but a personality never; that is the tremendous advantage of the latter. In this respect France evades all definitions. However sharply and clearly defined her outline may seem from a distance, she evades the hands that seek to grasp her. A personality implies in the minds of others a portrait and a life-history, and neither can be more than approximately and provisionally correct, and that only for the moment. A face that was finally fixed would be a death-mask, and a biography that did not end with a question mark against the future would be an obituary notice. A personality incapable of changing and developing and following unforeseen paths is a dead personality. That is the great danger for France today. In spite of all the convulsions to which she has been and still is subject, the great question against the future is whether she is capable of such change and development.

What follows is not intended to be a diagnosis, but an attempt to identify the characteristics of the France of yesterday that survive in the France of today. If in the pages that follow the reader is first confronted with Capets and Bourbons, with mediaeval jurists, and with representatives of the eighteenth-century enlightenment movement and contemporaries of Voltaire, it is not for the sake of historical study, but in order to draw up an inventory of what has survived, and also of what has become ossified, in the France of the present day. These characteristics are not the whole of France; by themselves they would provide only a caricature. But contemporary France still bears their imprint.

§ 2
THE STATE APPARATUS

WHEN the Christians of the west took up arms in the first crusade the fact that the King of France remained at home remained unnoticed, and nobody missed him. In the eleventh century France clothed herself with cathedrals, and the first notes of European poetry were sounded at her chivalrous courts; Norman French kingdoms were set up in England and Sicily; and the flower of the French nobility took up the cross in answer to the call of a French Pope at Clermont and ringed the eastern shore of the Mediterranean with French feudal states. But this tremendous century represented a point in the history of the French monarchy so low that it approximated to zero. No place in the *Gesta Dei per Francos* was found for Philip I, the fourth King of the House of Capet to occupy the throne of the western Franks, and the great events of his century seem to have affected him once only: he exploited the shortage of money of one of his vassals who desired to go to the Holy Land to buy his jurisdiction over Bourges, and thus established a first foothold for the royal dominions south of the Loire.

The clergy, who monopolised the writing of history, covered his reign of half-a-century with obloquy; we see him sitting in his court like a leper, abandoned by his lords and barons, living in open adultery, scorned and excommunicated, perjured towards his vassals, to whom he hired out his services like a mercenary, hawking the episcopal sees that remained to him in shameless simony, a minor brigand who plundered travelling merchants. Apart from the monarch's personal characteristics, the picture presented by his kingdom was pitiful enough. Even within the narrow limits of the royal dominions in the northerly Île de France to which his power and reputation were confined, he was scarcely able to move with safety outside his tiny city of Paris; a fortress or robber baron's castle on the road to Senlis, Orléans or Corbeil was sufficient to hold the King of France in check; and in 1081, when he bestirred himself to undertake the biggest military enterprise of his career, an expedition against the petty lords of Puiset, he suffered a disgraceful defeat outside the gates of Orléans at the hands of a minor vassal. The royal mantle had fallen on the shoulders of a scarecrow.

That, at any rate in so far as they paid him any attention, is how he must have seemed to his contemporaries. But in retrospect this nadir in the history of the French monarchy was the starting-point of an unswerving, rectilinear advance. The greatest historical achievement of this king was that he did not bestir himself. The first Capetians, like the last Carolingians, who had no home in their own country and were often at a loss about how to feed the royal train, had squandered their meagre substance on extravagant and impotent imperial gestures, laying claim to the inheritance of Charlemagne, engaging in magnificent dynastic meetings and alliances and absurd military expeditions to Lorraine and Aachen; and even Philip's father had exchanged diplomatic missions with Byzantium and married the daughter of the Grand Duke of Kiev. Philip was too dull and unimaginative for such flights of fancy; he was content to be a hedgerow king, whose France was not the realm of the Franks, but an area round Paris. He was mean and lazy, and with his resigned withdrawal into his own domains the character of the kingdom began to alter: a more-or-less nomadic monarchy with a retinue of turbulent vassals began to develop into a firmly anchored and organised institution. The court settled down. Paris became and remained the capital, the king's permanent retinue assumed the functions of the royal council, which should in theory have consisted of all the spiritual and temporal lords of the realm, and these functions shrank into the prosaic administration of the royal domains. The royal archives of Philip the Slothful plainly show the depopulation of the court. The chaos of signatures and seals of barons and magnates of the realm accidentally present at court disappears and gradually gives way to those of the great court officials. System is introduced, and in two legal documents at the end of this entirely lustreless reign the signatures of these officials appear alone. A haphazard medley of nobles has given way to a sharply defined body of advisers, much more like a Cabinet. The introduction of this element of permanence was as important an event in the history of the mediaeval state as was the transition to static settlements and agriculture in the history of humanity.

This unpretentious immobility led to nearly all the virtues of stability; henceforward there was a permanent centre of power, and the beginnings of an orderly and permanent administration and a documented legal system with established procedure; and after a few generations the hereditary nature of a Crown which nobody troubled about or contested came also to be accepted as beyond dispute. In its quiet historical backwater the French monarchy assured its own durability by sloth. There was little glamour about the achievements of the Capetians of the concluding period of the High Middle Ages. They waged laborious guerrilla warfare to clear their realms of lawless barons and robber-knights; they confined the unsafe streets of Paris within privileged communes; they established a militia independent of the unreliable feudal levies; they introduced order into their finances; and they carefully registered their legal titles and revenues. But when this monarchy again appeared in history and began pressing its wider claims, long habit had turned all these things into undisputed rights, no other centre of power or administration was conceivable, and the institutions had been created which enabled the royal writ to run.

After this there were periods of marking time, of confusion, and even of retreat; nevertheless developments followed their own inherent law and continued without a break. A century after the impotent reign of Philip the Slothful, his great-grandson Philip II could be given the additional appellation of Augustus without exciting ridicule, and at his court there had plainly crystallised out those institutions whose unremitting and impersonal operation assured the permanence of the state even when the ruler was incapable or took up the cross, as three kings now did in succession; namely the royal council, the present-day successor of which is the Council of State, and the Treasury, which still reigns supreme over the whole state administration. When Philip Augustus set out for the Third Crusade he entrusted the keys of his Treasury and the royal seal, not to a feudal regency council, but to a court official and a council of six citizens of his city of Paris with names as revealing as Theobald the Rich and Ebroin the Money-Changer; and in his will be called on "all the men of Paris" to safeguard his treasure for his son. Most important of all, his will shows that the *baillis* were already fully functioning. These officials remained the most effective instrument of the monarchy until the seventeenth century; their present-day successors are the prefects, the delegates of the central administration who supervise the work of the local authorities, proclaim the king's law monthly within their respective domains, and three times yearly give an account of their stewardship in Paris.

The century-long process of welding France into a state in the modern sense of the word began with the daily guerrilla warfare waged by these officials against all special rights and privileges, their unremitting efforts to widen the area within which all power belonged to the king, their zeal in never allowing a royal claim to drop, even if for the time being they were powerless to enforce it, and their vigour in exploiting every opportunity of establishing a precedent which might one day be used for making good a royal claim; and, while this mole-like labour went on remorselessly in every corner of the country, royal jurists like Fontaine and Beaumanoir transformed *le droit du plus fort* of early feudalism into the rigid, hierarchical, legal framework of the later feudal state. This led irresistibly to the conception that the Crown was the source of all power and privilege and that all land was held directly or indirectly in fee from the king; an imposing idea which overcame the disorders of early feudalism with its own inherent logic and ended by identifying France with the royal demesne. His kingdom might have fallen to pieces, but in gathering the fragments together again and welding them into a whole the king was only "re-entering into his own" and relying on the feudal duties which his vassals had never denied that they owed him. True, before the monarchy could put these legal claims into practice, it had first to establish itself on a firm basis of power and forge suitable instruments with which to exercise it; but the king's rights were "as clear as the day", and it was this that gave his claims priority over all others, and in the long run made the mole-like labour of his officials and jurists irresistible. The most powerful instrument in the century-long process by which France was turned into a nation—far more effective, enduring and irresistible in its effect than warfare, alliances and dynastic politics—was the patient, legalistic labour, concerned here with a right of way, a mill, a castle, an impost, a question of local jurisdiction, and there with a county or a dukedom; and as the country's frontiers, with their complicated and confused layers of legal, administrative and ecclesiastical rights, were in essence no different from those of a baronial demesne, this process of legalistic encroachment began as early as the late Middle Ages to extend beyond the French frontiers, and went on until the *chambres de réunion* of Louis XIV and, with somewhat altered procedure, until modern times. Such is the amazing continuity, undisturbed by wars, upheavals and disasters, which makes French history a process of continual and unswerving growth, like that of a natural organism, comparable neither with the national unity of England, which was established once and for all by a single historical incident, the Norman conquest, and was never challenged again, nor with the Spanish *reconquista,* nor with the national states of Central Europe which were established much later.

It is always a great temptation to project the result of a development back to its beginnings and to find history prescribed in advance on the map without taking into consideration how much the map itself has been transformed by history. The growth of France can be explained by the neat articulation of the French provinces round the nucleus of the Paris basin—the Île de France—or by the existence of a radial river system without high watersheds to act as obstacles to traffic, and her shape can be regarded as having been determined in advance by her "natural frontiers"—the Channel, the Atlantic, the Pyrenees, the Mediterranean, and the chain of the western Alps and the Jura, leaving only one side of an almost regular hexagon open to the north-east; and a contrast can be drawn with Germany, which lacks any natural frontier either to the east or the west and has no natural nucleus to hold it together; and the whole history of the two countries can be deduced from this state of affairs. But that is begging the question. None of these geographical factors had any reality, either in political or economic development or in the heads of the men of the High Middle Ages. Germany became a political unit long before France, and her "open frontiers", which, if anything, made a strong central power all the more vital, provide neither a sufficient explanation for her collapse nor for the tremendous transalpine adventure of the German Holy Roman Empire. The rulers of the Middle Ages had a supreme contempt for geography. The Capetians were not confronted with a predestined French "unity"; for it was they who first created it. The "kingdom" of Aquitaine, the *regnum* of Brittany, the vigorous dukedom of Normandy which continually sent out warlike expeditions in every direction, were independent entities every bit as powerful as the German hereditary dukedoms; and the ancient frontier of the Loire, which was only gradually broken down in the course of centuries of centralisation, divided France into two civilisations, distinct in speech, law, manners, and traditions, which differed at least as much as did north and south Germany. All the events of cultural, religious, and even warlike significance of the High Middle Ages took place independently of the Capetian dynasty. But, as all the paths of French history led eventually into the history of the French monarchy, the history of France has for long been written exclusively as the history of that monarchy; and historians and schoolmasters have thus completed the centralising labour of the jurists and the *baillis*—culminating in the celebrated Senegalese child spelling out the first sentence of its reading book: *"Nos pères li Gaulois . . ."*

The "natural frontiers" of France are nothing but a figment of the jurists, entirely devoid of reality. Centuries of mole-like advance were required of the French monarchy before it could think about, let alone come anywhere within sight of, the Pyrenees, the Mediterranean, the Alps, the Jura, and the Rhine. Until the end of the Middle Ages it was concerned exclusively with its own vassals, and those frontiers never provided it with security. They represented a claim, not a line of defence.

Here too historians and schoolmasters, by projecting the modern conceptions of nations and frontiers back into a past in which they had no meaning, have helped to transform the history of two peoples—Germany and France—into a desperate duel between them, and have seized with astonishing frivolity on every traditional old wives' tale, and every coincidence on the margin of the main stream of history that fitted in with this historical fiction: the notorious "battle of Tolbiac", for instance, which King Clovis probably never fought, but the imaginary date and circumstances of which were learned by heart by generations of schoolchildren; Jacques Bainville used it at the beginning of his *History of Two Peoples,* as it enabled him to represent the Alamanni—*les Allemands*—as Germans, and the barbarian Clovis as the first representative of Christian France; or the obscure family feuds of the last Carolingians, which are represented in certain German history books as "the first battle for the Rhine line", though one has to wait a thousand years for the second; and so on from Bouvines to Waterloo.

It is high time that an end was made on both sides of the Rhine of this sorry kind of history writing, not only because of its mischievousness, but also because of its stupidity, for it has contributed more than anything else to destroying understanding of the real historical nature of Germany and France alike. The Franco-German drama has dominated the recent past of Europe, and it is a matter to which in the course of this book we shall continually revert. It is therefore all the more necessary to state clearly and explicitly that the "duel" between the two nations is no historical necessity, but a mere episode, not yet a hundred years old, in their long history. The period of the formation of the French state was filled, not with national, but with dynastic conflicts of feudal origin. From its earliest beginnings until the fifteenth century the French state was struggling with its unruly vassals of the Anglo-Norman dynasty. From then until the reign of Louis XIV it was struggling to break up the Spanish-Burgundian-Netherlands inheritance which lay round France like a stifling ring—the fact that the Hapsburgs happened to be invested with the German imperial crown, which had degenerated into a mere symbol, was an entirely secondary consideration; and the conception of *la nation* itself, in the sense in which it set out upon its triumphal march with the French Revolution, cannot really be transferred to any other people. It was in reality nothing but a proclamation that France, "the creation of forty kings," had grown up and reached awareness of her own personality. It implied conflict, not with other nations, but with despotism, the transfer of sovereignty from crown to people, the transition from a group of subjects to a group of free citizens whose only distinguishing feature was the possession of liberty. Whatever may have happened in the subsequent quarter-century of revolutionary wars and the subsequent century of nationalism, the deputies of the nation —and with them the "patriots" of all Europe, for whom, as for Thomas Jefferson, France was "every man's second country"—believed at the moment of its ceremonial foundation that they were acting as the representatives of all mankind in setting up, not the French nation, but *la nation* pure and simple, the universal home of all who acknowledged the rights of man.

It is necessary to understand this concept of *la nation* as it was in its state of pristine innocence at birth if one is to appreciate the most fundamental characteristic of French history—namely that France, even when—and, indeed, particularly when—she has identified herself in her greatest moments with Christianity, the west, or humanity as a whole, has been fundamentally concerned only with herself. France has always seen and understood the world only as a projection of herself. The French state was not forged under external pressure, fighting for life behind threatened frontiers; it was not formed of blood and iron, though these things are not lacking in its history. It grew from a small nucleus, following its own laws of development, like a tree. The whole content of French history, from the pitiful initial struggles of the western half of the Frankish Empire to the full development of the French historical personality, consists in the drawing of all possible consequences from the fortunate situation of the Capetian royal domains in the heart of France, the extraction from the disorders of the Middle Ages of that ruthless feudal logic of which the final consequence was absolutism, and the exploitation of all the architectonic possibilities of the country and moulding them into a political system. To visualise the process that took place during the formative years of the French state it is sufficient to compare a map of the Roman period, or of the High Middle Ages, with the map of eighteenth-century France. In the former the great traffic arteries run like lattice work from north to south and east to west, along the Rhine–Rhône line and the rivers flowing to the west, among which the river-crossing at Paris was only a secondary traffic junction indistinguishable from a dozen others; and from this there gradually emerged the familiar spider's web radiating from Paris, where all the threads originate and to which all roads lead. Nature herself in this country assumed a rational form.

All the lines of force in France, in trade, traffic, politics, and things of the mind, ended by arranging themselves round this centre, like iron filings round a magnet. This logical pattern almost inevitably imposed itself on all subsequent developments, which thus made its geometrical rigidity more rigid still. The Revolution and the Empire eliminated the last traces of provincial autonomy and divided France with a ruler into artificial administrative areas with names divested of all historical or affective significance which are not generally used even to describe their inhabitants; the century of the railway accentuated the importance of Paris to such a degree that the way from one provincial town to another is nearly always by way of Paris; and the parliamentary republic made Paris the permanent place of assembly of the nation.

France's inner nature has impressed itself completely, perhaps excessively, upon her outward shape, and the complete immanence of her history represents perhaps her greatest danger today. The point that must be emphasised is the indisputable harmony of the entity that has thus arisen. Just as French history is characterised by the inevitability of an organic process, so does its result possess the convincing finality of a product of nature, in which state and nation, freedom and rigidity, mathematical accuracy and geological chance are reconciled. In a typical French landscape country and buildings form an inseparable whole, making one forget that one is confronted by the work of man. Similarly, when confronted with the over-all picture of France, an almost regular hexagon of coasts and mountain ranges, one tends to forget that it too is a work of man—a landscape planned by Le Nôtre. The secret of both is their durability.

Thus the history of France might be written as the history of an administration; an anonymous, prosaic, tremendously persistent, and in the deepest sense of the word non-political administration. The secret of the continuity of French history lies in this administration, and not in any particular far-sightedness on the part of her rulers and statesmen. It worked pedantically and unimaginatively, by its very nature it always took the long view, and in the long run it always regained what was thrown away or lost by blundering kings or ministers. For in short-sightedness, capriciousness, and frivolity the actions of French kings and their courtiers, and of later statesmen and popular leaders, were often comparable with those of any Balkan state. The spirit of continuity imprinted on French history was not seated on the throne. For centuries opportunities of attaining unity were light-heartedly thrown away by the dynasty, for the sake of setting up a second son, for the sake of a royal whim or love affair, or out of piety towards a feudal world to which the king and his courtiers felt themselves to belong; the dynasty itself created the complications which plunged France into the great historical disasters of the Hundred Years' War and the Burgundian disorders. There were periods, including some of the most idyllic in French history, during which the country was governed with an aristocratic gambler's elegant irresponsibility or a petty lawyer's second-rate slyness; the eighteenth century, for instance, in which the last monarchs of the *ancien régime* squandered an empire between two state bankruptcies, turned the exchequer of what was the richest country in the world into a disreputable gaming house, and sold offices and dignities to the highest bidder; or the Offenbach operetta period of the Second Empire, which had an unhappy ending, however; or the last decades of the Third

Republic, that provincial idyll between two world wars. But even the worst disasters left the foundations intact and the damage done was always temporary; and after a short period of remorse it was always these carefree periods of frivolity which in retrospect were transmogrified into "the good old days."

The recurrent French miracle has been the extraordinary invulnerability of a political organism which has suffered almost unparalleled convulsions. The French state apparatus with its thousand-headed personnel grew immune to the policies of its own controllers; the coach was not capable of being shaken out of the deep ruts of its routine. Forty kings and nearly as many revolutions and *coups d'état* came and went; but since the time of Philip Augustus a growing host of officials, jurists, clerks, and book-keepers has seen to it that no claim has ever been permanently dropped, that no chance has been finally given up for lost, and that no useful initiative has ever been finally abandoned. That is the constant factor in a story the chief surface feature of which is instability.

The continuity assured by this administration is above all that of the administration itself. It has survived all dynasties, revolutions, and catastrophes unscathed. Behind a constantly changing façade of feudalism, absolutism, constitutional monarchy, empires, and a whole series of republics, the great institutions and corporations of this state—and thus the state itself—have remained essentially the same. The *noblesse de robe* of the *ancien régime* and the *grand corps d'état* of the republic are of the same spirit and the same nature. Living images of the crow-like forms whose faces and deportment were immortalised by Daumier, clothed in their ermine robes, still haunt the grey corridors of the Palais de Justice, the old Parliament of royal times, about which there lingers the chill of the tomb. Even to Daumier these men seemed like a relic of the past; and for the layman, that is to say for the ordinary citizen, the law that is expounded here and the processes by which decisions are arrived at are as unfathomable as the astrology of the Chaldaeans or the symbols of the cabbala. The courts grind more slowly and more inscrutably than the mills of God, and sometimes, when there is a *cause célèbre* and a great tournament of legal eloquence takes place, they work in the full glare of publicity, with the result that the great lawyers vie in public esteem with the stars of literature, the stage, and the cinema. But the supreme luminaries who control the state itself, its legislation, its finances, and its personal politics, are totally removed from the eyes of the profane, and no breath of air disturbs the venerable dust of centuries that has gathered about them. The Conseil d'État will unhesitatingly interpret a law newly passed by the National Assembly in the light of decrees or regulations issued by Francis I or Louis XIII, and use the final and authoritative construction thus put upon it to pour back the new wine into the old bottles of an archaic jurisprudence. Before the last war the Cour des Comptes still used the antiquated accounting system, the same quill pens, and the same bewildering piles of ledgers that were used in the Chambre des Comptes of the last Capetians. The existence of the typewriter and the calculating machine was only discovered after the second world war.

In these sanctuaries of tradition there is much that is old and antiquated: the paper, the handwriting, the forms and precedents, the methods, the laws and regulations. True, in the course of time new laws, precedents, and regulations have been created, but none has ever been repealed, with the result that every reform, every new law, disappears into the jungle of existing laws and is swallowed up like a drop in the ocean of tradition. The very irrationality and obscurity of the processes and procedures have erected an insurmountable wall round the higher ranks of officials who alone can find their way about the labyrinth and are therefore irreplaceable; and their authority and prestige are based, not on the present or the future, but on the past. Moreover, the hereditary spirit of this high officialdom has again and again produced a *grand commis* of the type of Colbert, the great servant of the Crown and the *raison d'état*, infinitely superior to all politicians in his gravity and knowledge. But, as the Crown disappeared long ago, and as the Republic has seldom succeeded even in being taken seriously by its *grands commis,* the latter generally decide according to their own conscience and their own standards what is required in the national interest, and in their own manner and tradition, which is based nearly always on the spirit of the past.

Every new régime—and in the course of two centuries France has had more than a dozen new régimes—has come into power with a revolutionary programme of widespread state, administrative and judicial reforms, but not one of them has ever succeeded in bringing about more than a change of names and a change of personnel. After all the great upheavals, during the early years of struggle of the Third Republic and in the turbulent beginnings of the Fourth, all the newcomers who were introduced into these fraternities with a view to breathing a new spirit into them were rapidly either assimilated or eliminated; and the great central organs of the administration, the Council of State, the Inspectorate of Taxes, and the judicature, used these very periods to put their rights to irremovability and self-recruitment on an impregnable basis, either *de facto* or by entry in the statute book, and subsequently defended these rights against encroachment by any unorthodox alien body.

They constitute a supreme and sovereign self-recruiting body, immune from political intervention, responsible to no one outside their own hierarchy, a rock against which all political storms beat ineffectively and in vain; a completely closed mandarin system, even in the social choice it exercises in reproducing itself; its *esprit de corps*, the sense of belonging to a chosen *élite* fostered from childhood in the great boarding schools which prepare pupils for *la carrière*. These have to demonstrate their suitability to be received into the caste in the entry examinations prescribed by the hierarchy, and finally prove their worthiness to belong to it in the course of their novitiate. As the Council of State, in addition to all its other important functions, possesses jurisdiction over every state official, and as no Government or Minister is in a position without its approval to appoint, retire, or promote out of turn any prefect or financial agent, or even the chief of his own department or private office, the spirit of this gerontocracy has become the spirit of the French state itself The brief life of parliamentary Governments counts for little in comparison with this absolute permanence.

Here we have one of those characteristics of France which continually remind one of China of the past. It would not be far wrong to take its fundamental pattern to be that of the Académie Française, whose forty immortals, co-opted from the universities, the generals, the judicature, the *salons,* and the world of diplomacy, have for three hundred years been working on a French dictionary, and have again and again laid down a hundred years late how an educated Frenchman should and should not express himself. All the great organs of the state have emulated this pattern: the judicial apparatus, the police, the colonial administration, the foreign service, and the army; and if the last two did not entirely succeed in this aspiration—though in 1940 France experienced with painful surprise how close her general staff had come to the Académie Française pattern—it was only because limits were set to the cult of tradition by collision with a disrespectful environment.

It can be said, paradoxically enough, that in France politics and the state machine function in two watertight compartments. For generations France has been searching for a workable system of government without finding it; and the observer who looks only at the political façade, the Government, Parliament, and the parties, asks in bewilderment how a country can possibly manage to survive in such a condition, let alone preserve an international status. Is not the answer that it is because the administration works so well—or rather, whether it works well or not, that it works with such consummate smoothness—that the only field left to the politicians is that of ideology? If one looks at a constitutional handbook one will find no mention of, or at most a casual footnote devoted to, any of the great institutions on which the permanence of the state depends. Instead one finds a description of the lucid and logical theory according to which all sovereignty derives from the people, which makes known its will by its choice of deputies and senators; Parliament, wisely divided into Assembly and Senate, the engine and the brake, gives expression to the people's will in laws, resolutions, and orders of the day; and the Government responsible to it transforms these into orders to the civil service, which as a purely executive organ with no will of its own is worthy of no further comment. In the simplified form of this which in practice has been more or less fully adopted by each of the four French republics, France has been governed by an assembly of six hundred elected representatives of the people who entrust the conduct of affairs to a continually changing executive committee chosen from among themselves. But no mention is made of the Ministries which remain after the Minister of a day has departed. No mention is made of the Council of State which, because of its jurisdiction over the administrative machine, rules supreme over the instruments of state power, is indispensable to an executive incapable of carrying out its will without it, interprets according to its own code the true content of laws passed by Parliament or quietly buries them, and as the universal adviser of Governments usually gets its own way even in the formulation of Government policy, because it has authority and permanence, and the Government has not. No mention is made of the general staff of the financial administration, which is able to modify and interpret the budget passed by Parliament as autocratically as the Council of State is able to modify and interpret its laws, and by its control over state revenue and expenditure is able to exercise a decisive influence over the life and death of Governments. The only one of these institutions to find a modest place in the constitutional manuals is the independent and irremovable judiciary; room is found for it because it illustrates the otherwise completely forgotten principle of the separation of powers. But nothing is said about the powers of the Cour de Cassation, which lays down the content of civil law in as final and absolute a fashion as the Council of State lays down the content of public law; or about the disciplinary power it exercised until 1946 over the career of judges and officials of the judicial administration. For not one of these institutions is derived "from the people." They represent the state apparatus of the absolute monarchy, perfected and brought to its logical conclusion under the First Empire. When the crowned heads fell, the real sovereignty was transferred to this apparatus. But it works in the background, unobtrusively, anonymously, remote from all publicity and almost in secret; a monarch, a monarchy whose only surviving driving principle is routine. It is not so much a state within a state as the real state behind the façade of the democratic state.

This administration has impressed its characteristics upon the whole structure of the country. No move takes place in public life that escapes its supervision. No local council can have a water pipe laid, a street paved, or a school roof repaired without the official stamp and endorsement of the authorities at six levels of the central administration, from the sub-prefect to the officials of the Finance Ministry in Paris. With the best will in the world this process takes a year, and if an objection is made anywhere along the line it may never be completed at all. A whole body of law created by the Council of State has systematically deprived local councils of the slightest initiative in the economic, social, and public health fields, even in such matters as public baths or refuse collection. To an inconceivable degree Empire and Republic have completed the work of the monarchy and extinguished all trace of autonomy and independence in communes and departments. The first and most important answer to the question of who rules France must be that it is ruled by ninety agents of the Ministry of the Interior—not of the Minister of the Interior, who has long since lost the power of dismissing his prefects, and can at most promote them.

The empty and impoverished life of most French villages and provincial towns, whose monuments bear witness to a former vitality, is the result of this centralism. Not only was the road and railway map of France laid out like a spider's web radiating from Paris, but everything that used the web, men, goods, and energy, was caught up in it. All France was laid waste and her vital energy sucked into Paris.

The national economy itself developed according to the lines of force of the administration. A number of activities, such as mining and shipping, are of course bound to their localities, and some peripheral areas have maintained their economic autonomy, thanks to their distance from the capital and their contacts with the outside world. But there is scarcely a big concern that does not feel compelled to maintain its head office at great expense in Paris, the place of prestige, of useful contacts and combinations, and at the same time the only place where it is possible to minimise the fearful but inevitable bureaucratic complications by direct contact with the Ministries. Even the agricultural economy of this peasant country is directed towards Paris, or alternatively, where no contact with the "Paris network" has been established, has become ossified into a closed, archaic, village economy. More than half the French national income is concentrated in nine departments, or one-tenth of the country, with the Paris region as its centre of gravity; for more than a century these same nine departments have accounted for the whole of the increase in the French population, including immigrants, while since the middle of the nineteenth century a slow process of depopulation has been taking place in the remaining nine-tenths of the country; a process for which Ireland provides the only parallel. The circulatory system regulated from the heart at Paris reaches the whole country only in its most attenuated administrative form. One-half of France is in practice excluded from the modern economy and makes no appearance in the contemporary market either as producer or consumer. France, peasant France, has no organised provincial markets at all. Her agricultural market—another and a still more astonishing monument to the endurance of administrative shrines hallowed by tradition—is the Paris Halles, the picturesque, hopelessly overcrowded and overflowing "belly of Paris," bursting at all its seams, which has become the belly of the whole country. Its very situation is the most unsuitable that could be imagined: in the middle of a great city, with no direct access to a railway, hemmed in between narrow streets which are jammed with carts and lorries which disorganise the Paris traffic, which would be sufficiently chaotic without them. But the place is sacrosanct. Here was the market of the small Capetian city of the twelfth century, and here Napoleon III built the present Halles, which, like so many French antiquities, were a pioneering technical marvel of their time, a marvel of the first period of construction in iron. But in the century since the Second Empire, the century of giant strides in trade, of the capital's tremendous growth, and of the acquisition of a whole empire, it has been possible to expand Napoleon III's lay-out by exactly one-fifth, for no more space was available. What was a great pioneering achievement when it was built has become an archaism, an economic absurdity, perhaps the most absurd legacy of centuries of French centralism.

The Paris traffic arteries in a wide area round the Halles are jammed with vehicles taking their mountains of boxes and baskets and carcases to market from the stations and the slaughter-houses; crates of fruit rise in huge piles in all the neighbouring streets; every night a whole quarter of the city is turned into a welter of fish and blood and rotting vegetable refuse; the storage facilities are so inadequate that in the hot months a quarter of the produce goes bad. The cost of transport to the Halles from one of the Paris stations exceeds that from the most distant corner of southern France to Paris; but tomato boxes from Cavaillon, lettuce from Perpignan, cabbage from Brittany, have not just to be sent *via* Paris, but to be put through this incredible bottleneck in the centre of Paris, and to travel perhaps 1,500 miles and undergo five reloadings, from train to barrow and from barrow to lorry, before they get to market, from where they have to make their way back in the same way by another train, with all the wear and tear of the market behind them, only to end up at last in Bordeaux or Lille, perhaps only a few hundred miles from their place of origin.

There can be no serious checking of the deals and transactions that take place in the nightly pandemonium of the Halles, and no reliable figures can be given, but it is usually estimated that from one-third to a half of the produce sent to Paris from the provinces goes back to them, burdened with the huge costs of unnecessary handling and middlemen's profits incurred at every stage. It is here that there arises the incredible gap between the excessively low prices paid to the French producer and the excessively high prices paid by the French consumer. But the impregnable fortress of the Halles has rebuffed every effort at rationalisation, every attempt to institute a reasonable price policy, even every attempt to investigate the process by which prices are actually arrived at. In the autumn of 1952 an attempt was made to remove at any rate a part of the business of the Halles to spacious modern premises at the Gare d'Austerlitz, where the costs and amount of labour involved would have been reduced by half, but it was strangled with the aid of ancient legal texts by the Paris municipal council, and the seven-hundred-year-old monopoly of the Halles was legally confirmed. For the Halles are not just a place of business—their absurdity and their economic perniciousness have been undisputed for many years—they are a hallowed institution. Their privilege of holding France to ransom is bound up with this irrational site; for undisputed claims have existed for generations to every hole and corner of this cramped and terrifying labyrinth, to every table, every bench, every locker, every square yard of pavement on which a crate can be unloaded; and the oligarchy of dealers, concessionnaires, agents, middlemen, valuers, forwarding agents, etc., etc., each one of whom takes toll for the totally unnecessary ministrations which he is entitled by law and tradition to exercise, are protected by sheer lack of space from any attempt to break into their monopoly, for they are packed like sardines in a tin; and the supreme council of this hierarchy, the irremovable, irresponsible, and immortal *mandataires des Halles,* are in every respect a *corps d'état,* able to defy any Minister and any Parliament.

The Paris monopoly of the market applies to things of the mind just as much as it does to cauliflowers. Paris has turned the rest of France into an intellectual desert. The incessant, extravagant firework display which day after day and night after night arises from five dozen theatres, a hundred exhibitions, galleries, concerts, lectures, dress shows, literary circles, dinners, receptions, cafés, *salons,* first nights, scandals, controversies, and hoaxes, has its obverse side: the deadly boredom and leaden conformity of the provincial town, where nothing ever happens, or at most an occasional accident or crime, where intellectual life, except for the fleeting visit of an occasional travelling lecturer or second-rate theatrical company from Paris, is confined to the gossip of the Café de Commerce, and every young person's supreme ambition is to go to Paris. In intellectual life the Empire ruthlessly completed the process which centuries of monarchical policy, the building up of the splendour of the court and of the capital for prestige purposes, had only begun; and the republic loyally and zealously preserved the Napoleonic heritage. The whole intellectual life of France was centralised in Paris, and the state assumed responsibility for the whole education system, for universities, academies, art schools, conservatoires, schools of all levels, museums, libraries, records and archives, state and subsidised theatres, opera houses and orchestras, together with all the treasures and properties associated with them, the whole of their practising, technical, and teaching personnel from professor of philosophy to *balletteuse*, and all the titles, honours, and offices of official cultural activity. Cultural activity itself became an object of central administration, and practically the whole of French intellectual life takes place within its direct or indirect sphere of influence, whether in conformity or in opposition—for opposition itself is often only the reverse side of this "official culture"—and it is all concentrated into the narrowest possible space and takes place in an area nearly as tightly packed as the Paris Halles themselves.

All the parts of this well-balanced edifice prop and support each other. The absolutist state formed France in its own image, and the imprint its administrative structure left on the character of the French bourgeoisie was perhaps greater than the changes which have taken place in the latter in the century-and-a-half since the Revolution. For the *tiers état*, which in 1789 proclaimed that it represented the nation, was no assembly of merchants or capitalists; still less was it an assembly of peasants and artisans. It was almost exclusively an assembly of lawyers, judges, advocates, notaries, members of courts and councils of every kind, who had been formed and grown great in the monstrous and fantastic apparatus of justice established under the French monarchy, the clumsy machinery of which the *ancien régime* had complicated to the point of absurdity by the creation of parasitic appointments and offices, the sale of which had become its readiest method of raising funds. During two hundred years of absolutism nearly all the great names of French literature, from Corneille, Pascal, and Racine to Voltaire and the encyclopaedists, and nearly all the opposition trends from Jansenism to the enlightenment movement, arose from the *gens de robe*, that social group upon whom a deep unity had been imposed by the peculiarities of the uncomfortable position which it occupied between the nobility and the people. It was this group, together with a few renegade owners of church offices given away by the state, which provided practically the whole of the political personnel of the Revolution. The taking over of the state by the officials of the state apparatus was as fundamental an aspect of the Revolution as the taking over of the land by the peasants who tilled it. Just as the absolutist administration of the *ancien régime* created the bourgeoisie as a political class, so did the *ancien régime* in its other aspect as a mercantilist state create the bourgeoisie as a social class. For the great fortunes and the family dynasties which are so important in French economic development arose from the exercise of state functions or privileges granted by the state, from the royal manufactures or monopolies, from the farming out of taxes, from army contracts and other functions exercised on behalf of the state, but above all from the great financial operations undertaken on behalf of the court which in the eighteenth century developed into a state-organised looting of the national wealth.

It was the tradition of this mercantilist state, which gave official protection to every important form of economic activity and generally clothed it with the public sanction of official rank and dignity, which permitted so little enterprise, so little "capitalist spirit", to develop in France; and this tradition survived with astonishing persistence both Revolution and Empire, and even a few incursions of liberalism. Just as the *ancien régime* rewarded its servants with state and church offices, so did the French nineteenth-century state, under its successive monarchies and republics, reward its notables by granting them positions of economic power to which they were required to bring neither capital nor technical knowledge—just as it rewarded its humbler servants by granting them tobacconists' shops under the national tobacco monopoly. The Bank of France, the central financial institution of the state, which from its foundation to 1936 was the chief bastion of all the big private financial groups; the big mining concerns; heavy industry; the railways; the electricity industry; the colonial economy; all the strongholds of French economic life, were in the main built up, not with private capital and at private risk, but on a foundation of state concessions, with capital provided by the state, with guarantees which removed the element of risk, with the aid of public subsidies, and with deficits covered from public funds. Many of the family dynasties which have established themselves in these enterprises are directly descended from members of the revolutionary assemblies or from Napoleonic senators recruited from these; in these cases political influence was simply transformed into economic power. Looked at in this light, the acts of nationalisation carried out by the Popular Front and the Fourth Republic in the concessionary sector of the national economy were far less revolutionary in character than the controversies they let loose would have led one to suppose; and the only reason why it is so easy to discredit the performance of the industries concerned is that no one seems to remember the state of decay, bureaucratic sclerosis, and chronic deficit borne by public funds in which they were left by their private beneficiaries. Nationalisation was not unlike a reclamation of parts of the state domain which had been let out in fee, and the justification for it was practically the same as that with which the mediaeval feudal state justified such reclamations, namely disloyalty. However, this new demarcation of the fluid frontier between publicly and privately administered economic domains altered the general character of the French economy to a remarkably small extent.

From the management of the great state corporations, the public services and state monopolies at the summit, the concessionary and subsidised undertakings, and the great private concerns whose boards of directors traditionally attribute important national functions to themselves and appoint state councillors and inspectors of finance to positions of control, the pyramid broadens out step by step down to the teeming mass of little shops and factories. They are all imbued with the same spirit and the same mercantilist tradition, sheltered by the same legislation and legal tradition, which regards every *situation acquise* as worthy of protection and every *fonds de commerce* as a claim to a hereditary income; and they are all fenced round with the same protectionism, which has turned the whole of France into an artificial economic nature preserve, isolated from winds and storm. Nowhere is the economic man of liberal theory so little at home as in France, and nowhere has the cold accountancy of economic laws been so successfully eliminated. In the preponderance of the administrative function over that of the *entrepreneur*, of group solidarity over the principle of competition, of tradition over initiative, and in the loyalty to established routine and the respect for all *situations acquises* regarded as positions of licensed privilege, the way of life of an ancient state has survived in that of contemporary France.

§ 3

THE REPUBLIC

Is this country, so adult in the deepest sense of the word, the real France? The world oscillates in remarkable fashion between thinking of her as eternally the same and as eternally unstable. Both in turn rouse admiration and exasperation, and the two are in fact inseparable.

The picture of her fundamentally so harmonious and rectilinear past history leading directly to her present contains a great deal of France, but not the whole of her, and above all it omits the sense she has of herself; or rather it provides only the background of the sense she has of herself, the prehistory of her living history, which begins with sudden, tremendous pathos in 1789 and is still as vivid to her as the present day. Her earlier history is a book of legends, starting with yellow, faded, obscure pages on which there appear Vercingetorix and Clovis; Charlemagne, the great forerunner; Hugh Capet, the founder of the line; St. Louis, dispensing justice under his oak-tree; Philip the Handsome; and the horrors of the Tour de Nesle. Then, as if one were turning the pages of a family album, there comes more recognisable, more significant faces: Joan of Arc, the first embodiment of the national consciousness, and her meteoric career from Domrémy by way of Orléans and Reims to the stake at Rouen; Catherine de Medici, that bad fairy out of a story book, and the massacre of St. Bartholomew: the good King Henry IV, who thought Paris well worth a mass and wanted every Frenchman to have a chicken in his pot on Sundays; the *roi soleil,* glittering on his pompous throne, whose glory was celebrated by France and all Europe; and then, in the dim dawn of the coming day, the witty, frivolous, doomed world of Watteau and Marivaux, idling its way carelessly towards the abyss. All these are embodiments of *la personne France,* transfigured by the light of what was to follow. But with the assembly of the States-General at Versailles the present begins, the exciting, controversial present, a continuous and never-ending sequence of dramatic events, in which the people makes its first appearance in the struggle between light and darkness, liberty and tyranny, right and wrong; the people storms the Bastille, puts up barricades, cries "Up!" with this man and "Down!" with that, to the accompaniment of tremendous victories and bloody defeats—July 14th, the Oath of the Tennis Court, the breath-taking series of revolutionary dramas, the Empire, the Hundred Days, Delacroix's goddess of liberty on the barricades of 1830, the February revolution, the June massacre and then the Empire again, the Paris commune, Dreyfus . . .

Since 1789 events have been dated not by centuries, decades, or years, but by dates of the month. These dates are part of every Frenchman's life, and are invoked in every speech and political manifesto without any need to add the year; and anyone who has not grown up in this history and is not as familiar with these dates as he is with the birthdays of his closest relatives is apt to feel lost at a public meeting when he hears "the new feudal lords" being called on to perform their August 4th, or the terrors of Prairial are invoked, or the men of Thermidor or of Fructidor, or the spirit of August 10th, or the murderers of September, or the slaughterers of June; or when the people is called on to defend the republic against a new Brumaire 18th or December 2nd, or May 16th, or February 6th. On such occasions one feels one is among members of a family discussing personal experiences—a family in which no quarrel has been buried for centuries.

For all this is not historical reminiscence—or at any rate was not yesterday—but immediate actuality to which everyone responds. Every one of these battles is still in progress, and the issue is still open; every one of these dates still divides left and right, clerical and anti-clerical, progressive and reactionary, in all their historically determined constellations; and thus a century-and-a-half of history, or at any rate long stretches of that period, are involved in every big contemporary controversy. There is far more behind these phrases than the words of which they are composed. If the republic is declared every few months to be in danger and a call is made to organise its defence, what is referred to is not that form of parliamentary government which—except by a few romantic groups and in a few antiquated aristocratic *salons*—has not been called in question, save by its own impotence, for seventy years. The republic which is continually in danger, because it has never existed, consists of the principles of 1789, the rights of man, liberty, equality and fraternity, reason and virtue, the uncompleted work of an earlier generation, in comparison with the grandiose conceptions of which the Second, Third, and Fourth Republics have been only pitiful caricatures. The great Revolution and all the little ones which followed it have left in their wake the myth of the uncompleted revolution, which comes continually into conflict with the legitimacy of any existing order. Thus the great national drama continues to be acted with barely altered costumes and backcloth, and in forms and formulas which have little to do with the present and its problems, but have a great deal to do with tremendous and inspiring memories. All this history has turned into ideology, and it provides the whole content of a political agitation which exhausts itself in ideology, the revolutionary ideology of a conservative country; that is the apparent paradox.

True, the Jacobin political creed professed, say, by the Radicals or Socialist Radicals, those pillars of the Third and perhaps still of the Fourth Republic, or of the dignitaries elected to local and national assemblies under such alarming labels as those of the Republican Left or the Independent Socialists, causes nobody any sleepless nights. But they are not afraid of words, and their audiences applaud enthusiastically when they announce their determination to renew the assault on the Bastille and do away once and for all with the danger of reaction. They are relentless in their principles and unwearying in their battering at open doors; and they all profess themselves to be the children of the Revolution. Only the slightest ideological *nuances* divide the harmless Radicals, the liberal-minded clerk of the commune of Clochemerle and

Flaubert's chemist Homais, from the Communists. M. Herriot and M. Cachin, M. Daladier and M. Thorez, never had any difficulty in finding a common language; and in fact whole groups of electors, particularly in the word-intoxicated south, went over unitedly from the Radical to the Communist ticket, apparently without noticing the difference. In any other country a similar transfer of votes from a liberal to a Communist party would obviously be unthinkable. But there is no liberal tradition in France, where liberal practice exists only as an easy-going, unconfessable concession. Uncompromising rhetoric and the daily compromise with reality advance on parallel lines and never meet.

La Révolution est un bloc. That famous phrase of Clemenceau's has remained a dogma of the politicians, the historians, and the history teachers, who permit nothing of the great myth to be frittered away, and pass it on whole and undigested from generation to generation. The Revolution is exalted alike by official orators of the Republic and the revolutionary orators of the left. It proclaimed the rights of man, the sovereignty of the people, liberty, equality, and fraternity, and abolished feudal and class privileges and many ancient abuses. It also ran amok, and never dared put into practice either popular sovereignty or the rights of man. It drew up model constitutions by the dozen and never applied them, and laid the people it declared to be sovereign in the chains of an ever more rigorous dictatorship. It started with the storming of an empty prison and subsequently filled all the prisons in the country to bursting-point; introduced the technique of mass production into the business of sentencing and executing people and first created a "popular democracy" of terror and compulsory unanimity; made having "dangerous thoughts" or being a suspected person into capital offences, and elevated denunciation into the highest civic duty; and proclaimed the liberation of the peoples and filled Europe with satellite states ruled and plundered by Paris. But the Revolution which did all these things is as "one and indivisible" as the republic itself and must be accepted or repudiated *en bloc*; and accepting it is the hall-mark of republican mentality.

The ossified, absolutist state structure and the ossified

ideology of Jacobin republicanism belong together as parts of the same historical heritage, and both are equally remote from liberal democracy. There are many reasons for the strength of Communism in France; but that it should have established itself so naturally in the ideological world of the French left and set itself up with such ease as its legitimate heir presents no puzzle or problem; for it is the spirit of its spirit. The foundation of Communist ideology in France is Jacobin Utopianism, not belief in the revolutionary mission of the proletariat; even the combination of French chauvinism with submission to Russia, which appears such an alarming phenomenon today, can be explained simply as a projection. For the revolution which started in France a hundred and fifty years ago and was never completed is believed to have been completed in Russia, which has therefore become the home of the true republic; and even if all the things reported by anti-Communist propaganda are true, that does nothing to shake the belief of people who learned at school that the dictatorship of the Committee of Public Safety, the Terror, and the persecution of heretics constituted the hallmark of the inexorable spirit of republicanism. In the world of ideological abstractions and romantic historical pictures in which the French left lives, the Soviet Union is no foreign land. For it the Kremlin lies in the Place de L'Hôtel de Ville in Paris, where every republic and every commune was proclaimed, the Bolshevik revolution was only the last and the most thorough of all the glorious French revolutions, and if there were differences between them, they were only family differences, like the rows between Girondists and Montagnards, Dantonists and Robespierrists, Communards and Versaillais, which continue to be conducted with undiminished passion by historians and ideologists, but signify only shades of difference within the same republican family. No firm dividing line can be drawn between them without threatening with collapse the whole intoxicating world of revolutionary mystification without which the political life of France is as inconceivable as would be its social life without wine.

"The revolution is a *bloc*." The *bloc* includes not only extremely incompatible elements held together by a historical legend; it also excludes some extremely compatible elements, which are kept out only by the same historical legend. France is full of internal *émigré* groups which have remained outside the republic. Until the most recent times the biggest of these in this Roman Catholic country was the Roman Catholics themselves. For a century-and-a-half the rallying cry of the republic in every crisis was anti-clericalism, the one sure criterion of the progressive mentality; and the Church, which it had not been possible to eliminate from the face of France simultaneously with the monarchy, remained a continually visible incarnation of the enemy, *i.e.*, superstition, authority, unreason, and reaction. Anti-clericalism provided the common rallying-cry for all the traditions and all the heirs of the Revolution; it was shared by the tremendous war machine of the encyclopaedists and the enlightenment movement, the dry rationalism of the lay school leagues, the sceptical bourgeoisie of the masonic lodges, and the enthusiastic anarchists who peddled their anti-God pamphlets outside the church door on Sundays. The cry: *"Écrasez l'infame!"* was all the louder because it was the only surviving link between the bourgeois descendants of Voltaire and the proletarian descendants of the Commune, the grand masters of the masonic lodges and the revolutionary syndicalists, the court of governors of the Haute Banque Protestante and minor officials of the Socialist Party. Public acknowledgement of the principle of lay schools or quoting the old jingle about priests, depending on the audience, always sufficed to paper over the cracks. The classical example was provided when he first became Prime Minister by Raymond Poincaré, that supreme embodiment of all the virtues and failings which, in the eyes of an observer not brought up to the subtleties of French politics, are characteristic of the "diehard" conservative. When a Catholic deputy made a compromising demonstration of friendly feeling towards him, "M. Benoist," he replied, "between you and me there lies the whole gulf of the religious question!"

In recent years, however, a good deal has changed. The small "Catholic left" group, which, to the displeasure of the clerical hierarchy and the contempt of the keepers of the republican holy grail, sought in vain for a century for popular support, has at last fought its way out of its exile and broken the solid ranks of "right" and "left." A new and revolutionary element was thus introduced into French post-war politics, an alien body unassimilable by the ideological system of Jacobin republicanism; and the mere existence of this Christian Social movement, very different in spirit and origin from its central European counterparts, and its willingness to enter republican coalitions, shows that new questions and with them new antitheses—and no doubt new misunderstandings—are beginning to take the place of the old. But, though the new party has long been accepted in the political world of Paris, it still has difficulty in making headway in the country; a political tradition that has become instinctive does not change so rapidly. At Clochemerle the world-shaking struggle between enlightenment and progress on the one hand and authority and obscurantism on the other, between the state teacher and the Catholic priest, the similarly impoverished standard-bearers of the Revolution and the *ancien régime* respectively, remorselessly continues; and the families of the village, divided by heredity or tradition into republicans or reactionaries, are drawn up on two sides behind them, half-passionate and half-entertained spectators. This conflict is the fundamental rite of political life, and is conducted in deadly earnest, for people are used to it. It is no accident that at the heart and centre of the struggle is the schools question, the preponderant role of which in French politics often seems so unintelligible and absurd to foreign observers. For the conflict behind all political conflicts is about French history, and teachers of history are the priesthood of the republican faith. The teaching staff of the lay schools, centrally organised in hierarchical fashion like the priesthood of an anti-church, has assumed the functions on behalf of the republic which the clergy exercised on behalf of the *ancien régime*; they are the militant priesthood of the republican régime.

Though the Church and reaction have ceased to coincide, the Church continues to provide the rallying-cry for the right that anti-clericalism provides for the left. The loyalty to the Church of the French right has perhaps done more harm to French Catholicism than republican hostility; for it has been directed to the Church, not as a religious but as a political institution, not as a religious community but as the only surviving symbol of the old order, a *corps d'état* of the monarchy, that peculiar Gallican state Church, in whose eyes the king was a consecrated member of the clergy, the royal anointment was a sacramental rite, and the royal laying-on of hands was as effective to work miracles as were the hands of a saint. The Church which was the object of right-wing loyalty really was the Church of anti-clerical caricature. Charles Maurras, for half-a-century the "teacher" and idolised ideologist of the French right, merely rationalised this attitude in his noisy, provocative style when in his role as atheist and "Hellenist" he dismissed the Gospels as fairy-tales written by "four shabby Jews" and poured scorn and contempt on Christianity as a religion for the rabble, while in his role as reactionary political philosopher and pamphleteer he devoted all his noisy and compromising reverence to the Church as an embodiment of authority and order. This, in common with nearly all the other features of his counter-revolutionary doctrine, was in harmony with ancient, sceptical French traditions; only the aggressive fashion in which it was presented gave it an exciting flavour of intellectual boldness which delighted a *jeunesse dorée* nauseated by a plebeian world. The fact that the *Action Française* was repudiated both by the Church and the House of Bourbon dismayed these battlers for throne and altar not at all; for them the *ancien régime* was at bottom just as much an unrelated system of reference as was the Revolution for the popular orators of the republic.

The fact that Maurras was able for half-a-century, and with such undisputed political, literary, and above all social success, to maintain his position as the mouthpiece of ancient, aristocratic, Catholic, and monarchical France gives the full measure of the political sterility of the French right. For this blind misanthrope, this brawling littérateur, was precisely the opponent whom the republican ideologists required. Point by point, and taking pleasure in his very provocativeness, he made a doctrine of the opposite of "the principles of 1789"—*pour épater les radicaux*—and proudly threw over his own shoulders and those of his followers the cloak of reactionary obscurantism which republican orators had devised to frighten children in their political picture-books. In the eyes of Charles Maurras a hundred and fifty years of French history had been a hundred and fifty years of regicide and mob-rule, a criminal deflection from the true path, which must be undone. Democracy, the rights of man, equality before the law, freedom of religion, popular education, the eight-hour day, and all the other paraphernalia of so-called progress, constituted an alien poison introduced by Protestants, Jews, Freemasons, and other foreign bodies; and the poison must be eradicated with fire and the sword, making possible the restoration by counter-revolution of a reasonable and natural society of lords and labourers, educated classes and illiterate masses, aristocracy and the common herd. This amounted to demonstrating that the bogyman against whom the Jacobin popular orators so tirelessly defended the republic really existed. Indeed he did. All the limitation of outlook, all the arrogance and remoteness from life of the "upper classes" to whom the "people" refused due respect and the "régime" refused the place to which they were entitled—not so much the limitation of outlook, arrogance, and remoteness of the real aristocracy as that of the stuffy petty *rentiers* described with such terrifying truthfulness to life in French fiction—were expressed in the "total nationalism" of the *Action Française*.

But Maurras and the shindy made on the boulevards and in the Latin quarter by the *jeunesse dorée* never amounted to a serious political movement. He provided a literary high school of obscurantism, scorn, and hatred, the principal achievements of which were in the field of lampoon, slander, and personal invective. A number of the most brilliant French controversialists grew up in this school, though many of them subsequently left it. By the elegant style in which they clothed their scurrilities Maurras and his followers set the tone for the whole of the French right. François Mauriac summed up the experience of a life-time of controversy when he once said in the *Table Ronde*: "The dirt is always thrown from the extreme right." This contumelious literature did not fail to exercise a wider influence, however, but without promoting the moral regeneration which it proclaimed. Its only influence was demoralising. Thanks to it a whole French social *élite* put on their uniforms as officers at the outbreak of the second world war fully believing that their country was ruled by a dishonourable pack of thieves, swindlers, and traitors, and that it was rotten to the core; and the collapse came to them like a judgment of God, which they had expected, and for which they had almost hoped. For the theory of the corruption of the French state, the most easily popularisable part of the Maurras doctrine, had become familiar to a circle far wider than the readers of the *Action Française* and other, less elegantly written, organs of corruption, and was familiar to every waiter and butcher's boy. Maurras, when he daily dipped his brilliant pen in blood, appealed to violence, and began his article by demanding the head of the particular victim he happened to be attacking, was 'undoubtedly only practising his literary style and indulging in a literary excess. His misfortune was that he still believed it to be only a literary excess when France lay prostrate and the Gestapo and the Vichy militia saw to the complete and thorough carrying out of the things that he had preached. There is a grim symbolism in the last infatuation of this senile chauvinist, who had spent a life-time preaching hatred of the German enemy and now hailed with delight the "national revolution" he had longed for—brought about with Hitler's bayonets. The "true France", the *pays réel*, to the proclamation of whose advent he had devoted his life, was a historical myth, an empty ideology, the abstract antithesis of the official republican ideology, even remoter from France and her real problems than the electioneering speeches in the political market-place that he despised.

As a political factor the French right had ceased to count at least since the turn of the century. The *Action Française* and related groups were only its caricature. Nobody in the political battle—apart from a few backwaters where reaction still prevailed—confessed to belonging to the right, though everyone was willing enough to denounce his opponent as belonging to that category. At least two-thirds of the semicircle of the French Chamber was occupied by parties which proclaimed themselves to be, not just left, but Socialist, and in the immediate post-war period half the benches were occupied by the "extreme left" alone. Next to the "extreme left" comes the "centre", impinging dangerously on the right benches, however, though half of them label themselves "left-centre"; and to the extreme right of the Chamber there sit the "moderates", who do not, however, wish to be known as moderates, but as left-moderates, and obviously feel discomfort in close proximity with the few isolated conservative swashbucklers from the Vendée or the Basque country. The periodic swings of the pendulum between "left" and "right" thus take place within the "left" itself, between the extreme and less extreme left. In short, the republic is left, so completely left as to reduce the term to absurdity.

For all that the right is still very much alive, but not as a political party. It survives very vigorously as a *milieu* which has long given up trying to seek popular favour and has withdrawn to its powerful spheres of influence outside "politics", its key positions in society and the state. Not only the Faubourg Saint-Germain and the Académie Française, but the great offices of state, the *élite* of the *corps d'état*, the diplomatic service and the army, lie outside the plebeian republic. The French colonial empire, that last preserve of the *ancien régime,* lies completely outside it; the parliaments, parties, and broadly speaking even the governments of the Third Republic have exerted the smallest conceivable influence on its creation, administration, and politico-military defence, and the Fourth Republic seems to have finally and completely abdicated in the face of its local exarchs. The uninhibited scorn poured on the republic by Maurras and his young men was only vulgar or infantile mimicry of the lofty condescension with which *la vieille France,* as represented by the holders of the great offices of state, has served the republican régime. Some of the greatest crises in modern French history, above all the Dreyfus case, have arisen from the collision between the parliamentary republic and its practically sovereign *corps d'état*; and the Vichy régime which organised itself round the court of Marshal Pétain in 1940 after the collapse of the Third Republic was nothing but this sovereign state apparatus, which suddenly stood isolated as the naked "state in itself" deprived of its democratic and republican façade. During the four years of its existence it described itself as the *État français* without any qualification—an unvarnished laconicism which could not possibly have been more precise.

The state and the republic are two things which, except in times of crisis, never meet.

Thus this deeply conservative country has no conservative party; and this is no accident of nomenclature, explicable perhaps in terms of a political terminology which has never been able to differentiate between conservatives and reactionaries either on the right or on the left. In French political controversies there has never been any need of that minimum of objectivity and seriousness of discussion, of differentiation between the possible and the impossible, of respect for one's opponent, of appropriateness of tone and general sense of responsibility, which are essential for the proper functioning of democratic institutions if these controversies are to lead to the formation of a public opinion which expresses itself in elections and parliamentary debate and thus give a real direction to public affairs. The most that these passionately conducted controversies ever lead to is a change of Ministers in Paris. The irresponsibility of political controversy has its counterpart in its lack of consequences. The real decision in all matters, from the budget of the smallest village in the Pyrenees which desires to build a bridge or lay a water-pipe to the control of the national budget and the government of a great empire and the long-term conduct of foreign affairs, is in the hands of an administrative hierarchy which is practically immune from political fluctuations and, though it may sometimes be forced to compromise with a Minister whom Parliament sets before it, is always able to wait patiently until he and his ideas have departed.

Thus it came about, for instance, that a whole system of social legislation, passed by Parliament, signed by the responsible Ministers, and duly brought into force by publication in the official gazette during the stormy Socialist Radical period of the turn of the century, slumbered in the archives for thirty years on its way to total oblivion without any move whatever being made to put it into practice; it simply never reached the stage of administrative execution. A Minister is able to grant favours, pay particular attention to the interests of his own department of France, or the constituencies of his particular political friends; he can put in a word for particular promotions or particular subsidies, or influence the granting of state contracts; and above all he can distribute with open hands many hundred Orders of the Legion of Honour, for his Ministry gives him full control of its annual quota of these; so much is granted him by the rules of the parliamentary game. But he cannot carry out a policy of his own; and, indeed, he has no time to do so. The chief function of the ever-changing Ministers is to act as a buffer between the "left" Parliament and the "right" state apparatus; and the way to gain a reputation as a good, competent Minister with a reputation for efficiency is—notwithstanding the constitutional theory according to which a Minister is the executor of the people's will as expressed in Parliament—to be the spokesman and defender of competent departmental officials against the incompetence and demagogy of Parliament and perhaps one's own party. But a Minister, whether he is good or bad, independent or amenable, is soon exhausted and worn out by his function as a buffer between the turbulent wishes of Parliament and the unmoved permanence of the state apparatus. The high rate of consumption of governments is one of the things on the debit side of this system, in which the executive is reduced to paralysis between a parliament which regards itself as the government and an administration which regards itself as the state.

In seventy years of republicanism France has not once had a parliamentary working majority or a government coalition which could agree even on the foundations of a coherent policy, and it has never had a government which lived long enough to be able to work out and introduce such a policy. France is not ruled, but administered, and it is her apparent political instability which guarantees the stability and permanence of her administration. Thanks to this division of labour, politics remains with impunity the playground of ideology, abstraction, extremism, verbal tumult, and pure demagogy, because all these things hardly touch the life of the French state; and no counterweight to them is required, because they cancel themselves out. The republic reigns, but does not rule. Both the presupposition and the consequence of unbridled rhetoric is that it should work in a void.

There is another side to this elevation of political discussion into the realm of pure ideology. The French people, even when it goes to the polls, and its political personnel, even when it renders homage to classical Jacobin eloquence, by no means consist of exalted idealists. The French citizen is armed against the excesses of rhetoric with a sound dose of scepticism and calculating realism, and he differentiates sharply and instinctively between principles and practice. But this contributes little either to the principles or to the practice. He reads his newspaper without believing a word of it, and after enjoying its prose year in and year out is perfectly capable of voting the opposite way to what it tells him. But his offhand mistrust of all newspapers leaves him no better informed, and his newspaper is not improved by the fact that it is not taken seriously, and that any attempt at seriousness on its part would not be rewarded. He regards all the politicians who seek his vote, often rightly but sometimes wrongly, as ambitious buffoons, if not worse; and the fact that this is taken for granted does nothing to improve the political atmosphere. The celebrated remark that the Frenchman carries his heart on the left but his wallet on the right is undoubtedly true; but it is extremely questionable whether in the long run his wallet has fared better than his heart in consequence. The compromise between the grandiose nature of his principles and the pettiness of his practice results, not in equilibrium, but in caricature. The opposite pole of his high-flying ideology is not a responsible, realistic conservatism, but a teeming multitude of local and sectional interests, whose ruthlessness towards the national interest is if possible more profound, and certainly fraught with graver consequences, than the most uninhibited political demagogy. These local and sectional interests do not combine to form any political party or conservative right wing, as superficial political theorists might expect them to do; at most it can be said that as one goes from left to right on the parliamentary benches ideology is somewhat more thinly spread and the representation of special interests is spread somewhat more thickly and plays a somewhat bigger role. But it is a matter of shading; there is no demarcation line. If the representatives of the big financial and industrial combines traditionally sat for preference with the "left centre"—that small, select, and extremely loose group which throughout the history of the Third Republic was able to tilt the balance and provided an inexhaustible reservoir of its Ministers in spite of its insignificant numbers—the representatives of the small wine and brandy producers, the beetroot-growers, the owners of small transport concerns, and shopkeepers are distributed all over the House; and they are irresistible precisely because they are not organised in any group or party and have no solidarity other than the special interests of their clients, which are isolated from any connection with general political or economic ideas, and for that very reason can be advocated with complete irresponsibility. The deputy is just as well able as the citizen to have his heart on the left and his wallet on the right without their coming into conflict. The classical Radical politician who in one and the same rhetorical outburst upheld the sovereignty of the nation and of the individual, private enterprise, protection for the small trader, social democracy, the supremacy of the national interest, international conciliation and a frontier on the Rhine, a balanced budget, an improvement in morals and in the birth-rate, but above all state subsidies for the wine industry and public purchase of surplus wine, was certainly unaware of any inconsistency in his system of ideas.

The more limited and fragmentary is this representation of special interests, the more legitimate it is and the less danger it runs of coming into contact, let alone conflict, with the principles which are proclaimed. Only exceptionally does a systematic defence of nationally organised group interests, or of group interests that are seen in a national setting, demand a somewhat larger view and make a call on somewhat larger ideas. Normally each deputy, no matter to what party he belongs and independently of the political beliefs which he professes, proceeds from case to case, considering erratically and in isolation the wishes and demands of groups and leading individuals in his constituency. These may range from demands for subsidies and price supports for the agricultural products of the area, or a local railway connection or tax reduction, to a tariff for the benefit of a no longer competitive local industry. At this level no conflict of conscience ever arises between enthusiasm for progress in general and the artificial preservation of every hereditary structure and situation in particular; and the representative of local and sectional interests can go about his strictly practical business all the more undisturbedly because republican theory ignores his existence.

The French constitution indeed recognises no representatives of individual constituencies; in theory each deputy represents one six-hundredth of a single and indivisible nation. But the thorough-going centralism and the suppression of all local and regional self-administration, self-determination, and self-aid have left local needs and interests with no outlet through which to express themselves other than the national Parliament; and in Parliament these narrow interests—perfectly justified within their limits—continually overlay and distort those wider questions of national policy which it should be the object of Parliament to state and to solve. If Paris, through its prefects and sub-prefects, subjects to its yoke the politics of every parish pump in France, what alternative have the users of the parish pump but to take their local politics to Paris by way of their deputy? If their needs and requirements get held up somewhere in the prefectorial channels, how can they hope to get things moving again without the Minister's intervention? As soon as debate turns from its occasional high flights of abstract principle to the daily round of economic, administrative, or financial questions, the Parliament of the one and indivisible republic turns in the twinkling of an eye into a mosaic of six hundred local squabbles, and the corridors and committee-rooms of the Chamber and the Senate and the ante-rooms of the Ministries become lobbies for the greediest, pettiest, and narrowest local and sectional interests; this is a direct result of the very completeness of the centralisation of political life.

The incoherence of the resulting policies and resulting legislation, which calmly try to pursue all sort of irreconcilable aims at the same time, never choose between mutually exclusive ends and means, and often end with all the disadvantages of all the possible alternatives—pseudo-liberalism, pseudo-socialism, mercantilism, inflation, and stagnation—is not the result of a conspiracy of the "two hundred families", that mythological flower of radical eloquence which looms in popular superstition as the origin of all evil. It is the natural and inevitable result of the continually changing coalitions and compromises reached between erratic, short-sighted, self-centred interests, which always tackle every national economic problem exclusively from a parochial viewpoint, disjointedly, from day to day and from case to case, and are able to advance only along the line of least resistance; they are the natural and inevitable result of the defence of all *situations acquises,* or rather of the conditions in which they were established in the past, against the alterations required by modern economy; of granting state subsidies and state guarantees to every branch of the economy whose ways are threatened; of the shifting of deficits and the cost of surplus products on to the public purse; and of the uncompromising defence of an archaic fiscal system under which half the population have acquired exemptions and privileges which free them from the attentions of the tax-collector while the other half staggers under the burden.

The parliamentary history of the French republic offers some truly astonishing examples of co-operation between big financial interests and the pettiest parochial interests, into which the latter could have been led only by their guileless business instincts. One of these, the Freycinet railway plan, a huge and unconcealed raid on the state finances, caused a scandal which filled the history of the first decade of the republic. Another was the tariff legislation of the turn of the century which represented the popular will in such detail that paragraph after paragraph revealed, not just the branches of industry, but the individual concerns to be protected. A third is that monstrous growth, the alcohol administration, which for many years has enabled whole branches of the agricultural economy to produce at state expense, only for its products to be subsequently destroyed at state expense.

But behind this pseudo-economic activity there has never been any general idea, even in the narrowest sense of the word. Thanks to the importance to the great majority of deputies of the agricultural vote, "the interests of the peasants" have always been sacred, and their tax privileges—like those of the liberal professions, from which country and small-town notables, political committees, and deputies themselves were recruited—have always been untouchable; and agricultural protectionism and an ever-growing system of subsidies always hastened to the aid of the most retrograde and unproductive practices. But, in spite of all this electorally profitable but economically ruinous behaviour, the Third Republic never developed a coherent agricultural policy, or faced up to the fact that the agricultural economy of half the country was languishing and on the way to ruin; and in its excursions into the social field it was just as short-sighted and lacking in vision as in its a-social economic actions. The celebrated tenants' protection policy, which led in the course of thirty years of inflation to sitting tenants' being practically irremovable and living practically rent-free, to the ruin of the French landlords and to permanent lack of accommodation for those members of the coming generation who did not happen to be sitting tenants, is a symbol of the whole mentality of these direct representatives of sectional interests in their total blindness to the wider consequences of their actions. The daily work of Parliament as a "chamber of interests" can be summed up as sanctioning expenditure and refusing to meet it—an unusual reversal of the function which was the origin and is the reason for the existence of all parliaments.

The very inconsistency which often seems to be the only guiding principle of French political life fits harmoniously into the total structures of the French state. Parliamentary practice has adapted itself to the restricted sphere to which the administrative machine confines the activity of continually changing governments. The latter are unable to formulate or carry out a coherent policy; they are able to grant their clients favours, approvals, promotions, decorations, priorities for their local or sectional interests, and bigger or smaller titbits from the national table; and, as it is really one of the duties and responsibilities of the deputy for La Creuse in the council of the nation to wring from the republican budget the funds for the appointment of a *garde champêtre* at Chéneérailles-en-Combrailles, he has little time left to delve deeply into complicated problems of general policy; he has to content himself with his treasure-store of historical pictures and ideological certainties, from which he can incidentally draw rhetorical fireworks to illustrate the field watchman's republican functions. His attitude is that the ultimate reconciliation of all the resultant inconsistencies is a matter for the experts to work out. The only parallel to the capacity of the average politician alternately or simultaneously to uphold the most inconsistent principles with the same fervour and the same eloquence—demonstrated by both right and left alike but with the greatest virtuosity by the centre, which flirts with both—is the capacity of his audience indiscriminately to applaud it all, for at bottom everybody agrees with a wink on what it is all about.

Such are the politics of a country completely absorbed in its domestic affairs, completely unconcerned about the rest of the world and the future of its own state, a country resting so securely and so confidently on its ancient foundations that its citizens feel they have as little cause to worry about them as about the course of the stars.

There would indeed be no cause for worry if France were the fortunate isle she would so much like to be. The whole misfortune derives from the fact that she is not. For the most fundamental of all the inconsistencies which are upheld with equal fervour, the only one which is denied that delightful lack of consequences which characterises the domestic political game, is that between the parochial self-satisfaction and routine which the amiable philosophy of the radicals has elevated into a humanistic article of faith and the leading international role of the *grande nation* as a European and colonial power. The leading international status of France is both a proud Jacobin heritage and an assumption of the Jacobin philosophy; it is also a burdensome heritage of history itself.

In the inter-war period, no matter whether the governments of the "national *bloc*" pursued a policy of widespread alliances and simultaneous retreat behind the Maginot line and sacrificed the French economic potential to gold parity and the morale of investors; no matter whether the Popular Front, which succeeded to this hopelessly confused heritage, tried to introduce the five-day week and summer holidays for the whole of French industry simultaneously with a rearmament programme and the organisation of national defence;

no matter whether in the final utter confusion the "national parties" who had assumed the monopoly of patriotism came forward as advocates of capitulation and national abdication while the "unpatriotic and countryless rabble" of the extreme left became the uncompromising advocates of resistance and loyalty to alliances; no matter whether another change of line by Moscow and its French followers threw the whole pack of cards into hopeless confusion, so that nobody could see anything but treachery at work everywhere; the fundamental principle of French politics remained a blithe persistence in inconsistencies of which the politicians did not become aware until the final collapse.

This calamity was, however, regarded as a tremendous and incomprehensible intervention into the workings of a mechanism whose interior balances had worked so long and so satisfactorily. Not France but the outside world had changed. Anyone who is curious about the political climate of the immediate pre-war period in the light of the collapse of 1940, or about that of the *belle époque* after its test by fire in the ordeal of the Marne, should look at the French Press of that hot summer of 1914, during the weeks between the assassination at Serajevo and the outbreak of war, when, as we now believe, the whole world was waiting with bated breath. He should look, not at the newspapers of the extreme left, which were unswervingly hostile to the army as the breeding-ground of reaction and fought military credits as implying exploitation of the people by the armament manufacturers, dreamed of a general strike, and oscillated between horror of the Tsar and horror of the Kaiser; they were at least consistent, as long as they were allowed to be. He should look, not at the newspapers of the extreme right, which daily tore the republic to pieces in the name of the "true" France, just as they did in 1939. He should look at the serious, respectable, bourgeois Press, which with manifest patriotism applauded the army, the army estimates, the lengthening of the period of military service, and, indeed, every patriotic sacrifice—there spoke the heart—but in the same breath fought to the knife the revenue proposals designed to meet the cost of these things, and—in 1914!—attacked the introduction of income tax as being equivalent to robbery with violence. There spoke the wallet. When the solemn *Temps,* in tones as ominous as those of the Last Trump, called on public opinion to awake three weeks after Serajevo, it was not because it had been roused from its slumbers by distant thunder-clouds in the Balkans, but because Parliament after year-long struggles had at last passed the income tax Bill; and the aristocratic *Figaro,* the organ of the *salons* and the Académie Française, did not hesitate to descend to the most scurrilous level by overwhelming M. Caillaux, the Finance Minister who had at last succeeded in conducting this long-necessary fiscal reform through the House, with the lowest personal calumnies and "intimate revelations." In the last days before the outbreak of war the event that successfully competed in the Paris headlines with the news about ultimatums, mobilisation orders, and the starting up of the machinery of alliances was that of the melodramatic murder trial which crowned the *Figaro* campaign and supplied the newspapers with titbits from the Minister's old love-letters which were read to the jury. Four days after the verdict, which filled Paris with excited demonstrations and counter-demonstrations, there came mobilisation, followed a day later by war, which France was to survive only at the price of an irreparable loss of substance. . . . But it was not "little" history that had altered, but barbarous "big" history, which now brutally swept over her, entirely lacking in human proportion.

§ 4

HUMAN PROPORTION

Thus France, which has perhaps a more compact and self-contained personality than any other nation, presents herself as a confusing and unintelligible jumble of contradictions. For she is the home at one and the same time of the Messianic spirit and the parochial spirit, of universalism and provincialism, of modernism and antediluvianism, of intellectual rationalism and contempt of all reason, of ideological exuberance and the most petty and calculating narrowness. She is a country of the most extreme tolerance and the most malicious and virulent polemics, of democratic spirit and absolutist structure. She combines an imperishable structure with the perpetual preaching of insurrection; the deepest and most spontaneous national consciousness with the most complete and utter disregard of the state and the common good; she is the country of Catholicism and disbelief; tradition and impiety; stagnation and drama; order and anarchy She possesses the intellectual dynamite of a long tradition of rationalism which can find satisfaction only in logically, almost geometrically, constructed systems and yet manages most effectively to combine this with a radical individualism which is able to repudiate all empirically established and therefore viable systems and ends up finally by exclusively following its own will with a perfectly clear conscience. Where is the principle which holds all this together? It is not surprising if every observer has discovered a different France of his own.

There is no limit to such voyages of discovery. One man flees from the scintillating intellectual firework display and seeks out the "other France" of the archaic, austere, thrifty, bigoted, conservative provinces; another discovers against the background of its superficial lightheartedness and gaiety the austerity, almost gloom, of this country, which can be found by anyone who looks for it in the crystal clarity of its language, the bare and unadorned architecture of its villages and classical monuments, in the monkish discipline of its schools and intellectual work, and even in the unusually adult faces of its children; another indignantly rejects as a caricature the literature of adultery and sexual perversion, the life of the boulevards, and the whole cocktail of the foreign tourist industry of *gai Paris*, and discovers France to be the country with the most impregnable and self-contained family structure in the world.

All these things are true, and the only mistake is to pick out one of them as the "true" France excluding the others. It is also a mistake to regard them as isolated phenomena existing independently side by side. In reality they are all facets of the same one and indivisible national personality, of the France *une et indivisible* which the Revolution declared it to be: individual traits of the personality in which all these things are merged. The whole which is called France is neither a mere sum-total of heterogeneous parts, nor a modern structure of steel and concrete, but an ancient building of stone, bricks, and mortar which has grown up through the ages, made with men's hands, cracked and weather-beaten and overgrown with ivy, like one of those small country churches in which elements of the styles of many centuries are so marvellously harmonised.

The exciting secret of France is that an extremely durable order prevails behind its extremely apparent disorder. This order has become anonymous, unconscious, and imperceptible, but like a fine and impenetrable net it has caught up in its meshes absolutely everything, from the physical structure of the country and its road system radiating from the centre, and a now traditional system of political ideas which have been taken over uncritically from rebellious forefathers, to an amiable tyranny of conventions in speech, manners, conversation, cooking, menus, and the choice of drinks. Even the quarrels, the most unrestrained controversy and the vilest abuse, keep to canonically established forms, patterns, and references; and the heady wine of ideology is bottled and labelled in just the same way. The revolutionary and the reactionary, the aristocrat, the *clochard,* the bourgeois, and his son who rebels against God and his parents' house, the academician, the workman, the Bohemian, the priest and the anti-clerical, the Jacobin, the *communard,* the *camelot du roi,* Homais, Topaze, and Harpagon—to say nothing of their female variants—are established types strictly bound to their roles, which are indispensable to, and even in their extremes of individualism in conformity with, a way of life the fundamental law of which is perhaps summed up in the popular saying: *Il faut du tout pour faire un monde.* The true lawmakers and philosophers of France are the moralists, who drew up no code of morals or social doctrine or philosophical system, but in the course of centuries established the catalogue of types of the French species of man.

But if every individual has the most complete liberty to go his own way, even the most eccentric way, with the most complete ruthlessness and the utmost unconcern, for anybody else, how powerful must be the system which ensures and surrounds this liberty and invisibly supplies the guiding-strings, and demands no respect, no love, no discipline, no submission or even attention, but is simply there, and is only the more firmly anchored in the soil the more everybody shakes it and tugs at its roots. If a name is sought to describe it, it can be described as a civilisation; but it is a civilisation which has grown to be as much taken for granted as is nature herself; so familiar is it, so lacking in compulsion and the imposition of duties, that it might also be called a routine.

In his preface to the *Lettres Persanes* Paul Valéry sketched the process by which the complex social mechanism which we call order arises and subsequently decays, and he sought for the ideal moment in this process, in which the rules laying down what is sacred, right, lawful, moral, and praiseworthy and their opposites, all the remarkable practices of a tamed society which have grown unintelligible but were once imposed and borne in awe and terror, no longer seem to require force or moral compulsion to keep them alive. When this artificial social world, "this magical construction, which rests on texts, on obedience to words, on the keeping of promises, on the observation of customs and agreements, in short on pure fictions", has once come to seem as natural as nature herself, the hour of intellectual liberty has struck. Social conventions the origin of which has been forgotten and the ritual of which has degenerated into ceremonial are hauled before the judgment seat of the critical intelligence and found absurd; the sacred is regarded as superstition, law as an arbitrary system of local regulations, and the accepted moral code as current prejudice; and the enlightened set about working out schemes for a better and more reasonable society based on rational principles. The old order begins slowly to fall into disrepute, until the process of degeneration ends in collapse, followed by the violent and ruthless imposition of a new order. But what fascinates the dilettante M. Valéry is neither order nor disorder, but that ideal state of suspension in which the process of dissolution is just beginning, the stage reached in eighteenth-century France when it began its entrancing, bold, and superficial playing with ideas.

"Order is always a burden to man. In disorder he calls for the police or for death. Those are two extreme cases in which human nature feels uncomfortable. The individual longs for a thoroughly pleasant period, in which he would feel freest and most protected at the same time. He finds it at the beginning of the end of a social system.

"Then a priceless moment intervenes between order and disorder. All the benefits which can accrue from the establishment of public powers and duties have been secured, and it becomes possible to enjoy the first relaxations of the system. The institutions still survive in their grandeur and nobility, but, though no visible change has taken place, in reality all that is left is their fine appearance. They have produced all the good of which they are capable; the secret is that their potentialities are exhausted; they are no longer sacred, or rather they are no longer anything but sacred; criticism and disrespect have undermined them, and robbed them of all immediate value. Slowly and gently the social body loses its future. It is the hour of pleasure and general dissolution.

"The nearly always luxurious and voluptuous end of a

political edifice is accompanied by a glorious display of fireworks, in which everything which people previously feared to spend is spent lavishly.

"State secrets, feelings of private shame, unconfessed thoughts, dreams long repressed, the whole over-stimulated, gaily desperate background of human nature, are brought out and thrown into the public arena.

"A still fairy-like flame, destined to turn into a blaze, arises, and plays over the face of the world. It strangely illuminates the dance of principles and riches. Morals and patrimonies melt away. Mysteries and treasures go up in smoke. Respect evaporates, and all chains are softened in this ardour of living and dying, which rises to a frenzy.

"If the fates granted a man the free choice of a century in which to pass his life, I am sure that such a fortunate being would choose the age of Montesquieu. I am not without weaknesses; I should do the same. . . ."

Nothing is more intelligible than this nostalgia, to which M. Valéry confesses with ironic shamefulness, for a transfigured eighteenth century—the French century *par excellence*—even if historians might have some reservations to make about its delightfulness. M. Valéry and the whole of his dilettantish work are themselves the best evidence that the century of Montesquieu has not entirely passed away, and nearly every feature in his description is still a feature of contemporary France. The firework display of the iconoclasts of the enlightenment movement blackened the structure of the *ancien régime*, drove away its halo, robbed it of nobility, and nearly robbed it of greatness as well. But it did not cause it to collapse, and the firework display itself continues to this very day; the "priceless moment" is not yet over; and many men to whom the fates grant the favour of choosing the country in which they would most gladly spend their lives, or part of them, still choose France—for the same reason, the same mildly a-social, selfish reason which can be only shamefacedly confessed; namely to escape from the burden of obligations which the social order with its standards and duties imposes elsewhere.

It is not only in the French atmosphere that the eighteenth century is to be met. We have met it already in the course of this work, and the more acute becomes the conflict between the traditional French way of life and the technological and sociological pressure of the contemporary world, the more sharply there stand out the unaltered contours of old France, which were for a long time obscured by the busy, bourgeois activity of the nineteenth century. The characteristics of the still surviving *ancien régime* are all the more evident as France is again perceptibly living under an *ancien régime* which is heading for destruction, and its privileged citizens of today seem to be just as willing as the courtly society of yesterday to fritter away their future with an: "After us, the deluge!"

One *ancien régime* characteristic is the preservation of the state structure of the absolutist system; a structure which in spite of all revolutions only became more centralised, though in an anonymous form, exercising power in almost abstract fashion, divested of all outward pomp and ceremony, a monarchy without a crowned head, an administration which rules because the republic does not. Another is the ideologists of the enlightenment movement, drawn up in ossified battle-array against opponents as ossified as they, with the result that an impassable front line runs right through politics and society, introducing hopeless confusion into the approach to all more modern problems, modified though it is by the scepticism which attaches itself to any acknowledged state ideology; for the supreme and absolute claims of reason, which include the right to question anything and everything, go all too easily hand-in-hand with an only too practical reasonableness which tolerates all uses and abuses. Another *ancien régime* characteristic is mercantilism, which is ignored in theory but in practice is carried out in complete detail, combined with the *douceur de vivre* of a sheltered, protectionist, guild and patronage economy of acquired privileges; a planned economy without a plan but with innumerable administrations, without an engine but well provided with brakes, with forms but without statistics, or rather with false statistics, and provided with the huge reserved hunting ground of a colonial empire over which the *pacte coloniale* system of Colbert sleeps its Sleeping Beauty sleep, although two hundred years after Colbert that empire has been totally reconstructed. Another *ancien régime* characteristic is the world's most confusing and at the same time most oppressive and unproductive taxation system, which assumes as a matter of course in its calculations that whole groups of the population will defraud the revenue; it thereby not only justifies defrauding the revenue, but positively enforces it. The broad foundations of this fiscal system are a consumption tax on the lines of old *gabelle* and taxation of the "outward signs of wealth" on the pattern of the old window tax, which left a permanent mark on the appearance of French buildings, and it works on the principle that everything new and progressive shall be heavily taxed while everything old and traditional shall be exempt. The result is that the state is permanently short of funds and has to live from hand to mouth even in periods of the greatest prosperity. It is perpetually at the mercy of the "confidence" of its stocking-savers and gold-hoarders, its tax-evaders and exporters of flight capital. The national economy itself is rooted in the *ancien régime*. It clings obstinately to the obsolete methods of production of the age of France's power and glory, the typical features of which are the patriarchal small employer, a workshop industry relying largely on production by hand and preserving a corresponding economic outlook, and an agricultural system based on the peasant-family unit. The whole fights obstinately against mechanisation, rationalisation, concentration, depersonalisation, and proletarianisation at the price of individual and social impoverishment.

The harmony of this fundamental pattern is broken by the representatives of the machine age in the big industrial concentrations of northern and north-eastern France, the Paris basin, and the Loire, who have remained a disturbing and never properly assimilated alien body, obeying laws other than those which today more than ever isolate them from their context in the French national economy. They also constitute an alien body in the social and political sense. The industrial workers have never been properly incorporated into the nation, and today they form a new and powerful "internal *émigré*" group organised under that contemporary secessionary movement, the Communist Party. Another unassimilated body are the technicians, who since the second world war have placed on the order of the day the modernisation and regeneration of France in the spirit of modern techniques and have organised themselves into the youngest *corps d'état* on the general staffs of the nationalised industries and investment planning agencies. Moreover France's industrial workers can almost be described as alien bodies in the ethnical sense. For many years she has recruited them less from her own soil than from central and eastern Europe, Algeria, and her colonial empire, and in some industrial areas, notably the mining areas of the north, French workers have long since been a minority in relation to the compact national groups of foreign workers, just as they form a minority within the French nation itself.

The national interest requires that France should possess an efficient heavy industry, efficient sources of power, and an efficient transport system, and state intervention and the creation of this new *corps d'état* were required to rescue the keypoints of the country's economic potential from the stagnation of the rest of the economy. Here the technological and sociological pressure of the outside world is visibly at work, and is introducing new problems and new explosive elements into French society. But in every field which touches the daily life of the rest of France, in agriculture, in the building industry, in the consumer industries and markets, and in consumer habits, the effects have hitherto been effectively nipped in the bud and neutralised in the impenetrable thicket of the distribution system and the archaic working-up industries. The alien body has been isolated and made innocuous. This area, in which the classical standards of the French way of life no longer apply, remains an isolated enclave of modernism inside old France, which stands at bay against it with all its instincts and all the stubborn strength of its traditions.

For the secret of the invisible order which still embraces and holds together all the inconsistencies is—as is, indeed, taught as an adage in all French schools of every kind—proportion, that sense of proportion which is said to be the prerogative of the Latin and Mediterranean races, and is said to be denied to the Germans and the Slavs. The platitudinous nature of this commonplace should not prevent one from seeing its truth, to which the whole French landscape, style, and way of life bear witness. France has developed a whole philosophy and theology of proportion. The products of craftsmanship are held up against those of the machine, and individual taste against standardisation. The ethos of individual craftsmanship, which is not of an inferior but of a different nature from that of industrial society, cannot help but take pleasure in improvisation and resourcefulness, and it holds its ground triumphantly wherever insufficiency of resources has to be overcome by miracles of personal adroitness, in the luxury trades and in technically backward branches of industry; in fact, it is that very backwardness that enables it to survive. Manufactured goods are held to be ugly and bad in comparison, and it can indeed be said that the French consumption goods industries do everything to justify that belief. The same attitude of mind is to be found in the field of intellectual work. The highest scientific achievements go hand-in-hand with a complete lack of interest in their technical application, and the connection between science and industry, demonstrated elsewhere in the research departments of big concerns, in systematic market investigations, and in experimental building centres, remained as good as unknown until the second world war. The same mentality is also to be found in the French educational ideal, which fights with extraordinary obstinacy against lapsing into the sin of specialisation; this ideal is the *honnête homme, i.e.,* the formation, not of a useful member of society, but of an intellectually complete man. The most important unit for this philosophy is not society, but the individual, with all his peculiarities, and social organisation is not an end but a means; or rather it is a necessary evil to which the smallest possible part of the private soul, the private conscience, and also private selfishness, should be sacrificed.

Man, says this theory, is the measure and the centre of all things. However, he is not the centre of society as an object of public benevolence, but only the centre of his private environment as a sovereign individual responsible only to himself. In this individualistic ethic society is a bare abstraction, the state an adversary to be kept carefully within bounds, and the social conscience a rhetorical flower of speech. The matter-of-factness with which the individual is allowed to go his own way is only the obverse side of the matter-of-factness with which he is left to himself when misfortune overtakes him. If he goes under without any excessive disturbance of public order, no state, no police, no public authority will intervene to stop him. Irresponsibility towards society results in the irresponsibility of society.

This human mass has its trapdoors and its catacombs. In a society so completely organised round the private fortune of the individual, woe to him who loses his hold, and in age, illness, or misfortune is unable to fall back on personal solidarity: for he will find no public aid. Practically everything that comes under the heading of public welfare carries the stamp of damnation. There are countries, particularly countries with a Protestant tradition, in which all social matters are so well organised that it is practically prohibited and almost inconceivable for anyone to be poor and unashamed, to lose his way in life, or in the real sense of the word to have a personal destiny; and this strong social discipline, which is tolerable to some, to others can be intolerable and terrifying. But in France everyone is allowed his own destiny, and is allowed to follow it to the end; no man's hand will be raised to stop him. This, in other words, is the east, which really begins, not in Naples or even in Marseilles, but in the suburbs of Paris. But here it is intensified, and at the same time chilled, by the greater decomposition of pre-state forms of social organisation and by the extinction of the religious counterweight to individualism among the enlightened bourgeoisie and petty bourgeoisie. Moreover, the mentality of the greater part of the workers in small-scale industry is petty bourgeois. The whole history of the French working-class movement, with its brief flood tides and long ebbs, demonstrates that, apart from demands for higher pay, modern problems of social organisation are only beginning to dawn. Social movements are a sheer coincidence of private complaints, demands, and needs. But private liberty, the supreme 'imperative of individualism, is fundamentally liberty to behave in an a-social fashion; *i.e.*, liberty, not just to mark a voting paper every few months or years, as is the right of citizens of the great parliamentary democracies, but to do with one's life on every day of every week exactly what one wants to do, and to act, not in accordance with any social standards of behaviour, but in accordance with one's own standards, conscience, and abilities.

Nothing is more alien to this spirit of individualism than the modern welfare state, and the great effort of the Fourth Republic accordingly failed to make an impact. It represented an inroad of social categories into an individualistic society, and it was accepted sullenly, almost wrathfully, and was ruthlessly exploited and viciously fought.

It is significant that the whole structure bore the stamp of Catholic Social ethics, and that that exceedingly novel phenomenon in the French post-war world, the Christian Social movement, the M.R.P., or Popular Republican Movement, played a bigger part in it than the working-class movement. It was an emergency coalition of reasons of state and *caritas*. But such public, organised solidarity lies on a plane higher than that of the great human mass; the real, spontaneous, French solidarity is that of the private group, whether of relations, or friends, or customers, or colleagues linked by comradeships and complicities of all kinds, and the real structure of society is the complicated network of these relationships, out of which conspiratorial little *républiques des camarades* are formed at all levels of the state, political, and social hierarchy. They forgather, according to the classical pattern, round a table under the glittering chandeliers of a banqueting hall, or in a simple inn, and each item on the agenda other than straightforward matters of routine has to be ceremoniously introduced by a speaker, toasted, and sealed with demonstrations of friendship. In this network everything that represents a public necessity but a private inconvenience is caught up, sieved, and rendered innocuous. Objectivity is found to be inconsistent with "human proportion", and to be made acceptable it requires friendly treatment, a warming of the atmosphere, gastronomic preparation, much drinking of toasts, and a great deal of handshaking and slapping on the back.

"Human proportion" rounds off all corners, removes the sharp edges of principles, and in the last resort makes possible the reconciliation of all conflicts. The process of humanisation makes extremism flexible enough for the total result of all extremisms to be the middle of the road. That kitchen and life recipe *il faut du tout pour faire un monde* requires a supplement: but of nothing too much. A little Jacobinism and a little reaction, a little blasphemy and a little piety, a little aristocracy and a little *canaille*—everything has its place and its excuse, so that life and creation may be complete. But moderation and proportion must govern everything: reason, logic, emotion, use and abuse, and even honesty, justice, and truth. The key phrase is *tout s'arrange*—everything will turn out all right if only it can be tackled in human and sensible fashion over a glass of wine. The secret of the craft of politics and government is moderation and proportion, dexterity in the evasion of inexorable alternatives, never pushing matters to extremes, knowing even in moments of the greatest enthusiasm exactly how far it is safe to go, and being able to distinguish between words and deeds, because it is this which makes it possible to be uncompromising in one's principles. These are the principles behind all the eloquence which fills Parliament, the market-place, and the courts. The brilliantly developed art of conversation depends on the fact that it arrives at no result, is a game, depending on an equilibrium of thrust and parry. The name of Incorruptible given to Robespierre was a continual smack in the face to his colleagues and fellow-men; it has remained a bogy, summing up all the excesses of inhumanity, lack of imagination, and danger to the common weal. The intolerable aspect of the Terror in the French Revolution was the "tyranny of virtue"; for the fanatics who practised it had no human sense of proportion, and it is the only aspect of the Revolution which has no heir today. Absolutes, when they overstep the limits of abstract rhetoric, are the enemies of human society. Freedom is a modified form of compulsion, justice a modified form of injustice, and order itself is nothing but a modified form of disorder. Principles cannot be sufficiently exalted, for they are an indispensable element of social ceremonial, but of ceremonial only; and it is as well to rate them highly, because one so seldom comes across them in practice.

Insisting on one's rights beyond a certain measure, following one's goal too unswervingly, persisting in one's chain of argument too unflinchingly because one regards it as proved, is behaviour unbecoming to a civilised man: Kleist's Michael Kohlhaas is not at home here. France is a country with a thousand-headed and tirelessly active machinery of justice, and numerous important episodes in her history go to show how a legal case is capable of rousing her passions, or how her passions are capable of taking charge of a legal case. But that a country is full of lawyers, that her citizens assiduously go to law, and that legal rhetoric plays a big part in her public spectacles, does not prove that it is a country in which the rule of law prevails. A legal system which still regards as valid every legal decision made since the Consulate and every law, no matter how antiquated, which has not been specifically repealed is susceptible of greater variations of interpretation than a clear and unambiguous code which even a non-initiate can follow without the assistance of a horde of advocates, consultants, and notaries should he desire to draw up a contract, institute divorce proceedings, or make a will. Just as French democracy is an amalgam of absolutist administration, tumultuous public meeting, and latent anarchy, so is its legal system the outcome of a moderate amount of contempt of the law on the part of the citizen, the exercise of a moderate amount of arbitrary power on the part of the police, and a procedure the lengthiness, expense, and impenetrable labyrinths of which provide a man with incomparable opportunities for harassing his neighbour, but barely offer the ordinary citizen the prospect of securing his rights in his lifetime unless he possesses the immortality of the dead hand. If the other party to the proceedings has bad will and only a moderately good lawyer, within a year his case will have been completely swallowed up in a jungle of appeals, objections, questions of competence, etc.

What is expected of the citizen is the observation of legal forms rather than respect for the law, in the wilderness of which he cannot possibly be expected to find his way. For there are always legal ways of getting round the law, and between the legal and the illegal there is a broad zone of semi-legality in which advocates and notaries serve as expensive but reliable guides. Here too it is a matter of knowing how far one can go. It is difficult for the most respectable citizen to avoid this twilight zone, and for the business man it is practically impossible; and everybody enters it with a perfectly clear conscience, at any rate in so far as he does so at the expense of the state, the revenue, or the public interest. Law and order are general principles to which it is extremely desirable to adhere, but it is not always advantageous to do so, and only the ignorant and unimaginative would abide by them in all circumstances. When a breach of the law has occurred and proceedings are considered, the personalities of those involved, and their connections, and the extent to which the practice in question has become traditional and respectable, are taken into consideration, and where public interests are at stake the question of taking action is left to the discretion of the police.

For side by side with the slow, clumsy, official machinery of justice with its lavish equipment of formal guarantees, there exists another machine, which is bound by no rules and takes no heed of legal complications or the legal rights of the individual, *i.e.,* the police machine. Here again there is an equilibrium between two excesses. Human and civil rights are a French gift to the world, but she forgot to give herself a *habeas corpus* Act. Every French schoolboy knows that the worst blemish of the *ancien régime* was the *lettre de cachet,* and every year the French people celebrate the storming of the Bastille, which put an end to that stain on humanity. But the *lettre de cachet* has never been abolished; it has only been given a new name; it has, so to speak, been democratised. Under the Napoleonic code of 1811—the most up-to-date version of the statutes, dating back mostly to the seventeenth century, on which a prefect's powers depend—the Paris prefect of police, who unites political, administrative, and judicial powers in his own hands like an absolute king within his realm, can at any time, at his own discretion and upon his own authority and responsibility, and in the absence of any formal charge or evidence that a crime has been committed, and without the sanction of any judicial authority, issue warrants, keep people under arrest for unlimited periods, conduct interrogations and inquiries, order houses to be searched, confiscate letters in the post, hand people over to the machinery of justice, release them, or deliver them to a lunatic asylum. The police have, or assume, the right to hold a suspect, who may be an innocent from the country accidentally involved in a raid, in their own prisons, to subject him to interrogation, and to use their own methods to make him confess. The *bastonnade* is another blemish of ancient and despotic forms of government to which the republic turns a blind eye because it has given it another name. The current method of interrogation, sometimes carried out with an excess of zeal that leads to fatal consequences, is familiar to everybody—its popular name is the *passage à tabac*; the suspect is received with a luxurious dose of blows and kicks, and the treatment is repeated until he "sits down at the table", admits everything, and signs. Only then does the police consider that it has fulfilled its duty and hands over the guilty man to the protection of the courts.

It is perhaps a matter for surprise that the country of the Dreyfus case, a country of great traditions of justice, should accept such energetic police methods without violent protest, treat them as if they were a matter of course, as if it were necessary and inevitable that the police should behave in this way, and indeed regard them, if anything, as a subject for humour. But the preservers of order, though they daily and nightly hand out their beatings with pleasure and a sense of devotion to duty, do so with moderation and a sense of proportion, in so far as they seldom beat up a respectable bourgeois or a gentleman equipped with good references. But should such a person be unfortunate enough to be beaten, as is bound to happen from time to time in the pressure of business, as soon as a telephone call from an appropriate quarter confirms the error, he receives the police commissioner's personal apologies, and his over-enthusiastic subordinates are duly hauled over the coals. However, if the error is not confirmed, or if the police are not convinced that it was an error, the suspect, by now ranking practically as a convicted criminal, is, after a longer or shorter stay in police protection, formally charged and handed over to the machinery of justice; and the whole tremendous, wearisome ceremonial of the legal machine comes remorselessly into action against him. As French law sets no limit to the time during which a suspect may be kept under arrest, he may languish for weeks, or months, or, if he has no useful connections, for years in a remand prison before the appropriate court finds time to deal with his case; and his name, address, and photograph may have appeared in all the newspapers as those of a criminal and a gallows-bird, and his reputation and perhaps his livelihood may have been ruined before he has had a chance of defending himself. The principle that an accused is to be regarded as innocent until his guilt is proved is observed by the judge, but not by the police, the Press, or the public; and should it turn out in the end that no guilt can be proved against him, there is no question of any compensation for the beatings he has suffered, the time he has spent in prison, or the damage suffered by him in purse and reputation. He has to be thankful that he does not have to pay the costs of the prosecution and of his keep in prison, and at having got off so lightly. For no acquittal can shake the profound belief of the police that everyone has something to his discredit, whether it can be proved or not, and that everyone is a criminal, though some unfortunately cannot be caught; and, though respectable citizens seldom fall victim to the more severe methods of the police, the latter have no hesitation in following them into that twilight zone of semi-legality in which they suspect that they move. The prefecture of police, though it has no legal right to do so, openly assumes the right of collecting dossiers of damaging material about unsuspecting inhabitants of their city who have never been in the dock or even at the police station, based on gossip or information given by *concierges* or informers. The existence of these dossiers remains unknown to those whom they concern, and they have no opportunity of correcting them, because they are never aware of their contents. But from the police point of view it is always as well to be ready for all eventualities and "to have something in hand" against everyone.

A whole army of spies and obliging informers exists to supply the needs of the police and their insatiable appetite for knowledge; the network pervades every level of society, from what is known as the *milieu* up to the "best circles". The principal sub-divisions of this army are not only peaceable *concierges*, but pickpockets and gaolbirds tolerated because of their useful services, fallen women, shady financiers and business men, and café and night-resort proprietors whose more or less illegal activities depend entirely on the broad-minded tolerance of the police; and, as there are several kinds of police who wish to be informed about each other and hold each other jealously in check, there are several such armies. Every police force, every police commissioner, and every inspector, has his own special *protégés* among the community of crooks and criminals, and a gaolbird is more useful when at liberty, because then he can make reports. He may be out of harm's way when he is in prison, but on the other hand he is then perfectly useless.

Here too a tortuous, labyrinthine network of personal relationships is at work, an extraordinary traffic of give-and-take, of living and letting live, at many levels and with many wheels within wheels. In the long and rich history of French scandals there has hardly been one in which the police have not in some way been involved, either as accomplices, or at any rate as having had cognisance of what was going on. For the police too adhere to the principles of moderation and human proportion, and observe the wise maxim of Cardinal Richelieu, that great architect of the French state, who in his political testament said of the public failings of his time "that they could be tolerated in an old monarchy, the abuses of which have become established and the disorders of which not without advantage form a part of public order." The republic's roots are still in the soil of the monarchy. The public remains in spirit, methods, and personnel the police of Fouché, reorganised by the ex-convict le Vidocq, who was Balzac's Vautrin. The best way to gain an understanding of that spirit is still to read Balzac's novels. All the elements of the totalitarian state are present in the unlimited and impenetrable sway of this police system, and yet the atmosphere of the city over which they preside is that of the freest in the world. This freedom is best summed up in a remark of Yves Guyot in his classic *La Police*: "The citizen is free to do whatever he likes, but under police supervision."

That is how Paris lives, in apparently unlimited liberty and disorder, a city in which everything forbidden is tolerated and everything prescribed is disregarded, with its "great" and its "little" world, its half-world and its underworld, its quarters as quiet as villages and its noisy centres of the tourist and pleasure industries, its bourgeois-conservative city centre and its Communist outskirts, its juxtaposition of luxury and poverty, its aristocratic *salons,* the Bedlam of the Halles, the busy seriousness and disorder of the Latin quarter, its bourgeoisie, its Bohemians, its "little men", its proletariat, and its gallows types, all under the knowing eye of the police, who are aware of everything that goes on, allow it to take its course and even take part in it all, intervening sometimes kindly, sometimes disreputably, and sometimes brutally, depending on circumstances; and the life of the city proceeds rather like its traffic, which on the surface always looks like complete chaos and ought logically to lead to inevitable catastrophe; traffic through which everyone winds his own independent way as best he can amid the din and the expletives, under the indolent control of a talkative traffic policeman's baton; traffic that is yet quicker, safer, and more free of accidents than that of any other metropolis. Anyone who wonders how this state system can possibly work should watch the traffic at the Place de l'Opéra at a peak period. It is theoretically impossible, and yet it works. In France the circle is squared daily and hourly, and there is nothing miraculous about it, for it depends solely on the fact that nobody, except a few puritanical or Teutonic tourists, minds about the little bit of the circle that is left over.

Paris really is the concentrated result of this order, just as it is the concentrated result of French history. A thousand years of uninterrupted history have deposited all their splendour and all their refuse on the great, concentric century rings extending outwards from the small, ancient *cité,* with its adjoining villages on the left and its magnificent buildings on the right. In the boulevards ring all periods, styles, and distortions of style are reconciled—real Gothic with Viollet-le-Duc's pseudo-Gothic, the royal palaces and squares with the corrupt pomposity of the Second Empire, true Paris with false Rome, Byzantium with Manhattan, because the same black patina has overlaid it and the same gleaming, silky-grey light plays over it all; including the high, bare, party walls which give Paris the look of a ruined city, and the garish advertisements which conceal the real ruins. Outside the boulevards ring there begin the year rings of the industrial age, the ulcerous growths of the *zone* and the comfortless hideousness of the industrial *banlieue,* stretching endlessly over whole departments, with villages scattered about, and the parks and villa quarters here and there, an occasional skyscraper standing senselessly in the open country, or a wretched weekend colony site. But it is all on an individual, human scale, without system and without any trace of the colossal, rather as if a trumpery collection of toys had been upset on the floor. The first of these rings includes the Île-de-France and the last includes the whole country. The inhabitant of this city thinks of himself as being situated at the centre of the world. His conviction of this is not to be shaken by any evidence provided by world events.

He does so with a composure undisturbed by any metropolitan rhythm. The metropolis of Paris, the garishly illuminated centre-point of France, which like a bright light attracts from every corner of the country and from beyond its borders all that would rise and prosper, both the able and the parasites, both intellect and trash, is undoubtedly the most parochial of all big cities, with its quiet life in the quiet world of the *quartiers,* whose inhabitants undertake a journey of momentous proportions when they travel to the centre of the city peacefully to see the sights on Sundays. Paris is a city full of important personalities very much aware of their importance, the scene of international events and international conferences, full of spectacles for foreigners and provincial visitors (including the spectacle provided by the foreigners themselves, who imagine they come as onlookers, but provide the most amusing of spectacles for the city's inhabitants); it is a city full of speculation and intrigue and shady business, of police and spies and *concierges,* in which no one bothers you and no one cares what you do or leave undone. This city of pandemonium is a city of contemplativeness, which reduces everything to human proportions and integrates every eccentricity into the great *comédie humaine.*

In the midst of all the villages of which Paris consists there lies, rather like an abstract geometrical point, the centre of its political, cultural, and social life, the fascinating alchemist's laboratory of *tout Paris* which transforms success, talent, and money into fame and reputation. The capital, the cold heart and over-stimulated brain which rules and administers this country and represents it and surrounds it with prestige, is not the city in which the people of Paris live under the eagle eye and inscrutable colonial administration of the Prefecture of Police. They are even more completely divested of political autonomy and independent specific gravity than their provincial brethren; for until Paris was eliminated as a political factor French centralism did not reach its full perfection. The true capital of France is an artificial vacuum between the Palais Bourbon, the Hôtel Matignon, and the Elysée—the seat of Parliament, the Prime Minister's office, and the Presidency of the Republic—a space as restricted as that of a theatrical stage, on which there takes place the whole ceremonial of debates, coalitions, resignations, and crises, an endless succession of dramatic scenes; and on this stage there circulate, both before the footlights and behind the scenes, the whole political personnel of the republic, a throng little calculated to inspire respect. Another artificial locality, such as could be accommodated only in Paris, is that of the French Olympus, in which all the gods and demigods of literature and art are so herded together that an energetic reporter could with a little luck interview them all on the same day on the most pressing question of the hour—on which they would all inevitably have a view, which would count for more than that of the politicians and the specialists, for in reputation they stand far higher than all specialists as the embodiment of civilisation itself.

In the hierarchy of values this Olympus is the supreme and only unshaken summit. Here France is officially enthroned, the France which upholds the prestige of French as the international language of civilised man, the prestige of the French capital as the capital of western civilisation, and the prestige of French taste, fashions, and values as the internationally recognised standards. It fights tooth and nail to preserve this prestige, and it thus preserves its own self-esteem and at the same time is engaged in a very realistical and adroit campaign to maintain the French political and diplomatic position in the world, and even the position of French exports, against the whole structural revolution of the modern world.

At this summit everything falls into order. In France the supreme ambition of every politician, general, diplomatist, or leading advocate is not to win political, military, legal, or diplomatic success, but to acquire a literary reputation and end his career in the circle of the "immortals" of the Académie Française. At the same time this summit is under continual assault by a rebellious opposition of anti-bourgeois artists and writers who make the Left Bank reverberate with new feuds, manifestos, scandals, and revolutions, continually make fresh advances, and end by becoming successful and being appointed to the Academy themselves; while on the slopes below the summit are to be found the settled domains of political and legal eloquence, the activities of the Press, and the conversation of the *salons* and the cafés as sub-species of literature; *haute couture,* the applied arts, architecture, and gastronomy as sub-species of the fine arts; and the whole artist population of the cabarets and night resorts, with its ramifications into the half-world and underworld.

It is a world complete in itself; its life is lived to the hectic rhythm of the first night at three dozen theatres, the private views at a hundred galleries, the opening of *salons* and counter-*salons*, receptions at the Academy and the anti-academies, innumerable literary cocktail parties, innumerable prize awards, charity, and propaganda functions at which writers sign copies of their works, public debates, and manifestos, and controversies in dozens of pamphlets, cafés, clubs, and cliques. Writers are public figures to a much greater extent than politicians; the Press is continually at their heels, seeking their opinion on the latest constitutional issue, or international development, or latest trial, or on a colleague's new book. Practically every leading author is also critic, pamphleteer, leader-writer, or editor himself. Gossip and anecdotes about these Olympians, their friendships and enmities, their love affairs, their witticisms and malicious remarks about each other, their travels with reporters hot on their trail, their favourite dishes, their hobby-horses, and the bees in their bonnets, are given as much prominence in the Press as world events, and their diaries and private correspondence are printed in full during their lifetime, or at latest while the earth is still fresh on their grave. Nothing about them is private, and they resemble the gods of ancient Greece at any rate in one respect, namely that they walk in front of the footlights naked and unashamed. The astonishing thing about them is that in spite of all this they have time to write their works. France does not cultivate the solitary genius or the Faustian spirit; the French ideal is formal perfection, and the supreme aim is mastery of one's craft. The main stream of French literature flows, not from lyricism, but from the social art of conversation, and the gravest threat to it today is that conversation is gradually using up and pulverising all the elements of action. French writing consists of conversation drama, conversation novels, aphorisms and scraps of conversation out of diaries, in which everything is talked about and talked to pieces without its ever leading to anything; and this is also the gravest threat to France herself, for in this respect she faithfully reflects her literature.

In this hothouse atmosphere there are certainly aspects of inbreeding and sterility, but at the same time Paris is a tremendous communal workshop of the intellect and the arts, of a kind inconceivable elsewhere, and it is conducive less to the individual work of genius than to successful artistic co-operation. From time to time some unique and unrepeatable constellation turns this into visible reality, when half a dozen or perhaps a whole dozen great names in literature, music, the stage, the ballet, painting, *haute couture*, and production unite to make text or choreography, music, interpretation, scenery, costume, and orchestra; then the *Gesamtkunstwerk*, the total work of art, makes its appearance, not the ponderous Wagnerian steamroller, but a soap-bubble, brilliant, improvised, and transitory. On these occasions one feels that such pure and divine extravagance is possible only in this city, before this audience, and in this atmosphere. Artistic co-operation of this kind is at work every day and everywhere, but is most evident in the Paris theatre, which is still the chief amphitheatre of the French spirit. Practically every dramatist has or creates "his own" theatre, practically every theatre has "its own" author, and thanks to this relationship, which ranges from the loosest partnership to the most complete identification, France has every kind of theatre, good and bad, magnificent and vulgar, but no theatre that exists only on paper; there are no reading dramas, which fall to pieces when put on the stage. Even in the most trashy work the never-forgotten tradition of craftsmanship is observed. The author writes his play having in mind the specific actors who will play in it and the specific stage on which it will appear, and he polishes it at rehearsals with the players until he has brought words, interpretation, and scenery into harmony. That is how Giraudoux wrote for Jouvet, Salacrou for Dullin, Anouilh for the Atélier, Sartre for the Antoine, Montherlant for Hébertot, Gide for Barrault. . . . The limits that drama sets itself in this way are clear; it may revolt against god and man, but not against the laws of the theatre in which men co-operate to produce an act of the human comedy or tragedy.

It is no paradox that the most individualistic people on earth should have the most social literature. Both arise from the same exclusive interest in the individual; and the individual, being supreme, expects the sole object of literature to be to provide him with his own reflection. Morals are the most public of all institutions. The effectiveness of the wordless arts is limited unless they speak through the medium of literature or engage in a symbiosis with it. But literature, at any rate in its clichées, seeps in the form of the spirit of the times through all levels of society. Literature is involved as a matter of course in all controversies and disputes and takes a foremost part in them, and literature decides what is true and what is not; problems that do not come within its sphere have no reality. Everything flows into literature, and literature reacts on everything else. Literature, Victor Hugo said, is civilisation itself; a remark that could not have been made in any country but France. But literature sets up no moral standards, she draws the moral from case to case, and it is seldom an edifying one; it establishes no standards, but registers indifferently the types and the phenomena of the human comedy; an author, no matter whether he writes novels, plays, essays, or pamphlets, is in the first place a moralist, an observer, and describer of mankind, and it is interesting to observe how every new movement which, because of a growing sense of discomfort with the inadequacies of "human proportion" in the modern world, has sought to extend the field of literature into the super-personal, the ecstatic, or the philosophical, like surrealism yesterday or existentialism today, always and inevitably ends up with moral analysis of human motives, relations, or behaviour if it is not to degenerate into the flattest and most commonplace ideology.

France is a country of continual self-interpretation, entirely bound up with herself, mirroring herself with almost terrifying clarity, both in praise and in blame, in a literature which knows nothing of the outside world and attaches the same importance to a bedroom drama as to a national catastrophe, but reflects her own characteristics with unvarnished precision. The unremitting process of intellectualising everything human is the highest social product of France and that which is in most complete conformity with the whole French system, because it turns life itself into an intelligent work of art. Intellectual awareness of motivation and behaviour gives the French way of life an often delightful and often terrifying hard clarity which is more satisfying to the aesthetic sense than to the emotions. The fundamental impulse is not honesty, unless it is intellectual honesty; it is not morality, but intelligent understanding; it is not to do right, but to know what one is doing. Astute wickedness is more forgivable than folly of the heart; that is why the sentimentality of this people, which is as sentimental as any, so gladly takes refuge in the intellectualised form of melancholy cynicism which distinguishes the French popular *chanson*. In the mirror of French literature the eighteenth century is not dead either. The great undertaking of the encyclopaedists, the construction of a human society without super-personal connections as a pure intellectual work of art, is still in progress, and only the optimism has become somewhat damped.

In her enormous literary output France has expressed and interpreted herself perhaps more completely than any other country. She has revealed her most secret psychological impulses, and yet remains an unknown country, both to itself and to the world, defying all analysis. In France literature has taken the place of political economy, sociology, and statistics. Literature is the only possible and adequate social science of a society organised in innumerable groups held together by personal ties, each small enough to be surveyable by all its members and private enough to be impenetrable to outsiders, while in the mass their infinite divisions and subdivisions make them totally unsurveyable and incalculable. All the publications of the Statistical Office reveal less about present-day France than do the works of Balzac. Any observer who sets out to establish the laws which govern her functioning, or any reformer who would establish new laws by which she should function, may as well give up at the outset. For every statement about her is only half-true, every rule is valid only up to a point, every law is only formally valid, every principle applies only theoretically; everything happens with human proportion. This atmosphere, in which all sharp contours fade as in the diffuse light of the capital and all firm outlines are dissolved in playful ceremonial or in irony and scepticism, ends by smoothly and relentlessly swallowing up all enthusiasms and leading all rebellions along the line of least resistance back into the path of routine.

Everything gives and nothing yields. No firm boundaries are drawn anywhere, and it is possible to go just a little too far in every direction. But then the path simply stops. No country grants so much indulgence to its responsible politicians, those perpetual scapegoats for every public failing, or bestows so much admiration on the most modest achievements in statesmanship; and in no country is it so hard for a statesman to find a basis for taking action that departs by one iota from the accustomed. Organised anarchy provides an incredibly effective defence against any kind of social intervention. The system of personal relationships, the confidential nature of business transactions, the system of double bookkeeping, the unascertainability of production and turnover figures, the unsurveyability of markets, the universally taken-for-granted falsity of tax declarations, the fluidity and uncontrollability of gold-hoarding and flight capital, all these things provide a far greater protection for all *situations acquises* than could be offered by any system of authoritarian government, because they provide protection against the state itself. France, with her thousands of little factories and workshops, with her two-and-a-half million practically self-sufficient peasants, who could in case of need survive without any market outlet at all, has no "masses" in the modern sense, and is not susceptible to the contemporary techniques of impersonal mass organisation—from fiscal statistics and the control of consumption to *Gleichschaltung*; that is to say, in the modern sense France is not organisable. For her defence, not only against reformers and planners, but against conquerors, she relies on the secret weapon with the use of which she has by long tradition become so incredibly familiar, *i.e.*, her latent but ever-present anarchy. If France were willing to buy the survival of her traditional way of life by renouncing her national greatness, no doubt the ideal way of defending herself against all the revolutions of the twentieth century would be to have no nerve-centres which could be crippled, to have no organisation the destruction of which would have fatal consequences, and by ever-new improvisations to survive, unchanged and invulnerable. The most recent history of France is nothing but a tenacious, desperate, and acrobatic struggle to hold fast, in spite of all threats and catastrophes, to her way of life and to her national greatness, her admirable and terrifying equilibrium of incompatibles, in which she still succeeds in preserving the private small happiness of the greatest number.

France produces fewer goods and less horse-power per man-shift and works fewer hours per unit of population than most industrial countries, but she is full of men who preserve their own mind, their own individuality, their own fortunes and misfortunes, and are not organisable units of population, but individual men. They revolt with all the instinctive clarity of an ancient civilisation against being turned into modern mass-men. They refuse to take part in the Darwinian struggle for life, and at heart they look more with sorrow than with anger at the success of the nations which have so efficiently, progressively, busily, restlessly, organisedly, and competently undermined the former supremacy of the French nation; for they regard them as hordes of semi-animal, Neanderthal men making onslaughts on the painfully acquired human values the home of which is France, *la patrie de l'homme.* Is the price too high?

France, for him who looks for nothing else, is still the country in which it is supremely possible to live. The magic of the *douceur de vivre* is still unbroken. Paris, even the expensive and uncomfortable Paris of the second post-war period, is full of refugees from countries in which social discipline is excessive, social compulsions are inescapable, and the social machinery is incorruptible. Paris has become the undethronable capital of modern art precisely because it is the asylum of the individualist. There are Germans who hate Germany, Americans who are revolted by America, Swiss who feel stifled in Switzerland, Englishmen who say that England is impossible to live in; all these are marginal figures of an all-too-compact and well ordered society. But a Frenchman who is not in love with his country is hard to find. He may curse beyond redemption the French state and its institutions and the morals and manners of his fellow-countrymen, he may dismiss the French Government as a gang of crooks and the French administrative system as a racket, the most commonplace article of foreign manufacture may cause him to break out into a tirade and declare that only foreign-made goods are worth having, but at the end of it all he will passionately announce that France is the only country in which it is possible to live and breathe freely. What do technical achievements and social progress, efficient plumbing and lifts that work, amount to in comparison with the pleasure of being an unhampered individualist?

France has again and again succeeded in squaring the circle by miracles of dexterity and adroitness, and an unpretentiousness in matters of bodily comfort that approaches the miraculous. But the little bit left over every time the circle is squared has now grown so big that it can no longer be ignored. *"Pourvu que ca doure"*—the simple, anxious phrase of old Laetitia Bonaparte continually haunts those who walk through the streets of France and not only love this country enough to enjoy it as a work of art, but enough to be able to grieve for it.

§ 5

THE STRANGE DEFEAT

For generations France has been, not ruled, but administered. Is this not a secret fulfilment of the anarchist Utopia, the extinction of the state, which ceases to control the actions of men, but administers things only? The state survives, but confines itself to supervising the moderate current disorder, safeguarding the moderate current injustice, and controlling the traffic. Valéry's intellectualised memory of the "priceless moment" of the eighteenth century has its counterpart in the mind of the man in the street, who thinks nostalgically of happier and less anxious times before the war, just as during those times he thought nostalgically of the *belle époque* before the 1914 war. These lost paradises are always projections backwards of the present, day-dreams of a time when the *douceur de vivre* could be enjoyed without problems, anxieties, and dark forebodings. France, like the burning bush, in the course of centuries "burned and was not consumed." She produced, or devised, and then overthrew practically every form of social organisation of the final period of the European millennium, and ended by discovering what in its way was the final form of her civilisation, as final as was the Greek *polis*; and every time it is disturbed she seeks to re-establish it. She is so rich in history that she has had enough of it; history ought to proceed no further. The "priceless moment", though it recedes remorselessly into the distance, has not been savoured to the end; and every reconstruction, every liberation, every impulse of reform, develops imperceptibly and inevitably into an attempted restoration.

But France has long ceased to be happy except in memory.

Slowly and progressively, in one part of the social mechanism after another, here for a century, there for a generation, the stability that was so carefully preserved has been in process of transformation into stagnation and sclerosis. The whole process is inter-connected, and wherever stagnation is allowed to appear the fatal circle is completed, leaving no gaps. The population of France has been stagnating for a century; the rationing of the number of children in a family is so well calculated to preserve the family inheritance and the individual desire for happiness, and so fatal to the health of the nation. A stagnant market, in which every place was hereditary and which therefore vigorously defended itself against the incursion of outsiders, seemed to offer no more opportunities for development, and none was sought. A stagnant agriculture was sufficient for that market, and feared nothing more than over-production and foreign imports; and there was a steady decline in the rhythm of industrial development, the backwardness of which was revealed to all at that "industrial Sedan", the world exhibition of 1900, *i.e.*, when the *fin de siècle* period which has been transfigured in retrospect was in its heyday. Economic expansion did not come upon external limitations; its impulses had weakened from within. In the very years when France created her colonial empire she fell from second place among the world's industrial powers which she had occupied in the middle of the ninteenth century to fourth. In the period since the eve of the first world war, which has been a period of revolutionary developments, huge advances, and sensational collapses all over the world, France has barely maintained the level which she reached at its outset, or has laboriously climbed back to it again after every collapse. Thanks to the return of the industrial areas of Alsace-Lorraine, the re-equipment of her heavy industry financed by reparations and inflation, and the development of the new motor and electricity industries, ten years after the end of the first world war France had notably surpassed her pre-war level. But in the traditional fields of her national economy she had once more reached the level of 1913, just as in 1936 she was again where she had been in 1906—and in 1950 was again where she had been in 1929; and that is where she has since remained.

The first world war struck a social and economic body which had ceased to grow, and the damage and loss it suffered has never really healed. The huge gaps which the years 1914–18 left in the vulnerable French population structure moved year by year up the age pyramid, but were never filled. In the years during which the Nazi war machine was being built up on her frontiers the terrible losses of the first world war began to exercise their full effect when a weakened generation came of military age. From 1936 to 1940 the yearly call-up of French conscripts fell from 240,000 to 120,000—one fifth of that of 1914. Between 1930 and 1940 the number of marriages similarly dwindled by half, and after 1934 the annual number of deaths exceeded that of births. It is as well to bear these figures in mind before indulging in moral strictures about the instinctive inclination of pre-war France to accept anything rather than a repetition of that blood-letting and destruction. In 1938, between the Austrian *Anschluss* and the Munich crisis, when the completion of the reconstruction of the severely damaged cathedral of Rheims was celebrated, ruins and burnt-out façades of the first world war were still to be seen in the Place Royale, the heart of the city, and the question: What for? lay oppressively over the whole magnificent ceremony. Moreover the ruins of the second world war were soon to be added indistinguishably to the ruins of the first.

The history of the inter-war period, with all its confusion and inconsistencies, is the history of a hopeless attempt to shut the windows and bar the doors on the world, and to build round France a Great Wall of China. The counterpart of the Maginot line in the military sphere was her demand for "security" in the diplomatic sphere, her blind and pedantic clinging to the legal guarantees of the *status quo* drawn up at Versailles, her verbal intransigence, her illusory ossification in the pose of a victor, with all its irreconcilables and exaggerations, and the final inevitable capitulation of a system of power politics based on weakness. At home the supreme aim, nay, the moral imperative, of financial policy was the sacrifice of the country's economic substance for the sake of stability, the stability of incomes and the gold parity of the franc. But this only briefly delayed the decline of a currency whose economic foundation was crumbling away. France's answer to the world economic crisis was complete retirement into the autarky of her closed and self-sufficient economic life; this in fact succeeded in holding at bay the violent convulsions and huge readaptations of world economy, substituting for them a slow, effortless, declining spiral. France, a world power whose alliances spanned all Europe and whose empire spanned the world, visibly adapted herself to an economic system on the Spanish pattern, cultivating her artistic and intellectual prestige and her inherited treasure-store of great memories as an adequate guarantee of her greatness. The Quai d'Orsay sent to its eastern European allies its diplomatists, the Galas Karsenty and the travelling lecturers of the Alliance Française, which roused the enthusiasm of aristocratic audiences for French civilisation and the French way of life; and there was bitter disappointment when it turned out that more effective work had been a storey lower down by German commercial travellers with their bags full of samples of the goods of a material civilisation. Meanwhile the colonial empire, to which France thought of offering nothing but civilisation and from which she demanded nothing but soldiers, but with which in the economic sphere she did nothing whatever and had no idea what to do, went on sleeping its ever more restless sleep under the narcosis of the *pacte colonial*; and in 1940, when the question arose whether the war which had been lost in the motherland should be continued from North Africa, the hitherto unobserved fact came to notice, and weighed heavily in the scales, that after a hundred years of French colonisation North Africa was totally lacking in the essential facilities necessary to repair a rifle or a pair of boots, to manufacture a shell, or to replace the buttons of a uniform.

Stability in an unstable world has been purchased at the cost of a catastrophic shrinkage of the national capital and human substance, the consequences of which weigh heavily on post-war France today. But even in the happy inter-war period it was observed with growing concern that petty good fortune was being paid for at an alarmingly high price. Their *rentes*, the symbol of security and stability, started melting away faster and faster between the astonished hands of the

French bourgeoisie. The shopkeeper, *l'épicier du coin,* that quintessence of the modest and peaceable petty bourgeoisie, saw his customers becoming rarer and meaner. The peasantry, in a market protected by tariffs and quotas against the threat of dangerous competition even from the French colonial empire, found themselves faced with chronic crises of overproduction, and demanded guaranteed markets and prices. The young people of whole areas emigrated to the towns in search of a livelihood, but found only unemployment. Unemployment as reflected in statistics always remained relatively limited, however. Because of the archaic French economic structure it never became a mass catastrophe of the kind experienced in the great industrial countries; it took the form of working part-time or short time, of individuals drifting away from industry into every conceivable way of living from hand to mouth, and the continual latent threat to the innumerable small patriarchal establishments that tomorrow it would be necessary to put up the shutters and wait for better times. But in all its creeping and insidious forms the process served still further to depress the already extremely low standard of living of the French working class.

The final conclusion was that in some incredible and amazing fashion everyone had been robbed, and everyone set about searching for the surreptitious enemy who must be responsible for it all—the Government, parliamentary corruption, speculators, Communists, Jews, foreigners, the "two hundred families", the *affameurs et accapareurs,* according to taste. With the same earnestness, the same impotence, the same unlimited ignorance of economics, but with different slogans, both right and left entered a struggle against a lot of bogies, symbols, and figments of the imagination. The last ten years before the war were a time of growing unrest and bitter strife about a shrinking social product; the strife and unrest grew slowly and steadily in intensity and shook France to her depths. The semi-Fascist rioting of February 6th, 1934, followed by the Stavisky scandal and a whole series of others which, after the fashion of the Panama scandal, provided nourishment for a well orchestrated campaign of indignation against the "rottenness of the régime", led to no more than the resignations of a Government of the moderate left and its displacement by an equally short-lived Government of the moderate right. But the latent *coup d'état* atmosphere was maintained by the activities of the French pupils of Fascism. These were more grotesque than dangerous, but for want of wider possibilities they played at conspiracy and revolt and organised uproar and riot and senseless attempts at assassination. Even the riot of February, 1934, was no more than a particularly noisy disturbance outside Parliament, and would have remained an incident of no importance had it not provided the occasion for a great counter-movement of "anti-Fascism" and "republican defence". This, thanks to a complete reversal in Communist tactics, led to the Popular Front, and, after the 1936 elections, to the formation of a Socialist-Left Radical Government with Communist support. The new Government was greeted by a tremendous outburst of popular enthusiasm of the kind characteristic of anniversaries of the Revolution, and a spontaneous explosion of long pent-up social unrest. A wave of strikes and seizures of factories spread panic among the bourgeoisie and the employers, who unresistingly put their signatures to a social-political revolution: they granted a forty-hour week, and holidays with pay, only to sabotage them later.

It was a short interval of euphoria after years of discouragement, and once more France seemed to be the country which held high the torch of triumphant democracy in a Europe sinking into darkness and tyranny—"a great people on the march to the Elysian fields", as Bernanos put it. For two years at any rate the endless procession of tandems on which engaged couples, or married couples with children on the carriers, left town on Friday evenings for long week-ends in the country presented a peaceful picture of happiness which had at last become the common property of all. Then the whole dream collapsed in bitter disillusionment, and there was a rude awakening. A long overdue policy of social reform had failed because it sought at one blow to make good the arrears and omissions of half-a-century and was unaccompanied by even the beginnings of a realistic economic policy on which to base it; not even the levers needed to put such a policy into force had been present, and the consequences were the combination of inflation and depression which had grown to be so typical of France; the flight of capital; the series of devaluations; the civil war mentality with which the bourgeoisie and the middle classes answered the "rebellion of the masses", seeing even in the most justified social demands the diabolical figure of Bolshevism, for the elimination of which even Hitler, that scourge of God, would be welcome ("Better Hitler than Blum!"); the dishonest policy of the Communist Party, which simultaneously demanded "guns for Spain" and crippled the armaments industry by continual strikes, preached ideological war on tyranny in the best Jacobin style while bitterly opposing everything that made a policy of resistance possible, and finally, when war broke out and Stalin went fifty-fifty with Hitler, "turned its rifles" and declared war "on our imperialism"; the stupid, rampant reaction of the "national" parties, who turned the tables too and branded all who wished to organise resistance to Nazi aggression as criminal warmongers in the pay of Moscow, and when war finally broke out found nothing more urgent to do than to take revenge for the Popular Front under the pretext of the repression of Communism. All these things took place in the feverish years when the second world war was visibly on the horizon, and the denunciation of the peace treaties, the reoccupation of the Rhineland, Franco's military rebellion, the Austrian *Anschluss,* the Munich capitulation, the defeat of the Spanish Republic, the German entry into Prague, and the German-Russian pact succeeded one another like the hammer-blows of fate, lending an appalling unreality to all these domestic conflicts in a country whose very existence was at stake. In September, 1939, this people, in a state of complete intellectual and moral bewilderment, with mutual accusations of treachery and guilt ringing in its ears on every side and dazedly and bitterly convinced that for twenty years it had been deceived and betrayed, entered a war that it did not want, which it cursed in its heart and did not want to believe was true, a war which started with an endless, impotent, demoralising wait for the first shot to be fired: *la drôle de guerre,* the phoney war. . . .

Since then it has often been asked how it was possible for the French Communist Party, not only to survive its open treachery of 1939, the great shift from effusive patriotism to sabotage and defeatism, but to come forward a few years later as the great national party of patriotic Frenchmen and the most inflexible champions of French independence and national greatness, and how in the months of "purge" justice after the liberation it was able to assume the role of judge of the patriotic honour of all other Frenchmen. Thanks to the assumption of this judicial role, the party was able officially, so to speak, to rewrite the whole of the past, and with the logic and consistency of an Orwellian Ministry of Truth to bring into being a whole literature putting forward its own lying version of history, in which every detail was stood on its head, every date altered, and every document falsified. It was alleged, for instance, that Maurice Thorez took to the *maquis* in 1939 and as the *premier résistant de France* summoned the people to resistance in 1940 two weeks before General de Gaulle; and at the time hardly anyone dared to protest against this version of events, because it was made acceptable by all the means of mental terror at the Communist disposal and the tremendous prestige of their millions of followers. But that does not explain everything. For how did it come about that the Communists were able to assume this judicial role, and how was it possible for adult Frenchmen who had lived through the period in question to believe what the Communists said? Even the tremendous capacity of self-deception and readiness to forget characteristic of those years, and the eagerness to substitute a heroic legend for the memory of the dark period of war and occupation, with their atrocities, lies, and treachery, provide no sufficient explanation. "Big" history has no explanation to offer, but "little" history has; and, as these episodes from the last months of the Third Republic not only illustrate the oppressive, sultry atmosphere of the time of the outbreak of war, but were pregnant with disastrous consequences for the post-war period in France, they shall be described here.

After the great change of line to the Popular Front, the Communist Party had assumed and adopted as its own the whole Jacobin tradition of the French left, whose fundamental principle had always been the identity of the internal and the external enemy. French patriotism and Soviet patriotism, mortal hostility towards "reaction" and the Third

Reich, had been fused into one. The announcement of the German-Russian pact of August 22nd, 1939, came like a clap of thunder in a clear sky. The crisis that it caused in the party affected not only the leadership, but the rank-and-file; the shock was severe, and might have been fatal. Until that moment the Communists had been bellicose anti-Fascists, grimly determined to die for Danzig, and if the merest suspicion appeared anywhere on the horizon of any desire for "another Munich", a last-minute wish to conciliate Hitler or negotiate with him, *l'Humanité* snarled like a chained dog. It was an acrobatic leap from this to the view, announced a few weeks later, that "the French and British imperialists unleashed the war after instigating the Polish Government into refusing a peaceful settlement of the Polish Corridor question", and the French Communists did not accept it with the smooth unanimity of a party of automata. For a whole month, while the party leadership was left to itself without instructions or explanations from Moscow, it clung desperately to a daily more untenable double loyalty to the Soviet Union and to France. The last legal number of *l'Humanité*, which was confiscated by the police, announced that "the French Communists will stand in the front rank of the defenders of the independence of the peoples, of democracy, and of threatened republican France", and on September 6th the party leadership solemnly hailed "the mobilised deputies who have reported to their units with Maurice Thorez at their head." On September 30, after Hitler and Stalin had divided up Poland and Molotov and Ribbentrop had signed a joint declaration denouncing Britain and France as warmongers, and the party line was changed to a campaign against "the British imperialists and their French agents" and in favour of "immediate peace", the majority of the Communist deputies revolted when presented with a draft letter to be sent to M. Herriot, the president of the Chamber, calling on him to summon it to consider "peace proposals" of Hitler's which had not been made; this letter marked the final breach with the "national Communist" line which had hitherto been pursued. Because of the deputies' revolt M. Bonte, the general secretary, had to hand in the letter behind the backs of the parliamentary party. But even before that cracks had appeared, not only at the base of the pyramid, among the rank-and-file, who suddenly found themselves isolated by a wall of mistrust, fear, and aversion, but at the summit—not of course of the apparatus, but of the legal party, among the branch and local officials and the parliamentary party itself: twenty-one out of seventy-three deputies and senators repudiated the party; and open revolt prevailed in the "workers' and peasants' groups" which were re-formed after the banning of the party on September 26. The "diabolical" Moscow pact endangered the whole edifice.

What saved it was in the first place the blind, raging, pitiless assault which was let loose against the party without even waiting for its own members' reactions. Léon Blum was the only one who pointed out in the newspapers at the time what a gift from heaven it was for the Communists that on the third day after the announcement of the Moscow pact they were gagged by the banning of their Press. The issue of *l'Humanité* of August 26, which was confiscated by the police after it was ready for the press, was a glowing manifesto of patriotism, national unity, and readiness to fight Hitler. It would, of course, be absurd to assume that the party apparatus would have adhered to this patriotic line against the directives of Moscow which arrived a month later. But, for a great party which had advocated the *union sacrée* in defence of the nation with such ardour and enthusiasm, the change of line ordered a few weeks after the outbreak of war would have meant sheer suicide, and one may well wonder how many members would have followed the party apparatus into its self-chosen illegality. But instead the whole party was driven into illegality, isolated, and subjected to such an assault that it became morally and almost physically impossible to leave it.

The reaction of public opinion to the Moscow pact was perfectly justified and perfectly inevitable. But the motive of the onslaught to which the Communists were subjected was by no means mere patriotic indignation at their "betrayal of France", which was in any case primarily the work of Stalin and not of his French followers. In the first place, those who shrieked loudest for the banning of the Communist Party and for summary justice for its followers were now, as before, the *munichois* of yesterday and the fifth column of tomorrow

—Doriot, Déat, Flandin, and the infamous weekly *Gringoire*. But they had changed their ground. For months they had been clamouring for the banning of the party because of its "warmongering in the pay of Moscow"; now they wanted it banned because of its "treachery to France in the pay of Moscow". The German-Russian pact was not a reason, but a greedily seized pretext for an act of political revenge. The war in which their country was engaged was not their war, and its forthcoming defeat was not going to be their defeat, but a heaven-sent opportunity of getting rid once and for all of the "inner enemy"

To understand the extent to which all this came to the rescue of the Communist morale all the trivial, absurd, and hysterical details of the hue and cry must be borne in mind. But perhaps it may be sufficient to recall that the Prime Minister who carried out the repression was M. Daladier and that his Foreign Minister was M. Bonnet; that makes clear how questionable the judges in this trial must have seemed, both at the time and in the light of the following catastrophe and the universal cries of treachery of 1940. For the direct share of the French Communists in the collapse was modest. After the end of the "national Communist" period of August-September, 1939, they certainly did everything in their power to undermine their country's morale and material power of resistance. But their power to do so was in fact small, and their propaganda, so flagrantly in conflict with their previous line, had little effect. In the tumult of mutual accusations in a country almost every one of whose responsible politicians had been accused at least once of high treason in the wildly mendacious historical trials of Riom, Vichy, and Versailles, and after all the blood which the Communists had shed in the resistance after the German attack on Russia had brought French and Soviet patriotism once more into line, it was not too difficult to "drown the fish" in the resulting chaos. What with agents of Moscow, agents of London, agents of Wall Street, agents of Hitler, agents of Franco, the traitor Thorez, the traitor de Gaulle, and the traitor Pétain, it was difficult enough for anybody to find his way.

But the "national reaction" of autumn, 1939, was by no means directed only at the Communist Party and its submissiveness to Moscow; it was above all a pretext for taking a ruthless revenge for all that the Popular Front of 1936–37 had done in the social field. The social policy of the Daladier Government during the "phoney war" period was the most incredible example of ineptitude that can ever have characterised a country threatened from within and without. Not content with doing away with all limitations on hours of work and freezing wages without regard to the rise in the cost of living which had already begun, it not only did away with extra rates for overtime, but put a special tax of 40 per cent. on overtime pay which was estimated to yield more than a third of the revenue from direct taxation in 1940. *Faites payer les pauvres!* The Government and the employers declined all co-operation with the trade unions, which were deprived of all opportunity of effective intervention because all labour legislation was by decree. It needed the German offensive to bring employers and trade unions together, and on May 24th, 1940, after the Germans had advanced from Abbeville to the Channel at Calais, an agreement was signed between them, but in the general collapse it naturally remained a dead letter. In the circumstances the reorganisation of the C.G.T., the General Confederation of Labour, after the breach with the Communist trade union wing and the dissolution of all branches which had been under Communist leadership, was necessarily still-born. The attempt to re-form the dissolved organisations ended in fiasco; only in two per cent. of the factories engaged in national defence work was it possible to appoint delegates to the C.G.T. under M. Jouhaux. In the eyes of the French "national parties" destruction of the Communist Party and destruction of the workers' organisations was one and the same thing.

In the depressing atmosphere of the phoney war the chances of founding a Communist Party independent of Moscow which were created by the numerous public repudiations of the party at all levels of the hierarchy, and the existence of even more numerous silent dissidents within it, were condemned to be abortive. The names of the twenty Communist deputies and of all the Communist mayors and local councillors, party officials, and intellectuals who, when faced with the choice between Russia and France, chose

France, have long since been forgotten. The "great reckoning" of which the Communist Party dreamed throughout the war, which in 1940 it hoped in vain it would be able to carry out with the aid of the German occupation forces, but was able partially to carry out in the resistance movement and the post-war "purge", came to pass in at least one respect. The renegades of 1939, not just those who ended by collaborating with the Germans, but those who fought in the resistance movement, were ruthlessly liquidated in the "gorilla" justice of the resistance and the period of unofficial "people's justice" of the autumn of 1944; and those who had died in the struggle against the Germans were posthumously defamed as "traitors" without anyone's so much as turning a hair. When M. Marcel Cachin, who by reason of his seniority has taken the chair at every opening of the French Parliament since 1944, read out the list of names of deputies who had died for their country, he took the liberty of omitting these renegades; and M. Aragon, the party rhapsodist, omitted the works of Paul Nizan, a former editor of *l'Humanité* who died at Dunkirk, from the first post-liberation exhibition of the French writers' association because this "traitor" had opted for France two years before the party and M. Aragon himself. This was a worthy conclusion of one of the least known and saddest chapters of French contemporary history. The unbroken power of the French Communist Party is not to be explained by its nature and its history alone; the nature and history of French anti-Communism, its most loyal and effective ally, must also be taken into account. Both have learned little and forgotten everything.

More alarming than the defeat was the resignation, almost the haste, with which it was accepted. It came like something inevitable, half judgment of God and half natural catastrophe. In the two years after the defeat many voices spoke in the name of France from many places—Vichy, Paris, London, and Moscow—but none was able to overcome the silence of France herself. This long period was not a period of revolt or of submission; it was a period of self-communion. Never was France more completely occupied with herself than during this period, when the future was sealed, the national fabric seemed to have been smashed to pieces, and every individual was left alone with himself and his picture of France. The conqueror was in the land, but only in the physical sense; intellectually and morally he was not present, for what was there to say of Hitler and Goebbels, and what else of Germany was left? The object of France's soliloquy during that pause in history was not the harsh fact of military defeat, but her own dreadful interior collapse; and so complete was the collapse of everything that had seemed to count that even contemplation was difficult.

In the little book *A l'échelle humaine* which he wrote as his political testament in prison at Riom, Léon Blum wrote: "Peoples have an instinctive sense of justice. If they suffer a defeat, they need to believe that it was not undeserved. They look within themselves for what they may have been guilty of." Indeed, everyone started by attributing the blame to his particular political bugbear. The defeat must have been due to the bourgoisie, or the Marxists, or the collapse of authority, or the decline in public morals. During this period Paul Claudel pored over the Apocalypse, and discovered the etymological and semantic identity of Lucifer and the enlightenment; and if long passages of Blum's book are devoted to an ideological defence of the republic, which was poor in just that honesty which its defender treated so lightly, that is intelligible enough, considering that he was one of the accused in the grotesque Riom trial, in which the French politicians who with Marshal Pétain at their head had accommodated themselves to the defeat sought to fasten the blame for the defeat, and even for the war itself, on other pre-war politicians, and to surround themselves with a defensive barrier against the orgies of national self-denigration indulged in by the Vichy Press. But M. Blum expressed the essence of all the French self-communion of this period when he said: "The generation to which I belong failed in its task."

It was also strikingly expressed in the chaos of the collapse of the summer of 1940 by a distinguished scholar and patriot who had discarded his now useless uniform and waited for the time to come when there would again be something worth risking his life for. "The generation to which I belong has a bad conscience," he wrote. There is no better evidence of the struggle for clarity and the ruthless self-examination of those days than Marc Bloch's *L'étrange défaite,* published by his friends after his death and the liberation, a little book which is now almost as completely forgotten as are those days themselves. Bloch was a student of the Middle Ages who put the study of French social and economic history on an entirely new basis and shook a generation of historians out of their academic routine, and he carried out his "examination of a Frenchman's conscience" with the keen intellect of a historical critic, the experience of an officer in two world wars who was also a sociologist, and the inner excitement of a man who could write on the last page of his notes: "My only hope is that when the moment comes we may have enough blood left to shed. . . . For there can be no salvation when there is not some sacrifice, and no national liberty in the fullest sense unless we have ourselves worked to bring it about." Bloch subsequently worked for his country's national liberty and sacrificed his life for it. He became the unknown M. Blanchard of the resistance. Three weeks after the allied landing in Normandy, when the liberation was at hand, the Germans captured him at Lyons, and shot him without knowing who he was.

L'étrange défaite is a book full of sober indignation and a fearful clarity. Like Renan after the war of 1870, but with the precision of an eye-witness, Bloch starts by declaring that the defeat was primarily and above all an intellectual defeat. In the daily round of the various military headquarters, with their paper order but technical disorder, the smooth routine of which degenerated into chaos as soon as it was disturbed; in their incapacity for foresight or for reaction to the unexpected; in the tempo of their decisions, which corresponded to the speed of huge, clumsy, mass armies moving on foot and were always left hopelessly behind by the speed of the machine; in their bewildered helplessness in the face of the enemy's departure from established military doctrine—indeed, in the face of speed of any kind; in a hundred seen and experienced details the military clash had been a clash between two ages: the age of the ox-cart and that of the petrol engine. The metronome of the whole French military machine, says Marc Bloch, was always several beats behind, and "our war, up to the very end, was a war of old men, or of theorists who were bogged down in errors engendered by the faulty teaching of history. It was saturated by the smell of decay rising from the Staff College, the offices of a peace-time General Staff, and the barrack square. . . . But our leaders would not have succumbed so easily to that spirit of apathy which wise theologians have ever held to be among the worst of sins, had they merely entertained doubts of their own competence. In their hearts, they were only too ready to despair of the country they had been called upon to defend, and of the people who furnished the soldiers they commanded." Marc Bloch, having completed his soldier's eye-witness account, proceeds to examine his conscience as a civilian. The army, even in the isolation and alienation of the military hierarchy from its own people, was a replica of the nation. "Many men of what might still claim to be our ruling classes, since from them were drawn our leaders of industry, our senior civil servants, the majority of our reserve officers, set off for the war haunted by these gloomy prognostications. They were taking their orders from a political set-up which they held to be hopelessly corrupt. They were defending a country which they did not seriously think could offer any genuine resistance. The soldiers under their command were the sons of that 'people' which they were only too glad to regard as degenerate. . . . Our leaders not only let themselves be beaten, but too soon decided that it was perfectly natural that they should be beaten. . . . They accepted the disaster, but with rage in their hearts. However that may be, they did accept it, and long before they need have done. They were ready to find consolation in the thought that beneath the ruins of France a shameful régime might be crushed to death, and that if they yielded it was to a punishment meted out by destiny to a guilty nation. . . . Whatever the complexion of its government, a country is bound to suffer if the *instruments* of power are hostile to the spirit which obtains in the various branches of its public institutions. . . . A democracy becomes hopelessly weak, and the general good suffers accordingly, if its higher officials are bred up to despise it." The civil service and the army, the universities and the fields of politics were alike dominated by the principles of co-option from the narrowest social circles, promotion to the highest posts based on seniority and social and intellectual conformity, control in the hands of old men and model pupils, and confinement to the mental ruts of a gerontocracy: and both on the right and on the left "our party machinery had . . . begun to give off the smell of dry rot which it had acquired in small cafés and obscure back rooms."

Bloch has similar hard words to say of the low esteem enjoyed in France by scientific technique, specialised knowledge, or precise information, and of the untroubled acceptance of inconsistencies, commonplaces, and general impressions which nobody took the trouble to check, thus preserving an open field for every form of intellectual, political, and ideological fraud and falsity in a country so proud of its Cartesian spirit. The grotesque inadequacy of her statistics, which differentiated France from all other civilised and semi-civilised countries, the stuffy secrecy of her industry, which felt most at home in the semi-obscurity of *les petites affaires*, was matched by the inadequacy of the chief organs of public information, including *Le Temps*, which Bloch compares not without bitterness to *The Times*, and the *Frankfurter Zeitung* of the pre-Hitler and even of the Hitler period. "The wise man, says the proverb, is contented with little. In the field of information, our middle class has certainly been, in the sense intended by the sober Epicurus, terribly wise.

". . . Let us at least have the courage to admit that what so far has been conquered in our land is precisely the life of our dear, dead towns. The leisurely rhythm of their days, their crawling buses, their sleepy officials, the time wasted in their soft atmosphere of lethargy, the lazy ease of their café life, their local politics and petty trades, their empty libraries, their taste for the past, and their mistrust of anything that may shake them out of their comfortable habits. These are the things that have succumbed before the hellish onset of that dynamic Germany whose aggression was backed by the resources of a national life organised on the principle of the hive."

But it was not only the small-town *café de commerce* that lived in the past. History's death announcements, as Marc

Bloch puts it, had not been registered even at the Quai d'Orsay, the nerve-centre of French foreign policy. Its corridors were still haunted by Richelieu and the Rhineland policy, by Hapsburgs and Hohenzollerns, by the diplomacy of the *salons* and of the literary lecture room; and no one who has ever considered the social responsibility of the intellectual can read unmoved the last chapter of this testament of a scholar who had more right than many others to wash his hands of all these things: "The generation to which I belong has a bad conscience. . . . Many of us realised at a very early stage the nature of the abyss into which the diplomacy of Versailles and the Ruhr was threatening to plunge us. . . . The same, or roughly the same, men whom we have heard today preaching, before the last hour has struck, the gloomy wisdom of Louis XVIII were then urging us on to ape the grandiloquent arrogance of Louis XIV. We were not such fools as to believe that in a France impoverished, relatively undermanned, and capable of realising only a very small industrial potential, a policy of the kind they contemplated was advisable—if, indeed, it would have been so at any time. Not being prophets, we did not foresee the advent of the Nazis. But we did foresee that, in some form or other, though its precise nature was hidden from us, a German revival *would* come, that it would be embittered by rancorous memories to which our foolish ineptitude was daily adding, and that its explosion would be terrible. . . . We did realise that in the Germany of that time there were signs, however timid, of a new spirit of good will, of an attitude that was frankly pacific and honestly liberal. The only thing wanting was a gesture on the part of our political leaders. We knew all that, and yet, from laziness, from cowardice, we let things take their course. We feared the opposition of the mob, the sarcasm of our friends, the ignorant mistrust of our masters. We dared not stand up in public and be the voice crying in the wilderness. It might have been just that, but at least we should have had the consolation of knowing that, whatever the outcome of its message, it had at least spoken aloud the faith that was in us. We preferred to lock ourselves into the fear-haunted tranquillity of our studies. May the young men forgive us the blood that is red upon our hands!"

There were many such isolated voices. Then, as never before and never since, France was confronted with her own unadorned self. After the collapse of the republican façade the great hereditary administrative corporations of the France of the *ancien régime* went on working under foreign orders, unshaken and scarcely even disturbed. The archaic structure of her agricultural self-sufficiency, her small-town centres with their idyllic régime of notables, were now offered by Vichy the balm of that message of salvation: "Back to the land!" The artificial laboratory of Paris cultural activity continued unchanged to produce its *esprit* for the German conquerors, just as it had done under every other régime. The France which at the end of its long history was ready to decline into having no history had found its ideal, chemically pure, embodiment in the régime of the venerable patriarch of Vichy; and for that other France which was not prepared to abdicate, there it lay, visible and tangible before their eyes, like an anatomical model. In the discussions that went on in the earliest French resistance, and in the underground Press, which was the freest in the world, being written and distributed without censorship and without directives by individuals working at the risk of their lives, little self-satisfaction was to be found, and little of that most evil of the products of self-satisfaction, chauvinism. What had collapsed in 1940 seemed clear, and it seemed only too clear that it had collapsed for good. "France of the new springtime must be the creation of the young," Marc Bloch wrote in 1941. "As compared with their elders of the last war, they have one sad privilege: they will not have to guard against the lethargy bred of victory. Whatever form the final triumph may take, it will be many years before the stain of 1940 can be effaced."

But it turned out otherwise. There came the allied liberation, for which a small minority had fought, and on which a growing minority had gambled. But for the great majority it fell as a gift from heaven, accompanied by the unhoped-for prestige of a national victory, with all its possibilities of glory and self-deception. The nightmare was over, and it had not been true. There had been no 1940, no defeat, and no collapse; and once more the renewal turned into a restoration.

But since then the shadow has not lifted.

PART II

BACK TO THE THIRD REPUBLIC

THE Fourth Republic, like the third, began with a great historical legend. This was the legend of de Gaulle, the independent-minded colonel, whose voice in the wilderness calling for motorisation and tanks had for many years fallen upon the deaf ears of a General Staff inextricably tied up in its own red tape. After his recent promotion to the rank of brigadier-general and his appointment on June 5th, 1940, the first day of the final battle for France, to the post of Under-Secretary of State in the War Ministry, the man with the predestined name of "Charles of Gaul" on June 18th, 1940, in the midst of the general collapse, raised the flag of resistance in London and declared: "In the face of the confusion of French minds, in the face of the collapse of a Government which has fallen under the servitude of the enemy, in face of the impossibility of making our democratic institutions work, I, General de Gaulle, soldier and officer of France, know that I can talk in the name of France." He was followed, so the legend continues, like one man by the whole French people ("with the exception of a handful of traitors at Vichy"), first with fists clenched in their pockets, then in active conspiracy, and finally in open struggle.

All this was no figment of the imagination. On August 25th, 1944, when the two controlling bodies of the fighting French, the Government-in-exile of General de Gaulle and the Council of National Resistance which had been active in France itself, met and merged into the Provisional Government of the French Republic, it became an evident reality. There was no other France than this. Fears of civil war and revolution roused by emissaries of the Vichy régime, particularly in the United States, turned out to be groundless. "When I arrived in Paris on August 25th, 1944," General de Gaulle was able to announce a few weeks later, "I was handed a message from a representative of Marshal Pétain who was authorised by a written order dated August 11th to seek 'an agreement with me for the avoidance of civil war'. I showed him the door. Gentlemen, where is the civil war?"

The Vichy régime, in spite of the formal legitimacy bestowed upon it by the abdication of the last Parliament of the Third Republic, had been no more than the shadow cast over the country by the German occupation, and with the German withdrawal it simply vanished, leaving not a trace behind. No hand was lifted in its defence, no voice was raised to plead for it, no one had ever acknowledged it or had anything to do with it.

Those least surprised by this ghost-like disintegration of the régime which had sworn loyalty to Marshal Pétain were the departing Germans. As a German journalist grimly remarked in one of his last dispatches, the *attentisme* of Vichy of the last eighteen months had long since turned into *alibisme*. All who could had plunged into the resistance, headed by the police, who in Paris and many areas in southern France joined it in serried ranks. The cleverest people had long since established contact with it, the Vichy administration was riddled with Gaullist cells, and those sufficiently naïve to have procured no documents proving services rendered to the allies or to the resistance kept silent, fled, or pretended to be dead. The country's production and supply system, its administration and transport, were at a standstill. The railways, the canals, the harbours, the telegraph wires, were out of action practically everywhere, and not a single bridge was standing on the lower courses of the Seine, the Loire, or the Rhône. There was no telephone communication between Paris and central and southern France, and any vehicles that might still be available were requisitioned for the allied armies. German troops were still holding out in northern and eastern France and in the Atlantic ports. France lay literally in fragments, but everywhere one great cry went up in unison: France was Gaullist, and had never been anything but Gaullist.

Since then there has been uninterrupted historical controversy, in the course of which even those who shammed death at that time have found their voices again. Nevertheless the inner history of the resistance and the liberation remain obscure. No doubt a long time will pass before it becomes possible to write it, and perhaps it will never be possible to throw light on its darkest episodes and characters. All the various phases of the controversy, the *épurations,* the purges, with their expropriations and seizures of power, the struggle of parties, persons, and groups all claiming to be the true heirs of the resistance, lay under the spell of a Manichaean myth which divided all Frenchmen into heroes and traitors, the Vichy *bloc* and that of the resistance.

In reality the great majority of Frenchmen had belonged to neither. There had been no Vichy *bloc,* but only a stopgap régime which had sought to save out of the collapse what was to be saved, and opportunists, double-dealers, cynics, secret opponents of and open admirers of the Nazi "new order" had fought for control in it until ever more drastic German intervention had deprived it of the last semblance of freedom of movement and prestige; and the resistance was no *bloc,* but a great reservoir into which there poured all those who were driven into opposition, that is to say into exile or illegality, by patriotic impulse, political decision, the growing German terror, the drive to find labour for the German economy, or (perhaps most important of all) the prospect of German defeat.

The military collapse of 1940 overwhelmed the Third Republic, its leaders, its political habits, and its institutions, with the suddenness and completeness of a judgment of heaven. A natural catastrophe is something to which you have to adapt yourself; you do not take sides about it; and the general reaction was what it would have been to a natural catastrophe. Only the small, hysterical groups of the authoritarian right which had long since taken Fascism and Nazism as their models greeted the German victory, like Marcel Déat, as a "day of rejoicing". These people awakened no echo in the French people, though they thought they heard it in the thunder of the collapse. But it was not their hour that struck, but, as always in a defeated country, that of the defeated generals, who above all desired to maintain peace and order. It was also the hour of the reactionaries, in whose eyes there had at last dawned the day of judgment on a hundred and fifty years of French history, and of the conservative *Realpolitiker,* who regarded it as essential to maintain continuity, keep the state apparatus in being, and spare France the fate of Poland. Vichy was the paltry battleground of the Fascist and conservative wings of the French right; the "Paris opposition" of Déat and Doriot was a gang of desperadoes held in reserve by the occupying Power but never used, though some of them, consistently with their principles, went to the Russian front in the uniform of the Waffen S.S. and died there.

But this same environment, that of the army, the state service, the reactionaries, and the right extremists, produced the first impulse of resistance, the completely spontaneous, "non-political" reaction of downtrodden national pride which was embodied in such thoroughgoing fashion by the professional soldier Charles de Gaulle, who had grown up amid authoritarian and royalist traditions.

The Communist Party, which had been illegal since the beginning of the war, greeted the collapse of "French imperialism" as a revolutionary event, spent months in abusing de Gaulle and his first followers as deserters and agents of British high finance, and, deluded by its grotesque "dialectic", sought in the name of the Hitler-Stalin pact to outdo Vichy as a "peace party"; and between these extremists and those of the right nothing was left in 1940 but a huge, devastated no-man's-land in which there were no more political parties, but only individual reactions. It was personality, connections, and opportunities much more than membership of a political party or social group that decided who became involved in collaboration, who waited to see, and who escaped into exile. Recruits actually accrued to Vichy and the occupation régime from the pacifist wing of the Socialist Party and the trade unions. There were also some orthodox Marxists who over-reached themselves with their own dialectic and persuaded themselves that the historical path to Socialism lay by way of the Fascist instead of the Communist totalitarian state; there were also some members of the bourgeoisie, who used less casuistry in adapting themselves to "hard facts". A year later the German onslaught on Russia threw the ranks of the French Communist Party into the resistance movement as compactly as they had hitherto stood aloof from it, and, now that they were permitted to combine the cult of the Soviet fatherland with that of France, their long training in illegality, their iron discipline, and their technique of organisation and cell formation rapidly pushed them to the forefront of the resistance organisations. After 1942 Laval's return to "power", the drive for compulsory labour in Germany and on the Atlantic Wall, the allied landing in North Africa, and the German march into southern France mobilised a growing stream of man-power for the active resistance.

The dreadful eighteen months of waiting for the opening of the "second front" began, for the allied offensive in the west upon whose military support in the enemy's rear the whole organisation and policy of the Gaullist resistance was built up; eighteen months in which the Communists, by open and concealed taunts at the *attentisme* and inactivity of the other resistance groups and of the western allies—taunts which with the lapse of time were listened to ever more willingly—succeeded in drawing a veil of forgetfulness over their pre-1941 past; and they succeeded increasingly in gaining the lead from the older resistance groups which had been in the field longer than they. The party built up independently of the Gaullists its own resistance organisation, the National Front, and its own organisation of partisans, the Franc-Tireurs et Partisans; both were "cover-organisations", nominally entirely non-Communist in character, and they were carefully kept free of any political colouring or agitation; their declared aims were purely patriotic, or rather nationalistic, and their ranks were filled with unsuspecting fellow-travellers, but control was kept firmly in the iron hand of the party apparatus and was remote from all supervision or even observation by the liberation committees of London and Algiers; and it was these organisations which were the principal beneficiaries of the man-hunts of Darnand and Sauckel, whose "comb-outs" for forced labour in Germany drove a whole generation of French youth into the *maquis*. The *maquis* became the domain of the Communist Party organisation, which on the Yugoslav pattern conducted guerrilla warfare as a means of mass recruiting, did not shrink from militarily useless wastage of human life, and, in spite of all de Gaulle's orders to the contrary, indulged all the more systematically in individual acts of terror as every enemy reprisal merely drove more recruits into the partisan ranks.

Official co-ordination of the whole resistance movement came into being only in May, 1943, with the setting up of an underground national council for all the resistance groups in the country and the mutual recognition exchanged between this body and General de Gaulle's national committee in Algiers. But the mantle of the great comradeship of the resistance concealed a fierce and relentless competition for key-points in the struggle for power which would follow the liberation, and it did not lack its sinister episodes.

In the days of the liberation the competition to occupy the vacant positions of power resulted in a diarchy, and a most dangerous conflict between Communists and non-Communists, of which the public hardly became aware. It was masked by the existence of many intertwining political and other organisations, was surrounded by a kind of taboo, and was overlaid by another and more conspicuous conflict, that between the conservatives, in whose eyes the role of the resistance movement had come to an end with the liberation, and the revolutionaries, in whose eyes the struggle for the political and social regeneration of France was only just beginning. The "overseas" resistance that had now come to France from Algiers and the empire was engaged in rivalry with the "inner" resistance which had grown great in the underground struggle, both regarded with mistrust the return of the old, pre-war politicians, who had been more or less compromised by Vichy but had unquestionably been compromised by the 1940 collapse, and everyone united in common resistance to the latent allied attempts to exercise tutelage.

Meanwhile the war was still in progress. France had become a back area of the western front in which the allied command could tolerate no unrest, and the allies, particularly the United States, hesitated for two months before agreeing, with all sorts of reservations, to the recognition of the Government of General de Gaulle as the Provisional Government of France. The factor that held the resistance groups together was the universal determination that France should be spared an allied military government; they were resolved to conduct the inevitable struggle for power among themselves alone. It was the sheer stiff-neckedness with which General de Gaulle had insisted on French sovereignty from the first day when he went to the microphone in London, with no status and practically no following, and made his famous appeal to the French people, and claimed the right to deal with the allied governments on equal terms, and his uncompromising refusal to enter into the tactical combinations with Darlan and Giraud devised by American diplomacy after the landing in North Africa—in short the intractable stubbornness which got on the nerves of allied statesmen—that assured him the support of the resistance groups, and in particular, for very intelligible reasons, that of the Communists.

But behind the united front with which they faced the outer world a diarchy prevailed. Both the Provisional Government in Algiers and the C.N.R., the National Council of Resistance, which installed itself in the Ministries as a ready-made government in the days of the liberation of Paris, had made plans and preparations for the assumption of power, and whether the former or the latter in fact assumed it depended on whether an area was liberated by allied and regular French troops, or by a rising of the *maquisards*. Nearly everywhere south of the Loire it was by a rising of the *maquisards*.

This diarchy ran right through the provisional institutions of liberated France. De Gaulle's Minister of the Interior was M. d'Astier de la Vigerie, a representative of the C.N.R. who was very close to the Communists, and the Commissioner for Liberated Areas was M. Le Troquer, a right wing Socialist who subsequently became Minister of the Interior. In a frantic race with time each sent out his own emissaries to appoint the new prefects and local officials, and it was often a matter of pure chance who arrived first and consequently determined the political geography of France in those decisive weeks. Similarly, in the government of a day of the C.N.R. in Paris the Commissioner for the Interior was M. Parodi, a delegate of General de Gaulle's, and it was thanks to him that the Paris prefecture of police was prevented from falling into the hands of the Communists. Large areas of France were left completely to their own devices, and local and departmental liberation committees, purge committees, confiscation committees, factory committees, patriotic committees, militiamen and guardians of public order sprang out of the ground and took instructions from no one but the C.N.R., or sometimes the Communist Party leadership direct. In fact a whole machinery of government—an administration, a police, a militia, and a judicial system—sprang up parallel with the apparatus hastily salved by de Gaulle from the wreckage of Vichy and improvised from the cadres of North Africa. The new political, trade union, and military organisations and their hitherto illegal Press installed themselves by right of revolutionary seizure in the offices and printing works of the organs of the occupation régime which had vanished from the face of the earth, innumerable groups and committees which the day before had never been heard of started issuing orders and carrying out arrests and confiscations, and they were all in a hurry to present the world with accomplished facts.

For a few weeks the old language and cultural frontier of the Loire, the demarcation line between the occupied and the "free" zone which the armistice of 1940 had drawn across France, seemed again to separate two distinct countries. In the area south of the Loire, which the Germans occupied only in November, 1942, the resistance movement had for that reason secured a much firmer and earlier foothold, and a kind of "Soviet democracy" of liberation committees and their commissars continued unrestrained for weeks.

At Limoges, Toulouse, Montpellier, and Nice revolutionary Soviet republics were established to the accompaniment of noisy declarations of loyalty to de Gaulle. After the allied capture of Corsica in September, 1943, the so-called National Front promptly assumed control and, after summary "people's democratic" elections, presented the people in the marketplace with their chosen leaders and allowed the latter to be confirmed by their applause. The Provisional Government established itself rapidly and without friction in the fighting zone and the back areas in northern France, but had to feel its way forward cautiously as it extended its authority southward beyond the Loire. The difference in political psychology and temperature on either side of this dividing line across France remained perceptible for a long time.

The interregnum did not, however, go beyond the provisional and local stage. It allowed ample opportunity for acts of personal and political revenge, but this process, and the rush to secure the places left vacant by the change of régime, did not develop into a struggle for power. After a brief period of hesitation, the C.N.R. in Paris left the field to the Provisional Government, and its programme of political, economic, and social reforms, including the nationalisation of the key industries and the credit and insurance institutions became the official programme of the Provisional Government. The C.N.R. and its regional and local committees remained in existence as a kind of shadow government, claiming barely more than a moral role. The only semblance of a trial of strength developed when General de Gaulle decreed the dissolution and disarmament of the groups of *maquisards* who in many places were still exercising the police prerogatives that they had assumed and were causing increasing nervousness among the peasants because of their arbitrary acts of violence.

This was the first occasion on which the Communist Party came into conflict with the Government of which it was itself a member party. The National Front, the only body from which the "patriotic guards" would have accepted the order to disband, refused to obey the Government's decision, and invoked the support of the C.N.R. The campaign lasted for two months, and every railway accident, every attempted murder, every minor incident was exploited as demonstrating the necessity that the "people in arms" should exercise revolutionary vigilance against the omnipresent "fifth column". The Government carefully avoided resorting to force or, as was done simultaneously in Belgium, calling in the aid of allied troops against the Communist partisans. The order for their disbandment remained in a state of suspense. But two months later, on January 21st, 1945, M. Maurice Thorez, the general secretary of the Communist Party, who had just returned from Moscow, made the celebrated speech at a meeting of the party central committee which put an end to the first chapter of French post-war history.

"We Communists," he said, "at the present time put forward no demands of a social character. . . . We are animated by a single aim, as is the whole French people, and that is to win the war as quickly as possible . . . and in order to win the war we wish to act in harmony with all good Frenchmen, workers, employees, employers, intellectuals, and peasants." It was necessary, of course, "to smoke out enemy saboteurs, traitors, spies, and agents and bring them to trial", but this was obviously the task of the properly constituted authorities. The people had the right and the duty to raise its voice, but it was the business of the properly constituted legal authorities to undertake house searches, make arrests, secure convictions, and carry out sentences. During the period of armed struggle against the Nazi invaders and their Vichy accomplices the existence of the patriotic militia had been justified. But now the situation had altered. Public order must be maintained by the regular police forces, which existed for that purpose, and the true enemies of the people were those who perpetually talked of revolution.

Never had there been a more loyal advocate of bourgeois law and order. The revolution had been called off, and a new chapter in the political struggle began, the systematic exploitation of the positions of power secured in the chaos of the liberation and the party positional warfare that ensued.

§ 2

FROM "PEOPLE'S DEMOCRACY" TO RESTORATION

During the first eighteen months after the liberation the system of government in France exactly resembled that prevailing in most of the other countries of the European continent, the "people's democracies" in particular; *i.e.*, it was a régime of absolute unanimity. The Government and the Consultative Assembly were composed of representatives of all recognised groups and movements, the political weight and real influence of which were unknown quantities. The state of war and the absence in Germany of hundreds of thousands of prisoners of war, deportees, and forced labourers prevented any normal consultation of the people. The non-Communist parties were barely organised, the numerous resistance groups who for the time being dominated the stage were in an undefinable state somewhere between that of small, closely-knit conspiratorial groups and political parties, and an almost complete unity of slogans, symbols, and demands obliterated all the latent differences.

The unanimity was a consequence of the general confusion, and for the time being it was maintained. It also reflected the world situation, the spirit of Yalta, the desire to cling to the unity of the United Nations, and an obscure anxiety that the great alliance of democracies upon which the new world was to be built might turn out to be an illusion. Many exploited this anxiety as an instrument of mental terrorism. In France, as throughout Europe, there were words which were sacrosanct, and there were legends to assail which seemed treasonable and ideas to define which seemed a crime. French internal order depended on a dangerous equilibrium between the only two forces which had emerged from the chaos organised and ready to take over or share power. On the one hand was the state apparatus which had been built up round General de Gaulle in exile, with its ramifications in all parts of the country, and on the other was the Communist Party apparatus with its own ramifications. General de Gaulle was the symbol of the French unity which the Communist Party preached, and any attempt at discrimination between them seemed as dastardly as an assault upon the unity of the nation itself, from which only the Fascists could benefit; anyone who had dared make any such discrimination would have been denounced out-of-hand as a Fascist agent, and at any rate morally struck dead. In the "people's democracies" this process was carried to the bitter end, and in France, where it was arrested, the Communists called in just the same way for the merging of all resistance movements into their National Front and for the fusion with themselves of the Socialist Party which was in process of reorganisation. The first post-war elections in France were at local government level, and, if the Communists had had their way, these would have been held under the single list system. Seats would have been shared out between the parties in advance, which would have meant that the elections would have been merely a demonstration of approval for the resistance *en bloc*. The Communist Party nowhere fought the election under its own name, but as the "Patriotic Republican Anti-Fascist Union", under the banner of which great prominence was given to candidates of non-Communist affiliation.

Only the systematic confusion of ideas enabled unanimity to be maintained, and the most popular slogans, because they were the vaguest, began with *anti-* and ended in *ism*. The Communists were not the only ones to use these deadly and unanswerable slogans, but they used them with particular adroitness and effect. The Communist variety of anti-Fascism was not the only variety, but it was the most unquestionable and the most fundamental; other kinds were real only if they partook of the same essence. Conversely, according to a belief that far and wide no one dared to dispute, any public opposition to Communist policy was anti-Communism, *i.e.*, the distinguishing mark of the Fascist mentality and a deadly sin against democracy. There was no escaping from this dilemma, to which the many thousands of Communist dead lent the necessary silence-imposing pathos.

Indecent though it may seem to haggle about corpses, the number of these martyrs would seem to call for some comment. Who but the Communists would have had the courage to sort and count the dead according to their party affiliation? But with a massiveness and shamelessness which brooked no contradiction the Communists as the *parti des fusillés* exploited their "75,000 shot Communist patriots"—a number which from the first day of the liberation was hammered into the public mind with an intimidating intensity and was soon generally accepted as established, though no trace of evidence for its correctness was ever produced. At the Nuremberg trials the total number of Frenchmen shot under the German occupation was stated by the French Government to have been 29,660, and in eight years after the liberation the Communist Press was able to quote the names of only 176 Communists who had been shot. The difference between 176 and and 75,000 is too big to be accounted for just by variations of estimate, and this exploitation of the dead for propaganda purposes is made all the more horrible by the fact that it was based on a deliberate lie; moreover a lie on a subject which put a ban on all discussion.

The profit was a double one. The Communist Party possessed the power of the keys, that of absolution and damnation. In the role of public prosecutor it was able to silence almost anyone whom it disliked; by going sufficiently far back and appropriately applying the technique of generalisation and identification "guilt for France's misfortunes" could be fastened on almost any individual or group who had ever exercised responsibility. Safety from denunciation could be found only under the denouncers' wing; a party membership card excluded suspicion. The purge had devastating effects on the personnel of all other parties and organisations. The Socialist Party at its first congress expelled more than half its deputies and senators, and the reformist and syndicalist leaders of all levels who had continued their legal activity in the C.G.T. under the Vichy régime were purged in large numbers. But the Communist leaders and troops, in spite of their more ambiguous attitude before June, 1941, were spared all questioning, and their ranks were swollen by a big influx of individuals alarmed about their past to whom protection was willingly offered. The way in which the "purge" was carried out explains the most momentous success gained by the Communists at that time, their conquest of the trade union apparatus.

The "purging of France of traitors and collaborators" was the alpha and omega of Communist policy. All the lofty principles which it advocated in the name of national unity were pushed into the background, and it behaved with noticeable indifference towards all the structural reforms which had figured in the common programme of the resistance movement. It looked at the nationalisation of the key industries and public services, the reform of the administration and of the army, everything which during the resistance had been planned as the foundation for a new France, through the distorting lens of denunciation. In the purge it found a handy instrument for its cold revolution, the object of which was not to change the social and economic structure of France, but to get into its hands as large a number as possible of the levers of power and to neutralise the remainder.

The short-sighted cunning of these pseudo-Machiavellian technicians of power turned the liberation into a helter-skelter race for a number of key offices, wrecked the purge itself, and nipped in the bud the whole reform task of the resistance and the promising beginnings of a moral and political regeneration. The full extent of the damage they did became perceptible only years later. For the defence against them was organised in an equally anonymous, underhand, and mendacious manner.

All France was left wing, socialist, revolutionary, and all disputes about principles faded and grew dim in the atmosphere of anonymous unanimity. The purge got lost in its own endlessness and in the procedural jungle of a judicial system the representatives of which had almost without exception taken the oath of loyalty to Pétain and succeeded in adding a horrible flavour of judicial murder even to the conviction of Pierre Laval. The *esprit de corps* of the great mandarins, and all the toughness of a state apparatus which had survived unshaken a dozen revolutions and *coups d'état,* were mobilised to resist reform of the administration, the police, the machinery of justice, or the army, whether in personnel or in organisation; moreover the de Gaulle Government had no alternative but to fall back on this apparatus as the only substitute for the anarchic partisan régime of the "self-liberated areas".

In the course of this semi-underground struggle the great plans which had been worked out, both in the C.N.R. and at Algiers, for a more rational administrative structure, a regional organisation of France which would loosen the control of the prefects and increase local autonomy, disappeared without trace, and the outcome was that the bureaucratic centralisation of France became more stifling and the disorganisation at the top became more hopeless than ever. Thanks to the chaos created by the various economic Ministries, which were continually at loggerheads with each other, the chaos of the national economy was maintained. While M. Mendès-France, the Economics Minister, stood for a policy of austerity, strict regulation of prices and wages, and energetic measures to put the economy on a healthy footing, which would have involved a drastic currency reform on the Belgian or subsequent German pattern, the Finance Ministry chose the comfortable but disastrous routine course of bringing about a slight diminution in the flood of paper money by means of a "liberation loan", which neither put the currency on a healthy basis nor drove into the light of the day the enormous accumulated profits made by black marketeering, war profiteering, or operations which were actually criminal. There turned out to be sufficient solidarity between the unconfessed interests of the "collaboration profiteers" and the "resistance profiteers" (among whom the Communist Party chest, thanks to the activities of its partisan groups and their confiscation committees, was in the front rank) to prevent any proper currency reform; and, while the self-appointed "purge tribunals" blindly and arbitrarily confiscated "collaboration" and "war profits", the Supply Ministry had no greater concern than to avoid disturbing the economic administration inherited from Vichy, and to see that all its functionaries and committees, the general staffs of the semi-illegal black market and the *mandataires des Halles,* remained in office. The most contradictory things existed side by side: inflation and deflation, planning and disorganisation, strict regulation of retail food prices in the towns and complete lack of control of producers' prices and markets. Meanwhile chaos reigned in the wholesale and middlemen's trade, into the labyrinthine channels of which all rationed goods disappeared without trace; and in this jungle each party and each power-clique organised its own feudal domains and protectorates. The nationalisation of the mines, the gas, electricity, motor and aircraft industries, banks and the insurance companies, was carried out in a hasty, improvised manner between December, 1944, and December, 1945, but its first effect was only to transform the key positions in the French economy into political prizes for which competitors fought to the knife and in the control of which ever more numerous committees kept a jealous eye on one another.

In this positional warfare the great impulse of the liberation died a slow and painful death. The intermingled forces sorted themselves out in an atmosphere of disillusionment, or of actual demoralisation. There was too big a gap between the promise and the achievement. It was gratifying that the things that had to be patched up were patched up, that the transport system was put back on its feet, and that the surviving apparatus of production was got going again with astonishing energy and speed, but these things did not amount to a national regeneration. The state which had been set up as the instrument of social justice turned out to be impotent in the face of the black market and the inflation left behind by the occupation régime, and, under the banner of public control of industry, individuals, caring nothing for rules and regulations, did the best for themselves that they could.

There was no underlying political reality in the unspoken pact which held together General de Gaulle and the Communist Party, the two corner-stones of the coalition. For both, though they started from completely different premises, the inner life of France was merely the raw material for their world political mission; and it was remarkable that the heir of the oldest French traditions and the heirs of what had once been a world revolutionary mission should find common ground in the old grooves of the Rhineland policy of Richelieu.

The dissolution of the unity of Germany on the lines of 1648, the separation of the Rhineland and the Ruhr, which General de Gaulle once more made the grand design of French foreign policy, had always implied alliance with Russia, and in the European post-war situation it did so more insistently than ever; and General de Gaulle was all the readier for such an alliance in as much as his often bitter years of exile and the struggle for power in Algiers had left him with an incurable grudge against the English-speaking powers. De Gaulle's thinking, firmly anchored in history, was as firmly centred on the Rhine frontier and the idea of political and strategic guarantees against a fourth German invasion as if in the meantime the deluge had not swept over Europe, and his practical conclusions coincided with those of the Communists, whose thinking was centred on Moscow. De Gaulle declared again and again that France and Russia were united by history and geography in an indissoluble community of interests; his call for guarantees against a revival of German expansionism relied on the far more brutal pattern of Russian annexations in the east, and at the same time sanctioned it. His vision of a resuscitated France "in the first rank of the nations" could be achieved only if France were in a position to arbitrate between the allies; and, as the Anglo-American armies had opened the way for de Gaulle's return to Paris, it was all the more necessary to create a distance between France and her English-speaking allies. The first foreign policy move made by the French Provisional Government after its entry into Paris was General de Gaulle's and M. Bidault's flight to Moscow in December, 1944, to sign an alliance with the Soviet Union. More than two years were to pass before a similar alliance was signed with Britain, and that was in an entirely different political context.

This foreign policy set the seal on domestic civil peace. The Communists, de Gaulle's most loyal allies against all attacks—the Socialists in particular were already criticising both his foreign and his military policy—accompanied it and underlined it with the most bloodthirsty calls for revenge on Germany—an attitude entirely alien to de Gaulle himself—

and denounced all signs of that thinking in European terms which had made such hopeful beginnings during the war in the French underground movement. After the years of alien rule and humiliation there was ample scope for a party lacking in scruple to make play with hatred. Only years later did it become apparent that this harmony in foreign policy between the two protagonists of liberated France, de Gaulle and Thorez, was the most remarkable of the misunderstandings on which civil peace in France depended. This foreign policy certainly answered the needs of the wounded and sensitive national pride of the French at that time. It was nevertheless remarkably shortsighted, and it manœuvred France into a *cul-de-sac* from which she was able only with difficulty to extricate herself.

The year 1945 saw the disintegration of the resistance and liberation movements, which for a time had been going to give a new look to French politics, but resulted in nothing but a short-lived jigsaw puzzle of undecipherable initials. There is no need to follow the labyrinthine history of their splits, fusions, and ramifications over the political chessboard, though the system of personal connections on which those groupings were based is still active in the background of French politics. The bacillus of decomposition and decay was again the Communist "united front" tactics and their practice of planting cells. The outcome was the absorption of what the Communists were able to absorb and the destruction of the rest, but the end-result could not be regarded as very impressive from the Communist point of view. After a year of energetic fishing with all the artfully placed nets which the party contrived to use, it succeeded in pulling in very little more than its own original bait. The meeting of the local and departmental liberation committees in the "States-General of the French Renaissance" in the summer of 1945 was the last Communist attempt to use the C.N.R. as a potential counter-Government. With the inglorious failure of this attempt the political role of the resistance as such was finished, until two years later General de Gaulle revived "Gaullism" as an nationalist, authoritarian movement and once more gathered round himself the politically homeless remnants of the former liberation movement.

By October, 1945, when elections to a Constituent Assembly were held, a radical simplification had taken place in the French political scene. Three big parties shared in almost equal proportions three-quarters of the votes cast and four-fifths of the seats. At the top of the poll, with five million votes, came the Communist Party and the fellow-travelling organisations of the "united resistance movements". Next, with four-and-a-half million votes each, came the Socialist Party and a new party which had sprung up like a mushroom and had no pre-war parallel, the Popular Republican Movement (M.R.P.). Its nucleus was the small and plucky group of Christian Social "popular democrats", whose views had always been regarded by the Church authorities as smacking slightly of heresy. In the inter-war period these people had tried desperately to break down the equation of republicanism with anti-clericalism, the habit of mind which regarded the word "left" as implying, not a social or political outlook, but a shallow anti-Popery, and permitted the diehard Radicals to count as left wing because of their Voltairean tradition and their habitual denunciations of "black reaction" and "obscurantism".

The great comradeship of the resistance appeared to have attained one thing at any rate: French politics seemed no more to be centred on that outworn battle between the village teacher and the *curé* which has been celebrated in so many satires on French provincial life. The Christian Social movement and many representatives of the lower clergy had played a big part in the resistance, while the higher clergy had given their blessing to the clerical régime of Vichy. One representative of the movement, M. Bidault, had been president of the C.N.R. at the time of the liberation and had entered the Provisional Government as a representative of the "inner resistance"; and politically and personally General de Gaulle's own position was nearest to that of the Popular Republicans. True, the sudden development into a huge party of this small religious-social group, which previously had not really belonged to this world, was not without a certain ambiguity. The complete disappearance of the old parties of the centre and the right had created a vacuum into which the M.R.P. now stepped; to a huge number of conservative voters, silenced Pétainists, and local bigwigs, deprived of their accustomed political tools, they appeared to be the only party capable of providing a counter-weight to the Communist-Socialist *bloc*; and the episcopate, who had a great deal that it wished to be forgotten and was now delighted at the reappearance of its lost sheep of yesterday, backed them with almost compromising enthusiasm. The first beginnings of an anti-Communist rally gathered, at first very timidly and quietly, round the Catholic left.

With the election of this Parliament General de Gaulle's role as irreplaceable and absolute head of the government in reality came to an end. Hitherto he had been, not only the living embodiment and symbol of the resistance, but the representative of the legitimacy principle of free France, which, in contrast to all the other countries overrun by the Germans in the early stages of the war, had not been represented in the allied camp by a legal government in exile. It was through General de Gaulle alone that France had maintained a continuous foothold in the allied camp, and, if the legality of the Vichy régime were to be contested and the continuity of the republic upheld, it was necessary somewhat hazardously to resort to dependence on the solitary appeal to resistance made by de Gaulle on June 18th, 1940. Liberated France relied for the legality of its actions on General de Gaulle, just as the United States depended on George Washington and the Declaration of Independence, and the Soviet Union on Lenin and the October Revolution. But with the election of the National Assembly the legitimacy principle passed from the legendary founder-hero, particularly as a plebiscite coinciding with the election abolished the constitution of the Third Republic and gave constitution-making powers to the new body.

True, the plebiscite on the abolition of the constitution of 1875 developed in practice into a plebiscite for or against General de Gaulle. The "republican old guard", in the persons of M. Herriot and the not too greatly compromised leaders of the Radical Party, had returned to posts of honour under the Provisional Government as witnesses to its continuity, and, in spite of their imploring warnings, General de Gaulle had recommended repeal of the old constitution. This constitution at the time of its making had been agreed on as a compromise between hostile monarchist groups, and, thanks to the laconic brevity and elasticity of its provisions, it had been the most lasting of French constitutions, as lasting as all the twelve previous constitutions that had been adopted since the French Revolution put together. But to prevent an omnipotent assembly, unconstrained by any constitution or independent executive power, from running riot on the lines of the French Revolution, General de Gaulle simultaneously presented at the plebiscite a "law on the organisation of public powers", which in the first place limited the life of the Constituent Assembly to seven months and in the second place assured the Prime Minister, whose election was the Constituent Assembly's first task, and the Ministers appointed by him, of an almost impregnable position during the pre-constitutional period. It was as certain as anything human could be that the Prime Minister of this interim Government would be de Gaulle himself. Nearly all the parties, including those opposed in principle to altering the constitution, accepted this limitation of the Constituent Assembly's powers because of their fear of a "revolutionary assembly" régime. But the Communist Party mobilised all its strength and all its numerous affiliates against this proposal in the name of "the untrammelled sovereignty of the people", and in the process used the reconstituted C.G.T. for political purposes for the first time.

Unclear though the tremendous implications of this question were to the great majority of the electorate, confusing though it was to have simultaneously to cast votes for the election of a popular assembly and to have to decide whether or not it should be given constitution-making powers, and in addition to have to answer a subsidiary question expressing approval or disapproval of an interim system of government, the plebiscite was preceded by a hectic campaign. It took years for the laconic, scrawled phrases "Yes, yes," "Yes, no," and "No, yes," so puzzling to the uninitiated, to disappear from the walls and fences of France. The fact that the first question, whether the new assembly should adopt a new constitution, was answered in the affirmative by a majority approaching unanimity—18,600,000 votes to 700,000—and that the controversial proposal for the "organisation of public powers" was accepted by a clear two-thirds majority—13,000,000 to 6,500,000—was, taken in conjunction with the rejection of the Third Republic and the birth of the fourth, as a kind of ceremonial investiture of General de Gaulle. In retrospect this popular decision, even in its inconsistencies, looks like a historical landmark. For France had chosen a Constituent Assembly with an absolute Communist-Socialist majority, but at the same time covered herself against any adventure by voting for General de Gaulle. "Revolution" and "authority" held each other in check.

General de Gaulle was of course unanimously entrusted by the Constituent Assembly with the formation of a Government. But his solitary position above party was politically tenable only so long as he acted in a mediating role, *i.e.*, that normally played by the President of the Republic, and for this neither his highly authoritarian character nor his highly independent career suited him. He would neither condescend to become the leader of a party nor permit himself to be promoted to the symbolic dignity of a head of a state who "reigns, but does not rule". He wanted to be both, and lost both.

It remained for him to perform one last duty of which no one would have been able to deprive him—to refuse the keys of power to the Communist Party for the third time. The Communists, as the biggest and most powerful party, duly and democratically claimed the share in the Government to which they were entitled by the election results—in particular they put in a claim to one of the three key positions in the Government: the Foreign Ministry, the Ministry of the Interior, or the Ministry of Defence—and they made their entry into the coalition dependent on being given one of these. No one except General de Gaulle seemed to see how it could be denied them. Why should they, the most ardent and most tested patriots and resisters, be denied what would be freely granted to others?

What was at stake can be gauged only in the light of subsequent events in central Europe. Neither the Socialists nor the M.R.P. raised any objection, to the obviously democratic Communist demand, but General de Gaulle opposed it as categorically and obstinately as the Communists pressed it. After a week of vain negotiations he announced that his attempt to form a Government had failed, and handed his mandate back to the National Assembly. Next day, with a naturalness that unleashed a cry of indignation from all the guardians of parliamentary tradition, he went to the microphone and explained his action to the people over the heads of the National Assembly. "While I was fully prepared to admit the men of the party in question to the economic and social work of the Government and to give them appropriate portfolios," he said, "I could not see my way to conceding to them any of the three posts which determine foreign policy —diplomacy which expresses it, the army which supports it, and the police which covers it. Had I acted differently in view of today's international situation, I should have risked not being able to answer, even in appearance . . . for the French policy of equilibrium between two very great powers."

For the first time there was a public breach between the Communists, a "foreign nationalist party"—to use the celebrated phrase coined by Léon Blum in prison in 1941—and all the other parties. The blow struck deep, and the Communists protested loudly at this desecration of the memory of their dead comrades. But, as it seemed impossible to govern without de Gaulle on the one hand and the Communists on the other, after twelve days of deadlock a way out was found by a piece of political horse-dealing. The Communists were given the Ministries of National Economy, Labour, and Industrial Production, and as a makeweight M. Thorez, their leader, the deserter of 1939, was given a magnificent rehabilitation. He was allotted a place of honour at General de Gaulle's side as Minister of State. But, instead of one of the key positions they had demanded, they were given only the politically valueless Ministry of Armaments, a part of the Defence Ministry which was split off for the purpose. Its chief function was to supervise the return of the armaments industry to civilian production.

The crisis was a foretaste of what French politics were to be for years to come. The votes in the National Assembly, beginning with the unanimous vote appointing General de Gaulle into office, were pure formalities; the real decisions were the result of deals and negotiations between three party machines each of which controlled a quarter of the parliamentary seats. Not representatives of the parliamentary parties, but representatives of the party offices, called upon the Prime-Minister-designate, acted as their spokesmen, stated their terms, appeared in ever-changing groupings and constellations to make bargains and agree on tactics, and shared out portfolios among themselves. The partitioning of the Defence Ministry was the beginning of a long tradition. As the state apparatus had to be split up into party domains, each one of which was immediately established as a party stronghold and threatened to be occupied from top to bottom by men of confidence of the party in possession, the key Ministries, which no party was willing to leave entirely in the hands of another, were continually being reorganised into different component parts, for each of which a new bureaucracy had to be set up on each occasion; the sphere of activity of each was ill-defined, and, even when they did not deliberately work against each other, there was no tradition to help them to work together. After a number of reorganisations, the Defence Ministry came into Communist hands for a few months at the beginning of 1947, but it had been emptied of all content; its functions were merely to co-ordinate the activities of the Ministers of War, Air, and Marine, all of whom were violently anti-Communist and cared not a jot for the activities of their co-ordinator. The number and the functions of the economic and social Ministries varied in Proteus-like fashion in accordance with the changes in the party constellations. The consequences of this permanent disorganisation of the government machine were all the graver as, with the assumption of control of the capital and goods markets and the nationalisation of key industries, the French state had undertaken tremendous new responsibilities for which it was in any case ill prepared. Apart from other things, there was the whole structure of national defence which had to be built up again on an entirely new basis in view of the collapse of the old system; to say nothing of the fact that the whole of the state apparatus itself was in need of thoroughgoing reform if a modern, well articulated administration were to take the place of the traditional, stuffy, bureaucratic centralism. The only possible result of a division of power between rival forces which cancelled each other out was the pitiful failure of all attempts at reform in all these spheres.

On a Sunday in January, 1946, General de Gaulle, after presiding over this amalgam for two months, suddenly threw in his hand, without warning, without giving his astonished Ministers any explanation, and without any immediate occasion. With the self-assurance of a man who stood above the rules of the game, he proposed once more to broadcast to the people on the day after his resignation, explaining that he was tired of political squabbles, that he left the parties "to conduct their experiment alone", and that he proposed to remain aloof from their inferior machinations until a new hour of danger should strike. But the parliamentary régime was now more firmly in the saddle than it had been two months before, the broadcast was not delivered, and only more or less apocryphal versions of this condemnation of his creation by the founder of the Fourth Republic were circulated surreptitiously. The general withdrew into silent meditation, which lasted for many months; the object of his meditation was the same as that of the labours of the Constituent Assembly, namely the constitution of the Fourth Republic.

The year 1946 passed with the parties locked in hopeless confusion about the constitution. The Provisional Government lived on, in the new three-party form. The National Assembly and the Government showed themselves to be mere committees of delegates of the three party machines, which negotiated with each other as between Power and Power, assigned themselves and each other segments of the state machinery, but above all held each other in check. In this constricted equilibrium of forces all decisions were blocked and any long-term policy was out of the question; the three coalition parties were not too united to begin with, but the shortness of their term of office between two plebiscites ensured the impossibility of their agreeing on anything whatever. For after a few months the partners were destined to appear again as rivals at the polls, each denouncing the other two and exalting itself at their expense. The draft constitution produced by the seven-month Constituent Assembly in essence made permanent the "assembly régime" which for lack of other institutions was already functioning as the provisional French system of government.

The exclusive source of sovereignty under both the First Republic of 1793 and the Second Republic of 1848 had been a single elected assembly, and both had come to a swift end in dictatorship. But both were surrounded by the glorious halo of revolution, and the parties of the left, in unswerving loyalty to these models, had always condemned the two-chamber system, and the whole liberal constitutional system of checks and balances and the division of powers, as a reactionary barricade erected to obstruct the people's will. In the draft constitution some of these institutions survived only as mere decorative flourishes. The draft, however, passed the Constituent Assembly thanks only to the bare majority possessed by the Communists and Socialists combined, for the M.R.P., which had started by fully co-operating in these "popular democratic" ideas, ended by splitting with its partners over apparent trifles and calling on its followers to vote against it in the plebiscite. But even the Socialists breathed more easily when the people rejected the draft constitution by a small majority in spite of their support. Prisoners of their own principles, chained to the "brother party" by common slogans and a common clientèle, they were continually obsessed with the fear of an adventure *à deux* with the Communists, and their obstinate refusal, for which they found varying excuses, ever to decide between the other two big parties was the real cement which held the "three-party system" together.

The indecision of the Socialist Party led to its losing votes both to the right and to the left in the elections to the second Constituent Assembly in June, and left it so weakened that henceforth it was impossible to govern except *à trois*; for a Communist-Socialist majority no longer existed. With the new seven-month Provisional Government there began a pitiful period of impotence, the most characteristic and most disastrous example of which was the Government's complete abdication in the economic field. The Communist Party, its self-assurance shaken by the left-wing failure in the plebiscite, found it necessary to seek "closer contact with the masses", and four days before the elections to the second Constituent Assembly it sent the C.G.T. into the fray with a demand for a 25 per cent. all-round increase in wages, and this became its election slogan. This was like an opening of the floodgates. The demand that wages should be brought into line with the inflationary increase in prices had been held in check only by the iron Communist discipline in the trade unions. But now the Communists launched their campaign for higher wages at the very moment when the inflationary trend was becoming exhausted. What with the muddle and impotence of the state machinery, continual conflict with legal controls and regulations, in the impenetrable jungle of which nobody could find his way—though everybody had long since ceased taking any notice of them—the French had individually adapted themselves to the prevailing anarchy, set the archaic mechanisms of their national economy in motion again, and mole-like had dug their own channels parallel to the official channels of supply and demand. On the black market, the only market that worked, prices had begun to reach stability between a growing supply and a shrunken demand. A flood of paper purchasing power let loose on the market without a corresponding increase in supplies could act only like the crack of a whip on the expiring inflationary trend and set it rapidly spiralling again to new heights. M. Bidault's three-party Government could not make up its mind one way or the other, washed its hands of the matter, and summoned the representatives of the trade unions, industry, and agriculture to a conference to settle the question for themselves.

What happened was what always happens when representatives of sectional interests meet at a round table; they came to terms rapidly and harmoniously by generously granting all each other's demands; they agreed both to increased wages and to increased industrial and agricultural prices, and even the state got its mite in the form of an increase in the prices of the products of publicly owned or nationalised undertakings. But within two weeks, even before it became effective, the increase in wages was overtaken by a new increase in prices, the whole unstable price pattern was set in uncontrollable motion again, and the chance of stabilisation was postponed for another two years.

It now appeared that at all costs an end must be put to this rudderless drifting between two plebiscites. The new constitution, drawn up by the second Constituent Assembly in an anxiously preserved unity of the three parties, was in many respects a monstrosity in which irreconcilable principles had often to be reconciled at the expense of common sense, logic, and even elementary grammar. It contained complicated clauses which it was beyond the wit of man to understand, and trustingly left details on which agreement could not be reached to be solved by Providence in the future. Whole chapters, such as those on the organisation of the French Union and on "local collectives", have remained a dead letter, and the anxiously puzzled out provisions on the procedure of forming a Government, on votes of no confidence and the dissolution of Parliament have turned out in practice to be failures or to be simply unworkable. None of its creators was proud of this constitution, but it represented the best obtainable compromise, and at any rate it was better than risking another rejection by the people, and another Provisional Government followed by the threat of a landslide into chaos.

In view of the general weariness and the unanimity of the three parties, the second plebiscite would have taken place quite smoothly, had General de Gaulle not emerged from his solitude and thrown the whole weight of his authority into the scales against the "bastard project". The general, at a level ineffably remote from the daily grind and humiliating compromise of practical politics, delivered symbolic proclamations at Clemenceau's graveside, at the dedication of memorials, and at patriotic celebrations, reiterating thaumaturgically and with classically severe and abstract arguments, but never tackling the concrete difficulties, his ambiguous but plausible demand for a strong state with a strong leader, standing above the squabbling of the parties.

The effect of this dramatic intervention from off the political stage was as profound as it was embarrassed. It was obvious that de Gaulle was right in his onslaught on the "party régime" and the constitution which was to perpetuate it. But what did he want to put in its place? And what would happen if the result of the second plebiscite was also negative, and thus turned into a vote for the independent and autocratic de Gaulle and against the united *bloc* of the three parties?

The plebiscite resulted in a complete picture of confusion. The constitution was agreed to, but the number of votes cast for it was smaller than that cast in favour of the first draft which had been rejected in May. De Gaulle's intervention had more than compensated for the fact that the M.R.P., with its five million votes, had this time thrown its weight into the scales in favour of the constitution. Little more than one-third of the electorate accepted the act of foundation of the Fourth Republic as the lesser evil, nearly one-third rejected it, and the remainder were bewildered or disgusted, or simply stayed indifferently at home. This boded ill for the fate of a republic which had to be content with the lukewarm approval or toleration of one-third of its citizens, and, while balancing delicately on this slender basis, had to solve the problem of a democracy without a majority. Seldom has a new state begun its career in such an atmosphere of weariness, and with such slender reserves of prestige and self-confidence.

The elections to the National Assembly and the caricature of a Senate again confirmed the equilibrium of the three parties. In accordance with the familiar law of polarisation, the Communist Party, as the "bulwark against reaction", and the M.R.P., as the "shield against Communism", made the running against each other, while the Socialist Party in between was further worn away between the two millstones. But it was simultaneously held aloft by them. In its weakened state it became the indispensable pivot of every combination. It obtained in succession the presidency of the National Assembly, the Presidency of the Republic, and the premiership, and, at the high point of political confusion between the acceptance of the constitution and its coming into force, France actually had a purely Socialist Government, with Léon Blum as Prime Minister. The formation of this Government was purely a stopgap arrangement, but it was the only really effective Government that France had had and was to have for years. In the five weeks during which it "was entrusted with the conduct of affairs" by a unanimous

Assembly, *i.e.*, acted as a caretaker government, the Blum administration broke down France's diplomatic isolation by reviving the frozen relations with Britain, and, by introducing a strict policy of price reduction and wage stabilisation, took a firm grip on the rudder of economic policy which the Bidault Government six months previously had impotently let go. But this phase passed like a beautiful dream. No sooner had the transitional period ended and the new constitution come into force than the three-party system came into its rights again, just as if the Catholics and the Communists had not been hurling insults at each other; and by bringing in the Radicals the "régime of unanimity" was for the first time extended to this old party of the Third Republic. The Government was more than ever a mere committee of Parliament, reflecting all its conflicts, and the beginning of the duly constituted Fourth Republic was merely a continuation of the provisional régime. Over the entrance gate into the new France there was inscribed, with an ironic change of meaning, the opening phrase of Caesar's *Gallic War*—*Gallia divisa est in tres partes.*

The "three-party system" became a firmly established conception in French post-war history, and as it seemed to harmonise with a pattern—Communist Party, Socialist Party, and Christian Social Party—which seemed to prevail nearly all over Europe and could, moreover, be interpreted as a domestic political reflection of the world situation, a whole political philosophy on the subject was developed which persisted long after this state of affairs had come to an end; and in the form of neo-Gaullism it led to an authoritarian criticism of parliamentary democracy itself. The total blocking of the machinery of government and the splitting up of the state machine into party domains caused puritans to talk of corruption and the disappointed to talk of party dictatorship, while the apocalyptic-minded drew striking comparisons with the decline of ancient Rome and the anarchic beginnings of the feudal period. The state, which had just taken over large sectors of the national economy, had immediately handed them over in fee to the great parties, just as the Carolingians had once handed over crown domains; and the state had to tolerate the setting up of what was in reality an independent

Communist "people's republic" in the French mining area, where everyone, from the responsible Minister at the top, the boards of directors and managers, to the leading spirits in the trade union apparatus, the co-operatives, the canteens, and the sick funds, were devoted party members. Events reported in the newspapers continually provided fresh parallels, such as the local and regional autarkies which had arisen as a consequence of the war and still survived, a development which resulted in departments shutting out each other's produce and engaging in economic warfare with each other; the appropriation of arbitrary police and other public prerogative by representatives of sectional interests; the exuberant growth and multiplication of committees of all sorts, including committees representing suburbs and suburban housewives, which, in view of the impotence of the authorities, took over control of markets and shops on their own initiative, held up passing food lorries, confiscated their contents, and sold them to the local population at prices decided by themselves; the inevitable decay of respect for the law after so many convulsions and upheavals; and the exuberant growth of a new law of established custom, which in the extreme case of rents and the occupation of premises amounted to the right to stay where one was and to keep what one had once laid one's hands on, and must inevitably lead in the end to a *de facto* abolition of the laws of property. In this "return to feudalism" the party struggle of opinions and interests fused with all the surviving archaisms in France, the fundamental tendencies to regression which appeared all over Europe as a consequence of war, devastation, chaos, and social upheaval, and the surreptitious positional warfare in progress between the Communist Party, the counter-state which had established itself in all the nooks and crannies of the ancient edifice, and all the other forces in France. Under the influence of the Communist assault all the progressive forces in France were forced, or believed themselves to be forced, to support with all their might the wreckage of the old state apparatus. The Socialist Party in particular failed as a mass party because of the conflict between its conservative, defensive practice and its frantic clinging to a revolutionary theory.

But even the Communists were exclusively concerned, not with changing or overthrowing the state apparatus, but with gaining control of it. It would be a mistake to think of them only as a threat to the state; as a party to the Government coalition they constituted by far the most important pillar of public order. Only they could persuade the workers, who were the chief sufferers from the depreciation of the currency, the black market, and the failure of all attempts to control distribution and supply, to remain quiet, observe discipline, and fight a Stakhanovite battle for production. From no one but the Communists would a working-class brought up to believe in the doctrine of the class struggle accept as the last word in Marxist wisdom assurances that a strike would be a crime against the national economy, that only increased output could lead to a better life, and that there was a solidarity of interests between all sections of the population. The C.G.T. as reconstituted under Communist control had developed into something very different from the old anarcho-syndicalist C.G.T.; it was now a state trade union organisation in the hands of the Communist government party, and it was used, not to organise the working-class in its own defence, but to gain complete control of the working-class in the fashion in which the "Labour front" is controlled in every totalitarian state. The axiom, undisputed in France until 1947, that it was impossible to govern France without the Communists, depended on this phenomenon, for the Communists provided the backbone of the state; and the crisis that finally brought down the whole three-party structure came from the trade unions.

Trade union dictatorship without political dictatorship was a paradox which in the long run was untenable. The conflict in the strategy of a party which was both a pillar of the state and its irreconcilable opponent was nowhere so striking as in the fashion in which it used the C.G.T., now as a Stakhanovite body in the interests of the state, now as storm-troops against its partners in the Government, now as a convenient object with which to blackmail them. These excessive tactical zigzags constituted a threat to their hold on the C.G.T., which was firm, but by no means undisputed. The trade union bureaucracy's sudden change of front on the wages question before the elections of June, 1946, two months after the national congress of the C.G.T. had proclaimed the dogma of "Production, not wage demands!" and denounced the opposition as the *"agents provocateurs* of the reactionaries and the trusts", initiated the trade union crisis which in less than a year developed into a state crisis. The Communists proceeded to play a complicated game of chess with their coalition partners, involving innumerable twists and turns in the party line. The organised working-class was called on, now to make threatening mass demonstrations, now to demonstrate its discipline by swallowing pitiful compromises, and M. Héneff, the Paris regional secretary, was at one moment calling for "direct action" and at the next vigorously denouncing all strike action, passionately condemning one day the words that, according to his own party newspaper *l'Humanité,* he had himself pronounced the day before. All these things intensified working-class unrest and increased the resentment of the old trade unionists at being used as a strategic reserve in an unintelligible, or only too intelligible, party political game.

Opposition within the trade union movement had been beaten, but not eliminated, and all the active non-Communist left wing groups, from the anarchists and the Trotskyists to the survivors of the Vichy trade unions, rallied round the old trade unionists. The opposition visibly gained ground, and found support ready to hand from many who were not in the least concerned with the social position of the working class, but were very much concerned with breaking the Communist strength. Never had unofficial strikes and wage demands been so popular with the bourgeoisie, and—in the climate of "prosperity" induced by inflation—never had they been so little feared.

For eight months the Communist trade union Press raged against the "reactionaries", "Hitlerite-Trotskyists", and other *provocateurs* whom they held to be responsible for the smouldering strike agitation. They did so in the monotonous, denunciatory style with which the veteran rebel and syndicalist Monmousseau greeted in *l'Humanité* the first big unofficial Post Office strike of 1946. "The makers of this undisciplined movement," he wrote, "are a handful of agents who have got the telegraph and telephone system into their hands at various points and who collaborated with Pétain under the occupation régime. . . . The only aim of this strike is to exploit against the interests of democracy and the working class the justified dissatisfaction of Post Office workers at a moment when the only too obvious intention of the reactionaries is to provoke disorder," etc., etc.

But denunciation of undisciplined strikers as the agents of Hitler, Pétain, and Trotsky soon wore very thin; the success of the Post Office strike was the signal for the outbreak of an endless series of unofficial strikes of all categories of government employees, who set up unofficial strike committees in opposition to the official trade union bureaucracy, and organised opposition within the C.G.T. itself. Cracks began to appear in the powerful structure of the C.G.T. During the printers' strike of February, 1947, which left the French capital without newspapers for a month, Communist strike-breakers laid siege to the workers embattled in the offices of *l'Humanité* and there was a whole series of battles and *mêlées*. In April there were a number of signs which could no longer be overlooked. In particular there was the public failure of C.G.T. candidates in the elections to the administrative councils of the social insurance fund in the industrial heart of France; and an unofficial strike broke out at the nationalised Renault motor works in Paris, the biggest industrial undertaking in France and a stronghold of the French trade union movement. The Communist trade union leadership had been trying by every means in its power to nip in the bud the strikes that flared up now here, now there, now in one shop and now in another; but suddenly, in the course of a few days, practically the whole of the thirty thousand men employed at the Renault works downed tools, and the Communists had to look on while their Socialist and M.R.P. partners in the coalition with unconcealed glee fanned the workers' rebellion against their "bosses". Against the mobilised power of the Communist Party their opponents mobilised the ancient French secret weapon of anarchy.

The Communists, thus threatened in the central bastion of their power, carried out a sharp reversal of policy and with heavy heart resigned from the Government in order to seize the leadership of the strike for themselves and to put themselves at the head of the movement for higher wages in opposition to the official stabilisation programme. The parting shot of M. Duclos, the Communist leader, to his former Government colleagues was: "He who tries to attack the Communist Party from the left breaks his teeth." It was not yet clear to anybody that this incident marked the end of the period of the great alliance, in France and in the international field as well.

§ 3

YEAR OF DECISION

Only a few months before the inglorious end of the "three-party régime" Arthur Koestler had noted a remark of a Socialist deputy, who had summed up the prevailing state of mind by saying that, if the Communist Party should at any time wish to seize power, all they needed to do was to make a few telephone calls. But now M. Ramadier, the Prime Minister, taking a bold but legally irreproachable interpretation of the constitution, "released" the Communist Ministers of his Cabinet without its even causing a government crisis. The expected explosion did not occur. For a whole summer the Communist trade union leadership panted behind the incoherently rising and ebbing tide of unofficial strikes, incapable of either disciplining or organising it. With the collapse of this last element of order, anarchy, economic waste, and social club law reached their high point.

The French Communist Party had naturally never formulated the programme of "primary accumulation", combining the working conditions of early capitalism with the labour discipline of the police state, which their eastern European brother parties enforced as the alternative to "western capitalism"; it is a programme that can be enforced when one is in power, but cannot be proclaimed while one is still on the way to it. But the cult of production organised by the "party of French regeneration" had, in combination with the shamefully hushed-up credits received from the United States, helped to keep alive a belief in French revival by her own efforts. The departure of this party from the Government did not herald a crisis, but marked the end of many illusions. It left behind a Government without prestige, without propaganda, and without prospects; it did not fall, because nobody knew what to put in its place, and lived on credit from day to day. For week after week one industry after another was paralysed by unofficial strikes. The strikers demanded increased wages, but nobody believed that the result could be anything but a few additional worthless pieces of paper; some strikers downed tools without making any specific demands at all, merely as a token of disgruntlement and protest. At the glass factories of Saint-Gobain the workers smashed in the evening the mirrors, window panes, and glasses that they had made in the course of the day.

Later, when the Communist leadership had to some extent recovered control, all these extravagant and distorted forms of strike were admired as diabolically brilliant Communist inventions, involving far less risk than the "outdated strategy of the general strike" and making possible an equally disastrous crippling of the national economy; in reality the Communists, having failed to regiment the unruly and independent French workers into a well-drilled political army, merely made a virtue of necessity. The peasants, that powerful, shapeless mass of sovereign, economically isolated individuals, whose passive resistance defeated all attempts at planning, struck in their own way in an even more unruly fashion than the workers. In a rapidly spreading epidemic of "middle-class revolt" retailers, black marketeers, artisans, publicans, peasants, and housewives in some of the richest departments of France stormed the food and other government offices, emptied the files, and made bonfires of ration lists and ration cards. Private trade associations did away on their own account with the rationing of textiles and leather goods, and the Government meekly submitted, just as it submitted to the breaking of all wage regulations in private industry, which after a brief interval was again afloat on the mounting tide of inflation. Every economic group in France went on strike in turn—civil servants, teachers, students, industrialists, dancers at the Opera, taxpayers, tax-collectors, tenants, judges. All these delivered ultimatums to the Government, or, like powers at war, cut off each others' provisions, funds, electricity, coal, transport, etc. But public order was never endangered. The opposition was even more disorganised and at sea than the Government.

Six months later M. Thorez, the leader of the Communist Party, before departing for Moscow made a speech of several hours in which he confessed the errors and mistakes made by the French Communists during the last ten years and more. He said that a feature common to the Popular Front, the resistance, and the post-war policy of coalition with other parties had been a "united front" leadership in which the Communist Party had sacrificed its monopoly of salvation by recognising other parties at its side. After its departure from the Government the party "had seemed to hesitate in its opposition", and to be "accessible to the Socialist complaint that they were standing in the way of American credits and thus damaging France". "The root of these errors lay in the delay with which our central committee recognised and interpreted the regrouping of the imperialist forces under the leadership of and for the benefit of the United States. We therefore did not emphasise from the outset and with the necessary clarity that it was only upon the explicit orders of the American reactionaries that we were removed from the Government. We thus made possible the manœuvre of Blum and Ramadier, who wished it to be believed that it was only a difference of opinion about wages and prices. . . . We allowed the impression to arise that it was no more than one of the usual government crises." In short, the Communist Party, forgetting its mission, had taken part in the democratic party game and had "allowed the impression to arise" that its departure from the Government had arisen out of a mere domestic dispute, and not from the world conflict between the Soviet Union and the "imperialist camp".

France had in fact spent these years of domestic strife apparently completely out of contact with world politics. Public interest had been exclusively concentrated on her internal troubles, and her official foreign policy remained congealed in the fictional unanimity of its post-war point of departure and the blind alley of the German policy laid down by de Gaulle. She was still full of resentment against her war-time allies and anxious to play the intermediary between them. But 1947 was the year of decision, in domestic and in world politics. The façade of allied unity had broken down at the Moscow conference on Germany and Austria a few months before the French coalition broke down on a domestic labour issue. Immediately before his departure for Moscow M. Bidault, the Foreign Minister, still in the name of the policy of equilibrium, had thrown out the first diplomatic bridge to the west in the form of an offer of alliance with Britain, and he brought back from Moscow Anglo-American approval of the economic association of the Saar with France which Russia had refused to approve, and an Anglo-French-American agreement on the distribution of Ruhr coal.

More urgent, however, than any political problem was the persistence of the deficit in the French national economy, which manifested itself in the catastrophic foreign trade position, the progressive depreciation of the franc, and in social unrest. Nearly all the countries of Europe were faced in varying degree with the same problem: namely the impossibility in the foreseeable future of restoring their devastated economies out of their own resources without a severe lowering of the standard of living. In the last resort this meant choosing between Communism and dollar aid.

General Marshall, the American Secretary of State, made history in his Harvard speech of June 5th, 1947, by putting forward the first constructive idea to be tossed into the ideological craziness of the post-war world: namely that the nations of Europe, instead of remaining obstinately imprisoned in their own national difficulties, from which there was no way out, and continuing as best they could by securing what aid they could individually obtain from the United States, should get together and establish what they could achieve jointly and what they jointly needed to be put on their feet again. This proposal, which was put forward generously and unconditionally, could have turned into something much more than and quite different from the brilliant move on the chessboard of world politics into which it was transformed by the Russian veto. The Paris conference at which Mr. Molotov, in the name of the most reactionary of slogans, that of "national sovereignty", finally and dogmatically rejected any supra-national economic order and slammed the door behind him was the decisive rupture in the post-war history of Europe. Henceforward it was a fantastic game of dice in which America staked everything on the consolidation and recovery of western Europe while the Soviet Union staked everything on chaos and collapse. Everything that has since happened, from the brutal subjection of eastern Europe to the formation of the Atlantic Alliance, followed from that rupture.

Henceforward French politics were involved in this conflict. The Russians answered American aid to western Europe by rigorously associating all the national Communist parties in the Cominform, and the French Communist Party, like the rest, had to make everything else subsidiary to trying to wreck the Marshall plan. It did so by systematically whipping up all the chauvinism and bitterness of a nation whose traditional position had declined. It inveighed against the "national ignominy" of dependence on foreign aid, by denouncing Wall Street, and above all by fulminating against acceptance of "the hereditary enemy" Germany as a future partner in European co-operation; and it rose to occasional heights, such as the "sugar battle of Verdun", when the population of the French frontier departments were mobilised in the name of the dead heroes of two wars and the "starving children of France" to riot in protest against the progress through northern France of a barge bound for Germany laden with American sugar, or the mob scenes in Parliament when the Communists shouted *"boche!"* at M. Schuman, who was then the Prime Minister and is a Lorrainer. In this campaign everything was grist to the Communist mill—xenophobia, protectionism, fear of war, and chauvinism; and they were able to use all the positions of power and influence which they had acquired during the years when they were in the Government.

The driving to its ultimate conclusion of this debauchery of ideas ended by bringing down its own punishment on the Communists. After two years of senseless and fruitless agitation, the party's agitation had worn itself to a standstill. True, with the aid of the deliberate and inevitable anti-Communist reaction, they succeeded in laying down an impenetrable barrage behind which lay a quarter of the French population as in a gigantic, isolated pocket, cut off on all sides and subject to their influence only; but it was a dazed, hypnotised section of the population increasingly fit for nothing but to be led docilely to the polling booth. The principal features of this "cold civil war", the general assault on the French national economy in the autumn of 1947, the consequent split in the French trade union movement, and the much weaker second wave of the assault in the autumn of 1948, were episodes, not in French, but in western European post-war history.

The special feature of French domestic politics was not this stereotyped, sterile Communist propaganda, but the militant return to politics of General de Gaulle and "Gaullism". A month before the break-up of the Government coalition de Gaulle in a powerfully orchestrated announcement at Strasbourg had sent forth his call for a "Rally of the French People", and on April 14th he made his lapidary proclamation:

"Today the Rally of the French People is founded. I assume the leadership. Its aim is, over and above all the things that divide us, to promote a triumphant unity of our people in working for the renovation and reform of the state. I invite all Frenchwomen and Frenchmen who wish to unite for the common salvation to join me in the rally, just as they did yesterday for the liberation and victory of France. *Vive la France! Vive la République!*"

In all the years that have since passed, General de Gaulle has never condescended to define the programme of his "rally" more precisely than this. In the mystic vision of a new national unanimity round the leader of free France there seemed to be no room for such practical questions as how he proposed to attain power, how he proposed to exercise it when he had attained it, or what role would be allotted under the new system to the parties and institutions of parliamentary democracy. General de Gaulle never spoke of his followers except as the "rallied French people", he always referred to his aims as "the aims of France", and to his opponents as "those who do not play the French game". His object was to call forth an irresistible ground swell of national enthusiasm which would sweep away everything in its path and rescue France from her evil straits; giving details would have meant imposing limitations upon himself.

As the rally was supposed to be, not a party, but an association open to all Frenchmen without distinction of party, members of all political parties were admissible—with the exception, however, of Communists, whom de Gaulle characterised as "separatists" and thus excluded from the national community. All sorts of flotsam and jetsam were bound to be picked up and carried along in this tidal wave—all the reactionaries who were willing to plunge enthusiastically into any counter-revolutionary crusade, and all the innumerable collaborators who had been pushed out by the liberation and now, after years of political exile, thought that they descried under his banner an unhoped-for opportunity of getting their own back on the republic which they detested. But it did not matter. This was no time to pick and choose, but to let loose an avalanche, and to use its momentum to be precipitated into power and to achieve "the great, simple goals about which at heart all Frenchmen are united": order in the state, labour discipline, patriotism, revival of the French Empire, and the national greatness of France. . . .

The movement would be unintelligible if one failed to take into account the tremendous symbolic power of the name of de Gaulle, and his own conviction that in a short while it would be his mission for a second time to lead France through war and collapse under far harder conditions and against a fifth column in comparison with which that of the Nazis was a mere boy scout organisation. Notwithstanding the played-out pre-war politicians and the opportunists who hastily joined his movement in the next few months, its core was provided by companions of his London exile, men of the resistance who had been left stranded without a political home, idealists, adventurers, apocalyptics, and mythomaniacs; and it is as grotesque to compare, say, Malraux, who discovered the embodiment of his heroic vision in the superhuman proportions of the figure of General de Gaulle, with Dr. Goebbels, as it is to try to compare de Gaulle himself with Hitler, as was sometimes done. If the Führer was unable to visualise the world tragedy which he precipitated in his sleepwalker fashion except from the batrachian perspective of the Munich beerhouse *Putsch* and fourteen years of rowdiness at political meetings and elections, General de Gaulle was able to see the domestic troubles of France only in terms of a huge-scale world-historical battle of giants in which the parochial conflicts of daily politics shrank to the proportions of a childish, insignificant game.

De Gaulle was neither a *homo novus* nor a *uomo qualunque*, and Gaullism existed as a national myth long before a political movement sought to capture it and succeeded eventually in degrading it; and a plebiscite, the only method of accession to power that he publicly admitted that he would accept as confirmation of the legitimacy which he possessed in the eyes of innumerable Frenchmen and his own, was much closer to the deep-rooted French tradition of Bonapartism than to any contemporary totalitarian pattern. In January, 1945, de Gaulle had handed the republic "which he had picked out of the mud" back to the parliamentarians, "to allow the parties to perform their experiment", and, now that their impotence was manifest to all, he returned from the wilderness once more to take the country's destiny into his hands. Since his retirement in 1945 the monthly polls of the French Institute of Public Opinion had regularly reported that from 30 to 35 per cent. of those asked were in favour of General de Gaulle's return to power.

The state of the country in 1947 ensured a tremendous impact for the call for a "strong state", the vagueness of which obliged no one to work out the consequences for himself. The Fourth Republic had failed to achieve a satisfactory synthesis, French public opinion seemed to be intent on separating it out into its two original component parts, Gaullism and Communism, upon the unity of which the new régime had been founded in 1944, and both these components of the new régime were now engaged in an assault upon it. The civil war which had then been avoided now seemed inevitable three years later; once more the French domestic situation seemed a reflection in a broken mirror of the international situation resulting from the break-up of the great war-time alliance.

The local government elections of October, 1947, which by nature should have been so peaceable, were contested in an artificially whipped up civil war atmosphere between the anti-Communist "rally" on the one hand and the Communist

Party, which had dressed itself up as an "anti-Fascist front", on the other; and, in accordance with the law of political polarisation, both sides gained at the expense of the democratic centre parties.

The results of the election were startling, but purely negative. Nearly forty per cent. of the votes were for de Gaulle, thirty per cent. were for the Communists, and the remainder were spread over the remaining parties, which had nothing in common except that they were in favour of parliamentary democracy and abided by the rules. The Government's slender majority, even reinforced by the right wing opposition, no longer reflected a majority in the country, and it started crumbling away as individual deputies and whole groups from all parties from the Radicals to the extreme right went over with flying colours to the big battalions of de Gaulle or retired cautiously into neutrality to await the outcome, but in any case no longer desired to compromise themselves with a régime which appeared to be doomed.

General de Gaulle drew the logical conclusion and called for an immediate dissolution of the Assembly, which was barely one year old, and a general election, and he denied that the Government, "still in office but disavowed by the people", had any mandate; and with that the Fourth Republic again subsided into the blighting provisional state from which it appeared only just to have emerged, with the sword of Damocles of a plebiscite hanging perpetually over its head. The general held his first Press conference after the local government elections on November 12th, the day on which the M.R.P. tabled the resolution calling for a "strong and stable Government" which led to the crisis in which the Ramadier Government fell. On the same day the Communist Party opened the general offensive of the Cominform in western Europe with bloody rioting in Marseilles, and the C.G.T. issued a "manifesto to the workers of France" which led to a general strike. General de Gaulle spoke in that tone of phenomenal self-confidence and lofty contempt with which he henceforward referred to the régime as a "self-preservation society of the parties" and spoke of the "low intrigues" of its "so-called Ministers". He needed no power of foresight to be able to predict that the Rally of the French People would continue to grow and expand until it included the whole nation, with some obvious exceptions. There were the "separatists", for instance, whose peculiarity it was not to belong to the nation, and there were also some party general staffs without troops; and no doubt there would be a few sad and melancholy individualists as well. . . . The flood had risen, and it would grow until it carried away everything in its path. He could only feel sorry for those who refused to understand. If they sought to oppose this great force, which resembled those which, when they had appeared from time to time in their history, had swept everything before them, the only result would be that they would be overwhelmed; and if they remained blustering on the bank, they, or rather their execrations and hostility, would have no more effect than spitting into the sea. . . .

The resolution under which the Cominform was founded had announced the division of the world into two camps, of which one, the "peace camp", that of the Soviet *bloc* and its associated Communist agencies, had declared war on the imperialist "war camp". In France the two camps now stood facing each other, ready for action. Between them and civil war there seemed to be nothing but the pitiful, unpopular parliamentary régime, which had been rejected by the people and was creaking in all its joints. It looked like an unfortunate third party who had stumbled between the front lines and was the target of both until such time as the real opponents should come to grips.

After the Communist departure from the coalition the Ramadier Government managed to survive for six months. The Cabinet was several times reshuffled, and its slowly crumbling parliamentary majority permitted it just to keep its head above water, but would have been insufficient to permit it to be constitutionally invested with power as a new Government. It had no prestige and no prospects. The stabilisation policy of the beginning of the year had deteriorated into an incoherent and hopeless rearguard action against the tide of inflation, which had once more started to rise. A bad harvest, which brought little more than three million tons of wheat into the French granaries instead of the seven million tons of the previous year, and the usual eight, had exhausted the foreign currency reserves and left the Treasury bare. Real wages were half those of 1938, and social unrest was boiling up for an explosion.

The Government had no answer to all this except to scrape along from day to day with the aid of such expedients as the printing press, foreign exchange manipulations, and petty pinching and saving until salvation should arrive in the form of American aid. The exhausted régime of the worthy, colourless, tremendously industrious, and conscientious Socialist administrator M. Ramadier, who was almost literally bent to the ground by the weight of his insoluble task, started disintegrating when the general strike which started in the north and south spread and started surrounding Paris. M. Ramadier did not resign; with his Cabinet again reduced in numbers by half, his last official action was himself to engage in negotiations with the "grand old men" of the Third Republic over the formation of a Government of republican union, the flank guards of which to left and right were to be Léon Blum and M. Paul Reynaud—the Prime Ministers of the Popular Front of 1936 and of the war Cabinet of 1940 respectively. When this unusual government crisis, which had been latent for six months, at last broke out, the stage was ready. As always in great crises, the call went out to rally to the defence of the republic. But for the first time it was not the embattled left, but the last stronghold of the democratic centre which was endangered on all sides. Léon Blum, the last guardian of the Jaurès tradition of Socialist humanism, took up the battle on two fronts against Stalinism and "Caesarism" with his idea of the "third force"—which might perhaps have made history. The errors and illusions to which that idea led characterised a whole trend in European history; and Léon Blum failed with it.

The scene in the Palais Bourbon on November 21st, 1947, was not lacking in pathos. When M. Herriot, the president of the Assembly, mayor of Lyons and the tenor of the Radical Party for forty years, hoisted himself, wheezing with asthma, into the presidential chair on which on that historic day no one was permitted to take his place, and the aged, bent, aristocratic figure of the Prime Minister-designate Léon Blum, tall and slender as a flame on the point of extinction, rose from his lonely seat on the empty Government bench, mounted the rostrum, and shook M. Herriot's hand before beginning his speech, his audience were confronted in the flesh with the old, pre-war republic, which was apparently putting forth its last strength and refusing to die; and once more they were treated to the pre-war republic's parliamentary style, which, however questionable it might be, possessed an indisputable greatness, and now, in the person of its last representatives, towered over the hopelessly plebeian post-war generation.

Everything depended on a mere handful of votes; the few that were required to make up the difference between those which had enabled the Ramadier Ministry to survive and that extra number necessary to secure the absolute majority necessary to vote a new Government into office; and the only chance of securing these was in the border-zone between the old Radicals and the determined neo-Gaullists, whose political attitude, then as in every critical situation, was to raise a wet finger to test the direction of the wind. But Léon Blum spoke far over the head of this mediocre Parliament. "The republic, which for us is identical with our country, is in danger," he said. "Civil liberties, public peace, peace itself, are threatened. There is a double danger. On the one hand international Communism has openly declared war on French democracy. On the other, a party has been formed in France whose aim is to rob the sovereign nation of its fundamental rights. I am here to call for a rally of all republicans; a rally of all who refuse to subject themselves to the impersonal dictatorship, not of the proletariat, but of a party, and refuse to seek refuge from this danger in the personal dictatorship of one man." For the defence of this republic, "which was the creation of the people and is the people's own cause", it was necessary to make a call to the people, and above all to the workers, to distinguish between that part of the current strike movement which was aimed at the destruction of the institutions and principles of the republic and that which was a justified, or at any rate natural, expression of unrest and misery. It was necessary to appeal to co-operation against civil war, to social justice against hatred, to trade union democracy against the supremacy of the Communist apparatus. At the end of his eloquent appeal M. Blum quoted the words of the revolutionary deputy Vergniaud: "May our remembrance perish but let the republic be saved!"

But before he resumed his seat it was plain that such language found no echo in this Assembly, and the atmosphere of the "windowless house" sank oppressively. The handful of votes required melted away; those who might have exercised them decided merely to abstain. It was quite enough for them to think of one danger at a time, that of Communism; the other, that of "Caesarism", was in their eyes not so much a danger as a reinsurance. The great, exciting idea of the "third force", the idea of conducting the inevitable trial of strength with the Communists, not as a struggle *against* the working-class, but as a struggle *for* the working-class, was too subtle and alien to them. The situation allowed little elbow-room, and to hard-headed realists M. Blum's proposals might well seem those of an impractical idealist. The practical implications of the "third force" were vague, and "social justice" and "financial stability" were rhetorical flourishes which in practice could not have made things look very different. Nevertheless these ideas of M. Blum's might have altered the subsequent course of events. For the French working-class had been becoming increasingly rebellious to Communist discipline and was looking for some way out of the *cul-de-sac* into which the Communist Party was leading it other than merely resigning itself to its fate. Moreover Léon Blum was the last non-Communist French politician whose picture still hung in innumerable working-class homes and whose voice could still reach them above the barrage which Communist and anti-Communist hysteria had laid down over France. Perhaps the Fourth Republic that day missed the opportunity of daring to be great. It survived, however, but pettily, meanly, and half-heartedly, a republic without a people and without self-confidence.

Next day M. Robert Schuman, the Finance Minister of the old Government, succeeded M. Blum as Prime Minister-designate and secured the necessary majority without difficulty. All he had to do to obtain the unanimous support of the non-Communist part of the House was to omit all reference to M. Blum's "third force" and "second danger". But by the same token the defence of the republic was reduced to the level of a parliamentary manœuvre, and the big rally "from Blum to Reynaud" shrank to a little one "from Mayer to Mayer", *i.e.,* from the Radical Minister of Finance M. René Mayer to the Socialist Minister of Labour M. Daniel Mayer, whose Homeric duels on the subject of financial orthodoxy *versus* social generosity kept all the caricaturists and cabaret song-writers busy for months. It was inevitably a centre Government. General de Gaulle showed no haste to enter into his ruinous heritage, but left "the system" to complete its own liquidation and leave the rest to him; and in these circumstances it was voted into office with the toleration of the half- or quarter-Gaullists in Parliament, who were vacillating still, or perhaps again. It was obviously a transitional Government, incapable of striking a spark outside the four walls of Parliament, for it possessed neither an inspiring programme, brilliance, nor popular personalities, and it was lacking to an unprecedented extent in any trace of that eloquence which in times of emergency had always been the republic's favourite weapon.

Nevertheless the sum did not work out as expected. This nearly anonymous Government of administrators turned out to be a Government of *grands commis* in the old meaning of the term, and its achievements were in inverse proportion to its prestige. Beneath the mask of a dry, sober, close-fisted book-keeper the Prime Minister concealed the qualities of a great statesman which he later demonstrated in the international field, and the Socialist and Radical parties filled the key positions, the portfolios of Finance and the Interior, with their two hardest and coldest calculators who were least concerned with applause.

Jules Moch, a product of the École Polytechnique, technocrat by nature, strategist by inclination, and Socialist because of his love of organisation, a member of one of those French Jewish officers' families which since the Revolution have made a passionate cult of French patriotism, had had his first experience of strike-breaking during the long transport strike of 1947, when he built up a whole improvised system of goods and passenger transport out of the most variegated collection of requisitioned vehicles. As Minister of the Interior he now used a firm hand to discipline and reorganise the demoralised police force, which was penetrated through and through with Communist and Gaullist cells, and he also did something much harder, namely succeeded in instilling into the police a minimum of tact and self-control in dealing with strikers and demonstrators. His Compagnies Républicaines de Sécurité stood firm under showers of stones without retiring or infringing the order not to use fire-arms, and M. Moch laid the foundations of a new "science of war" which later, as Minister of Defence, he developed into a "dimensional strategy" for the conditions of modern warfare in which fifth columns and partisans operate behind the front. The Communists found this "police Socialist", whose name readily lent itself to a facile play on words, an easy target, and he was spared no insult, from "bloodhound" to "Fascist". His merit was that not only did he stand up to violence and terror for four crazy weeks, but succeeded almost completely in avoiding bloodshed.

About the personality of the Finance Minister, the second corner-stone of the Government, M. René Mayer, a member of the Conseil d'État and innumerable boards of directors, a cousin of the Baron de Rothschild and a former director of the famous bank of the same name, there was nothing new to be revealed. The list of his qualifications was sufficient to make the whole of the French left automatically hide its head. He took up the struggle, not just one or two fronts, but on all fronts simultaneously—in Parliament and in the International Monetary Fund, against the British veto and all the beneficiaries of inflation. He put forward an extremely unorthodox but adroit and radical scheme for restoring the health of the currency and the market by a series of ruthless measures of taxation and credit restriction, compulsory loans, and the sudden withdrawal from circulation of bank notes of big denominations, combined with an amnesty for past tax and currency offences, and the setting up of an open gold and exchange market in order to dry up the quagmire of inflation on which the black market had hitherto flourished. In the difficult winter months, after a year of strikes and a calamitous harvest, this was almost desperately swimming against the stream of rising prices and the prevailing inflation mentality, and the severity of some of M. Mayer's measures was justified only by the necessity of shock tactics. M. René Mayer soon managed to make himself the most hated man in France after M. Moch. But this belated and fragmentary attempt to catch up with the currency reform the opportunity for which had been missed in 1944 not only created the condition necessary to allow Marshall aid, which was now beginning, to exercise its full effect, but achieved something which, after the catastrophic winter, approached the realm of the miraculous; it turned the French franc into a "hard" currency. To the universal astonishment, the colourless Schuman Government turned out to be a "strong" Government—at any rate so long as the Communist onslaught kept Parliament in check and caused the Gaullist opposition to do the best that it could for France and for itself, namely pretend that it did not exist.

It is a sheer impossibility even in retrospect to discern in the French situation even a half-satisfactory explanation of what the aim of the Communist general strike strategy may have been. The slogan, in France as in Italy, was that of struggle against the Marshall plan and "enslavement by the dollar". But the severe damage to the national economy which was its only tangible result left France with no alternative but to stretch out both hands for dollar aid. The blind intensity of the wave of strikes and sabotage bore all the marks of an attempt at a violent seizure of power, and yet it was nothing of the sort. It had no explained or explainable aim; apart from being an act of sabotage directed against the French national economy, such as could be described only as a political crime in the French situation at that time, which was not a revolutionary situation but a *coup d'état* situation, the result could at most have been to put an authoritarian anti-Communist régime in the saddle against which an outlawed Communist Party might have been able to raise the flag of "republican resistance". But in practice the only result was in a few weeks to ride to ruin the French trade union movement, which had hitherto been the biggest power-factor in the Fourth Republic and the foundation of the Communist "counter-state" itself.

The old trade unionists who followed Léon Jouhaux objected to taking the "path to adventure", but M. Frachon, the Communist secretary-general, dismissed their protest with the contemptuous remark that "the mobilisation of millions of republicans in the factories, workshops, and local groups is more important than the chatter at the top"; and the Communist majority took the "path to adventure" with its "manifesto to the French working-class" of November 12th. It was a complete plan of campaign for a mobilisation of the masses. Agitation was to rise slowly to fever heat during the course of a month and culminate in an ultimatum to the Government on December 1st. This was to be followed by another meeting of the C.G.T. national committee on December 19th at which the next steps were to be decided on. The manifesto directed that meetings of all workers, whether organised or not, were to be held in all French factories in order "spontaneously" to decide on demands and a plan of action; and with this "appeal to the masses", which was alien to all trade union tradition, the apparatus, hoping that in the general chaos all resistance would collapse, itself unleashed the trade union anarchy which it had hitherto fought tooth and nail.

But no sooner had it been proclaimed than the whole programme was upset. On the same day the Communists mobilised the trade unions in their stronghold of Marseilles to demonstrate against an increase in tram fares, which had long been inevitable, but had been postponed by the previous Communist municipal council in view of the approach of the local elections; it had therefore to be enforced by their Gaullist successors—"on Truman's orders", as the unspeakably stupid and threadbare Communist propaganda insisted in all seriousness in accordance with the new Cominform *cliché*; and, what with rioting, pitched battles in the streets, assaults on the town hall and the Palais de Justice, and strikes in protest at the action taken by the Government to restore order, the agitation grew into a local general strike, which spread northwards from Marseilles like a spot of oil. Strike-leaders called the men out without even taking the trouble to state what they were striking for.

The coal-miners of northern France were called out on November 17th, and the mining areas became the second centre of violence. Here both management and the trade union apparatus—which had multiplied a hundredfold in comparison with the old C.G.T. apparatus of pre-war days—were in the hands of the Communists, who exercised complete and unrestricted control. Almost everywhere the men were called out without being consulted, and here as elsewhere pay and subsistence demands were hastily improvised only after the strike had begun. On the same day a strike was declared at a tumultuous *ad hoc* meeting held at the Renault motor works in Paris. No attempt was made to ensure that it was attended only by Renault employees, the strike was extended to other works in the same way, and two days later a general strike was called without even a beginning of negotiations with the employers. In other motor works in the Paris area the workers objected to being used in this way; they defended their place of work against the Communist emissaries and the gangs sent to occupy them, and in many cases, after the police had been called in, insisted on the taking of a proper ballot in which the strike orders were rejected by a big majority.

To break growing resistance within the C.G.T. the Communists carried out a *coup d'état*; the Communist majority set up an exclusively Communist "national strike committee", ousted the regular trade union leaders, and seized undisputed leadership of the movement for themselves. One trade union after another was now thrown indiscriminately into the fray, and every form of violence and intimidation was used. Places of work were forcibly seized and occupied. Communist strong-arm gangs conducted assaults upon non-strikers, tools were filched and put out of action, and work brought to a standstill by interference with the electricity and railway system and in other ways.

Nevertheless, outside the real strongholds of the party in the north and south, the strike movement was principally confined to the great nationalised industries of which the Communists had secured control from top to bottom during the years in which the economic Ministries had been in their hands. The France of small and medium-sized factories was barely touched by the agitation, and the Communist appeals to solidarity remained unanswered in all those publicly owned concerns whose workers and employees had succeeded in shaking off Communist trade union domination during the official "Stakhanovite" period. The C.G.T. tried three times in vain to bring the Paris public transport system to a standstill, and on the railways the strike spread only sporadically beyond the Paris–Marseilles line on which it started. Innumerable "spontaneous works meetings" were organised in accordance with the usual pattern, and strike resolutions were passed at them, but no stoppage of work followed; and on his return from his cross-examination in Moscow M. Thorez calmly took a train which, if the C.G.T. had had its way, would not have been running. But the more the movement degenerated into stagnation and was forced back to its starting lines, the more violent it became. In early December acts of sabotage and violence multiplied, and in many places in southern France where memories of partisan rule were still fresh the reign of terror of 1944 was temporarily resuscitated.

The last spectacular disturbances took place in the National Assembly, where the Communists, in five days of continuous uproar, fisticuffs, filibustering, singing of Communist songs, and forcible occupation of the rostrum, replayed in farcical fashion all the traditional scenes of the revolutionary picture-book in order to prevent the passage of a Bill "for the protection of the republic and of freedom of labour", while *l'Humanité* turned out special editions with blood-red headlines announcing the imminence of a midnight Fascist *coup d'état*. Once more the question arises whether this was sheer mental aberration or—as seems much more likely—the wish was the father of the thought. "Alarm!" *l'Humanité* declared. "They wish to murder the republic! The American party is tearing up the constitution! A plot for a reactionary *coup d'état* has been hatched for tonight! Workers! Democrats! Patriots! You have the power to prevent the crime which the exploiters and imperialists have ordered in New York!"

But it was only the Communists who lost their nerve. None of the daily and hourly acts of provocation that they piled up acted as the spark in the powder-barrel; the miscalculation was to take France for a powder-barrel. With remarkable calm, and with more surprise and disgust than fear or indignation, she allowed the frenzied onslaught to spend itself.

After the passage of the emergency legislation troops and police started clearing the strikers out of the factories and mines which they had occupied, and with that the fate of the strike was sealed. An unwritten law had hitherto allowed strikers to draw full pay for the period of a stoppage, and had thus turned strikes into a kind of paid, risk-free holiday. But this time it was quietly buried without the C.G.T.'s so much as daring to complain, and the paying out of social security and family allowances for the strike period was permitted only to those who were back at work by December 10th. In the areas where the strike first started want and hunger began to stalk. For ten days the strike was in a state of painful death agony. On December 8th the national strike committee disavowed the negotiations which had surreptitiously begun between the trade union opposition and the Ministry of Labour, rejected as a beggarly pittance the cost-of-living bonus which had been decided on by the Government weeks before, and uncompromisingly called on the working-class to "hold out and win"—only to admit unqualified defeat a day later and dissolve itself with another long "manifesto to the workers of France" in which it used remarkably military phraseology to order the troops who were still holding out to break off the battle.

They declared that the manœuvres of the reactionaries had succeeded in a number of places in breaking through their fighting front, and they did not want the forces of the working-class to be mopped up piecemeal. "Our strength must be rallied and regrouped for future hard battles. We assume the responsibility of ordering a general retreat. Those who have held out so magnificently and have maintained their strength and their fighting spirit intact will understand. . . . Workers, influenced, deceived, and demoralised by the lies, slanders, and manœuvres of our enemies, have gone back to work; others have been driven back by hunger. Show them understanding . . . but be pitiless to deliberate traitors and strike-breakers."

A "regrouping" in the trade union movement could indeed be delayed no longer. The C.G.T. was a monster with two heads. One of its secretaries-general was the "grand old man" Léon Jouhaux, leader of the French trade union movement for nearly forty years; in 1945, on his return from imprisonment in Germany, he had been put back by the Communists as a figurehead and symbol of the old trade union traditions. In his absence the C.G.T. had been purged and reconstituted, and he and the Communist secretary-general M. Benoît Frachon, who exercised the real control, were bound to part. But this meant leaving the old organisation and the old name as booty in the hands of the Communists, and the experienced veteran Jouhaux held out as long as possible against doing so. But now the breach could be delayed no longer, and on December 18th M. Jouhaux and his followers, and his newspaper the *Force Ouvrière,* broke away from the Communist-dominated apparatus. The assaults and violence of the last month made it impossible to remain with the "old firm", particularly for those officials who had held out against the Communist terror in the factories, and whole groups of workers and many individuals had broken away from the C.G.T. without waiting for the official split.

The hope that these people would join the breakaway organisation in large numbers turned out to be illusory. Membership of the C.G.T. dropped in the course of a few years from its proud peak of six millions to a mere two millions. But the great mass of the deserters went to swell the ranks of the unorganised, the disillusioned, and the apathetic; relatively few joined the Force Ouvrière, which could claim only half or quarter-success. This is to be explained partly by the sheer inertia which attaches to any mass organisation, partly by the whole tradition of the French working-class, which is able to cast aside its individualism only in periods of revolutionary enthusiasm such as that of the Popular Front or the liberation, but scatters to the winds after every defeat; and it is also to be explained by the nature of the new organisation, which shared the failure of the "third force" idea. It was set up with the aid of Government funds, and soon received grants from American trade unions; it started as the officially recognised headquarters of an organisation that barely existed, instead of as a crusade—a crusade such as had been conducted for three decades by the Christian trade union federation, which had started from the poorest and humblest beginnings, the fruits of which it now gathered as the biggest and above all the most respected non-Communist workers' organisation in France, without ever being able to overcome its denominational limitation. The proverb *pecunia non olet*, which applies universally elsewhere in France, does not apply to the French working-class, and the flavour of being a "scab" union always clung to the new organisation.

The Force Ouvrière was torn between half-hearted support of the official policy of stabilisation, the only consistently applied measures of which were "putting the brake on mass buying-power", *i.e.*, freezing wages at the lowest possible level, and hectic attempts to outdo the C.G.T. in demanding better living conditions, and it necessarily fell between two stools. Powerful as it had been as an opposition within the C.G.T., it was extremely weak as one of many competing organisations outside it. The trade union movement split into syndicalist, anarchist, Trotskyist, Gaullist, and really "scab" organisations, and at some points the competition was intense. On the Paris Métro, for instance, seventeen mutually hostile unions competed for the loyalty of the staff, and the resulting chaos ensured better than any state authority could have done that no strike action could possibly be successful for years to come; and in this sad decline the C.G.T., with the advantage of the durability and discipline of its powerful apparatus and its memories of the "heroic age" of trade unionism behind it, remained the "old firm" which was grieved for even by those who had disowned it.

But as a fighting machine it was broken. After a year of nursing its strength, cautious manœuvring, and organising a series of brief, local strikes, in which it sought to regroup and discipline its demoralised troops, it again attempted a major trial of strength in its most important and impregnable stronghold, the mining areas of northern France. In the closed and isolated world of the mining areas the unrestricted power of the C.G.T. and the laws of solidarity—a simple, crude, and often terroristic solidarity resembling that of a family or clan—survived unshaken. In particular the submerging of the original core of miners' families by a fluctuating, uprooted majority of immigrants and foreign workers made it impossible for adherents of the old, more democratic trade union traditions, who elsewhere had shaken the dictatorship of the Communist apparatus, to revolt. The great coal strike of 1948 was a grim and hopeless epilogue to the general strike of 1947, as hideous as the black horizon of the mines. Once more the C.G.T., now exclusively in Communist hands, deliberately omitted to carry out the first duty of a democratic trade union, namely to formulate demands capable of fulfilment in the existing economic situation, to negotiate with the employers, and as a last resort, but only as a last resort, to try to secure them by strike action. But again a strike was called without defined or limited aims, and the miners were deliberately led into the *cul-de-sac* of a violent trial of strength. The miners were mere pawns in a naked struggle for power between the state and a state-within-the-state, namely the Communist trade union apparatus, and the struggle was fought out with all the ruthlessness and brutality of a "cold" civil war. The C.G.T. threat to flood the mines, and thus eliminate one of the kingpins of the French national recovery for months or years, was averted only by military intervention.

Operations on the Government side were conducted as in a military campaign. Troops were strategically deployed, overwhelming strength was concentrated at key spots, raids took place at dawn, and the most dangerous centres of resistance were systematically isolated until they were ripe for unconditional surrender. The operations were conducted by M. Moch, the Minister of the Interior, with such careful timing, and with such an overwhelming parade of force, that bloodshed was almost completely avoided; police measures were supplemented, not only by the withdrawal of miners' pay, but of their family and pithead allowances, and the result was that after six or seven weeks the last strikers were forced to give in.

In the autumn of 1948 northern France was first a besieged and then an occupied zone, and, so far as the rest of France was concerned, all this took place in a foreign, unknown land; it was as if there had been a rebellion in Madagascar. All the efforts of C.G.T. headquarters to fan the dying embers failed;

their attempts to extend the strike to the engineering industry, the transport system, and the ports were abortive. A year before the C.G.T. had broken off the general strike too late to be able to make terms, but in time to beat an orderly retreat; a million workers were still striking in obedience to their orders. But this year the defeat was more severe and more striking; their orders to abandon the struggle came only after more than four-fifths of their troops had "deserted" and work in most mines had returned practically to normal. The management of the nationalised industry announced on November 26th, at the end of the eighth week of the strike, that, in view of the almost complete return to work, it regarded the strike as ended, and that workers who stayed out longer would be regarded as having been dismissed. This would in any case have been the end of the matter, even if the C.G.T. had not ordered a return to work next day. It was the unconditional surrender of the northern French "Soviet republic".

It was also the end of a cycle. The strike had been called in a mood of crazy, hair-brained irresponsibility and continued in the same mood by leaders who cynically left their followers in the lurch; and its end marked that of the biggest and most developed cell of the French "people's democracy" of 1945, the foundations of which had been the Communist trade union apparatus. Its leaders had succeeded without conflict of conscience in uniting in their own persons their position as trade union officials with those of Ministers, State Secretaries, and directors of the coalmines; it is sufficient to recall MM. Duguet, Delfosse, and Lecœur, for instance, who were general or regional secretaries of the miners' federation and simultaneously members of the board of the national mining corporation or State Secretaries in the Ministry of Production; or Comrade Marcel Paul, trade union secretary; or M. Thorez himself, miner's son and deputy Prime Minister in the de Gaulle Government, "upon whose call the miners entered the pits with redoubled energy." In the early, troubled days of the Fourth Republic in May, 1946, M. Auguste Lecœur, the Communist "miners' general", had attacked the already audible opposition of the old trade unionists in the style of the trade union officials of the "people's democracies".

"Where should we be," he asked, "if the miners listened to the bad shepherds who instigated them to strikes and smaller production and denounced as scabs those who did their national and proletarian duty? It is a slander to compare the nationalised coal mines of today with the capitalist coal mines of yesterday. The 'scab' of today is he who refuses to do his duty as a Frenchman and to take part in the battle of production. It is a lie to allege that today better conditions are to be obtained by strikes. The opposite is true. They are to be won from the ground with blows of the pick!"

This was the language of a totalitarian "labour front" leader; Dr. Ley could hardly have done better. However, the Communist-dominated C.G.T., with its Stakhanovism, its pennants of honour and special rations for the winners in "Socialist competition", its decorations and rewards for champion coal hewers whom it hailed as heroes of labour, had brought something more than propaganda into the pits; it had brought a myth that seemed to transfigure the miners' materially unaltered lot. They were no longer the galley-slaves of the pits, the "damned of the earth", but heroes of labour and the nation's truest sons, fighting in the pits for France's greatness and independence. The state to which the pits belonged was their state, the men who spoke to them in the name of the state were their men, even if they quietly cursed them in private as bullies and slave-drivers, and beyond the greyness of the present there loomed the prospect of *les lendemains qui chantent*. It was a myth, but myths count in a country's life. Whether the great mass of the working-class feels itself to be a responsible part of the nation or stands aloof and hostile to it makes the whole difference between the existence or non-existence of a sense of national unity, and, except for the brief honeymoon period after the liberation, the former is something that French democracy has never been able to achieve.

Even with the running amok of the cold war which the Cominform declared on France and western Europe, the fact that with the departure of the Communists from the Government this state within a state became a counter-state would have created an untenable position. The full extent of the breach was at first concealed during the difficult and hesitant transition period of the summer of 1947, when the Communists still counted on a speedy return to the Government, and M. Dupuy, a Communist deputy and secretary of the railwaymen's union, almost imploringly warned M. Ramadier, the Prime Minister, not to shake the power of Communist headquarters by making concessions to "unofficial" strikers. "Do not undermine the authority of the trade unions, which the country may still need!" he declared. But a few months later all this was put into reverse. First of all the slogan of the battle of production gave way to that of the Cominform, and "work, don't make demands!" was changed into "make demands, don't work!" Now that the party of the proletariat had dissociated itself from the state, what did the latter's nationalised industries matter? The French coalfields, having been nationalised, became the arena, not of a class struggle, but of a naked struggle for power. The strikes were only the dramatic climax of a daily process of sabotage, the methods of which are best illustrated by a memorandum submitted to the Government in the name of all the mining engineers, including members of the C.G.T., employed by the nationalised coalmining undertaking. It was a cry of distress issued a few months before the big strike broke out, declaring that all efforts to improve and rationalise methods of production and all modernisation of the mines were bound to remain fruitless so long as there persisted the atmosphere of suspicion and of terror which was systematically fostered by the trade union leaders. These did not hesitate to mobilise the most violent elements in the mines to exercise intimidation, and were continually devising new demands which had very little to do with practical mining-problems. For some time they had been practising a new method of intimidation, namely. making mass incursions into the manager's or engineer's office with a chorus of speakers and then, with unconcealed threats of violence, demanding that the manager or engineer should hold a "democratic discussion" with the whole body of employees of the mine. In an industry in which human relations played such a predominant role it was impossible in these conditions for a manager or engineer to preserve the authority essential to the exercise of his duties; even in the smallest mines a single engineer was responsible for the work of seven or eight hundred men.

In the isolated world of the mines the Government, officialdom, the administrative and political centres, were remote, and legendary forces which occasionally, in times of crisis, made their presence felt in the form of armed intervention. But in the end the troops always withdrew, and the trade union apparatus remained. That was the lesson that the C.G.T. pitilessly rubbed into the "renegades" after the strike of the winter of 1947. The only real and permanent power with which the works management were faced was the Communist apparatus; until recently the maintenance of all order had depended on this apparatus, and by the same token it had it in its power just as easily to destroy it. When the "guerrilla warfare" of local strikes and incidents in the mines developed into an all-out trial of strength, M. Lecœur, the Communist "miners' general", who had been such a magnificent advocate of work discipline in the pits, said during the parliamentary debate on the occupation of the mining districts: "Today the miners realise clearly that, if they had to do with a private employer, there would not be mobilised against them the formidable repressive forces of the state. A private employer would be forced in his own interests to take the workers' demands into account."

The coal strike of 1948 was the last big Communist offensive for many years. This time defeat was unambiguous and heavy with consequences. The Communists had staked all the power they had accumulated in the "revolutionary liberation" on a single throw which did not have the slightest chance of success. The years that followed were a long and painful decline, and, after a few final spasms, the Communist party and trade union machine, which had held all France in terror, was barely capable of organising a demonstration or causing a riot of any consequence. All efforts at "direct action", from attempts to interfere with imports of N.A.T.O. arms to calls for a general strike in protest against the arrest of Communist leaders, were totally ineffective. Nevertheless, throughout these years of impotence the Communist-controlled C.G.T. remained the great organisation of the French working-class, the embodiment of its impotence and disorganisation, and the Communist Party, though expelled from the national community, retained, unshaken even in its "exile", the loyalty of an electorate that included more than a quarter of the nation. Variegated though the fringes of this electorate might be, its core was the core of a working-class that felt itself expelled by the nation. They had given up a senseless and crazily conducted struggle, not because of any change of heart, but because of discouragement and demoralisation, and it left them with a bad conscience, the conscience of a deserter. Nothing that happened offered them any alternative to regarding the Communist defeat as their own; and in the victory of a Government in which since May, 1947, they had not felt themselves to be represented they saw the restoration of an order which refused them their share in the return of national prosperity; which was impotent against the malpractices and exactions of all the parasitical sectional interests; which showed itself to be incapable of imposing their due share of the burden of reconstruction and regeneration upon the other classes of the nation, but used armed force against wage-earners who rose in protest against their oppressive burdens. It would be false to see in all this only a question of the wage-earner's pay-packet. It can just as well be regarded as illustrating the disorder so precious to and well-beloved of all other sections of the population. France was treated to the paradoxical spectacle of a Government which was able to hold out without flinching against a two-months' loss of production by the French mines and calmly allowed rebellion quietly to be starved out, only a few months later to fall over some parochial squabble about three school buildings or an ultimatum from the brandy distillers. The alien body in the political and social organism was neither reabsorbed nor eliminated; it was simply segregated and sealed off. The way back to the good old times could begin.

§ 4

VICTORY OF THE SMALL TOWN

THE nightmare caused by the existence of a powerful Communist dissident state party and dissident trade union apparatus began to fade away; the sword of Damocles suspended over the Fourth Republic had dropped —and broken. The Communist Party was now deprived of all hope of gaining access to power either legally or illegally, not only by the defensive power of the state which had just received its baptism of fire, but by the united alliance of the west which was soon to be added to it. It remained a dangerous pocket, whose leaders, true, could no longer think of playing with revolution on their own account, but throughout the years of cold war awaited the day of salvation when the Soviet army would resume its march from its halting-places at Berlin and Vienna and advance the few hundred remaining miles which separated it from the Atlantic. It was necessary to hold oneself in readiness against this day, to prepare the way for it, and to stab in the back any attempt made to resist it. "The French people will never in any circumstances fight against the Soviet Union," M. Thorez announced in the spring of 1948, and this now became the *Leitmotiv* of all Communist propaganda. France was treated to the spectacle of Communist mayors, draped in the tricolour, calling on the newly enrolled recruits of their locality to vow never to use their arms against the Soviet Union. Nearly the whole following which this self-confessed "party of treason" had gathered round itself while it had been one of the Government parties of the Fourth Republic, a whole nation of five million voters, if not of five million militants, followed it into exile. But this hostile pocket on French soil consisting of a quarter of the French people, though it represented an immeasurable moral defeat for French democracy and caused all western strategists to have acute nightmares, turned out in practice to be a priceless factor of stability.

Since 1948 the Communist Party has counted in the political life of France only as a dead weight which has had to be taken into account as a negative quantity in all political calculation and has sterilised the votes, wishes, demands, and dissatisfactions of five million Frenchmen. True, most of these five millions had only a very unclear idea of what they were voting for. But they had an exceedingly clear idea of what they were voting against. However, the weight of their votes, which in a healthy democracy might have turned the scales in favour of economic and social reform, henceforward counted for as little as if they had left their voting papers unmarked or had stayed away from the polls.

This process of subtraction radically simplified the interplay of French political forces, and radically falsified it. The absurdly exaggerated parliamentary centralism of the French republic has limited consultation of the people to periodic elections in which the citizen totally delegates his sovereignty to the members of the consultative and legislative assemblies. For five million voters on the left the act of deciding what was the people's will degenerated into an empty gesture of protest or discontent. (In appearance this applied to an equally large number of voters on the right as well, but in appearance only, because of the double face of the Gaullist movement, which was on the one hand a party of national regeneration and on the other a party of reactionary notables.) As soon as the danger of a Communist rising, and the consequent danger of a *coup d'état* to save the nation from it, had been dispelled, this whole mass of votes was simply left out of account, not only in the process of forming Governments, but also in considering legislation and expenditure in general. These five millions were represented at the Palais Bourbon, not by deputies concerned for their interests, but by an obstruction and sabotage group which kept up a continual barrage against any sound policy whatever. They were the "dead" element in the electorate who had eliminated themselves from the discussion, and their votes no longer possessed any political purchasing power; the political purchasing power of the votes of all other sections of the population, round the struggle for whose favour the whole parliamentary and party game now centred, was enhanced accordingly.

Henceforward the republic was forced to resort to keeping two sets of political and economic account books. The first of these, with all their anxious tale of social disruption, military weakness, colonial unrest, war burdens, and national deficit, were those which statesmen overwhelmed by their appalling responsibilities laid before America and an anxious world; the other, in which no social, colonial, or world political problems figured, were those of the average Frenchman and his republican deputies, who now calmly went back to their petty local affairs and parochial squabbles. For the France which had victoriously survived the revolutionary convulsions which had occurred among the grey, oppressed masses of humanity in the industrial centres was the old France of the peasantry and the small town, whose clocks and whose problems had stood still for a century in spite of war, occupation and liberation, with their notables and small-scale workshops, their hereditary scarecrows and fetishes, their unshakeable peace and quiet, and their vastly entertaining ideological cockfights between the village schoolmaster and the priest. These flared up again as soon as the danger was over, and split the coalition between the Socialists and the M.R.P.—the party of the school teachers and the party of the priests.

Henceforward all politicians and parties squabbled and fought with all their might exclusively for the favour of this petty bourgeois electorate—the only one which marked its voting papers with cleverness or craft—and the swing of the pendulum between "left" or "right" depended on the success with which it was wooed. Even the Communists felt sure enough of the working-class, or were sufficiently indifferent to its fate, to rush headlong into a demagogic competition with Gaullists, Radicals, and independent notables for the middle-class and peasant vote. It was "party of the proletariat" which took the most prominent part in the onslaught on all attempts to bring about a juster or more rational distribution of the national income, to lay hands on the tax privileges of the farmers and traders into whose chests and stockings the greater part of the national wealth disappeared without trace, to set the blocked mechanism of competition going again, to stop the inflationary trend, and thus destroy the comfortable certainty of the middlemen of all types and descriptions, the number of whom had practically doubled in comparison with the pre-war period, that anything bought today could be sold at a higher price tomorrow, and that in this poverty-stricken country every fifth breadwinner could live for ever and ever on the "difference".

Some of the finest flowers of this middle-class demagogy were produced during the almost desperate attempt of the Schuman Government to stabilise the economy and restore its health. The capital and all the small towns in France resounded with the protests of all who made a living out of "the difference". The dairymen's association threatened to strike, and placarded Paris with bills threatening to withhold supplies. If people wanted milk, they must pay the price for it; the price of milk had increased to twenty-four times the pre-war price, while average wages had been multiplied by ten and average prices by fourteen. A "peasants' association", founded by a politically adroit lawyer, announced that "if the Government wants a trial of strength, Paris will have nothing to eat for a fortnight"; and in the course of a great demonstration of protest by the "small and medium businessmen" of Paris against M. René Mayer's proposed tax reforms the Gaullist president of the Federation of Small and Medium Businesses and the spokesman of the Federation of Trade and Industry, which was one of the many branches of the Communist Party, each accused the other of betraying the petty trader's interests. An article in *l'Humanité* illustrates the nature of this noble struggle perhaps better than any political analysis, which would be idle in this demagogic bedlam. A reporter sent by Communist headquarters to a meeting of small traders described the excellent reception he was given by the doorman:

"At the door of the Vélodrome d'Hiver I approached a steward wearing a green arm-band and said: 'The Press-box, please!'

" 'Which newspaper?' he answered in unfriendly fashion.
" '*L'Humanité.*'
"His face lit up. 'Oh, that's different!' he said. 'Please step this way, you're welcome!'
" 'Are you in the party?'
" 'I? Certainly not! But after what happened in the Chamber I can only say that the traders will be grateful to you Communists for keeping your word to the electors.'
" 'Yes, we don't act like the Gaullists!'
" 'But the Gaullists support us too. Just read this leaflet!'
" 'What? Don't you know that the Gaullist deputies voted for the Mayer plan?'
" 'Impossible! The dirty dogs!'
"However that may be, the traders know who are their true defenders," the representative of *l'Humanité* was able reassuringly to conclude at the end of this successful reconnaissance. The fact of the matter was that everyone defended the traders' interests, and the only inaccuracy in the Communist claim was that they were the only defenders of "trade and enterprise". The small groups of parliamentarians who had gone over to de Gaulle voted solidly with the whole of the right against M. René Mayer. Neither the general whose aim was the complete regeneration of France nor the party of the proletariat would permit a finger to be laid on a parasitical social structure in which productive labour was the only thing which in no circumstances could provide a man with a living. Both proclaimed an apocalyptic policy which promised that everything would be different on the day of their accession to power, but both fought tooth-and-nail to prevent anything whatever from being altered in the meantime; and the centre parties, from which the "third force" should have arisen, half-heartedly supported the unpopular experiment, sombrely aware that they were committing political suicide, and every now and then repealed what they had heroically voted for only two months before. They could still raise a majority in Parliament when necessary by temporarily reconciling their differences, but they had lost their majority in the country. This Parliament, in panic fear of elections which might have sealed not only its own fate but that of the republic, started fluttering like hens in a chicken-run at every

shot fired by right or left, and then, as soon as the scare was over, with the sure instinct of poultry, fluttered back into the same hopeless situation from which it had sought to escape. Saving the republic meant staving off elections, any kind of elections, even the most insignificant, including those due in the autumn of 1948 for the partial renewal of the departmental "general councils", which under the prefectorial régime fulfil the purely decorative function of holding one brief session a year for the purpose of passing ceremonial resolutions expressing the department's wishes. In the sultry summer of 1947 the National Assembly, in a frantic effort to postpone these elections and at the same time to withdraw from any popular influence the simultaneous election of the Senate by the general and communal councils of France, brought down three Governments one after another, and in three months squandered the remainder of its moral and political capital; until finally, after an unprecedented amount of haggling and horse-dealing, a chance majority was got together which enacted the postponement of elections until the following year. "This republic, which I picked up out of the mud," as General de Gaulle said, fought only to gain time, in the pusillanimous hope that time might bring counsel; and in this situation, whilst its representatives started losing all repute and dignity, General de Gaulle knocked more and more impatiently at the door. "Why and in whose name does this system, which means nothing but chronic weakness and perpetual crisis, endure?" he demanded. "As for myself, I declare that all is ready to ensure that the country shall be led to its salvation and greatness."

Perhaps what really saved the Fourth Republic was the fact that a determined and unrelenting opponent of General de Gaulle was in office as President of the Republic—an office the authority of which General de Gaulle had wished to increase during the controversies over the constitution of 1946, while the Socialists and M. Vincent Auriol, the president of the Constituent Assembly, had wished to restrict it to a purely decorative role. As the first President of the Fourth Republic, however, M. Auriol made of his role something completely different from what the creators of the constitution had foreseen: namely, the guardian and protector of the parliamentary régime against the suicidal tendencies of Parliament and the parties. Again and again he emerged from the restraint imposed by his above-party role, actively intervened in negotiations between the quarrelling parties, smoothed over difficulties, sought compromises, and in particular often enough called his former Socialist colleagues to order with paternal severity; and, with a frankness which raised storms of protest on the right, he gave it to be understood that he would never help into office "those who complain about the weakness and instability of the state power and are themselves most zealously at work undermining political responsibility, tearing down Governments, breaking up majorities, and sowing mistrust." In a speech at Quimper in the spring of 1948 for which the Gaullists never forgave him he declared: "On the day on which Parliament is no longer able to exercise control in the name of the sovereign people, the republic will no longer exist, and I assure you that I shall never look on at the downfall of the republic, but in case of need will resume the republican struggle by your side."

During the German occupation M. Auriol wrote an essay entitled "Yesterday and Today", a kind of political testament, in which he said that "experience teaches that persistency can achieve a great deal, even within a single legislative session." In the confusion of the Fourth Republic his was the only office in which persistence could be shown, and M. Auriol, the forgotten man in the Elysée, was certainly not lacking in persistence.

In the stuffy atmosphere of the Palais Bourbon the republic had an appointment with catastrophe once a fortnight. Political paralysis reached its lowest ebb. Government crisis followed Government crisis without intermission for two months, and at the end of the longest, sultriest, and most appalling session in French parliamentary history, all the political personnel of the Fourth Republic had been used up. Meanwhile its founder, General de Gaulle, appealed ever more urgently before ever more excited crowds for a repetition of the historic act of June, 1940. "If it should unfortunately happen that necessities are not understood in the place where they ought to be understood," he declared, "if men wish to remain in their places there to go on doing what they are doing now . . . then, I say deliberately in the face of France, we shall be confronted with the same duty as in 1940, namely to save the public good in spite of everything and everybody." After the failure of all attempts to form a Government, the President of the Republic in his hour of need sent out three candidates simultaneously in search of a Government and a majority, and none of them succeeded. The President then turned to his last hope, M. Herriot, the president of the Assembly, whose own party had just disintegrated, and M. Herriot excused himself because of his asthma. "Then in heaven's name who else is left for me to send for?" exclaimed the President of the Republic in his extremity? "M. Queuille," replied M. Herriot from his vast knowledge of the situation and of men.

General de Gaulle, like everybody else, had mistaken a parliamentary crisis for the end of the world. Everyone had seen him, General de Gaulle, standing at the gates, but it was not he who entered, but Henri Queuille, an inconspicuous Radical veteran and country doctor from southern France and a matchless embodiment of the "average Frenchman". Out of the mists of crisis and millenarianism which had overlain and concealed the real France for years the old, inglorious Third Republic, which everyone had supposed to be dead, trudged thoughtfully back into the light of day.

M. Queuille has become a legendary figure in French postwar history, and the sunset glow of yet another "priceless moment" has spread in retrospect over his period of government, as it has also spread over that of M. Antoine Pinay, another "average Frenchman". There exists in the folklore of many countries the tale of the cunning peasant who makes a deal with the devil and his grandmother, but ends by outwitting them when they call to collect their part of the bargain, his soul. It is a remarkably optimistic tale, for it rests on the assumption that the devil is stupid. The "average Frenchman" does not believe in the devil, but likes toying with him, and again and again the world allows itself to be taken in by the French talent for drama, and believes France to be rushing headlong to ruin with her eyes open when all she is doing is staging an exciting political cockfight. In

France a moderate, middle-of-the-road line has never been the result of a moderate decision; it has always been the resultant of two opposed extremes. Elections, when matters of principles are at stake, are won by Don Quixotes who storm windmills or Bastilles—and then either hand over the conduct of affairs to Sancho Panza or turn into Sancho Panzas themselves. Why should the good old times not return?

The old French party which still calls itself "Radical Socialist", in pious memory of its impetuous youth, had signed more than enough pacts with the devil in order to emerge from obscurity again. In the hectic dawn of the liberation it had been pushed aside as a discredited relic of a past which was never to return, and its political personnel, who, with a few exceptions, had failed to make contact with the resistance, disappeared from the scene, with the exception of a few respected veterans. Its first step on the stony road back had been a most unsuitable flirtation with the Communists, who were moving heaven and earth to drive a wedge between the Socialists and the M.R.P. and had resuscitated for this purpose the antediluvian war machine of the Popular Front, in which the Radicals, who were conservative to the core but anti-clerical as well as anti-Gaullist (in the sense of the word then current), were represented, but the "clerical" M.R.P. was not. This return to the old tram-lines of Clochemerle parish-pump squabbles, to which the liberation had for a short time put an end, was in itself an enormous triumph for Radical tradition over the new problems of the post-war period. The new men and the old exchanged credentials, so to speak, recognising each other as legitimate parties of the republican left. M. Herriot, the chairman of the Radical Party, did not allow his infirmity to prevent him from accepting the honorary presidency of the Communist "Republican Youth", and many prominent Radicals joined the Communist-controlled "National Front".

When the wind changed, however, the Radical Party plunged into an even more far-reaching flirtation with the Gaullist Rally. Having missed the opportunity of associating itself with the Gaullism of the first, heroic stage of 1940–44, it cashed in all the more enthusiastically on the electoral possibilities of the second stage. In the local government elections of October, 1947, the old Radical notables came flooding back into the communal councils of France which had eluded them since the liberation; and more than half the parliamentary party and groups associated with them under the odd name of "Rally of the Republican Left" identified themselves with the Gaullist Rally, and more or less energetically obstructed the Government coalition to which the other half belonged. This political "bigamy", as the Radical politicians with a worldly-wise smirk themselves described their "pact with the devil" tactics, was the fundamental principle of the success of a party which prided itself on being the guardian of tradition, and, like the great whore of Babylon, sat by many waters and slept in many beds.

It was here that the political quagmire was created in which French political climate was henceforward brewed. If General de Gaulle believed he could count on the loyalty of such a following, he was guilty of a quixotic mistake. This undisciplined gang of experienced and by no means martial local politicians, to whom it seemed advisable to have a strong man in reserve as a reinsurance against the eventuality of an attempted Communist *coup* and in the meantime to exploit his tremendous prestige for their own purposes, had not the slightest inclination to be ordered about by him, and were not suitable material for a totalitarian movement. While France impatiently voted right or left, the classical parties of the centre, of the middle classes, of the middle of the road, of the golden mean, returned to their traditional positions in between the two.

The apocalyptic struggle between Thorez and de Gaulle was won by *le petit père* Queuille because his strength lay in the very field where the immediate difficulties lay; namely the field of parliamentary routine. He had no strong views on all the controversial questions which divided the parties, that of economic controls, for instance, or nationalisation, or foreign policy, or the right to strike, but he knew how to handle an apparently ungovernable Parliament consisting of many minorities all bitterly hostile to one another, and he modestly and quietly solved the problem of government stability, which depended on a dozen vacillating votes.

His experience was unique; he had been mayor and deputy

of the little town of Neuvic-d'Ussel since 1914, and since 1920 had been Minister or State Secretary in more than twenty Governments, from those of Millerand and Poincaré to the Government-in-exile of de Gaulle. In the group photographs for which newly-formed Governments traditionally pose on the steps of the Elysée he had generally been half tucked away in the back row as Minister of Agriculture, Posts and Telegraphs, or Health. Since 1946 he had been chairman of the Radical parliamentary group, and his cautious eloquence made him the ideal spokesman of a group which split into two halves and voted on opposite sides on every important question. It could be said of him that he had nothing but friends in Parliament.

The Cabinet he formed was a Cabinet neither of personalities nor of experts, but it was big enough to ensure a majority if each of its thirty-two members could mobilise an average of half-a-dozen votes in addition to his own. The Ministries on which the whole edifice threatened to collapse were those of Finance and Economics, which no party was willing to accept itself or to see going to any other party; M. Queuille therefore courageously undertook both portfolios himself, and announced his solidarity with the measures taken by all his predecessors, Socialists and liberals alike. True, the immediate necessity of bringing the hopelessly confused budget into some sort of balance before the year's end allowed little elbow-room for the application of dogmatic remedies; there was but a meagre choice between the few well-tried recipes which the French financial and fiscal apparatus had had long practice in applying.

However, M. Queuille's remedies worked. Without noise and without planning, or rather in spite of noise and planning. France had crept back to her pre-war level of production, the excellent harvest of 1948 was ripening in the fields, Marshall aid was beginning to have its effect, and, if funds intended for reconstruction were exceptionally used for stopping a gap in the budget, the American authorities shut one eye; it was sufficient if additional disorder were avoided. When the winter, with its strikes and financial panics, was over the "sick man of Europe" discovered to his astonishment that he was almost healthy. For the first time since the war the budget was disposed of at the beginning of the year instead of at the end, inflation seemed to be over, and in the spring of 1949 the Government proceeded to launch an undated loan, to subscribe to which, in the Finance Minister's words, was not only patriotic, but good business. Many years had passed since patriotism and good business had been mentioned in the same breath, and M. Queuille's phrase seemed to augur a return to the golden age of pre-established harmony. The success of the state loan gave the Fourth Republic, the secret stain on whose escutcheon had hitherto been the low state of its credit, the *cachet* of bourgeois respectability. According to the French tradition, a state which tries to collect taxes is no better than a footpad, and self-respect requires that its exactions be evaded. But when the state takes the form of a beggar asking for a loan, and thus involves itself in an assurance of good behaviour towards its patrons, it deserves the confidence of all men of substance; and France discovered that she was by no means so poor as she had thought she was when she buried her riches in the ground for fear of war, revolution, and the tax-collector.

La belle époque had returned.

§ 5

ORTHODOXY v. SOCIAL CONSCIENCE

THE encounter in 1944 between the France whose history is identified with the fluctuation of *rentes* and that other France whose history leads by way of the bloodthirsty defeat of June, 1848, the Paris Commune, and the failure of the Popular Front to the revolutionary liberation of 1944 had turned out to be one more tragic misunderstanding. In the Communist counter-state the misunderstanding had congealed into an institution, and had been sealed off and made sterile. The defeated and outmanœuvred Communist Party remained the church of the working-class. True, a growing number of workers behaved like bad Christians, who go to church on special occasions, perhaps, but trouble themselves very little about their religion in their daily lives, are not prepared to allow it to disturb their peace and quiet, and are certainly not prepared to risk their livelihood for its sake. Membership of the party and the trade unions dropped, and it became more difficult to collect subscriptions. But that meant only a decline in the sense of communion; it did not mean that anything else took its place. The provincial, bourgeois, and peasant France which recognised its own image in Henri Queuille was not the France of the working-class. "France's prodigal son" was tired and discouraged, but not converted—and in the trouble-free world of the new golden age nobody thought of killing the fatted calf for his return.

At the opposite political pole the other myth of 1944, the myth of the mission of General de Gaulle, remained powerful long after its time was past, and it expressed a profound disbelief, not dissipated by the stabilisation achieved under M. Queuille, in the capacity of this parliamentary system to rise above its obstinate spirit of self-preservation and grapple with the problems and dangers of the contemporary world. True, there was a permanent misunderstanding between de Gaulle and the mass of petty bourgeois followers who gave him their applause. Under the Third Republic de Gaulle had been a non-political soldier; and his royalist inclinations at that time had been the symptom only of a revulsion against all politics. He had formed his political ideas in 1940, the year of catastrophe. The spectacle of the last Parliament of the Third Republic, which in the panic of the invasion had surrendered its sovereignty unresistingly, nay with a sigh of relief, into the hands of the aged Marshal Pétain, had made an ineradicable impression on him. So that was the inner strength of this talking-shop, which claimed to make history, but collapsed like a pack of cards at the first storm of world history! In this deep sense General de Gaulle was and remained a politician of catastrophe; he thought in terms of catastrophe, he judged men and institutions by their behaviour in catastrophe, and apocalyptics like Malraux who formed his entourage did nothing to counter this mental bias based on his profession and his experience.

The fundamental force which he had not taken into account and now confronted him, to his growing bewilderment and impatience, was the sheer power of survival possessed by any set of circumstances or institution in the absence of violent intervention from outside. The Parliament of the Fourth Republic was neither stronger nor more self-confident nor more respected than that of the Third, but the enemy was not at the gates of Paris and there was no rioting in the streets. In the sultry August of 1948, when Parliament seemed finally to have lost all sense of responsibility, he kept declaring before huge mass meetings, his long arms extended in gestures which were by now familiar to every Frenchman, that the whole people were rallying to him, and not to the official institutions. So where, he asked, did legitimacy reside? Legitimacy still resided in the Palais Bourbon, however, and its occupants had the longer breath; three years of their mandate, more than enough to exhaust the impetus of an extra-parliamentary movement, were still left to run, and people soon gave up believing in the imminence of catastrophe. Gaullism, which did not come into power in the hour of danger, could not hope to do so when the danger was past; and the lobby strategists and political jobbers of the Palais Bourbon were able unashamedly to continue with their business without having to fear the arrival of a national saviour who would drive the money-changers from the temple of national sovereignty. The anti-parliamentary wave started by General de Gaulle continued to be the expression of a deep sense of dissatisfaction with bare survival and muddling through, and of a vague desire for greatness and enthusiasm; but it was no more than that. When a general election came at last, four years after the movement had reached its climax, it was seen simply to have petered out, and General de Gaulle, shuddering at the thought of contact with parliamentary practice, withdrew once more into the Olympian remoteness from daily politics from which he had so incautiously descended, and left to his followers, who were no longer to be held back from them, "the games, the poisons, and the spoils of the system".

But the change of guard on the right had already long since taken place, practically unnoticed. When the departmental elections, the dangers of which had put the National Assembly in a panic only a year before, at last took place in every corner of France in March, 1949, the expected "swing to the right" duly took place. But in the new climate of civil peace, stabilisation of the franc, and the state loan, the beneficiaries were not the Gaullists—though many candidates to increase their chance had adopted the now usual and current practice of "political bigamy" and had secured the blessing of the Rally of the French People—but conservative notables who had no binding party ties, representatives of the local bourgeoisie who were re-entering their social and political positions of power.

On April 6th M. Paul Reynaud, the most brilliant mind and most ambitious politician of the French right and a perpetual prophet of disaster, both in the pre-war and post-war periods, whose mistake it was always to be right, formed a new constellation in the National Assembly, the Union of

Independents, consisting of a small group of twenty-six Independents and the seven members of the tiny Peasants' Party, which was destined to have such a great and confused future; and at an Independents' dinner, held to celebrate the triumph of bourgeois reason in the local elections, M. Reynaud assumed leadership of this amorphous, non-party mass of parochial politicians who were united only by their conservative instincts; and he sought to reduce to a common denominator the varied declarations of principles which these people had used in the elections. He wanted them to agree on a programme of orthodox liberalism, opposed to a planned economy and the welfare state. "A large number of Independent, Radical, and Republican candidates, both 'monogamous' and 'bigamous'," he declared, "wrote into their programme both a condemnation of administrative interference in the economy, with its consequences of fraud and corruption, and the aim of doing away with abuses in the nationalised undertakings and the social security system. Most candidates of the Rally of the French People agree with them on these points. In other words, a tremendous majority of the French people has expressed itself in this sense. Its wishes must be carried out."

The "tremendous majority" of Frenchmen in whose name he spoke was a group of notables successful in the local elections whose only common article of faith was the predominance over the general interest of every local, private, or sectional interest. True, in this they were the embodiment of a whole French nation. But this nation of notables was far from acknowledging M. Reynaud's claim to be their leader, or even their spokesman. Indeed, M. Reynaud was far too intelligent, far too modern, far too capitalist in the real and, from the French point of view, revolutionary meaning of the word, to be the political representative of the small town. In French politics he was and remains a solitary figure. His style has always lacked the emotional note so important at public meetings; he is witty, sarcastic, brilliant, but as cold as the unintentionally mocking, somewhat superior expression of his twinkling, gnome-like face, and his appeal is not to ideology, but to something different and unusual. "There is a French national asset of which we make exceedingly little use, that is to say, the French intelligence," he once said to a disconcerted National Assembly. "We must get rid of all the absurdities which complicate our lives and hamper our efforts. There is no sense nowadays in arguing whether we are for or against a planned economy; let us be intelligent!"

Challenging people's intelligence has never been a successful political technique; Machiavelli always preferred appealing to people's ideals. It was M. Reynaud's fate always to act as a destroyer of dreams. In 1938 he had the ugly task of destroying the peaceful illusions of the Popular Front and proclaiming the end of the "two-Sunday week" and the return to work, and to set war production in train, much too late, of course; and though his success in overcoming economic stagnation on this occasion gained him a reputation for wizardry among the middle classes and the bourgeoisie, in the eyes of the whole of the left he was henceforward the personal embodiment of the class enemy. His economic achievements told against him even more heavily than the fact that—at the same time as another outsider, Churchill, in England—he became Prime Minister a few weeks before the catastrophe of May, 1940, and thus ostensibly bore responsibility for the collapse which he had been prophesying for years. His lot was always to play the part of Cassandra, and Cassandra was never popular, least of all when she was right. But Paul Reynaud played the part with unconcealed satisfaction, and took pleasure in flying in the face of all established dogmas and ideas.

Saint-Just once said in the French revolutionary Convention that happiness was a new idea in Europe. That was at the end of a century of enlightenment, which believed in reason, and regarded the greatest happiness of the greatest number as a result that could be obtained like the answer to a sum in arithmetic. The bourgeois nineteenth century still lived in the prosaic belief that greater prosperity could be gained only through harder work. But in the meantime a new doctrine had made headway and found support in impressive theories, all of which rested on the assumption that the problems of production (*i.e.*, work) had been solved, and that only the problems of distribution (*i.e.*, happiness) remained. At the end of the bourgeois century the assumption was more or less justified; the failure to solve the problem of distribution was manifest, and fraught with momentous consequences. But, unfortunately, the distributors of happiness came into power after catastrophes which did not leave them with much to distribute. That, in a nutshell, was the tragedy of the Socialist idea. When its advocates came into power they had no alternative but to practise capitalism in the purest sense of the word. In Russia, as in Britain under the Labour Party, in spite of the tremendous differences in the methods used, capital had to be created at the expense of the consumer. In neither could there be much talk of happiness, except perhaps in the timeless and exalted sense in which Nazi propagandists talked of the thousand-year Reich. France, like a number of other western European countries, did not go through this process, in spite of the Stakhanovite efforts of the early liberation period. There were many reasons for this, but one was the competition between eastern and western Socialism, which collided in France and stood in each other's way. In competing for popular favour it is always better to talk of distribution than of production, of happiness than of effort, and the left-wing split in France resulted in nothing but mischief, confusion, and Byzantine ideological squabbles which left the fundamental problem untouched: the problem of how to shorten hours, increase wages, and provide social insurance from the cradle to the grave in a national economy in which, for both sociological and demographic reasons, the proportion of productive workers to the total population is abnormally low and, because of technical backwardness, the average productivity is far below normal. It was a fascinating problem, and all the ideologists and public speakers in France were occupied with it. What passed unnoticed was that the problem, stated in this way, is as insoluble as that of squaring the circle; and the nasal voice of Paul Reynaud seemed to be sarcastically echoing Saint-Just across the centuries, saying: "Intelligence is a new idea in Europe."

His diagnosis was unassailable. "The firm of France must be made to pay its way again." The deficit in the French economy had hitherto been concealed by innumerable devices; by the double book-keeping of the Budget, by foreign credits, by artificial prices and exchange rates, by the steady using up of capital, and by inflationary methods of finance. Since the end of the war France had literally lived at the expense of the American taxpayer, first through emergency aid and since 1948 under Marshall aid; a perpetuation of this state of affairs would make it idle to go on talking about national independence. Marshall aid provided a unique opportunity of restoring the national capital without excessive inroads into the standard of living; and, if it were not used for this purpose, but for the financing of consumption, the result in 1951, when the plan came to an end, would be double national bankruptcy, both political and economic.

After 1951 the sands would have run out; and M. Reynaud argued unanswerably that, if the French standard of living were to be increased, if she were to be made capable of surviving without perpetual foreign aid, if she were to regain the capacity to pay for her imports with her exports, there was no alternative to increasing the productivity of French industry and decreasing its costs. In the long run this must be done at the expense of the patriarchal business methods and parasitic profits with which the French economy was burdened, but the immediate, practical aim must be to tackle the only elements in the national bill of costs which were subject to direct influence, namely wages, the social security services, and "the costs of national administration" of the state. For, if all inflationary creation of purchasing power were consistently stopped, the pressure on prices must end by becoming so strong that the machinery of competition, which had grown rusty in decades of open or creeping inflation, would automatically be set in motion again, the parasitic elements in production and trade would be eliminated, and the remainder would be forced to return to that keen calculation of costs and prices which alone could produce a rational economy. But the state, which since nationalisation had become the biggest employer in France and controlled the levers of credit and wage legislation, must take the first step.

The misunderstanding between M. Reynaud and those whom he assumed to be his followers was hardly smaller than that between General de Gaulle and his followers. The great majority of the Independents in whose name M. Reynaud thought he was speaking were the representatives of the France which had hitherto so admirably succeeded, so far as itself was concerned, in squaring the circle and unloading its own deficit upon the state, leaving it to the latter to meet it as best it could. The liberalism universally professed by these "Independents" was riddled by so many special interests and special protectionisms that all that was left of M. Reynaud's programme of financial restoration and economic liberalism was opposition to the "social extravagances of the welfare state". But, on the basis of this very much reduced lowest common denominator of economic liberalism, M. Reynaud really spoke in the name of the conservative right, and his Union of Independents really gave the Fourth Republic a right wing opposition in the classic style of the Third, which spoke in the name of sound economic principles and financial orthodoxy and, unlike the Gaullist Rally, did not question the parliamentary régime, but stood ready at the first financial panic to take over the rudder from the "left-wing amateurs" without any convulsion or constitutional crisis in order to "save the franc" and "re-establish confidence". Thus, at any rate within the windowless premises of the Palais Bourbon, the return to the pre-war play of parliamentary forces was successfully concluded.

What M. Reynaud preached was precisely what was carried out, against wind and weather and with much creaking and groaning, by the Government of M. Queuille. To a certain extent it was a play with roles distributed in advance, and that too was in accordance with the traditions of the Third Republic. The right opposition, though only a small group of three dozen deputies, watched whip-in-hand in the name of the "overwhelming majority" of those who hid their savings in stockings or under the mattress over the orthodoxy of the "ruling amateurs and demagogues".

True, the whip was not, as in the past, the threat of a well-timed collapse on the Bourse, but the fear of a general election. The demand for a dissolution and an appeal to the people which had hitherto been the battle-cry of General de Gaulle became an effective weapon in M. Reynaud's hands when Parliament showed signs of degenerating into "social demagogy". Indeed, the freezing of wages, in other words, the holding down of mass purchasing power to the limit of what was socially tolerable, was the only effective means of stabilising the currency left to the Government after it had finally and to the general relief reverted to the free market and given up the price controls which had long since been generally ignored; and it was forced the more mercilessly to maintain the wage freeze in the private sector of the economy, because any wage increase would automatically have had repercussions among its own vast armies of employees and the employees of the nationalised industries, and all the dams of budgetary inflation would have been burst.

But for both the left-inclined parties of the Government coalition, the M.R.P. and the Socialists, whose supporters did not consist predominantly of wallet owners and both of whom had a following in the Christian trade unions and the Force Ouvrière, this path of "one-eyed liberalism", free prices, and frozen wages, represented martyrdom. In the summer of 1949 France's regained prosperity was strikingly evident in the luxury of her shop-windows and restaurants, the crush of expensive motor-cars, and the balance sheets of her industrial and commercial undertakings. It was necessary to go back a hundred years in French history, to the beginnings of the Second Empire, to find its like. Profits of the order of 100 per cent. on a firm's capital—it is true that this was nearly always grossly undervalued—were only a good average, and profits of 1,000 per cent. and more were not unusual exceptions; and resort had to be had to all sorts of devices, such as tucking them away among reserves, special reserves, exceptional reserves; and all sorts of other stratagems had to be resorted to to prevent the distributable and taxable declared profits from being swollen to an excessively provocative extent.

The non-existence of a willing capital market forced French industry to finance itself; but this meant that the burden of capital formation was shifted without any relief on to the backs of the workers and consumers. Meanwhile wages remained officially frozen on the basis of a monthly minimum of 11,200 francs, or the price which a tourist at a "lido" cheerfully paid for two bottles of champagne. More than one-third of the French working-class earned less than

15,000 francs a month, including all extras, and only a privileged minority earned more than 20,000 francs; and, while the French episcopate issued pastoral letter after pastoral letter denouncing excessive social injustices, and the efforts of the non-Communist trade unions to make a constructive contribution to a policy of stabilisation from which wage-earners would also benefit became a mockery to their own supporters, the Socialist and M.R.P. prisoners of the Government coalition had to face a crisis of their social conscience. They were forced to play the game to the end; there was no way of passing over into opposition, because neither in nor out of Parliament was there an alternative majority to which they could hand over responsibility. In the wise phrase of M. Queuille, they were "compelled to live together", like the damned in Sartre's hell, and there was no alternative to the policy of *immobilisme* which he prescribed. After the adventures and defeats of recent years even the working class were obviously resigned to their lot; they too feared a resumption of the inflationary spiral which had invariably caused them rapidly to lose more than they had gained by their nominal wage increases; and in the meantime a new fear, that of unemployment, had been added. But, just when the critical point was reached at which the unrelenting pressure on purchasing power really started exercising pressure on prices, social conscience suddenly exerted itself at a point where nobody had hitherto suspected its existence.

The "one-eyed liberalism" which regulated wages but left prices to take care of themselves would have been fully justified within the framework of a liberal policy of stabilisation if the laws of the free market had really been at work. The inflated price-level, which after the abolition of controls had practically everywhere remained at the level of the former black market and had led to the stabilisation of shortages and inflation, must inevitably have given way in the end. But the ordeal continued, and the "laws of the market" did not come into play. Everyone, from large-scale employer to the smallest greengrocer, obeyed the same inveterate and powerfully organised instinct rather not to sell at all than to sell more cheaply. The principle of small turnover and big profits became that of smaller turnover and bigger profits; and, if turnover approached zero, the shutters were put up for the summer to await better times. Under the banner of liberalism there flourished, not free competition, but a system of guaranteed profits that effectively blocked any solution of the "prices and wages" question from the prices side. But, as the laws of the market, mishandled though they may be, ultimately cannot be thwarted, but become effective in some way or other, the result was a repetition of what had occurred over and over again in France during the last thirty years. Every stabilisation that has been more than a mere pause for breath in the inflationary process has passed straight over into stagnation. At the end of a tourist season which brought swarms of tourists but few buyers, the warehouses were full, but the shops empty.

But now an attack on the Government's "one-eyed liberalism" came from a quarter from which it had hitherto had nothing but support. The financial and Bourse Press suddenly fell in with the trade union demands that the wage freeze should be ended, and *l'Aurore* presented the small commercial middle class, who had noticed that their customers were being much more careful with their money, with vivid descriptions of the appalling situation of hundreds of thousands of workers on short time whose pay had sunk even below the hunger-level of the legal minimum wage. Early in September *Le Monde* noted "the willingness of a section of employers to give way to wage demands rather than reduce prices" and "the organised and common resistance of the employers' associations, who are afraid of competition, and of the trade unions, who fear unemployment", to the intended tariff reductions and relaxations in import restrictions by means of which the Government wished to exert pressure on the prices of certain food items and manufactured goods. These were then joined by the association of agriculturists, who noisily demanded that agricultural prices should be advanced to the level of industrial prices and summoned its members to "active resistance with all the means at their disposal" to an agricultural policy "which is equivalent to economic suicide"; and M. Petsche, the Finance Minister, was obliged to resign from the rebellious Peasants' Party to which he had hitherto belonged.

Those who remembered the climate of the Popular Front, and the subsequent agreement of all orthodox economists that its policy had been catastrophic, must have been surprised when the chairman of the French employers' association announced after an interview with the Prime Minister that he had advocated a return to the free discussion of labour contracts "after the pattern of 1936–37". The employers' association supplemented this by announcing its opposition to an "over-hasty liberalisation of European trade", that is to say to the abolition of quotas, tariffs, and import permits which the French Government advocated in its negotiations with Marshall plan officials. Thus the cry for another injection of inflation led to the formation of a united front of trade unions and peasants, big employers and small tradesmen, all animated by their social conscience; it was the same united front which at that disastrous "economic conference" under M. Bidault's interim Government between two elections in 1946 had brought to grief the first attempt at post-war stabilisation. Rebellion against "one-eyed liberalism" was declared by another kind of liberalism, which was blind in both eyes.

For a fragile coalition Government made up of Radicals, Socialists, and M.R.P., it was impossible to refuse wage concessions "which even the employers agreed to", and its whole policy eventually shrank to beating about the bush, taking evasive action, haggling, and trying to gain time. It was inevitable in these conditions that public life should present neither a beautiful nor an edifying picture, and that "the state" should appear in the guise of an elderly miser denying a dry crust to its poorest children. But French politics have never allowed the Government to play any role but that of a scapegoat which bears all responsibility while the people, and the *élite*, wash their hands in innocence all around; and, when at last everyone is sick of the Government and it falls amid general execration, nobody knows or cares what has been the real reason for its fall, and the game can begin all over again. In France a Government crisis is a collective cleansing ritual.

The history of the "unique and exceptional bonus" for the most under-privileged group of all, the category of workers whose wage had really sunk below the minimum necessary for existence, which caused the downfall of the Queuille Government, is an edifying example of this process, the pitifulness and pettiness of which defy description. In July, when the retail price index, which had been slowly falling—the fall had just balanced the increase in rents and the costs of public services—started climbing again and destroyed the "loyal" trade unions' hopes of a solution of the wages question by a drop in prices, an agitation for a "holiday" bonus swept through France. This was the first round in the campaign for higher wages; the idea was that a special bonus should be given at the beginning of the summer holidays, which confronted many families with anxious problems. Many private firms fell in with this demand, and when the Socialist Minister of Labour granted it to the employees of the social insurance scheme he caused the first rift in the coalition. M. Queuille survived the last parliamentary vote before the holidays by only three votes. The floodgates still held, however. In September the agitation was resumed, and, as the holidays were over, the demand was now for a "post-holiday bonus". By the beginning of October holidays had lost all topicality, and the demand was for an "interim" bonus, to tide things over until the distant day of settlement of the wages question.

Now at last the Government crisis broke out, and after M. Queuille's resignation the parliamentary pendulum swung wildly for a whole month between "right" and "left", between M. Moch, the "social conscience" candidate, who was unsuccessful, and M. René Mayer, the similarly unsuccessful candidate of "financial orthodoxy", only to come down in the end non-committally in the middle with M. Bidault. Three weeks of intensive haggling about the amount, incidence, and timing of the "unique and exceptional bonus" made it plain to an incredulous public that what was proposed to be granted was "the maximum possible concession", and that "any step beyond it would inevitably lead to disaster". M. Reynaud produced a number of brilliant and telling arguments against granting anything whatever, and in the debate in which M. Moch unsuccessfully sought the approval of Parliament as Prime Minister a highly characteristic exchange took place between him and M. Reynaud in which the Socialist M. Moch presented himself as theoretically loyal all along the line to the tenets of financial orthodoxy, but felt it necessary to yield to the "requirements of life" and the "sense of social justice" which "weigh in the balance just as much as theory". True, the ineluctable laws of economics were important, but so were human feelings.

Public opinion and the Press regard these Homeric struggles in the parliamentary frog-pond with a certain irony, and with a modicum of this the whole crisis, with its dramatic incidents and *dénouements*, could be regarded as a prearranged performance, with roles distributed in advance, which permitted the Government parties united in an unhappy partnership to demonstrate in the eyes of the world their mutual hostility, and hence the justification for their existence as parties, and at the same time to make an impressive display of the fact that, although they would all have liked to have acted differently, any departure from the line to which they were committed was out of the question. Moreover, the crisis provided a whole month's breathing-space during which demands and agitation ceased. In all the years during which these storms in a teacup in the Palais Bourbon have alarmed the world these periods without a Government have been the quietest which France has enjoyed.

Consideration of this Government crisis will spare us consideration of all its innumerable successors. Its duration, its preposterousness, and the noticeable insignificance of the circumstances that gave rise to it are discouraging to any serious analysis, and its final solution by the appointment of a Prime Minister who was slightly more to the "left" and presided over a Cabinet which was extended slightly to the "right" was so devoid of any logic, or any connection with the concrete questions that had seemed originally to underlie it, that it is tempting to be satisfied with the philosophical observation of an American newspaper that France needs a new Government every now and then just as a woman needs a new hat.

But it is an empty form of democracy in which all decisions are concentrated in the hands of a small group of professional politicians, parliamentarians, and high officials, and the state apparatus is deeply involved in an unhealthy network of "personal connections" and business influences, and politics are reduced in the public eye to a fruitless swing of the pendulum between "left" and "right". The most striking characteristic of this crisis of October, 1949, was the profound lack of interest taken in it by the man in the street; he was able to see in it no more than a clash of personal rivalries which had nothing to do with him. Thanks to Dr. Queuille's chloroform treatment, this democracy had lost even the stimulus of a sense of external danger, and the crisis seemed all the more unreal in that it took place in the absence of any real opposition. Neither the Communist Party nor the Gaullist Rally played the slightest part in its outbreak, its course, or its solution, though *l'Humanité* daily celebrated the vicissitudes of the debates that followed the nomination of successive Prime Ministers-designate as triumphs of the imaginary "mass action" of the French people in favour of a "Government of democratic union", and General de Gaulle used the opportunity once more to thunder against the party system before audiences which had now noticeably shrunk. During these weeks of parliamentary anarchy, not only did the whole administrative clockwork continue ticking as usual, but there was not the slightest disturbance of public order, there were no strikes, and for the first time in such a situation there was not the slightest sign of either speculation or panic on the Bourse or the foreign exchange black market; the two most sensitive barometers of confidence in French economic stability remained at set fair practically without intermission throughout the interregnum. The price of free gold dropped, and *rentes* went up. M. Queuille's *immobilisme* could not more brilliantly have survived its ordeal by fire.

The policy of stabilisation continued under M. Bidault as it had under M. Queuille, and there was no other policy. But the stabilisation achieved was that of a market blocked by its own mechanisms at stagnation point. All true French liberals began to see that this economic, social, and psychological structure, distorted by generations of inflationary development, protectionism, regimentation by economic guilds and cliques, could not shake itself out of its state of ossified equilibrium, but that the shaking would have to come from outside, and that the lever by which this might be done was the "European market".

It has been nearly forgotten that at every European council or conference successive French Governments sought to promote the liberalisation of European trade, in spite of all resistance both from within and without. By cautiously opening windows, by progressive reduction of tariffs and quotas, the revitalising "fresh air of competition" was to be let in to the French hothouse. This was the spring-time of European integration, and at the end of this year of domestic stabilisation, if integration itself did not yet seem within range, French capacity to take an active part in a wider and more intensive economic circulatory system seemed to be in sight. French economic policy and foreign policy were in line, and M. Jean Monnet, the moving spirit in French economic planning and modernisation, became the inspirer of the Schuman plan, which on May 9th, 1950, was to open a new chapter in post-war European politics. The fundamental idea of the Marshall plan seemed to be heading for reality by way of new paths.

But barely two months later a new storm broke.

§ 6

HOLIDAY FROM POLITICS

IN the spring of 1950 political aims and economic developments seemed to be in line, but then they started drifting apart. The outbreak of the Korean War disturbed the still fragile internal and external equilibrium from which European integration was to follow. With positively elemental violence France eliminated herself again from the world economy. In the eighteen months after the Korean war began French wholesale and retail prices, borne aloft on the same wave of buying and speculation that affected world markets, rose by between 45 and 50 per cent., compared with about 30 per cent. in Britain, Belgium, and Germany, and about 15 per cent. in America, Switzerland, and Italy, and since then they have not descended from those speculative heights. Infinitely elastic as the French price structure proved to be in an upward direction, it turned out to be inelastic in a downward direction. The French balance of payments which seemed nearly to have been achieved in spring, 1950, gave way to a hopeless deficit, intensified by a renewed flight of capital. There was no inflation in the technical sense, there was no surplus buying power or shortage of goods, and all the experts tore their hair over the inexplicable behaviour of an economy which totally refused to adapt itself. Not only did price increases fail to stimulate production, but reduction in demand, when it took place, failed to bring down excessive prices; this economy even ceased alternating between inflation and stagnation, but managed to combine the two. The whole labour of Sisyphus of "European liberalisation" had to be cancelled out by a stroke of the pen, and the hothouse windows were shut again.

This was not due to rearmament, as France persuaded herself, for rearmament had hardly begun, even on paper. Price increases on the international raw materials market gave the process its first stimulus, it is true, but this had long since passed. The true explanation was the successful counter-offensive of the France of M. Gingembre—all the French traders and businessmen who for two years had been deprived of the opportunity of making an effortless living out of the "difference" between yesterday's price and today's, and now made up for lost time with compound interest. A general election, which could be postponed no longer, took place in 1951, under a new electoral law which had given the departing National Assembly terrible headaches and caused endless crises, but had once more ended only in rescuing the republic from the people by means of arithmetic, confusing all fronts, and outwitting democracy. Under this law the France of M. Gingembre triumphed, after a campaign in which there was no argument about the great issues facing France, but passionate argument about the lay schools question and passionate denunciation of the Moloch of taxation.

In the new Parliament there really was a majority on these two questions, for a politically indefinable horde of "Independent" provincial notables with 13 per cent. of the votes had secured more than one-fifth of the seats, and this group exercised an irresistible attraction for the dilapidated figures of the similarly recruited Gaullist Rally, who started coming over to it in groups. These people were determined that the monopoly of the "godless" state schools should be broken, that the Roman Catholic private schools should be subsidised, and that there must be no new taxes. But they constituted a majority on no other conceivable subject whatever, and no policy or Government coalition could possibly be based on them. In comparison with this "Assembly of six hundred local squabbles" the first Parliament of the Fourth Republic, which had ended its life in such bad odour, had been a positive miracle of objectivity, clarity, and seriousness. However, in one respect it was completely in harmony with the deepest popular feeling as expressed in that simplest, cheapest, and most popular of slogans under which these Independents had fought their campaigns and had spoken directly to the heart of all good citizens. This slogan was to the effect that an end must be put to politics, which were responsible for everything. The France of the small towns wanted to have no more of politics, of international complications, of the cold war, of Atlantic armaments, of European integration, of social problems, the welfare state, or expensive plans of industrialisation. Give us a good, economical administration and healthy finances and leave us in peace!

True, the "healthy finances" of these Independents were not those which had been preached in their name by M. Reynaud to the demagogues of the outgoing Legislature. Never did a Parliament so readily assent to all public expenditure likely to pay dividends at the polls, and never did a Parliament so obstinately refuse to impose the taxation necessary to meet it; and, when it came to making economies, never did a Parliament so consistently sacrifice productive expenditure—capital investment, housing, schools, the country's technical equipment—to unproductive expenditure. But this was not politics; politics had been abolished. Two Governments managed to keep their heads above water for a few weeks thanks to the number of their Ministers—the second, that of M. Edgar Faure, survived its first test by exactly forty votes, *i.e.*, the exact number of its Ministers and State Secretaries, only to fail at the second. Both these Governments exhausted their strength in manœuvres over individual votes and individual passages in the budget. By the end of February, 1952, the whole of the expenditure side of the budget had been passed, but two Governments had been brought down by the impossibility of passing the revenue side. The Bank of France had in all haste to lend 25,000 million francs to cover the current expenses of the next three weeks, and the European Payments Union had to advance $100 millions to meet the monthly trade deficit; and on leap year day, 1952, which was a day of wrath, the Governor of the Bank of France emerged from the quiet of his holy of holies and in a tone of paternal severity addressed himself to the conscience of the nation's representatives in a letter to the Prime Minister whom the latter had just overthrown.

"The general council of the Bank of France," he said, "has considered it necessary to lay down conditions, a maximum, and a term for the aid which has been asked of it, marking France's urgent need of a Government and a programme of recovery. . . . It is clearly evident that to meet the special situation in which France finds herself measures must be taken essentially similar to those which have enabled other countries confronted with the same difficulties to overcome them. This recovery programme, which is essential to avoid compromising what remains of our credit, our reserves, and our franc, must in the political and economic field make a clean sweep of all sectional and private interests, even apparently the most legitimate."

And in her dire emergency France again found the man of the hour. He came, as was now appropriate, from the ranks of the Independents, not in the suspiciously brilliant, caustic form of M. Paul Reynaud, but from the ranks of the truly non-political, unvocal, and unknown. M. Antoine Pinay, the new Prime Minister, the proprietor of a small tannery and the mayor of Saint-Chamond, was at first put forward only half-seriously, to fill a gap as it were, but almost overnight he became the most popular man in the country. He carried the day, not as the leader of a party or the representative of a programme, in short not as a politician, but as a personality; the true embodiment of the "average Frenchman" and ideal paterfamilias. "I speak to you with the temperament of a man whose first care is concern for settling day," he said in his declaration of policy, and, to the applause of all the non-politicals, he continued: "The remedies are neither on the left nor on the right. They have no parliamentary label. They are technical steps which must be taken in an atmosphere of political truce." This went straight to the hearts of those who wanted "no more politics, but sound administration". The public opinion which supported M. Pinay, and exercised tremendous pressure on Parliament itself, was the opinion of all who enjoy general respect and repute in small-town France. M. René Mayer, a politician who himself belongs to the business world—though not to the world of small business to which M. Pinay belongs—neatly described this "extra-parliamentary coalition" as that of the "French employers' association plus the general association of agriculturists, plus the general association of wine-growers, plus the association of small and medium businesses." The true France had again come to the fore, and its magic slogan was "confidence" again, as it had been in the better times of the Third Republic and the St. Martin's summer of the Queuille era—confidence in the franc, confidence in the healthy forces in France, confidence in the benevolent laws of a self-regulating economy.

The budget which Antoine Pinay now pushed through the National Assembly was an optimistic budget. The "no new taxes" cry which had been wrung from the bowels of the French provinces was at last listened to. The yawning gap in the state finances was to be met, not from taxation, which would never get at the gold buried under the apple-tree or the foreign exchange hoarded in the old oak chest or tucked away abroad, but from confidence, which would bring all the hidden wealth of France out into the light of day. All investment credits were to be blocked until the flotation of the new state loan, which was to be the solemn act marking the return of confidence; and the imminent economic upsurge, which would automatically increase state revenue from all sources, was taken into account in advance on the credit side of the balance. Thus the budget was balanced without sweat or tears; politics having been thrown out of the window, all its problems automatically disappeared.

This experiment in government by self-persuasion and recovery by suggestion started by being so strikingly successful that it seemed to herald the opening of a new era in French post-war politics: the Coué era. It was a year of clear consciences and a holiday from politics, and the psychological climate was made all the more receptive to the method of suggestion by the circumstances that all the things that were suggested were in complete harmony with its natural inclinations. But its greatest successes were gained, not in the economic, but in the political sphere. In the new "atmosphere of civil peace" party outlines began to blur, controversies were damped down, ideologies dropped off to sleep, and, in the face of the calm, unswerving reasonableness of that average Frenchman Antoine Pinay, the feet of clay of those two catastrophe-threatening spectres of French politics, the Communist Party and the Gaullist Rally, seemed quietly to collapse.

When M. Pinay formed his Government the dilapidated remnants of the Gaullist parliamentary party were no longer able to resist the long-suppressed call of the heart, and marched with colours flying into the camp of the classic conservative right; and General de Gaulle, after spending a year in trying to impose discipline on his remaining parliamentary followers, finally concluded that he himself was the only true Gaullist, shook the dust of politics from his feet, and left his followers to their own devices. The Communist Party, left headless and orphaned after the removal to Russia of its sick leader M. Thorez, alternated between inner crises, derisory attempts at "action", and a game of cat-and-mouse with the police, who exercised the wildest imagination in discovering Communist plots, arrested Communist leaders on the most hair-brained pretexts, and subsequently released them without anyone's turning a hair. The party was unable so much as to organise a proper protest march or protest strike; the working-class had "had enough of politics" too. The process of "depoliticisation" could almost be read statistically in the steep fall in circulation of the party political Press, which now suffered the fate which had already overtaken nearly all the organs of opinion of the liberation period. Party organs addressed to a wider public than that of their own immediate followers ceased publication one after another.

For another "priceless moment" M. Pinay achieved the ideal of a non-political Government which handled the country's affairs "like a solid little business", untroubled by unpractical ideologies; it was like an idyllic return to the monarchy which the country had so heedlessly discarded a hundred and fifty years before, the monarchy which at bottom it had missed ever since as a counterweight to its innate *fureur de raisonner*, the monarchy whose shadow it continually tried to conjure up in short and always unsuccessful periods of restoration.

In one sense the régime of the good paterfamilias Pinay, the former national councillor at the court of Marshal Pétain, was a melancholy St. Martin's summer coming after the Vichy restoration, which fitted in with so many French desires after the heavy burden and the glory of being a great Power had fallen from France's shoulders, and it was still possible to believe in an "honourable defeat" and an "understanding between one soldier and another". At the opposite pole to the France of Vichy, General de Gaulle, in his pride, his stubbornness, his incapacity to indulge in "low intrigues", stood for a lofty and ambitious vision of national greatness, which brooked no mourning over past glory and made no claims on the basis of past achievements, but aimed at pulling the nation together and creating the conditions for greatness. General de Gaulle, often tremendously overrating his own position and the quality of his following, had tried to carry this vision over into the years when the drive, the enthusiasm, and the illusions of the liberation had faded. When he withdrew in disgust to his hermitage at Colombey more was involved than the failure of a notably unadroit and unrealistic politician. The road from Charles de Gaulle to Antoine Pinay was a reflection of that travelled in eight years by the Fourth Republic.

The year of good consciences was another year of stabilisation—stabilisation in stagnation. Everything was put in order, but nothing was set in motion. With the help of the spring, falling world prices, and some subsidiary assistance from the trade associations, "price reduction by suggestion" resulted only in a stabilisation of prices far above the world level, and the best guardian of stability was now the sliding scale of wages which Parliament had agreed to immediately before M. Pinay came into office. The cost-of-living index was kept by the skin of its teeth, and not without occasional statistical sleight-of-hand, a few points below the fatal figure which would have brought the sliding scale into operation, and, as prices and wages were henceforward congealed in their old misrelationship to each other, a good conscience, but not France's capacity to compete internationally, was restored, and the domestic inelasticity of the French market was institutionalised, so to speak. Similarly the deficit in the external balance of payments was not overcome by export subsidies and import restrictions; rather was it stabilised, and the increased protectionist isolation from the world market which once more freed French producers from all external pressure on costs, prices, and profits had an effect exactly the opposite to that which the Prime Minister preached every

Sunday in his regular homilies on the virtues of a competitive economy.

The great state loan which was launched to the accompaniment of all the resources of propaganda was subscribed to without enthusiasm, and ended in a half success, or rather with the *status quo*. It was offered on terms which any other post-war Government could have offered, with or without "confidence in the franc". It offered a double guarantee, both against devaluation of the franc and a fall in the price of gold, and was thus "safer than gold" from the investors' point of view. But it succeeded neither in attracting notable quantities of hoarded gold nor in attracting flight capital back from abroad. French savers lustily applauded M. Pinay—candidates who used his name or could produce a letter of encouragement in his handwriting now triumphed in every local election—and they willingly exchanged a bundle of banknotes or sums invested in less favourable state securities for a stake in this new loan with its guaranteed gold value. But, after thirty years' bitter experience, they were not willing to exchange for any state security, even the best and most profitable, the gold they had safely hidden under the apple-tree or the hard currency they had safely accumulated abroad against all catastrophes, world convulsions, and tax-collectors.

The campaign that preceded the launching of the loan was conducted on a grand scale, and it could not possibly be repeated for a long time to come. Its results sufficed to keep the treasury's head above water for a few months, but financial recovery was as remote as ever. At the end of the Pinay year the budget, which had been so optimistically balanced on paper, showed a deficit of 800,000 million francs. This was concealed in all sorts of ways, but chiefly by the confusing accounting methods used, and what had become the standard practice of carrying payments forward into the next financial year. The 60,000 million francs of inflationary purchasing power which the treasury had pumped monthly into the market had just sufficed to prevent the hothouse temperature of the French economy from sinking below the minimum, and had served just to keep things more or less going. But now, as after every period of stabilisation, came the call for a stronger injection. When the National Assembly returned after its long summer recess—the first which a French Parliament had been able to enjoy since the end of the war—the "climate of confidence" was destroyed; and M. Pinay, who in his speech on entering office had declared his faith in liberalism, "but in honest liberalism, which continually seeks technical progress and social peace in a climate of healthy competition, not the blind liberalism of the jungle or the self-seeking liberalism of sectional interests," turned in his honest, naïve despair into the most severe conceivable critic of the sectional interests, of the blind selfishness of the "self-styled liberals, who are not only incapable of making the smallest sacrifice, but are also incapable of resisting the temptation of a special profit in a period of national recovery" and "dig the grave of liberalism in the liberal name." The optimistic experiment of trying to persuade a guild economy vegetating in a well-protected hothouse to gird itself up for battle by stirring appeals to liberalism had been a pitiful failure. If that lesson had gone home, the experiment might perhaps have been justified.

But, like other experiments, it ended in the confusion of a budget debate over some obscure trifle—a proposal to end some subsidy or increase some stamp duty. The Pinay Government had had to throw so much ballast overboard in the exhausting rearguard actions that it had been forced to fight that in the end the "Pinay policy" was so thin that a breath of wind was sufficient to blow it away altogether; and the day after its fall no one could remember who had overthrown it, or why. Had it been the M.R.P. on the family compensation issue, or the Radicals on the tax reform question, or M. Pinay's own Independents on the question of repealing the alcohol tax? But when M. Pinay, in an outbreak of long-suppressed indignation, at last threw in his hand without waiting for the result of a vote of confidence and walked out of the Chamber to submit his resignation to the President of the Republic and hand back the task of government to the professional politicians, he once more had behind him the whole public opinion of the *pays réel*; for he took his departure, not as a witness to the failure of his experiment, but as a martyr to liberalism; once more "politics" and the "politicians" were responsible for everything.

His successors were left to bear the burden. The deficit in the budget had meanwhile grown to about 1,000 million francs, and in addition there was the fact that the French Government was in the humiliating situation eight years after the end of the war of being the only Government left in Europe which was still living from hand to mouth with the aid of the printing press. Not only was it unable to balance its budget, but it was soon obliged to go hat-in-hand to Washington at the end of each month in search of loans; and it had to indulge in such dangerous feats of tightrope walking as using a dollar advance intended for the war in Indo-China for stopping a gap in its European balance of payments, or a credit granted for purposes of reconstruction for repaying a loan to the Bank of France, or financing the treasury at the end of the month out of the foreign trade deficit. But the French national deficit was not tragic. With a budgetary inflation which soon amounted to 1,000 million francs the French economy just remained in equilibrium, and bigger doses of the drug would have been needed to hasten its pulse. What was tragic was not the poverty of the state. This rich country, in which six times as much gold lay buried under apple-trees or hidden in stockings as was contained in the cellars of the Bank of France, had always liked to see its state reduced to beggary and forced to peddle for alms. What was tragic was that with this pitiful masking of the budget deficit the "politics" that had been thrown out through the door always climbed back again through the window, with the result that holidays from politics always ended in a rude awakening.

These holidays did not in fact begin with M. Pinay. Since French domestic politics had returned to the parliamentary tramlines in 1948 a remarkable narrowing of outlook had taken place. The one thing round which everything revolved, which caused old Governments to fall and new ones to be formed, which continually engaged the whole attention of the country—the *pays légal* as well as the *pays réel*, the National Assembly as well as the local political associations which deputies consulted every week-end to test the state of political opinion, was the budget. The budget, in short, was the alpha and omega of French politics. But the object of all this passionate interest was not the budget in its vast and incomprehensible complexity, into which whole sectors of the national economy had been drawn since nationalisation and through the manifold channels of which practically half the national income now circulated. The innumerable separate and special accounting systems of these were calculated to cause the keenest intelligences to lose their way; and in any case after the beginning of American economic and military aid the final word no longer depended on the sovereign will of Parliament. All these things belonged to a secret and mysterious sphere in which only the financial experts moved. The true object of interest was the budget as seen from the paltry level of the deputies and those who elected them; the civil service unions, who protested against any reduction in the number of state employees; groups of taxpayers who protested against the intolerable burdens to which they were subjected; the war-damaged departments clamorously insisting on the state's duty to provide for their reconstruction; the wine, fruit, and vegetable producing departments who insisted on having their surpluses bought up by the alcohol administration; the peasants' and trade associations who demanded their subsidies; the tenants' leagues clamouring for relief; to say nothing of social insurance and pensioners' claims and the claims of those with unusually large families....

Consideration of the budget, which had formerly been disposed of at the year's end, now lasted the whole year. It began at latest in November and was completed at the earliest in June, and the time left over, apart from the summer recess, was devoted to demolishing in detail what had previously been approved of in general.

The parliamentary time-table was as monotonous as a roundabout. Year after year, like phantoms, the same old problems swung unaltered into view in the appropriate clause or clauses of the budget, swung past, and disappeared, only inevitably to reappear again a year later. All the great reforms that had been put on the order of the day after the liberation—reform of the administration, reform of the machinery of justice, reform of the army, reform of the fiscal system—crumbled away in a mass of incoherent and disconnected detail. If some small economy or increase in taxation were urgently necessary, sanction to refill a temporarily vacant post would be refused, or a new clause would be added to the two thousand clauses of the fiscal code, without the state apparatus's becoming any more rational thereby or any relief being obtained by the unfortunate taxpayer entangled in its net; which continued, moreover, to offer just as many idyllic hide-outs as before to other, more fortunate individuals. It was rare indeed for matters of graver import than this to be debated by the sovereign Parliament of France. For years there was no discussion of foreign policy, except when the Foreign Ministry estimates came up for discussion in the course of the annual budget routine, and similarly there was no debate on the war in Indo-China, except when a part of the costs involved (which were never dealt with as a whole) came up in the estimates of one of the many departments involved. And if exceptionally there were such debates, they took place before yawningly empty benches and with no result—the ghostly debates on the European Defence Community for instance, which always ended with resolutions which were neither approved nor disapproved, or the debate on Tunisia to which the Assembly roused itself during the unrest of the summer of 1952, when it rejected one after the other all the proposals put before it and then adjourned and went to bed exhausted, without making any decision at all.

Moreover, from this groundling's viewpoint the great western alliance, which because of the inroads into national sovereignty it involves has caused the idea of national sovereignty itself to begin to crumble, appeared purely in the simplified and tangible guise of dollar aid, without which any budget at all had long since been inconceivable; and discussion of its consequences seemed all the more impractical because, as a result of the overlapping of the respective fiscal years, American credits were always taken into account in the French budget six months in advance, before they had even been approved by Congress, and you do not discuss the conditions of a loan you have already spent; and it was only from the point of view of balancing the budget that questions of social policy were ever discussed in the "windowless house" in which the representatives of the people met.

The representatives of the people discussed the budget and nothing but the budget, and the more they calculated the less the sum worked out. The public gazed transfixed at Parliament, the embodiment of national sovereignty, the engine of the republican régime, but the engine was running noisily in the void. Parliament was continually in violent motion without ever setting anything else in motion, except that every now and then it became upset and started playing skittles with the Governments which were compelled to appear before it for the sake of the budget, and only for the sake of the budget. All the remaining transmission gear of a parliamentary régime was conscientiously displayed. The Government was always glad enough to avoid all contact with this ungovernable Parliament when it could; unfortunately this was not possible in the case of the budget. The fundamental art of governing without a working majority, or indeed without a majority at all, and of getting along with chance majorities from day to day, was to be as unnoticeable as possible, to avoid parliamentary debates, and as far as possible to leave the assembly of the nation to its own gyrations in the void.

France is an old country, whose lawyers have long since made legal provision for almost every conceivable contingency, and, when the legislative machine, *i.e.*, Parliament, ceases to function, some more or less appropriate passage can generally be found in ancient legislation which can be more or less artificially interpreted to meet the new circumstances without troubling the legislature. This enables the Government to confine itself to its "executive" functions, *i.e.*, administration. What has been done in France has for years been done by administrative means, not as a consequence of new legislation, but by executive decree. The machinery has been kept in motion by Governments lacking in definite political colour, Governments which made themselves so small that they offered no surface for attack, caretaker Governments which have held the fort during Government crises; their Ministers provided the indispensable minimum of signatures on the documents laid before them by the officials of their departments. While for weeks at a time there was no Government, save a Government which had submitted its resignation and continued on a care-and-maintenance basis pending the installation of its successor, a hundred prefects continued to govern France. Whether a competent Minister was in office or not made no difference to the functioning or non-functioning of the public services.

True, high officials were dependent on a ministerial decision for their appointment, but once appointed carried out their duties very conscientiously themselves. Individual Ministers often remained in office when Prime Ministers or Governments were dismissed, and the more inconspicuously they did so, the better; and, as these many-headed Governments, to which Parliament never delegated fewer than thirty or forty men, were themselves nothing but parliamentary committees, Cabinet meetings were a complete substitute for parliamentary debates; even in the smaller body, a parliament in miniature, it was hard enough to reach decisions. The result was that each individual Ministry retreated quietly into its shell and pursued its own policy with the means at its disposal, without discussion and without making a fuss. Every Resident, every prefect, every ambassador, and every high official did the same. They acted for what they believed to be the best in the light of their knowledge and conscience, but no single political will activated the huge ramifications of the system because political will had dried up at the source.

All this amounted to a perfectly workable system of government, so far as keeping to the old tramlines was concerned; indeed, it saved plenty of useless unrest and innovation and taught the wisdom of sheer persistence, which Montaigne calls the "sparing of the will". But its workability stopped short at the point at which a new question arose requiring a new answer, a political decision, or legislative action—the alteration of a statute, the reform of an abuse sanctified by tradition, the ratification of an international treaty. At that point the machinery broke down.

So everything went on side by side, everything half new and everything half old, with books kept in separate, watertight compartments; a bankrupt Parliament of six hundred representatives of the sovereign people, concerned, not with the future of their country, but with re-election in the *arrondissement* of Saint-Coutufonds, and a bankrupt nation, which no longer had the resources to raise and equip fifteen divisions in its own country, but claimed as a European power to preside over the defence of the continent. As an Atlantic power she possessed a seat and a vote in the council of the great powers, as an African power she held Arab nationalisation in check, and as a Pacific power she waged war 7,500 miles away in the Far East. France was engaged simultaneously in world politics and parish-pump politics, the political and economic integration of Europe, and the defence of an archaic economic structure which could survive only behind firmly closed doors and windows . . . and only in the budget was it demonstrated that the sum did not add up. The politics of bankruptcy ended in the bankruptcy of politics.

André Siegfried, in his summing up of the Pinay year, wrote: "Just as there are operas in which the chorus sings 'Forward! Forward!' without moving from the spot, so are there years in which events seem to mark time. The year 1952 was one of these. We see the same problems turning up again without approaching a solution, and the persistence of the same situations from which there is apparently no way out. . . . In positive results there is little to report. But is mere survival nothing in the age of the atomic bomb?" From that point of view all problems solve themselves. France, small-town France, with the wisdom of bitter experience, prepared herself for the end of the world on the principle of every man for himself; with her little treasure-hoards under her apple-trees she even prepared for the day after the end of the world. A country can go on living and managing for years on the principle: "After us, the deluge", secure in the knowledge that there is still a priceless moment left to enjoy. But what happens if the deluge does not come, if all the bills drawn on the future, all the engagements freely entered into in the belief that they will never have to be met, are presented for settlement?

The year of good conscience was followed by the year of bad conscience. In the crisis of the summer of 1953, which beat all records in duration, irresponsibility, and using up of political personnel, all the bills and all the deficits were presented to this Parliament, and one Prime Minister-designate after another beseeched it to put an end to the mischief, to make up its mind, to choose between incompatibles, and to define the French attitude at a turning-point in world politics. The assembly of the nation sent them all packing one after another: and once more it found in its midst the man of the hour, the unknown quiet man from the quiet countryside, a superb embodiment of the virtues and cautiousness of the "real" France, a linen manufacturer from Vimoutiers in the Pays d'Auge, whom *Le Monde* next day introduced to a curious world as follows:

"In today's triumph of Joseph Laniel, the son of Henri, the grandson of Eugène, and the great-grandson of that Laniel-Fontaine who in 1806 founded at Lisores, outside the gates of Vimoutiers, the 'La Gousselinaie' laundry, Paul Bourget would have seen a confirmation of his theory that it is dangerous to advance too quickly, and that it is of better avail to advance slowly up the social scale, in the course of generations. In the end the time comes when a family's hard work, persistence, and virtues are brilliantly crowned in one of its descendants. If Joseph Laniel today becomes head of the Government, it can be said that it is not mere luck that has brought him to 'the top of the slippery pole' of power. Behind him is a century-and-a-half of hard work and honest toil. Just as one cannot separate the grandson from his grandfather, who built up a mechanical weaving business out of the 'La Gousselinaie' laundry, which, thanks to sound and honest management, withstood crises which were fatal to other mortals, one cannot separate his political career from theirs.

"Eugène Laniel, his grandfather, who had become an important manufacturer, was the first to demonstrate his interest in social questions and gained universal respect. His son reaped what his father had sown. In 1896, when the *arrondissement* of Lisieux was called on to choose a deputy, the seat was offered him. And just as Joseph Laniel succeeded him in control of his spinning mill, so did it seem natural that son should follow father into Parliament." The correspondent of *Le Monde* who reported all these things from Vimoutiers in the Pays d'Auge, the seat of the dynasty, went on to report with pride "the firm's mature respect for tradition and its loyalty to the manufacturing methods on which its reputation was founded." "We still lay the linen out to bleach in the field of Vimoutiers," he reported a representative of the firm as saying. "That may, perhaps, seem an offence against progress, but, thanks to this immutable process, our fabrics retain the same quality that they have always had."

In 1806 Napoleon fought the double battle of Jena and Auerstädt, made himself protector of the Confederation of the Rhine, and established his brothers as King of Naples and King of Holland. But what is left of that dynasty today? In the same year Jean-Joseph Laniel-Fontaine established the "La Gousselinaie" laundry "outside the gates of Vimoutiers", and his dynasty still flourishes. That is the sum-total of world history in the amiable Pays d'Auge.

PART III

OVERSEAS FRANCE

ONE of the revolutionary changes of the post-war world is that it is no longer possible to dismiss the French colonial empire in a footnote. It is only since this empire—the French Union, as it is called, though that is the expression of an aspiration rather than an accurate description—has been threatened on all sides with unrest and secession, and since France has been arraigned as an oppressor before the United Nations by the emancipated colonial countries of Asia and the Middle East, and charged with trampling on the rights of man, that France has slowly begun to be aware of her colonies, and to feel the weight of "greater France" upon her shoulders.

In the last years of the war Algiers was the capital of free France, and the Government-in-exile of General de Gaulle ceased to be a government-in-exile as soon as it had transferred itself to Algiers—which is as much a French city as Marseilles or Bordeaux, not the capital of a colony, but of a department of France. It was overseas France that stood the test of war, and provided France with territory, an army, and a fleet with which she was able to re-enter the conflict in its final phases. It was thanks to her colonial empire that her independent existence was in fact continuously preserved. But after the war whole libraries were written about the heroic deeds of the French resistance, which weighed terribly lightly in the scales of war in a material sense, though morally its weight was heavy; while there have been scarcely more than a few malicious attacks on, and irritated apologies for, those who held the French empire together after the defeat of the home country, under the Vichy régime but outside the range of German power. In the colonies other emotions were at work than in the home country. From time immemorial the traditional enemy had been, not Germany, but Britain; and the bombardment of Mers-el-Kébir, when the British Mediterranean Fleet sank all the attainable remnants of the French fleet ten days after the armistice, served only to fan an old resentment. Were the governors and residents-general of this empire to listen to the appeal addressed to them from London by a totally unauthorised, freshly-promoted brigadier-general to hoist the flag of rebellion—the flag of liberty, equality, democracy, and soon of the Atlantic Charter —against their legal head of state, Marshal Pétain?

One of them did so, a black citizen of the Antilles, the oldest and most assimilated part of the empire inherited from the *ancien régime*. The Third Republic had recently started recruiting civil servants for its African territories in the Antilles, and M. Eboué, the first of this new type, who had become governor of Chad, hoisted the flag of General de Gaulle's free France in the heart of Africa. He was an embodiment of the "greater France" of "a hundred million Frenchmen" of all colours and races; he was the great exception to the rule, the triumph of the Jacobin colonial idea over the colonial practice which everywhere else upheld peace and order in the name of Marshal Pétain until the allied landing in North Africa, when, again in the marshal's name and in that of peace and order—it was Admiral Darlan, the marshal's plenipotentiary, not General de Gaulle, who brought this off —they went over to the stronger camp of the allied naval Powers.

The apparently confused but in reality so logical history of the colonial empire during the war could not be fitted into the Manichaean legend of the revolutionary struggle for freedom; and its principal episodes, culminating in the grim and dramatic struggle for power between Darlan, Giraud, de Gaulle and their British, American, and Russian patrons, has remained secret history, wrapped in an atmosphere of doubtful intrigue. Only the heroic deeds of the Chad army gained popular renown. The "inner resistance"—and not only the Communist part of it, which had special grounds for doing so—watched the troops of the colonial empire entering France in the days of the liberation with deep, instinctive mistrust. Two alien, almost hostile, Frances then met; and in its first constitution liberated France hastened to abolish the colonial empire on paper. As usual, it was only the name which was abolished, but that was significant in itself. It had always been slightly improper to talk about the French colonial empire, of which Frenchmen knew little, but had all the stronger views about in consequence; it was something that existed, it is true, but ought not to have existed.

The truth of the matter is that the history of the French republic and that of the French colonial empire were impelled by different forces, went their different ways, and seldom met. Hundreds of histories of France, some of them first-rate, have been written in which the colonies were mentioned, if at all, only as an incidental curiosity, involving a number of doubtful and generally unsuccessful enterprises. Most of the episodes to which these histories confine themselves were, indeed, very doubtful, *e.g.*, John Law's Mississippi scheme; the throwing away of the valuable colonial territories in the reign of Louis XIV, "the few square miles of snow", as Voltaire contemptuously called Canada, and the fairyland of India; the story of Toussaint Louverture and the vicissitudes of the rights of man in the slave state of Santo Domingo; Napoleon's dreams of empire at the sight of the Pyramids; the diversionary manœuvres of the bankrupt restoration monarchy in Algeria, the adventurous expeditions of Napoleon the Little to Indo-China, Syria, and Mexico, the sharp practices of the Morocco crisis. In other words the empire was admitted to French history only by the backstairs, and its career was pictured as a perpetual variation on two equally displeasing themes—Panama and Fashoda. The empire was something with which the French people had nothing whatever to do, and its story was that of machinations of high finance, the Church, and the military caste, which tirelessly re-erected overseas the Bastilles which had been overthrown in France.

§ 2

THE TWO FACES OF FRENCH COLONIAL HISTORY

THE people, indeed, had nothing to do with the colonies. In 1830, when the Count de Polignac, a few weeks before his own fall and that of the monarchy, reduced to subjection the pirate state of Algeria and thus laid the foundation-stone for the reconstruction of the empire which had been lost in the Revolution, nobody thanked him. The whole enterprise was nothing but an election manœuvre, and the pretext that the French consul had been struck in the face with a fly-flap caused only angry laughter. "The attitude of a Government which accepts kicks from London but can think of nothing but to cross the Mediterranean to exact retribution for a slap in the face from Africa is indeed astounding," it was said. For four years the July monarchy, which took over this troublesome inheritance, could not make up its mind whether or not to remain in Algiers at all. In every budget debate there were tumultuous protests at the cost of this "crazy and useless" enterprise, but in the end the thrifty, unimaginative, unromantic Bourgeois Monarchy half-heartedly bowed to the necessity of continuing with something to which it found itself committed; colonisation and settlement had already been started for purely military reasons on the initiative of the generals on the spot. But the most celebrated and significant phrase from the debate on the subject was that used by the deputy Passy. "I would gladly exchange Algiers for the most wretched hole on the Rhine," he said.

The public reaction to the *fait accompli* of the punitive

expedition against the "Khmir bandits", by which Jules Ferry made Tunis into a French protectorate half a century later, was no different. Henri Rochefort, the Third Republic's most brilliant controversialist, opened his furious campaign against Ferry, whom he denounced as a corrupt speculator, an agent of Bismarck, and a madman, by saying: "There is an astonishing, grotesque, and crazy fact—there are no Khmirs." He went on to say that the Ferry Cabinet would gladly pay 30,000 francs to anyone who would find them a Khmir whom they could show to the army as a sample. Unfortunately, none was available. Who would be foolish enough to believe that they were spending millions, and employing more than forty thousand men, in Tunisia just to punish three Khmirs who from time to time stole a cow worth ninety francs from their settlers? Rochefort was tried for maligning and slandering the Government, but was acquitted by a Paris jury. Jules Ferry fell, but after a singularly confused parliamentary session in which no fewer than sixty resolutions were proposed and rejected one after the other, and in the end the indignant Chamber found no way out but solemnly to condemn the Tunisian expedition while approving the protectorate agreement of Bardo. France was in Tunis, so she remained.

Jules Ferry, the "architect of the French empire", was a symbol. Four years later he again confronted an angry Parliament to justify the expedition to Tongking, and Clemenceau's attack on him consisted of a succession of demagogic distortions and vilifications. "No discussion between us is possible," he said. "We do not want to listen to you any longer. We have had enough of you. A republican can have no more dealings with these Ministers, whom we accuse of high treason." This time the matter did not end in a simple vote of no-confidence; an angry mob gathered outside the Palais Bourbon and argued whether to hang Ferry, *le tunisien, le tonkinois*, from a street-lamp or to throw him in the Seine. He had to escape by a back door. But France stayed in Tongking too.

But the picture changed. When war broke out in Indo-China, which only a few years previously had been known as *la sale Indochine*, Parliament made no protest; it did not object to the "oriental despotism" of de Hauteville, the French Resident-General in Tunisia, or to the methods of the high officials of the Moroccan protectorate, who provoked riots and unrest on their own initiative in order to get rid of an inconvenient sultan. The critical role has passed to the United Nations, but the unpopularity of everything connected with the colonies remains.

Colonisation with a good conscience exists today less than ever. In dozens of demonstrations and debates the representatives of official policy have had flung in their faces the story of the German S.S. men who are said to have taken part in the slaughter of Oradour and to escape their punishment enlisted in the Foreign Legion to serve in Indo-China. A popular refrain among popular orators is: "We know today that France has Oradours and Lidices scattered all over the overseas territories." The colonial policy of the Fourth Republic has always been a difficult swimming against the stream of public and parliamentary opinion, and it would have been hard to have cut a worse figure in parliamentary debates or at party congresses than that cut by MM. Coste-Floret and Letourneau when they were Overseas Ministers. They were always made to look like men with bad consciences, lending themselves to a bad cause against all reason and justice. M. Schuman perhaps owed his fall as Foreign Minister to his European policy, but the opportunity for tripping him up was provided by the two protectorates of Tunisia and Morocco, which, by a tradition as unpractical as it is sanctified, are added to the Foreign Minister's other cares and responsibilities. The war in Indo-China as reflected in the French Press was largely a story of profiteering and corruption, an endless succession of scandals, from that of the "night-club Emperor" Bao Dai and the dinners given by his Paris agent Van Co and the "affair of the generals" of 1950, which, like another Panama scandal, for a moment seemed to shake the republic to its foundations, to the piastre scandal of 1953. Such is French colonial history as recorded in the French Press; an empire acquired by inadmissible means behind the backs of Parliament and people continues to be held together behind their backs by the same means.

Nevertheless a history of overseas France could equally well be written in which all the rows and scandals at home amounted to no more than troublesome interference by ignorant politicians and ideologists, who continually played havoc with a century-long, adventurous, but nevertheless deeply unified pioneering and constructive process, the results of which were always being thrown away on the Rhine and and in Flanders, if not in Paris budget debates and party manœuvres.

For France unquestionably possesses the oldest and greatest colonial tradition of all the European nations. Its traces are to be found all over the world. Between 1650 and 1750, before the English, the French created a protectorate over the Deccan, the last "five trading stations" of which, with their whole content of Franco-Indian schools, institutions, and traditions, are only today being absorbed by the new state of India. They opened up central North America to European colonisation before the English, and a compact French population in Canada and a garland of cities, lakes, and rivers with French names from Quebec, Montreal, and Detroit down to Louisiana, Baton Rouge, and New Orleans survive from the time when "New France" included the whole of North America from the Appalachians to the Rockies, from Canada to the Gulf of Mexico. France offers a unique historical example of a nation which built up a world-embracing empire, lost it with the exception of a few small islands and trading posts, and then made a new start, and for the second time became the second greatest colonial empire in the world. The forces behind this expansion varied. Feudalism and the Church, absolutism and mercantilism, and the financial and industrial capitalism of modern times all played their part in turn in the colonising process; but fundamentally it remained throughout the same *conquista* in feudal, absolutist, or imperialist guise.

For the empire of Richelieu and Colbert was not the first. French colonial history begins with the Norman expeditions at the beginning of our millennium and reaches its first climax in the crusades, when French feudal states were established throughout the Levant; it can even be said to begin with the beginning of French history itself, with the fusion into one of all the peoples who had successively settled on the soil of

Gaul, from the barbarian invasions until the most recent arrivals, the Bretons and the Normans. Barely a century after those pirates from Scandinavia, the Normans, had settled on French soil they started breaking out again as conquerors, transplanting French linguistic and social forms in every direction, from England to Sicily and Jerusalem. This was the first demonstration of the extraordinary assimilative capacity of a nation which until yesterday—let us leave open the question whether it still possesses it today—was able to absorb all who settled on her soil, and yesterday, to the concern of all birth-rate statisticians and students of eugenics, still believed that it would be able sooner or later to turn all the peoples of all the zones and races included in the French empire into parts of the French nation.

Underlying all the dangerous experiments of this "absurd dream" lay an infinitely naïve and calm confidence in the human and intellectual indestructibility of a nation which never aimed at "racial" unity, but at a cultural unity capable of assimilating all elements of human civilisation. Since the High Middle Ages a French "cultural imperialism" has been in existence which has remained a constant factor running parallel with all the practical economic and power-political elements in French colonial policy. But the reverse—not the dark—side of this was always receptivity. The oriental and Far Eastern influence on French philosophy, art, and literature, and later the influence of archaic and primitive cultures, has been incalculable, from the days of the great dialogue between the Arab and scholastic philosophers, the eastern Gothic of the Sainte Chapelle, the tremendous geographical and ethnological labours of the Benedictines, and the campaign, continuously conducted from Montaigne to the enlightenment period, against the illusion that European civilisation was the only or highest form of civilisation; and in recent times we have seen the violent incursion into the modern consciousness of east Asian, ancient oriental, Polynesian, and African cultures. France was never satisfied with being a European nation only, and to understand her more is required than a knowledge of her European face. The physiocrats tried to see an oriental people, a "western China" in France, and that undoubtedly contains a deeper reality than the stupid, unimaginative idea that France is "nigger-ridden".

Power to assimilate goes hand in hand with a capacity to be assimilated; you cannot have one without the other. Both depend on self-confidence, awareness of the possession of an intellectual superiority which is able to dispense with all outward signs of being "different" and has no fear of losing itself. For centuries France possessed this self-confidence, and the fact that it has now been shaken is her deepest crisis. In French colonial history there have been innumerable instances of Frenchmen who have gone overseas and become "natives", Indian chieftains, sheikhs, marabouts, rajahs, or Negro princes, as well as mendicant friars and fellaheen. There was René Caillié, the baker's son from the Vendée, who in the guise of an Arab pilgrim spent a year and a half wandering through the Sahara, was the first European to see Timbuctoo, the legendary capital of the Tuaregs, and was able to leave it alive because there was nothing about him to betray the European; there was Léon Roches, subsequently French consul in Tunis, who as the friend of the Algerian Mahdi Abd-el-Kader was accepted among Arab leaders and scholars of the Koran, the Vicomte Charles de Foucauld, who after a brilliant military career went into the desert and explored the forbidden territories of Morocco in the guise of a Jewish beggar, wrote a grammar and dictionary of the Tuareg language, and finally, as a Trappist in the solitude of the mountains of western Morocco, was honoured as a marabout until the day of his death, and in the first world war succeeded by his influence in preventing a rising of the Senussi.

The elements of this history are tremendously complicated. At the beginning of the seventeenth century the French Jesuit Alexandre de Rhodes went from Macao to Indo-China, established a Christian community among the inhabitants, drew up an Annamite catechism, and by his writings made Indo-China known in France. By 1660 French bishops were installed in Siam, Cochin China, and Tongking. French missionaries invented Quoc-Ngu—the literary language of Annam written in Latin characters—and a Compagnie de Chine was founded to turn these missionary successes into hard cash. A century later Pigneau de Behaine, Bishop of

Adran and Apostolic Vicar in Cochin China, signed a protectorate treaty with Louis XIV in the name of the kingdom of Cochin China. The French monarchy on the eve of its collapse was unable to exploit these possibilities, but the valiant bishop, with the aid of the French colonists of Réunion, then known as Bourbon Island, off Madagascar, organised an Annamite army, taught it bayonet fighting and how to build fortresses, and translated the works of Vauban into Annamite; French eighteenth-century fortresses in the style of Vauban are scattered all over Annam to this very day. Sixty years later, when the struggle for the China trade began and the Suez Canal project began to take shape, an Annamite bishop, Mgr. Pellerin, appeared at the French court to seek the aid of Napoleon III against a xenophobic movement. He was introduced at court by a certain Mgr. Bäuer, who as the agent of Rothschild's Bank had once arranged Napoleon III's Spanish marriage and had since insinuated himself into the position of the Empress's father confessor and apostolic observer at the imperial court. Their combined efforts succeeded in persuading the Emperor and Empress of the Christian utility of imposing a protectorate.

Superficially this enterprise appeared to be merely one of the many adventures indulged in by Napoleon the Little. Nevertheless it was the fruit of two hundred years of preliminary labour, and as in an allegory it displays the co-operation of throne, finance, and altar. Another allegory, an allegory of continuity, is provided by the fact that the plan of campaign used by Polignac in 1830 to capture the pirates' nest of Algiers, which was impregnable from the sea, had been worked out in detail under Napoleon I on the basis of advice supplied to Louis XVI by his consul in Algiers in 1783; the *ancien régime* had handed on the task to the restoration monarchy over the heads of Revolution and Empire.

One thing was common to all these stories. Those at home did not understand what was at stake and had to be presented with *faits accomplis,* distortions of fact, and stories about bandits, and appeals had to be made to doubtful ideals, second-rate material interests and national vanity, in order to persuade them to grant that absolute minimum of support to the work of colonisation with which it was in fact carried out. It was the achievement of men on the spot, settlers, legionaries, missionaries of the Church or of civilisation, adventures and *entrepreneurs* in the widest sense of the term. This sedentary and apparently so home-loving people has produced such men in astonishing numbers—lucky ones like Brazza and Lyautey, and others who were left in the lurch like Dupleix and Marchand. The men on the spot had to fight a hard and persistent struggle with the politicians, ideologists, and demagogues of the home country, who haggled over every sou in the colonial estimates and were always ready to "exchange Algiers for the wretchedest hole on the Rhine", in whose legalistic categories there was no place for rulers and ruled and in whose eyes the most urgent task was to apply the full doctrine of liberty, equality, and fraternity and introduce the forms of democracy and equality of rights to illiterates, fetishists, and head-hunters without suspecting the explosive force of unconsidered phrases and careless promises; who, in short, fostered agitation where the first principle should have been to tolerate no agitation, and made Paris the centre of all conspiracies and plots against the French empire. Such are the often indignant, often resigned reproaches levelled at their home country, "the France of the small town", by the Frenchmen of overseas France.

This empire indeed presents a different face of France. Here there is no languishing of the political will and no falling off of the *besoin de grandeur*; and the sleepy atmosphere of the small town is not to be found. All the strength and energy liberated by the republic which it has known less and less how to employ, all the pioneering spirits not to be satisfied with the petty gratifications of small-town life, and above all the prestige-conscious descendants of the *ancien régime*, the traditional servants of Crown and Church, a whole proud and ancient political class to whom their own country could offer nothing but a life of exile at home, found in the empire an unlimited field of activity. Another, greater, France was built up outside herself.

The great problem of this empire, strange though the word may sound, was that of its self-justification. France acquired her empire as a luxury, as a matter of prestige and power, not as a matter of necessity, or even utility. The self-sufficient home country did not know what to do with the work of its empire builders. The French empire has not, even in the mildest sense of the word, developed an imperial economy. Between France and her overseas territories there circulated officials, officers, soldiers, teachers, students, representatives of the state authority and civilisation, but few goods and little capital. Before the first world war, when France was the world's capitalist, she invested 45,000 million gold francs abroad; only one-tenth of this reached the colonies. The France of the Third Republic subscribed to loans issued by the Tsar and all the other monarchs whom the first world war swept away together with their debts, but she did not invest. She spent 10,000 million francs on the military conquest and the security of her empire, but not half that sum on opening it up and developing it. In the budget year of 1938, the last before the war, the French state devoted two-and-a-half per cent. of its total expenditure to the colonies, and four-fifths of this expenditure was military.

The tremendous colonial expansion of the last quarter of the nineteenth century did not prevent the onset of the trend to stagnation both of the national economy and the population statistics of the French homeland; on the contrary, the empire, by its protected markets, from which competition was even more effectively eliminated than it was at home, spared French industry the need to make efforts to hold its place on the free world market. Under the protection of the mercantilist *pacte colonial* traders with the colonies drew their revenues from the sale to the inhabitants of the traditional manufactured goods and by importing the traditional colonial products to the homeland; the big banks drew their revenue from state loans and state-guaranteed investments; the landowning companies drew their revenue from state and tribal lands cheaply acquired after being declared to be ownerless. It was colonisation on a mercantilist, almost feudal pattern. No plantation economy, exploiting native labour, was set up; but large-scale ownership of land was introduced and trading stations were established. The biggest and proudest achievements of this colonisation were in the fields which characterised Roman colonisation, namely road-building and administration.

In the economic sphere the colonies were extensions of the homeland; they were not supplementary to it. The economy which has developed in Algeria after a century of French rule is symbolic of this, though it is true that elsewhere it has not been possible for the process to go so far. In Algeria the French settlers are engaged exclusively in the production of wheat and wine, though the over-production of wheat in France makes restrictions and price supports necessary; and, as the North African population is forbidden by the Prophet to drink wine, there is no market for the wine produced in Algeria save in France herself, which is already suffocated by the weight of her own wine surplus; in other words it is a form of production for which there is literally no demand. Algeria has really become a continuation of France beyond the Mediterranean; the settlers have so effectively transplanted the home country to North Africa that the former has had to protect herself by the imposition of duties against Algeria, which is supposed to be politically and administratively a part of the one and indivisible republic. Algeria is the extreme case. But up to the first world war practically nine-tenths of French imports from her empire consisted of foodstuffs, and even the progress of banana cultivation in West Africa caused an intelligible panic among French fruit-growers. The groundnuts and palm oil of West Africa threatened the French olive oil industry, and West Indian rum threatened French liqueurs and spirits; there was hardly a colonial product which escaped the duties with which France protected the products of her own soil. The mercantilist strait-jacket which confined the empire to an unreceptive home market which was incapable of expansion simultaneously excluded it from that market; and, apart from the exploitation of certain raw materials, there was no industrial development whatever, even in the modest sense of local working up of agricultural products; the first principle of the mercantilist *pacte colonial* is the industrial monopoly of the home country.

There are two territories in this profoundly pre-capitalist colonial régime which are exceptions. In Morocco and Indo-China, the two youngest and most modern French colonies, the financial empires of the Banque de Paris et des Pays-Bas and the Banque d'Indochine, the spirit of modern capitalist development has been at work: in Indo-China because its great distance protected it effectively even against the French protectionists, and in Morocco because of the vision of Lyautey, who launched the country like a commercial enterprise, and even more, perhaps, because of the international "open door" statute, which has excluded Morocco from complete economic incorporation into the French colonial system. Here the French spirit of enterprise has been exposed to foreign competition, and has proved that all it needs to be able to stand up to it is the necessity of having to do so.

The humanity of French colonisation has often been only the more attractive obverse side of its uneconomic nature. But there is another and more significant side to it. What France expected from "greater France" was the production of Frenchmen; French citizens in the future, but here and now French soldiers. The narrow way to citizenship for the native *élite* has been education, but the broad way has been by war service under the French flag. All the assimilation laws and all the big advances in the granting of citizenship rights bear the date of wars—1870–71, 1914–19, 1943–45; and the saying that France consists, not of forty, but of a hundred million Frenchmen, which did a good deal to restore the self-confidence of the *grande nation*, is generally attributed to General Mangin. The ideology of assimilation, the great dream of turning people of all nations and races into the children of France, found in this its firmest foundation. The colonies provided soldiers, and the army, which keeps the spirit and tradition of the *ancien régime* even more alive on colonial soil than it does at home, has become the great melting pot. The army has made French patriots of Arabs and Berbers, Senegalese and Madagascans, while the schools have only too often produced intellectuals who revolted against French colonialism in the name of republican principles. Perhaps the most striking proof of the effectiveness of this melting pot is the Foreign Legion, which consists neither of French citizens nor of members of primitive races.

§ 3
A HUNDRED MILLION FRENCHMEN

ALL French ideologies meet and harmonise in the idea of a greater France of "a hundred million Frenchmen". It has the true French *élan,* and combines the French love of a resounding phrase with the hard French spirit of realism; it is humanitarian in spirit, takes into account the military necessity of recruiting, and at the same time implies that subtle form of "dividing and ruling" which consists of setting up a privileged and assimilated *élite* over against the primitive masses and thus depriving the latter of their natural leaders. It provides common ground for the egalitarian idealism of the Jacobins and the Christian missionary ideal of the *ancien régime,* the worldly and the religious form of that "imperialism in its civilising role" which is inseparable from the French national idea; in short, it envisages a whole great section of humanity on the march to absorption by France, the civilised nation *par excellence.* He who treats this phrase as a mere phrase—and often enough it is used only as such—and is unable to understand it as a myth will always lack a key to the understanding of French thought, its greatness, and the crisis it is undergoing. True, sixty of the hundred million were still far from the goal, without rights or with only very slender rights, and often enough they were far from anything which could be described as human dignity, but they were on the way, and the chosen who had already arrived held out a beckoning light to them from far ahead. Governor Eboué, *le premier résistant d'Afrique,* provided the assimilation idea, not only with its most convincing symbolic confirmation, but with its most fiery advocate.

The first imperial conference of free France, over which

General de Gaulle presided at Brazzaville in January, 1944, made it more specifically than ever the basic principle of imperial policy. In one of those bold anticipations of a distant and hypothetical goal which distinguish so many French utterances on the colonial question, M. Pleven, the Commissioner for the Colonies, opened the conference with the following words: "We read from time to time that this war must end with what is called an enfranchisement of the colonial peoples. In the greater colonial France there are no peoples to enfranchise or racial discrimination to abolish. There are populations who feel French and wish to take, and to whom France wishes to give, a bigger and bigger part in the life and democratic institutions of the French community. There are populations whom we intend to lead step by step to personality, and the most mature of them will be given political franchise, but they desire no independence other than French independence."

Had M. Pleven not been speaking of ideals, one might have accused him of a lack of frankness. But, just as the Ten Commandments, speaking of what people ought to do, say "thou shalt", so do French politicians, speaking of the colonies, say "it is" when they mean "it ought to be". The final resolution of the Brazzaville conference drew the practical inference of the whole of French colonial history when it announced imperatively "that the aims of the work of colonisation which France is pursuing in her colonies exclude any idea of autonomy and any possibility of development outside the French empire *bloc*; the attainment of self-government [the word was left in English in the French text, an alien body unassimilable even linguistically] in the colonies even in the most distant future must be excluded."

This proclamation, delivered in the capital of the French Congo in the presence of the black Governor Eboué, lost nothing of its effect. In black Africa, where the French national idea and French civilisation have no effective competitors, the mystical process of transubstantiation which by the process of education brings forth an *élite* of "Frenchmen by creed" as the advance guard of whole races and peoples, preserves its strength unbroken; significantly, it fails only in that part of black Africa where the exceedingly active mission of Islam was established first. However, even without that, the difference between theory and reality was always big enough. The black citizens and soldiers of the "five old settlements" on the Senegal and the coloured Frenchmen of the West Indies have for long and with unbounded pride sent their deputies to the French Chamber, and these dozen picturesque figures have never raised in acute form the question whether sovereignty over the French homeland is one day to be shared with sixty million Africans and Asians possessing equal rights, and whether three-fifths of the seats in the Paris Parliament of the one and indivisible republic are one day to be evacuated to make room for them. But the idea of assimilation became sacrosanct, and blocked the way to coming to an understanding with all those inhabitants of the French empire who possessed ancient civilisations of their own, and did not want to become Frenchmen, but free citizens of their own countries.

The more commercial British Empire had already, even if only for administrative convenience, granted some measure of local autonomy to every African tribe, but the idea of granting the slightest measure of autonomy to the Arabs of North Africa, the Hovas of Madagascar, or the civilised peoples of Indo-China, was even more inconceivable to the "revolutionary" colonial reformers of the French left than to the hard-boiled colonialists of the right.

Boissy d'Anglas, presenting the revolutionary constitution of the year III to the Convention, declared: "There can be only one kind of good administration. If we have found it for the European countries, why should the colonies be deprived of it?" and the Jacobins remained loyal to this article of faith. Federalism, local autonomy, decentralisation, differentiation, have always been alien and suspicious conceptions to French politicians and jurists. Federalism implied reaction, the Vendée, the *Action Française*, provincial clericalism, Vichy; and all who labelled themselves progressive, from the Radicals to the Communists, rallied to the Jacobin "one and indivisible republic". The first Constituent Assembly of 1946 solemnly condemned colonialism, and dealt with the general constitution and institutions of the French empire in a mere sub-section of the unified constitution of the French republic.

"The colonial empire is dead," M. Pierre Cot, who acted as *rapporteur* in the matter, solemnly declaimed. "In its place we set up the French Union. France, enriched, ennobled, and expanded, will tomorrow possess a hundred million citizens and free men." This paper revolution, the proclamation of a 'French Union resting on consent" (the colonial peoples' consent was taken for granted, for they were not consulted), significantly enough papered over all the complicated problems of a world-wide empire with the principles of the Brazzaville imperial conference. The Fourth Republic dashed with all the fury of idealistic logic into the blind alley of accepting assimilation as being indisputably the only way of progress. As the logical consummation of its work the first Constituent Assembly unanimously passed the new Lex Caracalla of May 7th, 1946, which remained in force even after the rejection of the first draft of the constitution. "From June 1st, 1946," it said, "all subjects of overseas territories, including Algeria, possess the quality of citizens with the same rights as French citizens in the home country and in the overseas territories." The nation of a hundred million citizens with equal rights had come into being.

Whether such promises are meant seriously or rhetorically, the results are equally disastrous. Making play in this fashion with labels and ideological slogans can end only in complete irresponsibility. The proclamations which had been made could not be taken back, and the second Constituent Assembly in essence confined itself to minimising the damage that had been done. The constitution of the French Union which came into being in this way was a complicated jumble of clauses which cancelled each other out, and it was left to history and the lawyers to decide between them. It established a maze of mutually overlapping centralised and federal institutions. Some of them remained on paper, others were purely decorative, while a few dry paragraphs at the end in essence left everything where it had been before. Legislation for the overseas territories remained in the hands of the French Parliament, and their administration was left in the hands of governors appointed by the French Government, who enjoyed sole responsibility. The theory was assimilation by the grant of civil rights; the practice was administrative levelling out. However questionable it may be for a constitution to state, not what is, but what may perhaps one day happen in the future, the fact remains that a promise was solemnly given in black and white which was henceforth in complete conflict with reality.

The public first became aware of the crisis of the French colonial empire as the crisis of the idea of assimilation. The schoolroom example was provided by Algeria, that French creation on the other side of the Mediterranean which had become an integral part of the home country. Nowhere else had there been such a successful synthesis between east and west; and nowhere else—except in those relics of the empire of Colbert, the old overseas departments of the West Indies and the island of Réunion—had political and administrative integration with the homeland been so systematic and so complete. But now, when thirteen Algerian deputies—elected on an unequal basis and in separate electoral colleges—sat in the Constituent Assembly for the first time and, because of the unstable and shifting majorities in that body, were often able to swing the balance, it came as a shock to French public opinion to find that these men represented, not French, but Algerian or Arab national feeling.

There were continual clashes, now grotesque, now tragic, between an old, sentimental, fixed idea of progress and a newly discovered living reality. "I am here to represent the interests of my country," said Ferhat Abbas, the leader of the "Algerian Manifesto" independence movement which was the rallying ground of all politically active Algerians. At this there were indignant cries from all quarters of the House, pointing out that his country was France. Official France recognised no Algerians or Algeria, but only the department of France of that name beyond the Mediterranean, which, like all other departments of France, was governed by prefects subject to the Ministry of the Interior. The Algerian deputies should have acted as symbols of greater France, which recognised no racial prejudice or colour bar, and here they were abusing French tolerance by standing for something other than the French national ideal. Instead of acting as symbols of a future equality, they were making an outrageous attack on the inequality that still survived. It was their duty to feel in exactly the same way as other deputies, and their presence filled the Constituent Assembly with pride. But it was also their duty not to forget that they were not exactly the same as other deputies, but as M. Herriot, the president of the Assembly, liked to put it, "their younger brothers, not yet of age," and that they ought to exercise with reserve their strange privilege of being able to vote on laws and taxes which did not apply to their territories.

It is impossible to illustrate the abyss of misunderstanding and the hopeless tangle of this situation better than by this extract from the verbatim report of the maiden speech of the Algerian deputy Hadj A. Saadane in the *Journal Officiel* of August 23rd, 1946:

M. Saadane.—I feel somewhat embarrassed in addressing this Assembly, which consists chiefly of Frenchmen [violent interruptions right and centre] because I fear I may not be able to make myself understood . . .

[Voices from several parts of the House.—There are only Frenchmen here!]

M. Edouard Depreux, Minister of the Interior [Socialist]. —M. Saadane has made a mistake!

M. André Le Troquer [Socialist].—A very significant one!

M. Saadane.—I am really embarrassed at these interruptions, because until now I have not known what I am. [Interruptions right and centre.] Am I a French subject? Am I a French citizen? [Renewed interruptions from the same benches. Exclamation from the extreme left.—Hear, hear!]

The president.—M. Saadane, you are speaking from the rostrum of the French Parliament! [Applause right and centre.]

M. Maroselli [Radical].—Only French deputies can speak from that rostrum, so you are a Frenchman!

M. André Le Troquer.—We are in a French Assembly!

Voices from the right.—If you don't know that, you had better go! [Exclamations of protest from the extreme left.]

M. Saadane.—If France does not give us the rights which she ought to give us in accordance with her philosophical tradition and her history, we shall go! [Exclamations of

"Hear, hear!" from various benches on the extreme left.] I say that, speaking from this French rostrum to an Assembly in which Bretons, Alsatians . . . [Violent interruptions left, centre, and right. Calls from many benches of "Frenchmen!"]

M. Bougrain [Republican].—There are only Frenchmen in this Assembly!

M. Le Troquer.—The Bretons are French!

The president—Please allow the speaker to continue.

M. Bouret.—Breton autonomists have been put in prison.

M. Saadane.—Speaking from this rostrum, and trying to speak words, not of hatred . . .

M. Roclore [Independent].—Of appeasement?

M. Saadane.—. . . but of truth, in full awareness that, in spite of the difference of departments, a Breton or an Alsatian is a Frenchman, then I am afraid that I, an Arabic-speaking Mohammedan, when I speak to Frenchmen who come from their own Brittany, who are of the Catholic faith . . . [Interruptions right and centre. Protests from the extreme left.] . . . It's enough to make one despair!

Different views are possible of the parliamentary adroitness of the deputy Saadane and of the parliamentary manners of his European colleagues, but his fear that he would be unable to make himself intelligible to the latter turned out to be justified from the very start. The rest of what he was able to say before his speech was finally drowned in tumult was in its deliberate moderation perhaps the biggest challenge to which the Palais Bourbon had ever had to listen:

Many people say to us: Why do you not accept the policy of assimilation? We are making Frenchmen of you. Why do you reject the honour done to you? . . . In a community like ours the national stage is an inevitable and natural stage of development, and I do not understand how any members of this Assembly, either on this side [the right] or on that, could possibly condemn national feeling. You brought us your civilisation—that above all I honour in the record of France—the ferment which should make possible the enfranchisement of man. You showed us the way, you gave us the taste of liberty, and now, when we say that we do not want the colonial spirit or the spirit of colonisation, and that we wish to be free, to be men, no more and no less, you deny us the right to take over your own formulas, and are surprised, you Frenchmen, that a few spirits among us aim at independence. That, nevertheless, is a completely natural attitude. [Interruptions.]

M. Le Troquer.—This language is unheard of!

M. Pierre-Grouès [M.R.P.]—Say that still more plainly!

The president.—M. Saadane, I have already reminded you that you are speaking from a French rostrum. I now invite you to speak as a Frenchman. [Applause left, in the centre, and on the right.]

The report of the unlucky maiden speech of Hadj Ahmed Saadane, who "did not know what he was", has all the features of a great comedy and a great tragedy: the tragedy of an ideology that was once the boldest and most advanced in the world and now finds itself in a void. The grotesque forms often assumed by the clash of this ideology with reality, and the intolerable arrogance or tragic pathos with which it is sometimes expressed, should not cause one to forget that it was one of the most powerful forces of modern times; and it has fused so completely with the French national consciousness that its crisis has become the crisis of France herself; *i.e.*, the crisis of the claim to universality of French civilisation, the claim that it is identical with civilisation itself.

The fact that there are peoples who are not French is admitted, though it is a rather strange one; but that there should be people who, confronted with the opportunity of becoming French, do not desire to avail themselves of it, but nurse the ambition of attaining human dignity by other routes, is utterly beyond the understanding of a number of minds brought up in the best traditions.

The hardest question which confronts France, alike in her colonial empire and in her relations with Europe and the world, is whether her idea of civilisation is capable of renewal—renewal by receptivity to the alien and the novel without which it can itself have no radiative or assimilative power—or whether it will degenerate into that crabbed and narrow cultural chauvinism which nowadays characterises so many manifestations of the French spirit.

§ 4
CATASTROPHE IN THE DISTANCE

THE first and most pressing problems presented themselves in a form far more brutal than that of a conflict of conscience. The war and post-war period had subjected the French empire both materially and morally to the hardest conceivable test. When the war was over, it was like a parched and mutilated tree. All connection with the homeland had been severed for years, and each of the territories lived a separate life of its own. The thin layer of settlers, who had lived all too long without recruitment or support from home, was decimated, exhausted, and discredited in the struggles between Gaullists and the adherents of Vichy which rent the colonial empire, and rent it still further in the course of the post-war "purge". Though the forms of French sovereignty were preserved, the allied entries and landings, and the display of American technical equipment which made the free French forces look like shabby auxiliaries, did French prestige no good in the eyes of the inhabitants. France, economically disrupted and bled white, had nothing to offer the overseas territories, which had borne the whole burden of recruiting and requisitioning in the last years of the war; it could provide neither men, nor foreign exchange, nor manufactured goods, nor even the ships in which to transport them.

One of the keys to the disaster in Madagascar was that Madagascan soldiers, set free after four years of German imprisonment, had to wait in French camps for two more years until ships could be found to send them home; and one of the keys to the disaster in Indo-China was that at the time. of the Japanese capitulation that country, in view of the position the French Government was in, was unattainably remote. It is almost superfluous to speak of the psychological effects in the colonies of war in Europe; for the second time within a generation Europe had crippled herself, morally and materially. It is sufficient to recall the often-quoted speech made by the ex-prisoner-of-war candidate at an election meeting in Madagascar a few weeks before the rising there. "Do you know," he said, "what the Germans gave the French to eat during the occupation? Bran, just like pigs!" France was not the only country to discover in 1945 what had happened to European prestige in south-east Asia.

It had become a commonplace that the age of colonisation was over. The messages of the Atlantic and San Francisco charters had a tremendous echo among the highly developed colonial peoples. Henceforward the existence of colonial territories was a fact without moral justification, the relic of a past which the conscience of the world had solemnly repudiated. When international protection and trusteeship for all not yet independent territories was proposed at the United Nations, the remaining European colonial powers found themselves confronted with an overwhelming majority of nations who were radically opposed to colonialism: the former colonies of North and South America, starting with the United States itself, the Arab and Asian delegations, and the Soviet Union and its satellites. Moreover, the colonial powers were far from acting in harmony among themselves. British policy in south-east Asia put every conceivable obstacle in the way of the return of France to Indo-China, as it did to that of the Dutch to Indonesia. In the Near East France, under the pressure of a British ultimatum, which rankled for a long time, had to abandon her mandate over Syria to which the French Government sought to cling after the legal expiry of its term; and the Arab League, in which Britain hoped to find support for her Near Eastern policy, became a centre of agitation for all the aspirations to independence prevalent in French North Africa. The age of colonisation was over; had the French Constituent Assembly itself not solemnly announced the abolition of the colonial empire? Words, proclamations, and phrases so lightheartedly bandied about in the Palais Bourbon became dynamite thousands of miles away at election meetings at which new citizens, who yesterday had been recruited for compulsory labour by French settlers, now gathered to elect their deputies.

The rising which on March 29th, 1947, broke out simultaneously in many parts of Madagascar, that Asian island stranded off the African coast, was like an explosion in an isolated laboratory. The after-effects of the war and the occupation by the British, upon whose withdrawal the maintenance of order was left to an absurdly small French police force of a few hundred men; the lack of imports; the immediate abolition of compulsory labour—an obvious consequence of the grant of citizenship to all the island's inhabitants—which left the plantations without labour at the time of their greatest need; the open hostility of the settlers to all the measures ordered from Paris; the agitation conducted by the new native parties; the echo of the declaration of independence in Indonesia, from which the Madagascan ruling race had once emigrated; all these things created an explosive atmosphere, and only a spark was needed to set it alight. Nevertheless the rising came as a complete surprise. Upon an invisible sign it started spreading throughout the island like a spot of oil dropped in a pond, and its suppression involved the use of large numbers of troops and "mopping-up" operations which lasted for months. The rebels adopted the principles and slogans of the "democratic renewal movement of Madagascar", which had just previously won all the seats allotted to the people of Madagascar in the French Parliament, but no definable political aim was discoverable behind the revolt. The big centres of settlement were spared, but a wild massacre took place of more than eight hundred Frenchmen living on isolated plantations and their "collaborating" natives. The Hovas, the Madagascan "master race" of Malay origin, who before the French colonisation had exercised a hard feudal tyranny over the original inhabitants and still form the island's native *élite*, provided the leadership of the revolt, but the primitive black tribes, some of whom had been cannibals until a few generations ago, were caught up in the maelstrom, and the outbreak was of unspeakable savagery. Bands of hundreds of fanatics, armed with knives, fell on the settlers and murdered them, their wives, and their children, as well as native farm workers who often tried to defend the settlements and plantations. The rising, which lacked central leadership or political prospects, lost itself in the bush and the swamps, and isolated groups carried on a desperate and hopeless struggle for months until rendered innocuous district by district in protracted military operations. The suppression of the rising perhaps exceeded the rising itself in horror, and involved at least a hundred times as much bloodshed. The explanation, if not the excuse, was the anonymity of the rising, its fragmentation into innumerable, leaderless gangs of murderers and fire-raisers, with whom any kind of negotiation or coming to terms was impossible.

These people were in the clinical sense of the word guiltless and irresponsible. But who was responsible? As always in such cases, opinions were diametrically opposed. While the French left, in accordance with its political principles, laid all the blame on the colonial régime for coming into conflict with Madagascan aspirations for liberty, the right, and above all the settlers, blamed the "blind liberalism" of M. Coppet, the Governor-General, who was soon afterwards relieved of his post, on the ground that he had fostered the "renewal movement" as a legal party, tolerated its agitation, and encouraged the storm to break loose by his failure to take effective action. According to this point of view, the rising was due to the reforms, which had gone to the natives' heads, to education, to the granting of relative freedom of the Press, and to the abolition of compulsory labour.

As always in such cases, the trial of the Madagascan leaders, which took a year to go through all the courts, failed to throw any light on the matter. The preparation of the case against them was left to the local judicial authorities, to whom it was necessary at all costs to find persons to whom political guilt could be attributed, and this made the trials only too questionable; the confessions extracted by the inquisitorial methods of the local police magistrates, on whose omnipotence there was no check, were too numerous and too complete; and too many important witnesses had been caused to disappear under the emergency regulations before the proceedings became public and the accused were able to avail themselves of their constitutional rights. The result was "another Dreyfus case", the prelude to many similar cases in Tunisia and Morocco, and it took a long time for the excitement to die down. But the three seats in the National Assembly which had been reserved for Madagascans remained unoccupied.

Meanwhile the revolt itself was practically forgotten. Nobody had wanted it and nobody had started it; it was just a tragedy of irresponsibility. But the endless, eloquent pleadings in which the Madagascan politicians—doctors, lawyers, journalists, and politicians by profession, many of whom had been trained in French universities—described their careers and their adherence to French republican principles, perhaps provided a key; it was not only a tragedy of intellectuals torn between two cultures, one primitive and the other overdeveloped, but a tragedy of uprooted ideals.

These men had imbibed at the Sorbonne, at political meetings, in the radical, intellectual circles of Paris, the message of the French Revolution, had taken it home with them, and had handed it on to their compatriots in a language, which, besides other *nuances,* fails to differentiate between the indicative, the conditional, and the subjunctive. Their compatriots had learned how to go to the polls and vote, and sent them back to Paris as their deputies. That, perhaps, satisfied the deputies' ambition, but not that of their compatriots; and one evening the village medicine-men had stalked through the bush with lanterns, announcing that the ancestral spirits were dissatisfied, that the white invaders must be exterminated, and that the divine dynasty of the Hovas must be restored to its rights.

Perhaps in the strict sense of the word no one was responsible for the Madagascan massacres. But the French settlers' Press, and to a lesser extent the colonial politicians at home, took the opportunity of the blood-bath to condemn the "artificial breeding of *élites*", and to claim that the task of education in French overseas territories must be to produce, not intellectuals, but skilled workmen. They said wisely that idealism not based on a solid foundation of reality led only to death and arson. But they forgot to add that colonisation based solely on the rulers' claim to rule is also without a solid foundation, not just for France, but for Europe and Europeans as a whole.

The rising in Madagascar was a dull and distant echo of the revolution in eastern Asia; it was ruthless, isolated, and amenable to suppression by a hastily-got-together punitive expedition of the traditional kind. In even more remote Indo-China France was confronted with the Asian revolution itself; and here the attempt to return to the old position of power led straight into a long and hopeless *cul-de-sac* from which no way out was to be discerned. It is easy, and at the same time futile, to suggest policies now which might have prevented the disastrous situation in which from 1946 onwards France wasted her strength in a struggle that grew more hopeless as time wore on. In the case of Indo-China it was not so much that a wrong policy was pursued as that there was no policy at all; or rather that every kind of policy was followed at the same time, which is the same thing. Reconciliation, reconquest, recognition of independence, suppression, and restoration were all tried simultaneously, and there was too little of each. In a situation in which it was necessary to sacrifice a great deal in order to retain anything at all, military force was used, but there was too little of it to be effective; political negotiation was tried, but without generosity, and generally without sincerity; and small concessions were made with one hand and taken back with the other. For years the French colonial politicians stubbornly refused to see that this was no local colonial revolt, but a revolution; and they were continually forced to abandon on paper, piecemeal, "too little and too late", what they had already lost in reality.

After seven years of being hopelessly on the defensive, all the concessions, refusal to grant which had been the original cause of the war, had been wrung from them, and they had surrendered much more than the privileges for the retention of which they had originally started fighting. This policy, with its stratagems and illusory cunning, presented an appalling picture of indecision, ambiguity, impotence, and lack of vision. But there are two things that no critic should forget. In Indo-China France was faced with the same problem which confronted Britain in Malaya, Holland in Indonesia, and to a certain extent America in China and Korea, and the national blinkers of all the western Powers for years concealed the full extent of what was going on in these places. Each one of them dealt with the situation on its own and used its own methods, and each acted independently, if not in opposition to each other, and the resulting situation as a whole gives little right to any of them to criticise the mistakes of others. In Indo-China, the most threatening area of them all, France was presented with the problem in its most acute form. Leadership of the Viet-minh was assumed by the Communists, and what that means is clearer today than it was then.

The attempt of France to re-establish herself at the other end of the world with the weak forces at her disposal after the complete loss of power and prestige involved by the Japanese occupation was an adventurous step in the dark. In the absence of all French forces, the country had been divided at the sixteenth parallel on the Korean pattern between British and Chinese occupation troops. The Japanese had left behind time-bombs in the form of revolutionary committees and armed bands; all sorts of pro-Chinese and secret societies were introduced in the wake of the Chinese troops, and all the old Chinese claims to suzerainty over Indo-China were revived; and the Americans suggested handing the masterless country over to the United Nations. In this darkness and confusion the French emissaries clung to anything that seemed to offer any sort of support; to the restorable remnants of the old régime in the south and to the spirit of Annamite nationalism in the north. In order to get rid as quickly as possible of the British, and above all of the Chinese troops, the French High Commissioner, M. Thierry d'Argenlieu, a Carmelite provincial, clutched at the first straw that offered: the revolutionary government of Ho Chi-minh, who had proclaimed an independent republic of Viet Nam on the day after the Japanese capitulation and—as he too wanted to get rid of Chiang Kai-shek's soldiery—declared himself ready to co-operate with France in return for an assurance of Viet Namese independence within the framework of the French Union. This formula was wide enough to permit almost any interpretation, and after their attempt at the political and military reconquest of Indo-China Ho Chi-minh had just as much right to complain that the French broke their word to him as *vice versa*. Nowadays it has been almost forgotten that in the summer of 1946 Ho Chi-minh was ceremoniously received by the French Government of M. Bidault as the recognised head of a friendly state in order to settle the details of "Viet Namese independence within the French Union", but that on the day of his departure for Paris the French High Commissioner proclaimed an "independent republic of Cochin China", with a Government nominated by himself, in that part of Viet Nam of which he had military control.

This was the first act in a series of events which led five months later to open war. The Paris Government had one policy and its officials in Indo-China another, and both were hesitant and groping, and followed many paths at once. The greater the indecision and confusion became, the more decisions in fact depended on sectional interests, local commanders, and the manœuvres of mutually hostile groups. The tragedy began as a war in the dark, and it continued as a war in the dark. In French official language the head of state Ho Chi-minh was slowly transformed again into a leader of rebellion, though they failed to give any authority whatever to any of the local authorities whom they appointed in the old colonial style, and it became harder and harder to find Indo-Chinese personalities prepared to undertake the deadly risk of "collaboration". When the government of Ho Chi-minh took to the mountains a complete political void lay between it and the French expeditionary corps; and slowly, terribly slowly, French policy set about the task of finding a new ruler for Indo-China whom it could oppose to Ho Chi-minh. More than two years slipped by in backstairs negotiations undertaken by intermediaries with Bao Dai, the former Emperor of Annam, who had abdicated on the day of the Japanese abdication and had put himself at Ho Chi-minh's disposal as an adviser before going into exile on the French Riviera.

All over the world, from the Lake of Geneva to the Along-Bai, go-betweens of the French Government and the Emperor in exile pursued and avoided each other. The Emperor felt no burning desire to return to a hostile country as a French shadow prince, and demanded the highest possible price, namely the real independence which France had refused to the republic of Ho Chi-minh. Once more it was a case of too little and too late. Not till the Chinese Communist armies had advanced to the borders of Indo-China did the French at last make up their mind to try an experiment which their endless haggling had almost completely discredited in advance. Once more they solemnly proclaimed the "independence of Viet Nam within the framework of the French Union" and sent Bao Dai back to Indo-China, not as a restored Emperor, but with a strange, undefined, and circumscribed mission of "pacification". With the diplomatic recognition of the Government of Ho Chi-minh by the Chinese and the Soviet Governments, and the collapse of the French attempt to maintain a military barrier along the Chinese frontier, all prospect of an early military decision had disappeared before the French made up their mind to stake everything on their last card—now much depreciated in value.

They agreed to the Annamite restoration, and granted the Viet Namese "head of state" and the Kings of Laos and Cambodia the external attributes of independence; and these monarchs, sitting on French bayonets, replied by behaving more and more nationalistically and repudiating French suzerainty, just as Ho Chi-minh had done. In the autumn of 1953 the Viet Namese national congress appointed by Bao Dai passed a resolution declaring the vague phrase "within the framework of the French Union" to be unacceptable, and every conceivable pressure had to be applied to have it subsequently modified by the addition of the words "in its present form". Only Governments as uncompromisingly opposed as the Communists themselves to the last relics of French colonial domination could hope to compete with the Vietminh; and so France, after eight years of exhausting struggle and even more expensive corruption in Indo-China, was left officially with only one surviving war aim: evacuation of the country. But even that seemed as far off as the long-since-abandoned prospect of reconquest had been.

For, while Indo-China, the former jewel of the French empire, had been sinking deeper and deeper into a chaos of terror, fear, hatred, and treachery, the international face of the war had altered. An isolated, local war had turned into a struggle for a key position in the front line between two worlds, a front line which stretched from Korea by way of Formosa and Indo-China right round the continent of Asia and through Europe. Yesterday it had been a "dirty colonial war", condemned, not only by the Communists, but by the western, and in particular the American Press. It had turned into a war, fought in one of the outposts of the free world, for the defence of all Eurasia against the advancing tide of Communism, and the French ceased to be fighting just their own battle, but that of the whole of the west; and, as the Americans increasingly financed it, it came to be regarded in France as an American war, in which France was playing merely an auxiliary, mercenary role.

But for the men on the spot the face of the war did not change; it remained a hopeless, unending struggle between two interlocked opponents who could neither go forward or go back, fought over an exhausted country whose towns were controlled by the French and whose hills by the Communists, while the rice fields and villages of the fertile Red River delta were controlled by French patrols during the day and by Viet-minh guerrillas at night; while in the towns, above all in Saigon, advantage was taken of the respite to engage in all sorts of speculation and corruption.

The war in Indo-China turned into a war of indefinitely prolonged stagnation. Was it inevitable? Was there a way out? Indo-China was a bottomless pit into which France poured practically double the amount she received in Marshall aid, and nearly all the young officers she needed so desperately to train her army in Europe. This remote, detested war, which for a long time she fought as a police action, almost secretly and with a bad conscience, which never became a national cause, and in which the Government never dared employ any but North Africans, Foreign Legionaries, professional officers, volunteers, and men specially recruited, consumed to an unassessable extent, not only the resources that France needed for her European policy, but also the spirit needed to conduct such a policy.

§ 5

NORTH AFRICAN BASTION

IN the midst of all these convulsions the great, compact block of the French empire in North Africa remained unshaken. But here too France was confronted with great tasks for which neither the old French methods nor the old national exclusiveness were adequate.

French North Africa is divided politically and administratively into the three departments of France which constitute Algeria in the middle, and two protectorates—Morocco and Tunis—on either side. The former come within the province of different Ministries, and are even divided by customs barriers from the latter. There is historical justification for the division of this great geographical, geological, and ethnical unit of the Maghreb, the former Africa Minor. In North Africa the word colonisation still preserves its full, ancient meaning, *i.e.*, settlement. Moreover, French colonisation took place upon the site of ancient colonisation; the Mediterranean civilisation of antiquity had been overlain on its southern shores by Islam just as on its northern shores it had been overlain by Christianity. So far as Africa is concerned, argument about dependence on or independence of the home country is mere talk; it bypasses the real problem, which is that created by the third factor in the situation, namely the European settlers. All the present crises in North Africa spring, not from the relations between France and her North African possessions, but from those between the local European population of close on two millions and the indigenous population of nearly twenty millions. The problem that arises here is *sui generis*, and arises in a different form in each of the three

North African territories. But fundamentally it is that of the co-existence of a European minority, far superior in standard of living, economic power, and political development, and an indigenous population which outnumbers it by ten to one and is increasing rapidly.

The postulates of egalitarian democracy involve the stating of all questions in terms of numerical majorities without regard to stages of national or social development, and this has undoubtedly complicated the problem and made it more intractable. In Algeria democracy has to be betrayed daily. But that is only the surface of the problem. The truth of the matter is that the problem of the co-existence of different races at different levels of development has never been satisfactorily solved, except where it has been disposed of by the practical extermination of the native peoples, as in North America and Australia, or in Latin America, where the religious and cultural identity of the indigenous population has been as good as exterminated. It is the hardest problem with which colonial policy can be faced.

There can be no more wrong-headed or grotesque analogy than that between the liberation of America from the former British and Spanish domination and the Arab independence movement in North Africa. In America it was not the native population, but the European settlers, who threw off the European yoke. The true parallel would be a defection from France of the French North African settlers. Actually this is not a totally fantastic idea, but a threat which reappears whenever French colonial policy appears too ready to meet Arab aspirations for emancipation. The South African policy of Dr. Malan might perhaps provide the pattern for such a development. That it would be a disaster for everybody concerned does not prevent such ideas from being toyed with in Algiers and Tunis, if only to recall to the minds of the Paris "ideologists" and "politicians of liquidation", who "desire to hand over the French of North Africa to the Arab mob", that the European population has a voice of its own. Separatism is an idea by no means confined to Arab heads, and it is a fact that up to the second world war those who benefited by all the developments tending in the direction of Algerian autonomy were not the Algerians, but Algeria's ruling population of European settlers. In the difficult three-way exchanges on the subject of North Africa, of which it is impossible to understand a word if the third partner is left out of account, the home country holds the balance. In times of conservative government or political weakness at home the influence of the home country seems to flag, and sometimes to disappear altogether, and the reins are left completely to the settlers; then the situation threatens to lead in the direction of the "holy war" which in Algeria, as in all Arab countries, is always lurking beneath the surface, and in North Africa it would be a civil war. But in the long run the colonial tradition of the French homeland, *i.e.*, the tradition of assimilation, always exerts itself again. In the exchanges between the inhabitants of the same country it could assume a different and far deeper significance than in the ideological battles of the Palais Bourbon. Assimilation is perhaps a discredited phrase nowadays, but, so long as the great aim of making two peoples into one is maintained, it will not lose its meaning; its implications are the direct opposite of *apartheid*.

The most favourable conditions possible seemed to exist for this policy in North Africa, at any rate in Algeria. Algeria really is a natural continuation of France beyond the Mediterranean, and really is a French creation. When the French originally went there they were confronted, not with a people, a nation, a state, but a nest of pirates who had crippled navigation in the western Mediterranean from a rocky fastness which had been impregnable for centuries. The place was ruled by janissaries under nominal Turkish suzerainty who tyrannised over the bare, thinly populated interior. Even the name of "Algeria" was first given to this sterile, nameless, and history-less country by the French. The history of this country before their arrival is a monotonous story of endless fiascos. These inhospitable highlands, impregnable from the sea almost along their entire length because of their steep cliffs, but helpless in face of invasion or nomadic incursion from the east, the south, and the west, never developed any trace of inner unity, of any centre of their own; there had never been even the beginnings of historical continuity, and the area had never enjoyed a moment of independent existence. Again and again in the course of centuries urban civilisation had tried to establish itself on this inhospitable soil, but not a single embryonic city survived for more than three generations before a nomadic incursion levelled it to the ground; and Algeria's only historical memorials are the traces of perpetually changing alien rule. Its French colonisers had no organised force to contend with, except the wild and anarchic resistance of its mountain and desert tribes to any kind of rule or any kind of state order, and in thirty years of military operations this resistance, together with the tribal organisation itself, was broken by ruthless and purely military means.

"Do you see the ripple in the sea when the bird touches it with its wing-tips? That is what your expedition to Africa amounts to," the Arab tribal leaders wrote to General Lamoricière after the defeat of Abd-el-Kader, and history seemed to show that they were right; that is what every previous conquest of Algeria had amounted to. But the French colonisers started ploughing up this country and organising it by Roman methods, the only methods which were applicable here. They set about their task by annexing territory and progressively incorporating it into the home country. The settlement of ex-soldiers on the land was organised by the state, and French towns and villages were built which looked as if they had been lifted bodily from France; and the domains of rebellious tribes and "ownerless" land, that is to say, land which was not in private possession as understood by French law, was confiscated, reclaimed, and distributed. One half of the fertile land in Algeria is land reclaimed from salt waste, steppe, and bare heathland now cultivated by the French. It was the economic conquest which followed the military conquest that turned Algeria into a part of France.

When the policy of assimilation was introduced in 1865 it could really be said to start with a *tabula rasa*. There were no relics of a past for Algerian national consciousness to cling to, and the only conceivable future for the country seemed to be complete absorption by France. True, nowhere else do Europe and the east seem to have mingled so successfully. But the mixture led to no synthesis. France established herself in Algeria, but the great mass of the indigenous population remained outside her schools, her system of justice, her democratic institutions, in the tragic position of a people whose status in their own country was something like that of homeless aliens. They were neither "subjects", a status unknown to French law, nor "citizens" in the full sense of the word. Their language was officially a foreign language, and their religion was officially a sect; they constituted an "inner proletariat" in the full sense in which Toynbee uses the term; they were as much aliens on the outskirts of the French towns in Algeria as in the proletarian outskirts of Paris, Lyons, and St. Etienne.

Many reasons can be produced to account for this failure, and at first sight the most important seems to be the abyss which divides the Arab standard of living from that of the European. But in Algeria there is a European proletariat and a prosperous Arab bourgeoisie; the demarcation does not follow this line. To talk of a racial barrier is more meaningless in North Africa than elsewhere—the "Arabised" Berbers of North Africa are not "coloured", but "white"—and there has never been any talk of segregation. The only barrier, and it is an insuperable one, is Islam. Post-revolutionary France inherited, not only whole colonies, but a whole tradition of Catholic missionary zeal. Like the Church, France recognises no racial barriers, but only barriers of faith superable by individual decision. The French state has only secularised this tradition by substituting for religion the "transition to civilisation", or, in legal terms, the production of evidence of education which leads to the granting of civil rights. But in practice the barrier remained insuperable. In North Africa there is no colour bar and no racial discrimination, but something fundamentally different, which forbids comparison with other territories with mixed populations, namely the clash of two civilisations which make the same universal claims and possess the same pride and the same coherence. To avoid a further error, let us repeat that we are confronted here with a clash of two civilisations rather than of two religions. The colonial policy of the French republic is completely secular, and it has avoided any attempt at religious conversion. True, Islam is a religion, but it is much more than that; it is a granite block on which Europeanisation beats as ineffectively as does Christianisation.

It has become a commonplace to talk of modern totalitarianism as a twentieth-century version of Islam. There are many objections to making a comparison between the two—chiefly from the point of view of Islam—but, if the phrase has any validity, it ought to be put the other way about; Islam is a totalitarianism that has grown old and has become ossified. The word "Islam" means "submission", not just to a religious faith, but to a total religious, political, legal, and social system which includes and regulates all fields of behaviour. There is a radical simplicity about the Muslim faith, which is a severely rational monotheism abstracted from Judaism and Christianity, but divested of their mysteries, and can be summed up in the statement that "God is God"; and there is a similar simplicity about Muslim practice, which can be summed up in a few rites and precepts. This gives it an irresistible appeal to people who are at a stage of development more or less corresponding to that of Arabia in the time of the Prophet. The conversion of all Africa to Islam is an entirely plausible prospect. But the practice of Islam means being drawn into a social system which acknowledges no community outside the religious community of Islam, no law outside the Koran and the Sunna, no truth other than that revealed by the Prophet, and no wisdom other than the exposition of that truth. True, every religion is in a sense a "totalitarian system", but what has set Islam apart since its first foundation has been its obstinate negation of all difference between the worldly and the spiritual—between religious and secular authority, between spiritual and worldly law, between physics and metaphysics. The realm of the Prophet was completely "of this world"; he was founder of a political religion, prophet, chief of state, and conqueror in one.

Arab colonisation was as total and enduring as no other has been before or since; not because it was particularly terrible or intolerant—on the contrary, from the first it practised a supremely contemptuous tolerance of all who remained outside the fold in the ghettoes and the Christian quarters, an attitude that was more effective than any persecution or proselytising zeal. Its secret was its monolithic nature. But the factor which gave this political religion or religious imperialism its strength and greatness turned out also to be its weakness. The society that it created and the law that it laid down were final and unalterable, and that finality and unalterability extended to every field of mental and material, political, and private life. The heyday of Arab civilisation and learning in the High Middle Ages as exemplified at its chief centres, Baghdad and Cordoba, in comparison with which contemporary Europe lay in deepest barbarism, ended with the rapidity of a firework display; the display was the rain of sparks which accompanied the forging of the oldest cultural centres of the Mediterranean into the Islamic block, and it ceased when the raw material was exhausted. Since the fourteenth century Arab civilisation—these very summary remarks apply only to the western branch of Islam, in which religious conquest and Arab colonisation coincided —has produced nothing creative in the fields of art, philosophy, science, or politics, and has produced no personalities, either individual or national, other than war leaders, despots, and imams. Just as Arab art became ossified in arabesque, so did literary Arabic become ossified in the style of the Koran, a language of prayer and learning as unintelligible to the Arab people as Latin is to the Latin peoples. Jurisprudence and philology remained the only branches of knowledge taught at Arab universities; they were taught as subjects auxiliary to theology, for the purpose of expounding the Koran.

The most impressive symptom of this ossification has been the failure of the Arab empire and its successors ever to produce a political constitution. They never advanced beyond trying to rule a huge empire with the institutions and forms of organisation of the tribe Koreish with which Mahomet and his companions set out from southern Arabia to conquer the world. The powers that the Prophet and his immediate followers united in their own person as simultaneous head of state, war leader, prayer leader, religious, political, and civil lawgiver and judge were never separated, or at most in circumstances which made separation temporarily necessary. Not one of the Arab dynasties which inherited the empire when it split ever succeeded in creating a binding law of succession; state power remained the prerogative of the family of the Prophet, the tribe Koreish, to which every Arab ruler or band leader still has his ancestry traced back, governed by the same law of collective inheritance that prevailed in the pasture lands. The system is regulated in practice by the right of the stronger—"despotism modified by assassination" in fact. Through thirteen centuries the Islamic group, whether we meet it in the form of a state, a church, a tribe, brotherhood, a group of Mahdi warriors, or a political party, has remained basically unchanged; it consists of a leader and his followers of the faithful. It is hopelessly misleading to apply to the Muslim world ideas taken from another historical world, such as "state", "nation", "democracy", "monarchy", or "feudalism". One might imagine that this form of religious-political organisation would be inevitably condemned to anarchy and self-destruction; its immense durability in fact depends on its capacity to re-arise phoenix-like from the ashes of every destruction and defeat, whether in a valley in the Atlas mountains or in a hut settlement on the outskirts of Paris. Moreover, there is another factor in this durability which should not be forgotten: namely the women, who remain veiled, ignorant, submissive, and segregated from public life. In spite of all revolutionary changes in the outside world, the Arab woman, and therefore the Arab family, is preserved from infection by modern life, and every new generation is therefore born and brought up in the same unchanging tradition.

Is there an Arab renaissance at the present day? It has become obvious and familiar to every newspaper reader that the Arab world, the weight of its numbers, and above all its geographical position at the meeting-point of three continents, have become an important factor in international affairs. But that is a purely external matter. It is also obvious that for a century western technique, western schools, and western political intervention have been slowly eating away and undermining this ossified civilisation. But on closer observation it turns out that the surface has barely been scratched. A tremendous social and religious revolution took place in Turkey, but it remained for more than thirty years an isolated phenomenon in the Muslim world, and anathema to the spokesmen of the pan-Arab idea. But Turkey is not an Arab country. Leaving aside the special case of Turkey, the convulsions by which the Muslim world is agitated are more like those of an organism trying to rid itself of an alien body, "the western poison" which has gained an entry to it, with all the attendant symptoms of xenophobia, religious fanaticism, and reactionary traditionalism—all of them at bottom variations on the "holy war" theme.

The fever which in recent times has been increasingly affecting the Arab countries is commonly called nationalism. That is another word which has been transplanted unthinkingly from a completely alien world of ideas. Outside Arabia there is no Arab people, but only an Arab civilisation, to which nothing is more alien than the concept of "nation". Islam is supra-national and universal, and Arab colonisation totally extinguished the individuality of the nations which it overran. What is called Arab nationalism has thus generally been, not the expression of national feeling, of loyalty to a nation, but of loyalty to Arab civilisation and Islam, and its content has been, not national emancipation, but revolt against the west. This revolt happens to have been taking place in several distinct national territories, but is nevertheless deeply unified. It is new in name, but not in substance. One of the most promising phenomena of recent times is that there are signs in the Middle East that the era of the pan-Islamic dervishes may be followed by an era of internal reform on the Kemal Ataturk pattern in Turkey, which is Muslim, it is true, but is no more Arab than Persia, Pakistan, or Indonesia. But the scales are still hesitating between a self-renewal, which is terribly difficult for Islam, and the always tempting "holy war".

In French North Africa opposition to French predominance is present in every form and variety, from the atavistic fanaticism which can always easily be set alight to nationalism of a modern kind, generally of Young Turk inspiration. One looks forward, and the other back; one looks spiritually towards Cairo, the other towards the west. Movements like the Party of the Algerian Manifesto and the Neo-Destourian movement in Tunis show that here an *élite* has passed through the schools of French political thought. For one of the paradoxes of the French empire is that practically all the anti-colonial emancipation movements have their roots in

Paris. The Algerian People's Party of Messali Hadj was founded in Paris after the first world war as the Étoile Nord-Africaine, and its greatest strength is still among the Algerian workers in France. The Moroccan Istiqlal was founded with a manifesto issued by Moroccan students in Paris. The Party of the Algerian Manifesto and the Neo-Destour are supported in both countries by a Europeanised educated class thoroughly impregnated with the French spirit, which, as it says itself, "has taken the French school books seriously." That is a feature common to all parts of the French empire. Communism was exported to Indo-China, not from Moscow, but from Paris, and Ho Chi-minh served his apprenticeship as a political agitator in Paris, the incubator of all rebellious ideas. Hence the phenomenon, astonishing at first sight, that the most radical advocates of independence in the French empire continually emphasise their love of France—not the France represented overseas by French Residents and governors-general, but the France of "the ideas of 1789".

No greater mistake could be made than to regard this as insincere. In spite of all the differences in the situation, the political debate between the settlers and the indigenous population is to an astonishing extent a replica, in style, terminology, and mental attitude, of that between the "two Frances" at home, with the settlers playing the part of the conservative right and the indigenous nationalists that of the radical left. The resemblance is so close that the superficial observer is in continual danger of forgetting that he is not in Europe. Apart from the aged Abd-el-Krim, the hero of the Riff war, whose experiences and thinking stopped still at the holy war stage, none of the North African leaders has got on well with the pan-Arab and pan-Islamic leaders in Cairo; in the society of these dancing dervishes and cynical pashas a Habib Bomguiba and even a Messali Hadj, the Algerian prophet, feel much too European.

If one speaks of the French policy of assimilation in North Africa as having failed, that does not mean that it has not had its successes. But these have been of a kind different from those expected by the ideologists. For France lives in the hearts of those who rebel against her. Perhaps for that very reason France is equipped to be the great intermediary between Europe and Islam, just because her own civilisation possesses unmistakable affinities with the rigidly logical and abstract structure of Muslim civilisation. Indeed, common possession of so many elements both of greatness and weakness intensifies, not only the fruitfulness, but the sharpness of the clash between them. There is an element of tragedy in the Franco-Arab conflict that is completely absent from the difficulties experienced by the British in the Near East: an element of disappointed love. The Arabs of North Africa will never be Frenchmen—that great dream is over. "The time has passed when an Algerian Muslim wanted to be anything but an Algerian Muslim," Ferhat Abbas wrote in the Algerian Manifesto which he submitted in the name of the notables of Algeria on February 10th, 1943, in the midst of the political confusion that followed the allied landing, to the representatives of France, Britain, the United States, and the Soviet Union in order "purely and simply to demand the recognition of the Algerian nation". But the personality of Ferhat Abbas forbids one to smile at the dream, which was dreamed not only by French ideologists; and there is an undertone of regret at disappointed hopes in the Algerian Manifesto. For it is not very long ago since a North African *élite* regarded fulfilment of the dream as tangibly near.

During the second Constituent Assembly's debate on the colonies, the debate from which we have already quoted the tragi-comic contribution of the Algerian deputy Saadane, M. Maurice Viollette, a Radical veteran who was Governor-General of Algeria during the Popular Front period, said: "I am one of those who tried to carry out the policy of assimilation in that country. I remain faithful to it. . . . I believed that it would be possible by successive great surges through the lock-gates to integrate into the French unity the whole of the population that I saw suffering and often despairing all about me, and that France would thus become the greatest Mohammedan Power in the world. It was a great dream that I nourished, and it seemed to me to be not unworthy of my country to desire that from the North Sea to the Congo only a single heart should beat for France; it was a policy which carried me away. Romanticism, one may say. . . ."

It sounded tired and resigned, like an obituary notice. M.

Viollette was the originator of the reform project, still known under his name, which was laid before the Chamber by the Blum Government in 1937. It proposed the granting of civil rights to about 30,000 Algerians, soldiers of the first world war, officials, teachers, and those who had completed a school education, and its "revolutionary" feature was that it did not demand a transition from Koranic to European civil law in advance of the grant of civil rights. At that time, only six years before the Algerian Manifesto, Ferhat Abbas wrote another profession of faith which became famous: *La France, c'est moi.*

"If I had discovered an 'Algerian nation,'" he wrote, "I should have become a nationalist, and should not have blushed for it. . . . I did not find it. I consulted history, the living and the dead, I visited the cemeteries; and no answer came. . . . You cannot build on air. We have driven away the clouds and chimeras in order once and for all to bind our future to the French work of construction in this country. Six million Muslims live on this soil which has been French for a hundred years; they live in hovels, go barefoot, without clothing and often without bread. Out of this hungry mass we shall make a modern society . . . elevate them to human dignity, so that they may be worthy of the name of Frenchmen . . ."

The Viollette plan, which nourished these dreams, failed, like so many earlier plans, because of the bitter resistance of the French settlers, who feared that this first great "surge through the lock-gates" would open a breach which would submerge them, a privileged minority of barely a million citizens, in a rapidly mounting flood of indigenous Algerians, who today number nearly nine million. A general strike of Algerian mayors and the opposition of all who "reproach us for having taken their school books seriously", as Ferhat Abbas then said, forced the "crazy Paris ideologists" quietly to bury the project.

The reforms and the granting of civil rights carried out in Algeria six years later by the Free French Government of de Gaulle were substantially those of the Blum-Viollette project. But this belated and limited gesture now roused no echo; in the interval the Algerian intellectuals had discovered the

"Algerian nation". Opportunities during which generosity can be rewarding are sometimes short-lived, and French colonial history so often appears to have been a series of such missed opportunities. Algerian "nationalism" is based on the simple and self-evident desire of a people who, in spite of all hopes and promises, have remained outside the one and indivisible republic to be given at any rate a home in their own country.

The Algerian statute, which came into force in 1947 and for the first time recognised the "territorial unity" of the three Algerian departments and gave them administrative autonomy and a parliament of their own with very restricted powers, went half-way to meeting this demand. It bears all the marks of compromise, and is remote from fulfilling the revolutionary promises of the first Constituent Assembly. Its most obvious and most controversial characteristic is that, in spite of a general grant of civil rights to all the inhabitants of Algeria, it preserves the demarcation line between "old" citizens and "new". Europeans and assimilated Algerians are in one category and those who previously did not possess citizenship are in another. They vote in separate electoral colleges, and, though the second category outnumbers the first by eight to one, both send the same number of representatives to the Algerian, and for that matter to the French, Parliament. That this division between the two categories is not a mere arbitrary disadvantage imposed on the majority is shown by the fact, for instance, that votes for women were granted in the second electoral college just as naturally as they were in the first, though in the second the privilege is not taken advantage of, and no indigenous politician has ever suggested that votes for women should be granted to women living under the Koranic law. The Algerian constitution did not grant universal equal suffrage, but it was aimed at creating a new equilibrium and at giving the indigenous population a voice in affairs without introducing a sudden reversal of power relationships which would have been dangerous for the future development of Algeria; and it succeeded at any rate in introducing a period of internal quiet and diminished tension. But the fundamental conflict arising from the existence of two Algerias, one a Mohammedan country and the other an area of European settlement, cannot be done away with by constitutional decision. It could be modified and made fruitful only by constructive collaboration between the two.

Neither autonomy nor independence offer an answer to the vital question for this country, which is how an Arab population is to live in harmony with a compact, hundred-year-old settlement of Europeans who have long since felt themselves to be Algerians—and have often felt themselves to be the only true Algerians, just as the Afrikaners feel themselves to be the only true South Africans. Only the crazy imagination of the "holy war" dervishes could play with the idea of "throwing the Europeans of Algeria into the sea". That the appeals to the religious fanaticism of the largely illiterate and *déclassé* mass of electors of the second electoral college indulged in by the extremist Algerian People's Party of the wandering prophet Messali Hadj should for the time being fall on more fertile soil than the more complicated ideas of the Party of the Algerian Manifesto is as natural in such a population structure as are the blind outbursts of fear and hatred indulged in by the European settlers. On the one side the inferiority complex is numerical, on the other it is political and moral. The experiment of Algerian "colonial democracy" can be understood only in that light.

The first effect of the proclamation of the Algerian constitution was a wave of extremism in both electoral bodies. Algerian local elections were held a few weeks later, and in the "European" college the Gaullist Rally, under whose banner were united all those who were opposed to indigenous aspirations, from officials anxious about their posts to the big landowning and mining interests, won all along the line. In the other college the more moderate Party of the Algerian Manifesto, whose aims were directed more to practical reforms than to the stimulation of hatred and fanaticism, was completely swept away by the extremist and terrorist Algerian People's Party of Messali Hadj, though a year previously it had won 70 per cent. of the votes. An Algerian parliament elected on this basis would have been an arena of wild and sterile fanaticism; tumult and agitation could have been expected from it, but neither useful work nor a relaxation of political tension. The French Ministry of the Interior and the Governor-General of Algeria whom it selected for this purpose extricated themselves from the quandary in a not very elegant but hardly avoidable manner. The Algerian parliamentary election of 1948—and to a scarcely less degree the partial elections of 1951—were shamelessly rigged, and, except in the big towns and larger centres where public opinion acted as a check to secure honest elections, the representatives elected to the second college and sent to the Algerian Assembly were nearly all official candidates—"yes men", as they are called locally. The result is a parliament in which the representatives of the first college fight the settlers' cause with great energy, while the cause of the mass of the indigenous population is represented, with the exception of a handful of nationalist deputies, by docile creatures of the Government, a great many of whom are of very mediocre quality.

The argument of the responsible French authorities, when they talk frankly, can be summed up somewhat as follows: Universal suffrage, which often works havoc even in old-established democracies, in Algeria would be an infernal machine which would blow up everything if it were not carefully manipulated. The Algerian people are ignorant and immature, and there is no limit to their capacity to be led astray. Leaving the fate of Algeria to their moods and impulses would mean handing it over to the most uninhibited demagogues and dervishes. The people do not know what is good for them; they must be led by the hand, like children. The elections are not an act of self-determination, but of political education; in going to the polls the voter is slowly learning to understand problems about which his descendants will one day be able to make up their minds freely for themselves. He is learning to make the fundamental gestures of democracy; but he must be told how to fill in his voting paper, and, if he chooses wrong in spite of that, we must be able to correct the results.

As it is difficult in the face of world public opinion to state this argument publicly, the political atmosphere of Algeria is heavy with hypocrisy.

But is the argument wholly false? It is the argument of

enlightened absolutism, which was everywhere the necessary prelude to democracy. The question is whether the emphasis is on "enlightened" or on "absolutism". The task of government in Algeria is the reconciliation of the irreconcilable, and the new institutions which have arisen there since the end of the war reflect the whole paradoxical nature of a situation for which there is no general solution; there are only endless conflicts which have continually to be bridged. The Algerian parliament is a step towards the autonomy which has been alternately or unitedly demanded by the Algerian nationalists and the European settlers, but for conflicting reasons; the representation of both sections of the Algerian population is an expression of the policy of assimilation, which has been described as dead but continues nevertheless to be pursued, and of the centralism which transformed Algeria into three departments of the one and indivisible republic. The Assembly of the French Union at Versailles is an embryonic central parliament of the French "Commonwealth" which at the end of the war was the great dream of the French colonial reformers and has remained a dream to the present day. In other words we are confronted with three institutions which are fundamentally irreconcilable and project into the future three different and irreconcilable solutions of the colonial problem; and yet each is a balancing factor and a contribution to the great and complicated experiment which is going forward in North Africa.

The most promising feature of the situation is that a search for a solution has now begun on the Algerian side. The ideas, manifestos, and proposals for reform of the leader of the Party of the Algerian Manifesto are the product of real political thought which is not satisfied with sterile hatred and historical complaints against imperialism, but accepts the historical events of the last hundred years as irrevocable. From there it goes on to devise ways and means by which Algerians, who, as a consequence of the existing situation "are at home neither in France nor in Algeria", can be given a national life of their own. The pattern to be followed is not a return to the Middle Ages as advocated by the Arab League, but the Turkey of Kemal Ataturk, whose picture is to be seen in every office of the Union of the Algerian Manifesto.

This is a sign of a new awareness that the Muslim population of Algeria must be emancipated, not just from European domination or European influence, but from their own past, though it must never be a repudiation of that past.

The revolution that is taking place is not apparent in any election statistics; its progress is slow and molecular. The meeting of civilisations takes place, not only at the *élite* level at which the educated, Europeanised, higher classes in North Africa come into contact with French orientalists, but at a less respectable but more momentous level, that of the lowest level of the fluctuating proletariat. Hundreds of thousands of Algerian workers have lived for a longer or shorter time in France, and thousands have married Frenchwomen—even Messali Hadj, the prophet of Algerian nationalism, has a French wife; and similar mixed marriages are to be met with everywhere in the politically leading indigenous section of North Africa. A growing number of young Algerian men, and, what is perhaps more important, young Algerian women, have been born and grown up in France, and have come into hopeless conflict with the archaic forms of Islamic family life.

This mingling of civilisations generally takes place in very unpleasing conditions, in the Arab quarters of Paris, Lyons, and St. Etienne; and the fact that the Algerian proletariat in France was the point of departure and still provides the mass basis of Algerian nationalism shows the double-edged nature of the process which is at work. But we are still at the beginning of a drama which a few decades ago began to affect the small educated *élite* of Algeria and is now extending to broader and broader levels of the Muslim population. After a century of colonisation there began a contest between western civilisation and Islam in which, if it is to be fruitful, there must be neither victors nor vanquished. Only harm can come of overlooking this greater problem in the stress of immediate current problems, and of trying to force quick, ready-made solutions.

It is less in the political than in the economic sphere that French colonisation in Algeria has landed itself in a deadend which must eventually result in the stagnation of its civilising influence, the slow poisoning of its political and even human atmosphere, and the decay of the central bastion of the empire itself. A century of the *pax franca*, of orderly administration, of opening up of communications, and of laying the foundations of hygiene and medical care which French civilisation has taken wherever it has gone, has broken down the barriers which nomadic raids, tribal feuds, epidemics, and famine had previously set to the uninhibited fertility which is the law of all oriental peoples. This country, which in 1870, when the military conquest was completed, had little more than two million inhabitants, now has ten millions, with a yearly excess of births over deaths of between 150,000 and 200,000. The drama of all European colonisation has been that it brought into being a number of mouths that demanded to be fed that far exceeded the number of jobs, the amount of housing, and the opportunities for prosperity that it provided, and we shall come across another illustration of this later in the notorious *bidonvilles*, the petrol-tin towns of Morocco. But the increase in population in Algeria, unlike Morocco, is taking place in an area where the colonial system is of the Colbert type, which has no answer to it. This system reproduces on African soil the economic structure and economic mentality of the home country in the greatest and most absurd detail, and since the first world war it has stood still at that point. The pitiful, squalid dwellings made of rags and boards which cling to the slopes of the Kasbah and the edges of the big Algerian towns are not the emergency housing of a rising industrial proletariat, the hideous excrescences characteristic of every incipient industrial revolution, such as are the petrol-tin towns of Morocco; they are the chance dumping-grounds of a hopeless and timeless destitution.

The *bidonvilles* of Algeria are not in Algeria, but in France. The fluctuating mass of Algerians who seek work in French agriculture and industry now exceeds 300,000. In 1951 alone 150,000 Algerians entered France and 100,000 returned to Algeria, and the great majority of this wandering mass of seekers for work and a decent life, most of whom lack the slightest training or qualification, are reduced to casual labour or the lowest forms of employment. In present-day France they constitute a sub-proletariat which in the big towns has created a special problem of "North African crime". This Algerian emigration acts as a safety-valve which diminishes the risk of an explosion resulting from the pressure of Algerian population, but it is no solution; and the social and moral plague of this sub-proletariat is the price paid for the economic annexation which has brought Algeria completely into the closed, protectionist French economic circulatory system.

The European settlers have organised Algeria and made it sufficiently fertile for their purpose, and since the turn of the century the flow of new settlers from the home country has practically dried up. Algeria has practically no industry or preconditions for industry, and even the industrial working up of agricultural products is still in an embryonic stage. In the last ten years, during which there has been so much talk of the industrialisation of Algeria, about 20,000 new jobs have been created altogether. Its economy meets, or rather exceeds, the needs of the home country and its own stabilised European population, and the marketing of Algerian agricultural produce has become a practically insoluble problem; but it does not meet the needs of the growing Algerian population. So little do the needs of the latter—the greater part of whom vegetate on the borderline of destitution and have no purchasing power—weigh in the scales that settlers surrounded by this chronically undernourished mass grow wine, wine, and still more wine, the cultivation of which offers welcome opportunities of work to Algerians who as Muslims would not be allowed to touch the wine thus produced even if they could afford to.

It is the same old vicious circle of stagnating production and a stagnating market. In the past ten years tremendous plans for development have been worked out, such as the Shott-esh-Shergi project, which would use the subterranean lakes of the central Algerian salt waste to water the department of Oran. Beginnings have been made with such projects, but they have invariably been dropped again, and it is hard to see where the necessary drive and resources will come from. The drive will certainly not be provided by the present Algerian settlers; and, as for the industrialisation of Africa which M. Schuman, in announcing his plan for the European Coal and Steel Community, mentioned as an all-European task, interests on both sides of the Mediterranean have since drawn a thick veil of silence over it. Let sleeping dogs lie....

The things that it has been possible to do in the absence of a tremendous capital investment policy have in the course of a century mostly been done, and the principal beneficiaries, the European settlers, have a tendency to be content with that and to rest on their laurels. Thus colonisation in its most advanced positions is today in retreat. On the other hand indigenous farming is gradually taking to European methods. The administration, in spite of the slender resources at its disposal, is actively helping in this with its network of agricultural modernisation centres. In other words, indigenous agriculture is slowly advancing, and in this molecular process in agriculture, as in administration and politics, the Algerians are carrying out a gradual reconquest of the country. The areas where this is taking place, particularly in the western part of the country, where an Arab middle class and peasantry has partly maintained itself and partly built itself up anew, are strongholds of the Arab reformist movement, the Party of the Algerian Manifesto. The greatest hope of this unhappy people, which in the whole course of its history has been bandied about between one overlord and another, lies in this slow and laborious development of a modern Algerian *élite*. But without help from outside their road will be long and bitter, and today they have a right to feel that the world has left them in the lurch.

§ 6

THE ADMINISTRATION AND THE PROTECTORATES

THE problems of the two North African protectorates which flank the central bastion to east and west are apparently quite different from those of Algeria.

Here are two states which have preserved their individuality, their hereditary state form, and awareness of their own history. In Morocco and Tunisia nationalism was presented with a framework and a programme in advance. Here are two ancient monarchies on which a French protectorate has been imposed for some generations which want their independence back. In comparison with Algerian nationalism, which had a difficult search for a definition of itself if it was to avoid running headlong into a dead-end, the nationalist movements in Morocco and Tunisia had an inestimable advantage. They had a living past to build on instead of having to start from scratch. They were spared a new beginning, and their activities have been directed backwards towards a restoration of the pre-colonial period. But a similar framework contains very different things. Between the colonisation of Tunisia and that of Morocco there lay the difference of a generation —and between the spirit of nationalism in the two territories there is a difference of centuries.

It was the good fortune of France and of Morocco that the exercise of the protectorate over the former was for the first fifteen years in the hands of one of the greatest colonisers of modern history, who understood, loved, and admired this country and its people, and made it his aim to turn it into a modern nation while fully preserving its characteristics and traditions. On the one hand he demonstrated a brilliant flair for publicity in launching Morocco as a new country and promoting capital investment in it, and on the other he demonstrated a conservative zeal for the preservation of its state and religious institutions, its towns, its antiquities, and its natural wealth. The opening up and exploitation of the Moroccan phosphate mines, which gave the country its first big industry, and their nationalisation for the benefit of the Moroccan state, which was thereby put on a sound financial footing, bore witness to a far more vigilant concern for the country's interests than had been shown by any sovereign ruler in the Middle East at that time. The "spirit of Lyautey", which is still invoked by the Moroccan nationalists in their polemics against present French practice, was a strange mixture of extreme modernism and the colonising spirit of the *ancien régime*, which regarded colonisation, not as a business and not just as a matter of prestige, but as a mission.

Few of Lyautey's successors at the Rabat Residency have possessed the same spirit, though all of them have zealously invoked it. French suzerainty over the Sherifate as Lyautey conceived it had a glamorous quality of chivalry and feudal loyalty, which fitted in well with the character of Morocco, but badly, as can be imagined, with the spirit of the plebeian republic, and worse with the type of hard and unscrupulous money-seekers who were irresistibly attracted by the North African "California" which was now opened up. Since the French settlers in Morocco succeeded in enforcing the departure in 1947 of M. Eirik Labonne, the last Resident-General in the Lyautey style, and the substitution for the latter of the "strong first" and barrack-square style of Marshal Juin, the memory of Lyautey has been rather unpopular in the Rabat Residency. On August 20th, 1953, French tanks surrounded the palace of the Sultan Sidi Mohammed ben Youssef, the Commander of the Faithful, and he was unceremoniously bundled off to Corsica in a transport aircraft. This put a full-stop to the policy under which the protectorate had been founded. On the heights of the Residency the "spirit of Lyautey", if it is invoked at all, has become an empty phrase, and in the hum of business activity in the mushroom cities of Algeria nothing whatever is known about it.

But all this is not the whole of Morocco. The political crisis affects only the surface of a country which is still in a state of rapid economic development and social transformation, and in which those engaged in constructive work are still in the ascendant. In this rough and inhospitable country the proud, simple people of the mountains demand respect and reply with respect, and here the last Arab theocracy persisted into the twentieth century "in a state of glory", completely isolated from the outside world—until a few decades ago it was brought sharply and unpreparedly into contact with the modern world; and in Morocco the word "colonisation" still retains the meaning and resonance that it had in olden times and at the beginning of modern times. It calls for pioneers and missionaries, and this type of humanity is sufficiently represented in the outposts and outlying districts of the protectorate to set the tone.

Here all the traditional pictures of the "paternal colonisation" picture book still correspond with the truth. A French officer, alone with a few men in the steppes of the Atlas representing the *pax franca* over a huge area, drinking tea with the village *caid,* spending the night in his tent, is accepted as the mouthpiece of wisdom, justice, and peace; the teacher of the newly opened school in the *bled* has to go out in search of pupils, and has to convince their elders of the usefulness of learning; the worldly missionaries of the agricultural modernisation stations draw up contracts with individual families and whole tribes, see to the digging of wells, the distribution of seed and animals for stock, and above all persuade the Moroccan peasants by practical example of the advantages of regular sowing in furrows, of proper manuring, and the choice of the most suitable seed. Colonial outposts become centres of social life, schools, kindergartens, hospitals, and the source of help and advice in all situations in life; the doctors and nurses placed in strategic positions in dispensaries and hospitals round an old Arab quarter, where everything has to be taught and demonstrated—how to cook a baby's food, put on its napkins, and keep it clean, instead of leaving it sewed up in its rags for days and weeks on end. . . .

All these are aspects of a process of colonisation which is still young, has a missionary drive behind it, and has not yet had a chance to start growing old and stale behind closed doors. French prestige in Morocco still depends on these things. But slowly it is beginning to be overlain by something else.

There is a characteristic of this protectorate which its officials are less willing to expose to the eyes of a foreign observer: the living conditions of the new Moroccan proletariat, the first generation of which has gathered in the overcrowded Medinas and *bidonvilles* on the outskirts of the industrial and commercial towns. On the other hand they are the first thing which the propagandists of Moroccan nationalism hasten to show to foreign visitors, and that is why the dominant impression of the Moroccan protectorate taken away by so many tourists and journalists is of these "blots on civilisation". The minimum programme of the conducted tour through this inferno on which the local agents of the Istiqlal conduct every reporter sent from Paris or New York includes the two huge "petrol-tin towns" of Casablanca, Ben M'Sik, and Carrières Centrales. Each of these contains about fifty thousand inhabitants, and the rectangular streets, the whitewashed wooden huts, shops, and mosques roofed with sheet metal, and the guard-houses situated at frequent intervals, are as terrifying as a concentration or displaced persons' camp. The next stage in the pilgrimage is the smaller, more colourful, and more improvised hut settlement of Bochka, the provocative nature of which depends on its situation in a deserted quarry at the edge of one of the best quarters of Casablanca, immediately adjoining a big, almost luxurious, dog-breeding establishment. "A palace for dogs and stables for men, that is colonialism!" the guide remarks.

The contrast is indeed shattering; it would be equally shattering in the Paris *zone,* the *borghate* on the outskirts of Italian towns, the slums in western industrial countries, which are far more hopeless and inhuman, to say nothing of the poor quarters in the Middle East, through which conducted tours for foreigners are unfortunately not organised. Here, on the periphery of the new Moroccan industrial towns, we see a repetition of the picture presented by the rapid growth of towns in Europe in the nineteenth century, and more recently in the Americas, where it exists in some places still. But in Morocco the contrast between two worlds and two ages increases the effect to demagogic explosive point. It is, after all, fundamentally just as natural for European settlers, industrialists, business men and officials to bring with them to this new country their European living habits, often grossly exaggerated on a "colonial" scale, as it is for the newcomers streaming in from the Atlas, the high plateau, and the oases to transplant their straw and clay dwellings and tents to their new homes.

The problem is neither of a political or even of a town-planning nature; throughout the east it is the same. In 1910, before the setting up of the protectorate, Morocco was able to provide a bare living for about three million inhabitants, and drought, famine, epidemics, high infant mortality, and perpetual feudal and tribal wars saw to it the population was kept stable, or was periodically "corrected". The security guaranteed by the protectorate and the pacification of the country, which was completed in 1934; the successful campaign against epidemics, which since the end of the thirties have disappeared; the importation of food in the years of harvest failure which recur from time to time because of the variations in the Moroccan rainfall; the reclamation of land; and the process of industrialisation have combined to burst the dam. Today Morocco numbers nine million inhabitants, and with every day that dawns there are five hundred more who require food, clothing, and housing. Rapid as the economic development of Morocco has been in the last thirty years, it has not kept pace with this population flood.

The Istiqlal claim that the Moroccans' land was taken away is simply not true; the million acres of European-owned land is concentrated around Meknès and the Atlantic coastline from Casablanca to Rabat, and before 1912 it was bare, treeless, and sterile. Between the two wars the area cultivated by Moroccans increased between from five to twelve-and-a-half million acres, and an irrigation project now in hand will make fertile new land sufficient for about eight hundred thousand Moroccan families. But one of the incalculable freaks of the Moroccan climate, a drought such as that of 1945, is sufficient to cause havoc among the pastures and fields cultivated by the primitive, archaic methods of the indigenous inhabitants of the Moroccan hinterland, and to send the surplus population of the worst-hit areas streaming into the towns; for the opening up of the country's communications permits them this way out of what in former times would have meant irremediable catastrophe. Whole families, whole villages, pledge their land and migrate to the industrial towns and the ports to eke out some sort of a living as miners, harbour workers, porters, bootblacks, street traders, or beggars, to tide themselves over the emergency and keep themselves alive until the next harvest, always hoping one day to be able to redeem their land. In fact thousands of millions of francs saved from wages earned in the *bidonvilles* of the north flow yearly into the mountain villages and oases of south and east Morocco. A sedentary Moroccan proletariat is only slowly beginning to emerge. The backbone of the population of the "shanty towns" still consists of simple, frugal peasants' and shepherds' sons, men of few needs, who want nothing from the towns but some quickly earned money with which to return to their villages; and they feel far happier in the huts at the outskirts of the town, where they live together in a tribal manner, than they would in the stuffy Arab quarter.

No town-planning policy has been able to cope with the spasmodic, seasonal influx which overwhelms every European settlement, even places like Port Lyautey, where no trace of an Arab settlement existed before. In all these places a fivefold number of Moroccan migrants gathers immediately. As soon as the old Medina at Casablanca became filled to overflowing, a new Medina immediately formed. After the end of the second world war a much too small, too ambitious, and too expensive Arab model settlement was built which offered homes to one hundred and sixty thousand Moroccans, not including about ten thousand Arabs scattered about the European quarter. But since 1912 the population of Casablanca has grown from twenty to nearly six hundred thousand. This desperate situation is repeated everywhere, and the biggest criticism that can fairly be levelled at the French administration is that it started trying to cope with the situation very late, not until after the second world war, after a flood of hostile criticism had descended upon the French protectorate.

But it has begun to cope with it. Since the end of the war the number of Moroccan children who attend French-Moroccan schools has increased in geometrical progression—between 1944 and 1953 it grew from 33,000 to 190,000. In 1953 two new classes were being opened daily, and one new school was being opened every three days. The pace of this development is not limited by lack of school buildings and is no longer hampered by lack of funds, but by the shortage of teachers, who have to be trained. This is another field in which everything had to be created out of nothing; the only schools in this country were mediaeval Koran schools, in which groups of children of all ages were taught, not to read and write, but to chant the Koran in chorus. Progress has been made by leaps and bounds; and yet, with a yearly surplus of births of between 150,000 and 200,000, it remains a drop in the ocean. Only the medical service, which covers the remotest corners of the country with its system of hospitals and dispensaries, can be said to be reasonably adequate, at any rate in the material respect.

But those who keep their eyes open, not only to what is still lacking, but to what is being done, will not rate the French colonising work in Morocco lightly; at any rate it has nothing to fear from a comparison with the conditions prevalent in the sovereign states of the Arab League. Even the jerrycan towns of Morocco, in spite of their horrible promiscuity, offer a less hopeless picture than the poor quarters of the Middle East, because they are the sign, not of a hopeless and incurable poverty which is accepted with a shrug of the shoulders as inevitable, but as the growing pains of a young country growing out of an old one. The same applies to the Morrocan towns themselves, which are bursting on all sides out of their red earth walls.

Morocco is neither wholly Arab nor wholly French; it is neither only Africa nor only Europe. It is the strategic turntable of the west, the land of huge American air bases, a fortress between the Mediterranean and the Atlantic. In the economic sphere it is the country of the at any rate half-open door; and, thanks to this outlet to the world, it is the promised land of French flight capital, which is sent here partly out of fear of war and exchange controls, but partly also to escape from the all-too-fenced-in nature of the French economy; and here it engages in constructive enterprise, which it does to such a very limited extent at home. It illustrates what North Africa could be—the Far West, the California, or, as M. Eirik Labonne, the former Resident-General, once said, "the Urals of Europe".

Morocco, if no political collapse brings its stormy development to a halt, will be in a position to absorb and feed its rapidly growing population. The French in Morocco have not failed in tackling economic and social problems, and they have not failed with the mass of the population. But they have failed in the very area in which Marshal Lyautey desired to lay the protectorate's firm foundation; they have failed with the Moroccan *élite*, who here as elsewhere have taken to nationalism. It was this that led to the crisis which brought about a complete reversal of the former declared French policy of building up the unity of the Moroccan nation round its Sultan.

The European-educated Moroccan intelligentsia from which the Istiqlal, the nationalist party, is recruited is as young as the colonisation of Morocco, and as young as its proletariat. It is a narrow segment of the population, almost exclusively descended from the rich and powerful families of traditional Morocco, and it made the jump from the school desk to politics almost without transition. In 1934, just when the authority of the Moroccan monarchy, thanks to the suppression of the last dissident tribes in the Anti-Atlas, had for the first time been extended over the whole area of the country, a group of Moroccan students in Paris, in co-operation with some French left-wing journalists, produced a "reform plan" for the barely articulated and pacified state demanding the immediate grant of a modern, democratic, parliamentary constitution. That was how the Istiqlal was born. Morocco then had twenty young men who had completed their secondary education. They were all young enough to hope that one day they would become Cabinet Ministers, and that was what they wanted to be.

In all Arab countries the most profitable occupation has

always been the exercise of power. The educated class in Morocco has not yet produced any scientists, engineers, technicians, or agricultural experts, and it has produced few doctors. But it has produced many lawyers; in other words the form of education chosen is that best adapted to a political career. The total lack of native cadres on whom the independent administration of a modern and democratic Moroccan state could depend seemed to worry the leaders of the Istiqlal but little. Were all the institutions of the old Sherifate not still present and ready to resume their role? What they wanted was perfectly intelligible; in what until a century ago had been a sovereign state it was more than intelligible; they wanted to exercise power themselves—as in the old days. After the idealistic beginnings of its democratic "reform plan", the Istiqlal quickly turned over a new leaf and disclosed its real nature as a party of "revolution from above", *i.e.*, restoration; and since the end of the second world war the whole of its propaganda has been concentrated on one point, the claim to sovereignty of the Sultan of Morocco, who as Sherif, Commander of the Faithful, and descendant of the Prophet was the embodiment of all spiritual and temporal authority. The Sultan became the symbol and idol of Moroccan nationalism.

This identification of the Istiqlal with the royal cause was never explicitly approved but was never repudiated by the young, modernistic Sultan Sidi Mohammed ben Youssef. But it was taken up enthusiasically by his eldest son, the "Crown Prince", in whose favour Sidi Mohammed sought to introduce the western principle of primogeniture in place of the traditional method of succession, the "selection" of a suitable member of the family by learned doctors of the Koran. It was this that provided the background of the Moroccan problem in the form in which it has become known to the world since the war; in Morocco an organised state and its recognised chief have been protesting against the protecting Power, which is accused of violating the international treaties by which both the protectorate and Morocco's domestic sovereignty were established.

Thus Lyautey's basic idea has in a certain sense been turned against France. His determination to preserve the old institutions of Morocco intact allowed the traditional apparatus of Government to survive in an ossified form, and thus preserved the theoretical possibility of a restoration of the Sherifate to its former sovereignty and glory—theoretical because it is totally inconceivable in practice that a metropolis like Casablanca could return to the archaic theocracy of the "Commander of the Faithful". Such an illusion could arise only because of the artificial preservation of the old Morocco, which persisted side-by-side with the new without knowing it or coming into contact with it. But the simultaneous co-existence within the same frontier of two totally different countries was in harmony with French policy, which here as elsewhere sought to reconcile the irreconcilable. "The conception of the protectorate," Lyautey reminded the French administration in 1920, "is that of a country which preserves its own institutions, rules and administers itself with its own organs, under the simple control of a European power which undertakes its representation abroad and the general control of its army, its finances, and its economic development. What distinguishes and characterises this conception is the formula of control as distinct from that of direct administration. . . . But," he added, "we have direct administration in our blood. . . . We do not speak Arabic, and we have no patience, but, to establish useful co-operation with the indigenous population much patience ought to be exercised, at least in the initial stages and for a long time afterwards."

The French officials and settlers indeed had no patience, and they regarded the protectorate statute just as Lyautey feared they would, as nothing but a preliminary, transitional régime, which was bound in the end to lead to annexation and administrative assimilation, and the sooner the better. In the ten years after Lyautey's departure—he was, as he bitterly remarked, "shown the door by his own administration"—officials from Algeria and Algerian administrative methods were systematically and increasingly introduced into Morocco, and flew in the face both of the spirit and of the letter of the protectorate agreement. A highly efficient, active, and completely European "direct administration", which worked hand-in-hand with the important settlers and big colonial enterprises and fell in with all their wishes, did a great deal for the economic development of Morocco, and the "Californian" rate of growth that ensued would scarcely have been conceivable without it. But by reducing to a shadow the native Moroccan institutions, which were artificially preserved in spirit, so to speak, and by excluding both the old and the young Moroccan *élite* from any genuine participation in public affairs, it created by its own hand hostility to the protectorate, both on the part of the old state and of the educated youth of the country.

"It would be a grave illusion to believe that the Moroccans will accept this exclusion from public affairs. . . . They are neither a barbarous nor a dull-witted people. They are curious about world events and are well informed. They are thirsty for education and very adaptable. A young generation is growing up which wants to live and to act, and has a taste for education and public affairs. As our state offers them so few and inferior openings, they will seek their way elsewhere, partly with European groups all of which are ready to accept them and use them against France, partly with Mohammedan groupings outside Morocco; and in the end they will all join together to make their demands. . . . We can be certain that all round us and without our knowledge ideas are seething, secret meetings and conversations are taking place about world events and the position of Islam, and that one day all these will break out and take shape, unless we concern ourselves with these things and straight away assume the leadership of this movement ourselves."

These prophetic words were written by Lyautey in his cry of alarm written in 1920, fifteen years before the first beginnings of an organised nationalist opposition in Morocco. No attention was paid to them. Lyautey's personality and his legendary prestige continued to be invoked, but the administration and the settlers were far too busy, and materially far too successful, to "listen to the heart-beats of Morocco", as this "romantic" did. All the material successes of the protectorate did not alter the bitter fact that Morocco was obviously not on the way to the promised emancipation, but was being involved more and more deeply in the French colonial administration. Thirty years later the crisis had grown to maturity.

An abyss of non-understanding, mistrust, and resentment had arisen between the settlers, who felt themselves to be no longer guests but masters in the Moroccan household, and the awakened forces of this country, which the process of colonisation had itself shaken from their sleep.

The international reverberations which the Istiqlal raised by the skilful statement of their case under international law, reinforced by the amplifier of the Arab League and the great interest taken at times in the matter in America in the postwar years, were probably greater than the reverberations it roused in the protectorate itself. But international sympathy with the Istiqlal, and above all its role as mouthpiece— whether legitimate or not—of the "captive" Sultan, presented the officials of the protecting Power with a problem which was capable of being disposed of by force, but was fundamentally practically insoluble: the problem of defending against the Sultan a protectorate the purpose of which was declared in treaties to be the unification of Morocco around the Sultan himself.

The Istiqlal as the "party of the Sherif" had become a state within a state, something both less and more than a political party. It very effectively combined the beginnings of a modern mass organisation with the characteristics of an archaic band loyal to its leader—which was preserved in all its purity in the sister party in Spanish Morocco deliberately fostered by General Franco. It was a *Fronde* of the mighty in the land with their clientèles. The Moroccan "trade unions", whose cells were identical with those of the Istiqlal and always became active when it was deemed desirable to organise demonstrations, unrest, or protest strikes, were no more than the party's lengthened arm and proletarian clientèle; and in its private schools, in which several thousand sons of the Moroccan aristocracy were brought up in a strictly nationalist, pan-Islamic spirit, the Istiqlal had turned inside out a characteristic idea of Lyautey's, that of recruiting the future cadres of the protectorate from the country's traditional *èlite* by means of "schools for the sons of notables".

For years the Residency met this situation by the doubletracked methods which have grown up everywhere in the French empire as a consequence of the unclear division of power between a weak and indecisive Government in Paris and a very independent colonial administration affected only by local influences and outlook. The trade unions and the schools, indeed the whole activity of the Istiqlal, depended on mere tolerance and were without any legal foundation; and, indeed, all political activity in the protectorate took place in a twilight zone of semi-legality. A state of emergency had been "put on ice" for forty years, but had never been raised. The inhabitants of Morocco not only did not possess the right of assembly, or of having their own Press, but all personal rights existed only provisionally, to the extent and for the period that seemed appropriate to the French police officials, or to the extent that these officials were restrained by Paris. The result was the development of a game of cat-and-mouse between the nationalists and the Residency, the changing fortunes of which provided an inexhaustible source of nationalist propaganda; and the protecting power's obstinate refusal or incapacity to create clear legal conditions makes idle all discussion of guilt or responsibility. Where legality does not exist, the word "illegality" has no meaning.

The question of the legal relations between France and Morocco was not settled—or even properly stated—any more than was that of Moroccan political rights. A straightforward transformation of the protectorate into a colony under direct French administration would unquestionably have conflicted with the international treaties on which the French mandate in Morocco rests. But when Sultan Sidi Mohammed made efforts to come to an understanding about the basis of Moroccan policy, to discuss a reform of the régime or a revision of the protectorate treaty of Fez, he could find nobody with whom to discuss the matter. At Rabat he was confronted with a sergeant-major who told him brusquely that it was his business to maintain peace and order and not to conduct diplomatic negotiations; and when he wrote to Paris, or—to the deep displeasure of his nationalist followers—paid a state visit to the capital in 1950, he was received and entertained with the greatest pomp and ceremony, but again found nobody to negotiate with, but only chiefs of protocol who politely referred him back to the Resident-General at Rabat. Throughout these years, indeed, French policy was conducted, not by the Government in Paris, but by the local officials at Rabat and the leaders of the French colony at Casablanca, who now, to outmanœuvre both the Sultan and the French Government itself, took a further step in the repudiation of the actions and policy of Marshal Lyautey; they incited the Berbers of the Moroccan hinterland against the Arab monarchy, which had become a nuisance to them.

This plan was in harmony with the classical recipe of "divide and rule" and had long been advocated in influential colonial circles; it found a willing and energetic ally in El Glaoui, the Pasha of Marrakesh, the most prominent Moroccan beneficiary of the protectorate, who as "France's most loyal friend" had risen from being an unimportant tribal chief to the richest feudal lord in Morocco, and the real "sultan of the south". In February, 1951, Morocco was treated to a kind of dress rehearsal of a performance which took place in earnest two years later. As in the old days of anarchy and tribal feuds, warlike tribes came down from the Atlas mountains and advanced mounted and armed upon the old capital of Fez; and, under the pressure of this carefully staged "Berber rising", the Sultan, who appealed in vain to the President of the Republic to act as umpire, dismissed the supporters of the Istiqlal from the royal cabinet, proclaimed his loyalty to French Moroccan co-operation, and caused the activities of the Istiqlal to be specifically condemned by his Grand Vizier. The world was now treated to the moving spectacle of the Sultan of Morocco's resorting to publicity. In an interview with the Egyptian newspaper *Al Ahram,* which was smuggled past the censorship, he announced that he had acted under duress; and this was amply confirmed next day by another interview, this time given by General Juin, the Resident-General, who said that he had informed the Sultan that he had been in danger of "being deposed by his people, who were dissatisfied with the activities of the Istiqlal" and had invited him to see reason "before a catastrophe should arise". Any understanding between the Sultan and this Resident-General was henceforth impossible.

Once more this catastrophic policy was brought to a temporary halt. General Juin was appointed Commander-in-

Chief, Allied Forces, Central Europe, and was soon promoted to the rank of Marshal of France; and his successor at Rabat, General Guillaume, behaved at any rate at first in a more polite and conciliatory manner. But the threads of protectorate policy remained united in the same hands, and after the French elections of 1951 there ceased to be any French Government able to oppose the colonial *Fronde*. A year later the intrigue, which was in conflict with all French contractual obligations and was disavowed to the last by all French official spokesmen, began to develop publicly. The police officials of Morocco opened a *battue* against the Istiqlal and other objectionable Moroccans and Frenchmen, while the Pasha of Marrakesh organised a conspiracy of the tribal chiefs. The leaders of the religious brotherhoods condemned the Sultan's "modernism," and *caids* and indigenous police magistrates loyal to the régime put their signatures to a rebellious petition against Sidi Mohammed; and Marshal Juin in his speech on election to the Académie Française exalted the services of El Glaoui, who was present in the audience, and mocked at "sensitive Christian souls" of the type of François Mauriac who were growing more and more hostile to these tactics, which were so unworthy of French traditions.

Once again the same scenario was enacted. While "indignant Berber tribes" from El Glaoui's realm marched on Fez and Rabat under the indifferent eyes of the French police, the Sultan, now thoroughly "softened up," put his long-refused signature to a *dahir* in which he abandoned his legislative power to a "council of viziers" consisting of palace dignitaries and French protectorate officials, and thereby surrendered his only weapon against the Residency, namely the power to refuse his signature to decrees laid before him by the Resident. By now things had gone too far to be left half way. The conspirators of Casablanca and Marrakesh had a free hand. In Paris a Government lacking both prestige and power was paralysed by a civil service strike, and General Guillaume, the official representative of France in Morocco, prudently withdrew at the critical moment to spend his leave in the Haute Savoie. Upon the Government's urgent appeal to him to return, he reached Rabat just in time to sanction the *fait accompli* with the classic phrase: "We did not wish for this," and to carry out the Sultan's deportation.

Had this been the result of a well-considered and clearsighted policy and not a capitulation of the French Government to the tactics of a local clique, there might have been a good deal to say in its favour from the point of view of *Realpolitik*. The power and prestige of the nationalist Istiqlal was in fact chiefly confined to those areas and those sections of the population which looked up to the Sultan as their sanctified, traditional ruler. In other words, it had been more or less confined to the Arab town population, and hardly extended to the Berbers of the highlands and the desert, who before the French colonisation had been largely independent and had conducted a continual struggle against Arab rule. The traditional conflict between Arabs and Berbers, which the "Machiavellians" of the French administration started exploiting immediately after the pacification of the country against the Sultan's claims to sovereignty, is no artificial creation of the colonial politicians. The "Arabisation" of Morocco was in fact far more superficial than elsewhere in North Africa, and barely extended beyond the towns and the north-western lowlands; the chiefly nomadic Berbers of the mountainous hinterland had persisted in revolt, and had successfully maintained their ethnic, linguistic, and to an extent even their religious, identity. Nearly half the population of Morocco has never adopted Arabic as the language of everyday speech, though Arabic, the language of their religion, is the only written and literary language of the country. Under Islam Morocco remained a country of magic, sects, local cults, and mystical confraternities; and Marrakesh, the capital of the southern part of the country and of the domains of El Glaoui, is a town full of heathen gaiety, in the sharpest possible contrast to the strict orthodoxy of Fez, the ancient seat of the Sultan.

The mountain tribes were actively insubordinate to the Sultan whom France supported only twenty years ago, and when one leaves the immediate neighbourhood of the towns the slowly crumbling fortifications which surround even the poorest villages consisting of nothing but tents and huts are a reminder of a recent past of feudal and tribal warfare, looting expeditions, and continual insecurity. The internal unity of Morocco is still a very fragile structure, and it is exceedingly questionable whether in the absence of the protectorate it could be held together under the banner of Arab nationalism, which still awakens in the minds of the Berbers the fresh memory of another, more tyrannical and more oppressive alien rule.

But the wisdom of a policy which takes back with one hand what it gives with the other and blows on the embers of past anarchy, imperilling the unity of Morocco which was its own creation, is just as questionable. If French colonial policy, which until 1934 was based on the more advanced town population and the Sultan, now looks for support against the awakening national consciousness of the latter to the formerly dissident mountain tribes and rebellious pashas, and tries to play off primitive tribal autonomy against mediaeval theocracy, El Glaoui against the Sultan, the country against the town, the Berbers against the Arabs, from the short-range point of view the French position in Africa may be consolidated, but in the long run it must inevitably put France on the losing side. For the French, whether they wish it or not, cannot avoid pursuing the work to which they have set their hand of fusing the various sections of the Moroccan population into a nation. The Berbers could retain their individuality in the remoteness of the Atlas mountains and the steppe, in inaccessible valleys cut off from the rest of the country, so long as they preserved their primitive tribal ways and a nomadic life. But the establishment of peace and the Sherifian authority, the opening up of communications throughout the country, extending even into the remotest valleys, the economic and social revolutionising of the country, and Berber mass migrations, whether temporary or permanent, into the rapidly growing towns of the north, where they are "Arabised" in a very short time, all combine to work in the same direction. Morocco is on the way to becoming a nation, and an Arab nation. To prevent that from happening France would have to destroy her own handiwork.

The astonishing success of the *coup* of August 20th, 1953, also demonstrated the weakness and immaturity of the young Moroccan nationalist movement. The identification of its cause with that of the Sultan gave it a momentary strength, but also a fundamental fragility. Oriental tradition knows no legitimacy in the western sense, and deposing a ruler and substituting for him another representative of his innumerable kith and kin is by no means such an earth-shaking event as might appear. True, Sultan Sidi Mohammed had made a claim to such legitimacy and had striven for the "regular succession" of his eldest son, but he had not been able to appeal to any deep-rooted tradition. Istiqlal propaganda had made him the embodiment of Moroccan national consciousness in the eyes of a whole generation of nationalist youth, but this made him too much a party sultan. The Istiqlal as a party of restoration fell with its idol. Ruthless police intervention sufficed to put its active minority out of action, arrest, scatter, or intimidate its leaders, smash its "trade unions", close its schools, and disintegrate its clientèle. "Quiet prevails in Morocco."

The Arab world, in spite of its outbursts of hot blood and its rodomontades, is a world of great patience, always ready to adapt itself to the compulsion of facts. But it would be a disastrous illusion to suppose that Moroccan nationalism has been done away with for good. The "legitimist", boastful, and fundamentally so naïve restoration movement, which took its stand on treaty texts and the French word, appealed to the world's conscience, to America, and to Arab solidarity, has been decapitated and defeated, and has disappeared. If the country's fate is left to the coalition of colonial magnates, feudal lords, and police commissioners which triumphed on that August 20th, a revolutionary movement, nourished in hatred and hardened in terror, will start slowly growing in the dark; that can be the only result of the political lawlessness to which the Moroccans are subject, and of their lack of social protection and opportunity to manage their own affairs. Hitherto the Moroccan crisis has been a political crisis on the surface of a country in a state of soaring advance. Forcing it from the surface means driving it into the depths.

In no other field do the French zigzag so much as in their policy to their protectorates. At the very moment when the Laniel Government was impotently bowing to the *fait accompli* in Morocco, it pulled itself together to introduce "a policy of reconciliation" in Tunisia and withdrew the Resident, M. de Hauteville. This was a characteristic instance of the technique of concession. Members of the Laniel Cabinet who favoured a policy of liberal reform in North Africa were given a late and platonic sop to make the Rabat *coup* acceptable to them.

In United Nations debates and in the world's press Moroccan and Tunisian crises have always gone hand-in-hand, and the formal resemblances between the two are indeed striking. But in Tunisia we are confronted with a later and more mature stage of the same conflict. This third and smallest country of the North African triptych has all the features which should make it the happiest and quietest of the three. After the wildness of the Moroccan interior and the inhospitable high plateau of Algeria, we come to a broad stretch of country sloping gently down towards the sea. It has a Mediterranean climate, and is the most fertile, the most uniform, and the most self-contained of the three countries of the Maghreb. The pressure of population is smallest, the social conflict is weakest, the standard of living of the indigenous population is highest, and it has the most favourable combination of factors for independent national development. The traditional framework of the old Turkish regency had been driven into bankruptcy by the mismanagement of its beys and the adroitness of the international financiers who had lent it money, but it was capable of regeneration; the Tunisians are an intelligent and gentle, almost effeminate, people, who after the almost endless succession of civilisations and colonisations which have flourished on their soil from the time of the Phoenician colonisation of Carthage to the establishment of the French protectorate, have acquired the extraordinary quickness of understanding characteristic of mixed races. An Arab proverb says: "The Moroccan is a warrior, the Algerian a man, the Tunisian a woman"; Tunisia has the biggest and most developed educated class in North Africa, and is both more completely "Arabised" and more deeply impregnated by French influences than either Algeria or Morocco; it has a prosperous indigenous bourgeoisie and peasantry, a real indigenous trade union apparatus—in fact the only real trade union organisation in the Arab world—and the most "western" nationalist movement.

It is significant that it was in Tunisia that conflict became most acute. Tunisia provided a schoolroom example of the degree to which colonisation, the justification and declared aim of which is always emancipation, changes into "colonialism" which seeks to destroy its own work. The Franco-Tunisian crisis, which after 1951 drove deeper and deeper into a *cul-de-sac*, was not the first of its kind, but it was the most serious and most unfortunate, because it followed directly on a promising experiment in co-operation. In the existing situation it was demanding an almost suicidal degree of moderation of an Arab nationalist party such as the Neo-Destour to expect it to shake hands with a European protecting power over a "gradual transition to internal autonomy"; and if it adopts such an attitude and is repaid with a smack in the face the hope of a repetition of the experiment is slight.

Such an experiment began in the summer of 1950 with the setting up of the Chenik Government, which was not a mere Regency shadow Cabinet, but reflected the political trends in the country and had the official blessing of Tunisian nationalism, because the Neo-Destour was represented in it; and it started out with an apparently straightforward programme of political reform, which was approved both by M. Périllier, the French Resident-General, and M. Schuman, the French Foreign Minister. This foresaw the gradual handing over of internal administration to the Tunisians. Thereupon the "third partner" noisily entered the conversation and started steering everything to disaster. The French settlers started a furious assault upon the Resident-General, and the Foreign Minister: Franco-Tunisian negotiations—the French side was hamstrung by Radical opposition inside the Cabinet —broke down; the Tunisians complained to the United Nations; M. Périllier was recalled; the reactionary M. de Hautecloque arrived in a warship to take his place, had the Chenik Cabinet arrested on his own responsibility, established a regular "Asian despotism" in Tunisia, and in the course of a year deported more or less the whole of the Tunisian political *élite* to desert fortresses in southern Tunisia.

This brutal turn of events was possible because of the existence in Tunisia of the same twilight of semi-legality which we have already met in Morocco. Even while the Neo-Destour was holding public meetings, was officially invited to take part in the Government, and its secretary-general was appointed Tunisian Minister of Justice, it remained an officially forbidden party, subject to police persecution; and, by virtue of the state of martial law which since 1938 had been partially forgotten but never lifted, it was possible to let loose the police against this Government party, its leaders, and its Ministers, and against all Tunisians guilty or suspected of political activity; and it was similarly possible to order the Foreign Legion to conduct a "comb-out" of the villages of Cape Bon for followers of the Neo-Destour. What arbitrary power had granted, arbitrary power could take away.

Franco-Tunisian negotiations had first come to a standstill and then broken down because of a conflict of constitutional views which these events threw completely into the shade and caused to be almost completely forgotten. True, in the subsequent polemics neither the French nor the Tunisians went out of their way to define it, as if they feared to state too plainly a problem on which honest differences of opinion were possible and which could not be solved in the twinkling of an eye.

The question of the economic, political, or strategic positions of the French in Tunisia was not at issue. The Tunisian nationalists were ready to make their country the first completely independent member of the French Union, but they were not ready to share its internal administration with the French settlers, and no step towards democratic self-administration was possible until there was a clear decision of the question of who was to be qualified to send representatives to the elected bodies of Tunisia. In its celebrated Note of December 15th, 1951, which led to the breakdown of negotiations, the French Foreign Ministry, under the pressure of the "colonial lobby" in Parliament and in the Government, for the first time specifically adopted the settlers' case. "The French of Tunisia cannot . . . in view of their share in the economic life of the Tunisian state and its contributions to its budget, be excluded from a share in its political institutions," it declared.

This was the principle of co-sovereignty, which Tunisian spokesmen of all shades of opinion denounced as a heresy in state and international law. True, they said, Tunisia was today a French protectorate, and tomorrow might become a member of a federal "French Union", but its individuality as a state had never been in dispute. The protectorate treaty was a treaty between states, and the French Resident was accredited to the Bey of Tunis by the French Foreign Ministry. Therefore the French settlers in Tunisia, like other immigrants who had not individually acquired Tunisian nationality, were clearly and unquestionably aliens in law; and who had ever heard of aliens being permitted a vote in countries in which they were guests?

This, on a higher level of political development, was a repetition of the conflict between colonial practice and the legal basis of the protectorate which we have already met in Morocco, and in their rejection of co-sovereignty the Tunisians had behind them the whole logic of international law. But it was perfectly natural that the French settlers, who had hitherto felt themselves to be masters of the house in Tunisia, should regard it as intolerable to be suddenly regarded as aliens, with no voice in the running of the country. They regarded modern Tunisia as their creation. They had administered it and provided it with irrigation, housing, and electricity. More than half the present European population had been born in Tunisia, and, if France failed to defend the rights they had acquired, they would fight for themselves. This talk of civil war turned up in conversation with practically every French settler in Tunisia at that time, and it came only too near to becoming a reality. This game was not so dangerous to the settlers as it was to France herself; for it was a certainty that no French Government could leave its settlers in the lurch when rifles started cracking and shells bursting, and in relying on it the settlers were justified by the result.

At first sight the furious reaction of the "French of Tunisia" appears not entirely intelligible. Tunisian self-administration threatened none of their rights, and the undisputed suzerainty of France offered sufficient guarantees for their security. The fact that the question became so acute is intelligible only in the light of the peculiar structure of the European colony in Tunisia. Had they formed a real, massive settlement, anchored to the soil, as in Algeria, the question of their being "aliens" could not seriously have arisen. Had they been employers, pioneers, developers of a country emerging from the Middle Ages, as in Morocco, the question of their share in the domestic political organs of Tunisia would not have been a question of life and death to them. But the bulk of the European colony in Tunisia is the unhappy product of an unsuccessful policy of enforced settlement on the Algerian pattern, carried out, however, without the reserves of population which France still possessed at the time of the colonisation of Algeria. Settlement took place in competition with Italy, which was making claims based on the far larger numbers of Tunisian settlers of Italian origin. The "French of Tunisia" consist to a large extent of Sicilians, Maltese, and Spaniards, who have acquired French citizenship by "automatic naturalisation" and are superior neither in skill nor in mentality to the Tunisian "orientals"; and they proclaim their loyalty to France all the more noisily for the fact that during the war they showed it to be exceedingly questionable. The land owned by the French consists chiefly of a number of huge plantations in the hands of absentee landlords whose activities are more closely related to financial speculation than to opening up the country; and as for the real French settlers, the majority constitute less a French than a Corsican colony; people who have settled like rats in the cheese of the protectorate and have populated every office building, down to the last post office, bank, and tax-office counter, with members of their clan. After the second or third generation nothing European is left about them except their trousers.

This kind of colonist has everything to lose: the assurance of a carefree livelihood justified by no particular service rendered, and all the privileges of colonial civil servants, who automatically enjoy higher pay than their colleagues of equivalent grade at home; comfort; cheap native service; and a feeling of importance and dignity which is all the greater the less justification there is for it; and for this reason these people proclaim with irritated violence their belief that the Tunisians would never be able to administer their own country, or even serve behind their post office counters. Nearly half the working population of French citizenship in the protectorate are installed behind its desks and counters; and they were not satisfied with the fact that the Tunisian reform plan guaranteed the *situations acquises* of all existing office holders, their well-earned office chairs and pension rights; in other words, that their posts should pass into Tunisian hands at the rate at which vacancies occurred because of normal promotion, pensioning off, and deaths, which would result in the Tunisian administration becoming Tunisian at the end of a generation if new appointments were reserved for Tunisians. In July, 1952, the French civil service trade union in Tunisia passed an angry resolution which said: "The promised respect for *situations acquises* is nothing but a deception so long as no guarantee is given for the children of personnel in office at the present time." In other words they demanded, not only security for themselves, but hereditary rights for their children and children's children, who were to occupy the holes in the Tunisian cheese in perpetuity.

No satire could more pitilessly illuminate the spirit of this race of officials. They stand, not for France or for any civilising mission, but for their own personal livelihood, for which they fight with all the violence of the superfluous. The toying with the idea of civil war, which culminated in the murder of the outstanding and moderate Tunisian trade union leader Ferhat Hached—and in the systematic failure of the French police to bring the murderers to light—was a tactical move which in the short run was infallible. For the deeper was the abyss between the French and the Tunisians created by terrorism and counter-terrorism, the more inevitably would that priceless product of colonial education, the readiness of the Tunisian political *élite* for conciliation, be thrown overboard. The leaderless, defeated, and resentful Tunisian masses would be left to their instincts; and the more inevitably would the weak French Government be forced to stand behind its "threatened sons" in Tunisia. The bill would be paid by the real pioneers and settlers, compelled to flee from their property and plantations scattered about the countryside.

"Above all do not make Tunisia a colony of officials," Paul Cambon, the first French Resident, had said to the assembled colonists on July 14th, 1885. But Lyautey was right: "We have direct administration in our blood." French colonial practice has irresistibly followed the course of the French state; the descent from the "spirit of Lyautey" to the rabid hereditary dynasties of Bouvard and Pécuchet. The French state apparatus has lost the aristocratic gift of being able discreetly to direct the destinies of a country from a few key positions in the background with a minimum of personnel and a minimum of friction. This was what Lyautey and Cambon wanted to do, and Britain in many parts of her empire succeeded in doing. It is the natural tendency of a bureaucracy to appropriate to itself all the functions of administration from top to bottom, from the formulation of policy of the detailed control of its execution. The advantages of civil service colonisation on this basis are undeniable. Its grip is firm and practically unshakeable, and is independent of the political strength or weakness of the home country—on the contrary, the weaker the home Government, the more unhampered are the officials by liberal inhibitions and counter-influences. The remarkable solidity demonstrated by the French empire throughout a war in which the home country was occupied by the enemy, and throughout a post-war period in which all colonial régimes were shaken, in which the United Nations put the colonial Powers on the defensive, and the French Parliament itself solemnly declared the colonial empire to have been "abolished", is to a large extent to be attributed to this compact bureaucratic structure. The process which in the course of centuries moulded France into a unit has extended to "greater France". But it takes hold of territories, not their inhabitants; it creates objects of administration, not a "hundred million citizens"; and the administrative assimilation triumphant everywhere comes into more and more violent contrast with the human and civilising kind of assimilation which is inscribed on the banner of the French colonising mission.

The further the process has gone, the harder it is to put it in reverse; in any case it would mean increasing the immediate risk for a distant and not absolutely certain gain. But such a long-sighted policy can be imposed only by the home country; it cannot be expected of settlers and colonial officials whose mind is on the conduct of immediate, day-to-day business and the maintenance of peace and order in the police sense. But how can Governments which themselves live from hand-to-mouth, or a country which cannot agree on its own immediate future problems, hope to carry out such a long-term policy, with all its risks and hazards, in the teeth of those on the spot who are fighting for the maintenance of their own positions, and, unlike the Ministers who are supposed to control them, know exactly what they want?

M. Schuman, who as Foreign Minister for four years carried official responsibility for French policy in the protectorates, after his resignation provided a clue to the French colonial crisis in an article in *La Nef* in March, 1953. The authority of the Government, he soberly stated, was "one of those fictions on which the democratic system rests.... Before deciding the policy we should adopt, we must ask ourselves whose task it is to make this decision in the name of France.... The creation of *faits accomplis* is the great and constant temptation which Residents-General deserve credit for resisting, to the extent that they do resist it and do not succumb to it. Moreover, they themselves are in a similar position in relation to certain services (police, intelligence, etc.), which enjoy very great independence and, for the lack of a public opinion, which elsewhere acts as a salutary rein, easily escape any effective control.... I have come to the conclusion that without a return to precise ideas of responsibility and hierarchic subordination there can be no significant reform in the relations between France and Morocco or Tunis." And in an interview he added: "We have not been able to choose any policy for North Africa, and, if we had chosen one, I am afraid that in the present state of the French administration and its relations with the home country it would be impossible to carry it out. We have put up with the formation of groups and cliques in the bosom of the administration which block certain mechanisms. Do you know, for instance, that it is very difficult and sometimes impossible to transfer an official who has failed to carry out instructions in the sense that was desired?"

The crisis of the French empire is above all the crisis of the French state itself, whose power to rule and capacity to form a political will have crumbled between an irresponsible Parliament and the sovereignty of a *corps d'état* and administrative dynasty which are similarly irresponsible. The French edifice in North Africa is threatened, not from without, but from within, and it is most threatened by those who talk loudest in the name of France. It has become urgent that France should once more resume her role. In the bewildering complication of its problems and populations the Maghreb must not wantonly be exposed to destruction. In French North Africa not just one of France's last chances, but one of Europe's, is at stake.

For the end of colonisation which was everywhere proclaimed in 1945 is, like every end, only a new beginning, a return to the old and real meaning of the word "colonisation", which is not conquest and suppression, but building, pacification, the introduction of order, the opening up of new territory, the foundation of towns, the clearing of land and making it fertile; and the history of colonisation is that of civilisation itself, from the ancient civilisations of the Mediterranean, from Greece and Rome, to the tremendous adventure of European expansion, which in four centuries altered the face of the world. The age of the *pacte colonial*, of colonial *rentes* without colonial development, the age of "white gods", and of ruling immature peoples for ruling's sake, is over, no matter what interests still cling to these things. If there is one right that can never become hereditary, it is the right to rule, which can never become a *situation acquise*, a source of revenue, or a sinecure. The tremendous epic of triumphs and catastrophes, achievements and crimes, which has been in progress since the end of the Middle Ages, and has transformed the economies, the racial structure, and even the landscape of whole continents, and has annihilated whole nations, put them in the melting-pot and reforged them, and has involved greater and greater masses of humanity in mutual contact and conflict, is not yet over. Its deeper meaning—and it is at the same time the elementary and tremendous proviso which a thousand years of the French spirit of colonisation has to contribute to the robust ambitions of the new age—is the triumphant progress, not of technical civilisation, mass production, and television, but the arising of humanity.

PART IV

THE FULCRUM

For a half-century which was a period of profound change throughout the world France succeeded with an astonishing and admirable obstinacy in preserving her inner shape and her style of life, though at the expense of defencelessness and impoverishment. Two wars in the course of a generation, in both of which she was invaded and in the second of which she was overrun, did not act on her like the crack of a whip, but had a terrible paralysing effect. While the other warring countries were the scene of frantic activity behind the lines, France was the battlefield over which armies swept, like the plagues of Egypt, leaving a trail of looting, destruction, corruption, and demoralisation. When the second world war broke out the destruction and the losses of the first had not been made good—the scars had not even grown over the wounds. No grass yet grew on the battlefields of Champagne and Picardy, and a generation weakened both in numbers and self-confidence walked between the graves. Awareness of the irreplaceability of every man and every building, concern for the preservation of a diminished substance, lay like a heavy shadow, more instinctive than conscious, over France's whole way through the war and the defeat. The systematic declaration that every town of over twenty thousand inhabitants was an open town, which in 1940 so incredibly facilitated the German advance over intact bridges, was a symbol; the towns and the bridges were destroyed all the same, not in 1940, but in 1944.

A stranger walking through the streets of a town like Rheims today cannot distinguish the ruins of the first world war from those of the second. Paris, that most lively monument of western civilisation, is outwardly undamaged, but he who looks more closely can discover a dying city, almost a city of ruins. Nowhere is the loss of the national economic substance so plainly visible as here. There has been no violent destruction, but everywhere, in practically every street even in the most prosperous quarters, there are uninhabitable, collapsing, or demolished buildings, yawning gaps behind the bright deceptiveness of the advertisement hoardings, gates behind which no building is left, empty façades, cracked walls, houses on crutches. After the first world war little building was done. Since 1939 there has been no building at all, and little repair work. During the German occupation not even the most essential maintenance was possible, and there was not even that minimum of heating which is enough, not to keep people warm, but to keep houses intact. Rain seeped through the holes made in the roofs by *Flak* fragments, beams rotted, walls cracked, and now it is too late. Whole quarters in Paris consist of the wreckage of houses, which, thanks to the brilliant French talent for making-do and mending, may remain habitable for many years, but cannot be saved. Every year another two thousand houses in the French capital reach this condition.

Over these unsound buildings there lies a kind of gloom that is quite different and is more subdued and tired than that of a shell-pitted battlefield. Here everything goes on as it did before, life clings to every crevice like ivy to the door of an empty church, and Paris seems never to have been so intensely alive as since the death-worm has been at work in its walls. The French version of existentialism, in so far as it was an expression of the mood and atmosphere of the immediate post-war period, was a reflection of the unease of living in rooms threatened with collapse. This was not destruction, but decay. Was it worth while beginning all over again? Would not a new beginning for the first time make visible the whole extent of the irremediable breach in continuity which has taken place in the uninterrupted, organic, thousand-year-old growth of this city? The first new buildings which started slowly going up here and there in 1952, seven years after the end of the war, created the impression that the destruction was just beginning, and seemed to confirm the irreplaceability of what was decaying. The tall structure of the new Faculty of Medicine, the steel framework of which was completed in 1938 and for ten years stretched up into the void like a huge skeleton until work on it could be resumed, is like a restless, white, bare monster, wrecking the harmony of one of the most beautiful quarters of Paris, and suffocating the ancient little church of the Feuillants with its hideous mass. Behind the two beautiful Renaissance façades which shut off the Ile-de-la-Cité, "the cradle of Paris", on the west a huge whitewashed wall has destroyed the most magnificent view in Paris. In all past centuries, in spite of all stylistic horrors and distortions, the new always fitted in with the old, was a continuation of it, but now the continuity has been broken, and it will be a long time before the new and the old grow together again. For a whole generation Paris ceased to build, and it has almost forgotten how to build.

Architecture is always a symbol of the state of a civilisation. Other countries in Europe were materially harder hit than France. But what is important in this context is not the extent of the destruction, but the nature of what has been destroyed. The younger and more unformed a nation is, the more easily does it recover from such blows. Here something that seemed finished and complete, something in which everything which we mean by the "west" had reached its fullest flower, was severely, almost mortally wounded.

The decline of the west? Something of the sort broods over the post-war history of France. But only over that which is complete and finished—in that strange double meaning which is associated with that word in all languages. Nothing alive is ever finished. The seventh day of creation, which France, that apparently so sceptical country, wished to believe was dawning, never came.

§ 2

DOUBLE BOOK-KEEPING

THE model chosen by Karl Marx, the economist and sociologist, for his study of the laws of capital was Britain, where the industrial revolution had transformed a whole society and created an almost chemically pure capitalist system without upsetting the institutions of the state and without causing the political pendulum to swing further than to the Whigs and the Chartists. For his demonstration of the class struggle the other Karl Marx, the revolutionary journalist, turned to France, an essentially peasant and artisan country, so little capitalist that big industry was practically the creation of absolutism and "Colbertism", control of the heritage of which was everlastingly disputed by revolution and counter-revolution without any profound effect on the country's social structure. The first was characteristic of Britain, the second of France. But Marx projected the British economic revolution and the French political revolution into each other, as if they were two halves of the same thing, substructure and superstructure of the same social reality. That was how he produced the explosive mixture of his messianic vision, and that was the warped starting-point of an ideology which has ended in total perversion.

On the map the amalgam has long since fallen apart. Capitalism and Communism have gone their several ways, and have met only in border zones where the offshoots of industrialism have made devastating inroads into archaic agrarian societies. In France, as indeed everywhere where the millenarian doctrine of Marxism has met with success, its influence does not depend on the existence of a mature capitalist economic and social structure, but is propped up by decaying or shaken pre-capitalist structures and myths. The Jacobin tradition provides a most fertile soil for this ideology, which drew such a lot from Jacobinism itself. But France, an old country which has achieved only a minimum of real change in the last century-and-a-half in spite of a record number of revolutions and *coups d'état,* has long since developed, not only every kind of poison, but every kind of antidote, and a revolutionary "all or nothing" attitude has often enough been an excuse to leave things as they are. In a paradoxical and perhaps dangerous manner Communism itself has become a factor in French stability, a dead weight standing in the way, not only of any revolutionary change, but of practically any reform. The classic country of revolution is in reality the most conservative country in the world, and its latent anarchy has itself turned out to be the most effective self-defence against any fundamental intervention from within or without.

Since the turn of the century the France of the small town, the small workshop, the small plot of land, has slowly spun itself into a cocoon of established rights and privileges for everything that is small, old, traditional, irrational, and stationary, and of bans and penalties on all disturbing innovations. These range from the protective tariffs of the Méline period to the practical exemption of small-scale trade and production from taxation and competition in the inter-war period; from the state-guaranteed prices and markets for agricultural produce to the legally enacted ossification of the milling industry in its existing condition; from the exclusion of foreign shipping from the colonial empire to the systematic preservation of administrative and judicial offices which have ceased to perform any useful function, and exist only to preserve an appearance of life and activity in stagnating provincial towns. The end result of all this was that every acquired position was transferred into a source of income in perpetuity and the business of living was protected from any alteration in tempo. France, with her social equilibrium, her stable population, and her devotion to the rhythm of this style of life, sheltered from the technological pressure of the outside world by this all-embracing umbrella as well as by her own self-sufficiency, lay in the middle of her huge oversea possession like a beautiful garden, which had slightly run to seed behind the high but uncompleted wall which she had built between herself and a threatening, desperate Germany, which was suffocating in her own industrial power and finally broke loose.

The running amok of the Third Reich, that barbarous form in which a technological and population flood-tide broke over France and swept the wall away, led to two different and opposite reactions which can only very crudely and approximately be identified with Vichy and the resistance; the conflict between the two, greatly distorted and often effaced, runs through all parties and groups. One is the tendency to return to the old passive resistance; the other is active acceptance of the challenge in a sense far wider than the purely military. Nevertheless it was the first of these, the spirit of passive resistance—not "collaboration", which was never real if more is meant by it than the absorption of northern French industry into the German war machine—which was the fundamental attitude of Vichy France; while the first great impulse of liberated France was the administrative, social, economic, and technical modernisation of the country, never mind the conflicting ideas about the means by which this was to be achieved. Leaving aside all political labels, which on this fundamental question are liable only to be misleading, the question of which of these two attitudes will eventually gain the upper hand is still open; and after eight years, in which the same question has assumed a completely new form, Vichy is often no longer to be found in the places where out of custom and convenience one has grown used to looking for it, while the drive of the resistance is no longer where it was, or said that it was.

Vichy represented, not just a repudiation of the Third Republic, but also the completion of many of its secret trends, namely the driving of the administrative, guild, and corporation state to its last logical conclusion and organisation of the economy by the economic associations themselves as a system of privileges and monopolies. Moreover, this inheritance of Vichy has turned out to be most enduring, much more enduring than the ideology connected with it, which was rejected with horror in 1944. Indeed, the doctrine of the return to the land and to the good old traditions of craftsmanship, the exaltation of the traditions of peasant France unremittingly broadcast by the Vichy loudspeakers, only too obviously proclaimed how well the ideals of Marshal Pétain and his courtiers fitted in with the conquerors' wishes; the Germans could ask no more than that France should never again be able to rise against the master race, and should decline to the status of a purely agricultural country after the "aberrations of the enlightenment, the revolution, and faith in progress".

In this matter both sides were guilty of self-deception. Peasant peoples are not so tractable as all that; the French Jacques Bonhomme has never had the reputation of being willing to bend his neck. But more fundamental and more enduring than the state apparatus of Vichy was the fashion in which the French, in spite of all forms of external disorganisation, organised themselves individually, at first with the simple and immediate objective of keeping themselves alive. Galtier-Boissière, in that new *Journal d'un bourgeois de Paris*, his diary of the occupation period, noted on February 1st of the last winter of the occupation: "The winter of 1940–41 was the hardest. Self-supply was organised from year to year. This winter everyone on every floor, from the *concierge's* lodge to the attic, had his parcels from the provinces. We were provided for from the Mayenne, Normandy, the Puy-de-Dôme at practically normal prices." Apart from the official distribution and marketing systems, and behind the backs of the occupation Power and the official Vichy rationing and supply system, the French economy undermined the zone barriers and mole-like grubbed out "parallel channels" for itself which survived the war and the occupation.

This was not the black market, which was on the whole confined to the occupation régime and its fancy-men, and remained inaccessible to the man in the street; it was the grey market, the system of personal connections, built up of relatives, friends, people coming from the same neighbourhood, chance contacts; and, in spite of all its dark and unedifying aspects, its creation amounted to an act of solidarity, almost of resistance, by which a country full of small, unsupervisable farms and workshops conspiratorially withdrew itself from foreign intervention, requisitioning, and involvement in the war machine. The underground network of the resistance in all its complicated and often doubtful ramifications was at bottom built up no differently from these "parallel channels". The obverse side of the French lack of specialisation, division of labour, and technical organisation is a fantastic adaptability and capacity for improvisation. Most independent of all was the antediluvian farm—it was independent of outside supplies, petrol, machinery, spare parts, manure, foreign labour. Most useful of all was the most primitive workshop, which could make or repair practically anything; the most old-fashioned printing shop was the safest, the most ancient houses had the most hiding places; the most remote corners in the country were the freest.

For more than two years the Germans occupied only the industrialised north, leaving the southern part of the country to the twilight régime of Vichy; the demarcation line exaggerated the impression that France was taking refuge in her backwardness. The war increased the value of all the archaisms in the French national structure, strengthened them, almost turned them into pathological fixations, and the feeling of helplessness itself became a factor in encouraging persistence in the old ways. Its effect was not just negative, encouraging the fear of investing money, the custom of burying gold in the garden and hiding it in the walls of the cellar, reminiscent of the times of the barbarian invasions; it was given a positive fillip by actual experience of the advantages of this archaic, economic self-sufficiency, the almost unassailable position of the minute community, the circle of personal connections, local autarky, all those forms of anarchistic self-aid which can only be misleadingly half-described as "black marketeering" and *débrouillardise,* and make it possible to survive in the absence of all public order and in spite of all public disorder. Out of this high school of passive resistance the old France, uncontrollable, unorganisable, and ungovernable, arose again. The first post-war decade, in which France was first a field of manœuvre for the Cominform and then a N.A.T.O. back area, did nothing to encourage the French to bury what they had learned to trust as their secret weapon, the only effective weapon against conquest and tyranny, the weapon of latent but perpetually mobilisable anarchy. This country, over which four invasions had passed in less than a century, has organised itself for the life of a battlefield.

One should beware of hastening to make a moral condemnation of this attitude. The wisdom of peasant peoples has always been to allow catastrophes to pass over their heads and pass away, while they remained, hung on, clung fast to the soil, and it was always their way of turning out victors in the end. France is inconceivable without her strong peasant foundation, and without the contemplative rhythm of her small-town life she would not be the France that we love. Her self-defence, her struggle to maintain a structure and personality which, from the point of view of mass production, technical efficiency, and even of war potential, is so backward, irrational, and expensive, but from the human and cultural point of view is so rich, is part of the defence of the west. But France is more than an agricultural country, a country of provincial peace with a cultural chemical laboratory in Paris. This was not the France which became the first nation of Europe, the first national state in Europe, proclaimed the civilising mission of the *grande nation*, claimed European hegemony and built an empire, and it is not this France which will maintain her traditional position as a great power. The French intellect and the always living French need of *grandeur*, all the forces which set the pace in the active resistance and occupied the centre of the political stage during the years after the liberation, repudiated the "Chinese attitude" of bending the back and lasting out. The great slogans with which the liberated republic started its career were modernisation, development, productivity, technical equipment at the highest contemporary level, "catching up and overtaking".

The overriding maxim which M. Jean Monnet imposed on all the activities of his planning commission was "modernisation or downfall". In his first declaration of policy to the National Council of the Resistance General de Gaulle spoke of the "voluntary discipline of a strong people" and the "labours of a great period", and in his presentation of the

French programme of reconstruction to the first Consultative Assembly, while the battle for the Rhine was still in progress, he said: "The events which threatened France with literal extermination have shown in the most glaring light the absolute necessity of a national revival. A return to the condition in which catastrophe overtook us would not only obviously condemn us to destruction on the next occasion; we also know that, in the exceedingly hard and busy world which is to be discerned ahead after victory has been won, all those things which constitute our life and our values will not weigh in the scales heavily and for long if we do not once again in our history make ourselves strong. . . . A country like ours which in the east, the west, and the Massif Central possesses the richest supply of iron in all Europe with the exception of Russia, in whose rivers and streams there is stored up an extraordinary treasure in the form of electrical energy . . . such a country, I say, has all it needs to provide itself with a huge heavy industry, able to produce locomotives, wagons, rails, ships, aircraft, machines, tools, weapons, building materials, and all the needs of mechanical and chemical industry. The output of our agriculture, which has the advantage of a very rich and very varied soil, can with suitable equipment and organisation be doubled . . . and . . . our North Africa . . . our West and Equatorial Africa, our Indo-China, Madagascar, Guiana, to the opening up of which much has been done but so much remains to be done, call for the enthusiastic efforts of France. . . ."

The age of the pioneers and technocrats was to begin.

Its embodiment was the "plan for modernisation and equipment", generally known simply as "the plan", or the "Monnet plan", after its high commissioner. There was much doctrinaire or sceptical discussion at the time whether such a thing as a Monnet plan really existed, and whether M. Monnet's team of apostles and technicians of modernisation were on the side of liberalism or of state control. In fact this experiment in "liberal planning", which flew in the face of all doctrines and labels, was the most original and fruitful contribution to the economic thought of the years of liberation. M. Monnet, its leader and driving spirit, was for France a new type of "manager", at once *entrepreneur*, "civil servant" in the British sense, and international economic negotiator. He inherited a little Cognac business in the town of the same name, and looks like a peasant from the Charente with the features of an Anglo-American financial diplomatist. He was French delegate to the Inter-Allied Transport and Supply Commission in the first world war, which surprised him among the trappers of Hudson's Bay. Between the wars he was deputy secretary-general and financial adviser of the League of Nations, and was entrusted with financial and economic missions to Poland, Austria, Rumania, and China. In between he was sent for by his father after his elder brother's death to restore the fortunes of the family business, which had been shaken by the post-war crisis; and he was a partner in American-French-Chinese banking syndicates. In 1939 he was called back to government service as chairman of the Anglo-French co-ordinating committee. During the French collapse he took an active part in the desperate attempts which were made to bring M. Reynaud and even Marshal Pétain to London and to proclaim the fusion of the British and French Empires. Subsequently he was sent by Sir Winston Churchill to Washington as a member of the British purchasing commission for the purpose of bringing into action the "arsenal of democracy", and in 1942, in the confusion of Algiers, he was the go-between and man of confidence of the rival French government teams and allied missions; he was the Provisional Government's commissioner for supply and equipment, and negotiator of nearly all the supply and finance agreements with the allies. These are some of the significant entries in the biography of this international personality, who is at home in all questions of national and international co-ordination, planning, diplomacy, and discreetly conducted publicity.

The statement of French economic needs, difficulties, and potentialities with which M. Monnet flew to Washington in the spring of 1946 in the wake of M. Blum was used by the latter as the basis for the loan negotiations the results of which enabled France to keep her head above water until Marshall aid came into operation; it was, in fact, the first draft of the Monnet plan which was put into force during the following winter by M. Blum's short-lived interim Government. This was the beginning of that original experiment, which remained the only really constant factor in French politics for the next few years, and survived unscathed all convulsions, crises, and devastating budget debates. Thanks to an elasticity unintelligible to lovers of ready-made systems, it was always able to adapt itself to changing situations, and in its final transformation ended by over-stepping the French national frontiers; a good deal of the spirit and methods of the Monnet plan migrated with its originator to Luxembourg and the European Coal and Steel Community.

M. Monnet's planning commission was in every respect the opposite of a planning bureaucracy exercising exclusive control. He started with a small team of generally very young "planners" whom he found in industry and the universities. Their number never exceeded forty, which was the maximum laid down at the outset, though the specialised committees for individual branches of industry soon approached a hundred, and the more or less permanent voluntary workers for the plan ran into thousands. The latter were all living forces in the academic or official world, employers and civil servants, directors and trade union officials, technicians and experts of all kinds, who were drawn to the periodic committee meetings because of their specialised knowledge or activities and their willingness to co-operate; and anyone else who had knowledge or ideas to contribute, whether French or foreign, was invited to consultations round the green table of the commission's headquarters in the Rue de Martignac, or more informally to a meal at a restaurant.

The "planning" was done on the one hand by bringing together and comparing all development plans worked out for individual industries or industrial units, and on the other by drawing up a balance sheet of all available resources in raw materials, labour, and capital; and in most cases the general view so obtained of available resources and requirements was sufficient to exclude overlapping and the misdirection of capital and to produce agreement on a list of priorities among all concerned. The commission had no powers of coercion; its field was restricted to that of capital investment, and did not extend to such controversial questions as wages, prices, taxes, and the budget, though its "national balance sheet" provided a background for the objective consideration of these questions, and thus influenced them. But, because of its voluntary nature, it succeeded in bringing about agreement among all parties and economic groups on the long-term aims of French economic policy, and in giving these aims, and the Monnet plan itself, a moral authority which was accepted both by the big economic associations and by Parliament, in spite of the latter's meanness with the purse-strings.

During the early months of the plan M. Monnet brought about a real "unity of will" between industry, large and small, the trade unions, both Communist and Christian, the state economic and financial bureaucracy, Parliament, and public opinion. The "plan" was the great unifying legend of this period, during which the Communist trade union leaders directed the Stakhanovite "coal battle for France's greatness and independence" and exalted the heroic nature of labour, Lorraine heavy industry was busy with great schemes for transferring the industrial centre of Europe from the Ruhr to north-eastern France, and the country almost on its own overcame the great "bottle-neck" of its disrupted transport and power system; and, thanks to the key position which the planning commission, largely because of American aid, came to occupy in relation to the dried up French capital market, the impulse once given was maintained even when the illusions of "people's democracy" and the "social republic" collapsed in inflation and social disintegration and, with the gradual return to the Third Republic, the Monnet team of technocrats was put under the tutelage of the Finance Ministry and the Banque de France, which, in the spirit of classical financial orthodoxy, saw the cure for inflation, not in increased production and economic expansion, but in restricting credit and consumption; and it survived even when investment credits were the first to be sacrificed in making budget cuts. Moreover optimism was maintained about the plan's ultimate aims—it was almost the only real optimism there was in France during those years; and it was nurtured by all the resources of publicity, including reports of the plan's triumphs in the course of its advance along the road to economic revival, and a good deal of artificial manipulation of the methods of presentation of the results obtained which concealed its retreats and its postponed objectives and target dates.

Apart, however, from the solid results achieved, the Monnet "brains trust" made an invaluable contribution to preserving France's faith in herself. M. Jean Fourastié, the chairman of the production committee under the plan, displayed this modernistic spirit in its most robust and ingenuous form in his books on "The Civilisation of 1960" and "The Great Hope of the Twentieth Century" in which, in bold defiance of all orthodox, traditional, or revolutionary doctrines, he held up productivity as the sole criterion of economic forms of organisation, and for the first time made many Frenchmen—including many French teachers of economics—aware of the connection between productivity and the standard of living. The controversy between planned and liberal economy was completely alien and academic to these practitioners of organisation; to them planning meant the concentration of all energies in the service of aims which had been jointly agreed on and recognised to be correct. What counted was the visible result; everything else was mere theory; and, leaving aside for the moment the question of who paid and who got the benefit, their achievement was indeed immense.

The Monnet plan was extended for two years to coincide with the Marshall plan, and when it ended vital sectors of French industry had overtaken the arrears of more than thirty years. The French steel industry now possesses the most modern equipment and the most efficient rolling mills and uses the most up-to-date coking methods in Europe, which have for the first time made low-grade French coal usable in blast-furnaces. The French coal mines, in spite of relatively much less favourable natural conditions, have nearly attained the productivity of the Ruhr. In six years French electrical industry doubled its productive capacity, and, taken in conjunction with the Rhône valley irrigation scheme and the work undertaken to make that river navigable, constitute an enterprise which can claim without blushing to be a European counterpart to the achievements of the Tennessee Valley Authority. An oil industry with the most up-to-date refineries and pipe-lines was created out of practically nothing. The

French motor industry is working in top gear, and even the aircraft industry—in the pioneering days of which the French industry led the world—which long before the second world war had lost touch with international developments, has, after eight years of agony and failures, to the universal surprise once more put itself in a position to re-enter the front rank. The French railways are today among the best, fastest, and most punctual in the world. Total industrial production has increased by one half in comparison with 1938, and productivity per worker has risen by nearly a quarter. Year by year the President of the Republic was able to report new records in material progress—the biggest power station in Europe at the Génissiat dam, the biggest lock at Donzère-Mondragon, the biggest coffer-dam in the world at Tignes; and in face of these achievements he was able solemnly to remind the world and France of these achievements of French labour and French technique, which need fear no comparison.

Why, then, was the echo so sceptical? Why, when President Auriol at Donzère and a year later at Tignes eloquently claimed that this was the true face of France, was it not only malicious foreigners, but the man in the street himself who had the impression that the true face of France was that of a farmcart stuck in the mud? Why that shrill cleavage of view among visitors who, depending on what it was they were observing, were either amazed at the extent and speed of French reconstruction or else appalled at French economic stagnation and decay? How is it that one sees progress and another stagnation, one modernity and the other archaism? Why the bewildered questions of Americans, who ask where all their money has gone to, and how it is that not a single French Communist has been convinced of the advantages of western democracy? Why the disenchantment after all the proclamations of increased productivity, which should provide the French people with a more worthy standard of living?

An example of this disenchantment was that of the French Christian trade unions in the autumn of 1952, after a patient experiment in co-operation between employers and employed for the purpose of increasing production and reducing costs. They then announced: "It has been demonstrated that it is possible to increase the output and productivity of industry; but it has been no less clearly demonstrated that this progress nowadays benefits neither consumer nor worker; it has only increased profits."

If one searches for the effects which the tremendous constructive achievements of the French key industries have had on the daily life of France, they all seem to run away between one's fingers. Even in those sectors of industry which remained fully within the realm of the Monnet plan when the creeping bankruptcy of the state and the transition of private industry to self-financing slowly undermined the commission's direction of investment planning, the limits of what was achieved can be read in a sometimes almost dramatic fashion.

Among the tasks which the Monnet plan set itself was the technical equipment and modernisation of French agriculture, and the first "four-year plan" of 1946 set the target of an annual production of 50,000 tractors in 1950. This objective, which was several times revised downwards, was one quarter fulfilled in 1950 and barely half fulfilled in 1952. This was not because of any lack of industrial capacity—at the present time the French tractor industry is using only one half of its capacity—but because French agriculture would not absorb these tractors. French agriculture is congealed in its archaic habits, and hampered over large areas by the splitting up of land into tiny plots which makes any rationalisation of methods impossible. After years of post-war market conditions, it again confined itself within the straitjacket of an autarkic market which can cause any increase in production to be catastrophic for the producer, and it had no use for the "industrial revolution" proposed for it.

In view of the enormous requirements of French reconstruction, the first four-year plan set the cement industry the target of an annual production of 13,500 tons in 1950. But the reconstruction did not get going, building activity was confined to the state-financed restoration of destroyed towns, and the report of the Monnet plan for 1949 stated resignedly that the yearly production of between seven and eight million tons which had been attained "appears sufficient for the years ahead". This figure was not exceeded until 1953.

France today possesses the industrial productive capacity of a modern country, but everywhere, as soon as production began to approach the level of consumption, it appeared inexplicably to flag. A multitude of open sluice-gates seemed to be inserted between the magnificently equipped key industries and a stagnating market which drew off the increased social product and caused it to run dry before it reached the consumer, and thus the building up of heavy industry soon reached its limits. Five years have passed since the triumphant announcement in the winter of 1948–49 that French industry had again reached the maximum output in its history, that of 1929, and no further advance has since been reported; and if French production is stagnating about a high point reached a quarter of a century ago, without any apparent prospects of ever exceeding it, French wages are stagnating below the depressed level of 1938.

This fantastic juxtaposition of progress solemnly announced in official reports and ceremonially acclaimed at opening ceremonies and an all-pervading, insuperable stagnation has made its mark on the whole political, social, and moral climate of France. The French wage-earner hears that France has got back to her best pre-war level, and when he sees the full shops of the capital, its streets jammed with motor-cars, and all the luxury of the tourist industry, he is prepared to believe it. But what is more important to him is that the average wage index in depreciated francs has become stabilised at fifteen times the 1938 level, while the price index is twenty-five times the 1938 level. True, French statistics are questionable, and we shall have more to say about them later; but the wage-earner can tell from his experience that these figures are roughly correct.

His wages are sufficient to live on, that is to say, to enable him to eat, and to pay his rent, if he belongs to the privileged class of "old tenants", who live absurdly cheaply in slowly collapsing houses at rents which are kept down by law. But even a pair of shoes is a great luxury. If he is not one of these favoured "old tenants", whose lease, granted fifteen or twenty years ago, has become a kind of perpetual right of usufruct, he is unable to make ends meet. Hundreds of thousands of young French families are unable to find a home; in Paris alone eight years after the end of the war there are 90,000 young married couples, including 35,000 families of three, four, and more, who live in a single room or cheap hotel bedroom, or live as sub-tenants in a housemaid's attic, generally without water or the most primitive hygienic installation, and pay more for it than the fortunate "old tenant" pays for his whole flat; and an inquiry in twelve country departments in 1952 showed that more than one family in three was living in a single room in indescribable hygienic conditions. True, no buildings were destroyed in Paris during the war, but in Paris, as in the whole of France, the rate at which houses become uninhabitable because of age and neglect exceeds the rate at which they are built.

The population grows while accommodation decreases. The deficit which has been accumulating for twenty years now exceeds two million houses, and this figure is increasing by at least 100,000 a year. The consequences of this social plague are only now beginning to fill the crime and disaster columns of the newspapers with accounts of family tragedies, the break-up of marriages, the murder, maltreatment, and neglect of children, drunkenness, and juvenile crime. Moreover, the housing shortage has itself become a factor in the congealment of French society. The worker's feeling that it is better to go on living where he is, however miserable he may be, rather than move on somewhere else where it will almost certainly be impossible to find a roof over his head means in practice that his freedom of choice is abolished, and that he is bound to his place of work just as the mediaeval serf was bound to the soil. The housing situation has become the most striking of the external signs of stagnation. A country in which no building is taking place is a country in decay. In short, the fruits of this national economy, which has in appearance returned to full, "normal" working, seem to slip away down dark, mysterious channels without ever reaching the great mass of consumers and without benefiting the country in any visible way. What is the "small man" to think except that there is an evil conspiracy—he generally calls it "capitalism"—which skims the cream of the result of the nation's labours and secretly squanders it on good living, buries it, or smuggles it abroad?

Were it really a tiny group of "big capitalists", a dozen "trusts", or "two hundred families" who were making off with the profit of French labour, as is alleged in the current demagogy, the solution would be simple—just as Italian land reform would be simple if the land were owned only by a few big landowners. In reality, however, a whole population is busily engaged in "skimming the cream" of the French social product, the whole idyllic, old-fashioned France of little shops and small factories. To differentiate it from the France of M. Monnet, let us call it the France of M. Gingembre, the valiant chairman of the Association of Small and Medium Businesses. French society is in reality divided, not into "little" and "big" men, "capitalists" on the one hand and "exploited" on the other, but into three almost equal categories. These are the independent peasants; the fixed wage or salary earners all the way up to the level of members of the Council of State and the permanent heads of government departments; and the "business people", the great majority of whom are active, not in production, but in distribution. The first and last categories benefit from protectionism, increasing prices, and shortages, or at any rate think that they do, while the third is smothered between them; it is this third of the nation, from working men to the holders of the highest administrative and technical positions, which has borne all the burdens since the end of the war.

The devastating policy of low wages and high prices, of small turnover and big profits, has been conducted exclusively at their expense; and the whole social policy of the Fourth Republic has consisted in levelling out wages in favour of the lowest categories, who live on the border-line of the minimum necessary for existence. The natural consequence is that the attraction of skilled work has disappeared, and recruitment for jobs which make high technical demands has threatened to dry up. The only career that has offered the prospect of prosperity has been "business". In the period of dear living and shortage of goods between 1939 and 1950 the number of registered businesses of all kinds increased by 300,000, *i.e.*, by nearly one-third, and it has reached the fantastic level of one business to every thirty-two inhabitants, women, the aged, and children included. The shorter the supply of goods, the higher the toll that can be extracted from them. The industrial and agricultural productivity of France, backward as a consequence of generations of technical and organisational stagnation and the elimination of competition, is burdened by a parasitic structure which even the most flourishing national economy could hardly bear; and it was with this social structure that France tried to mend the destruction of war, restore the carefree inter-war period, overtake the arrears of generations of backwardness, balance her foreign trade, the deficit of which before the second world war had been covered by investment income which was now lost, build up her national defences, hold her empire together, reconquer Indo-China—and establish a welfare state.

The word "parasitic" has an evil sound. But a parasitic existence is not necessarily care-free, profitable, or prosperous. All the honest vine, fruit, and turnip growers who just keep their heads above water thanks to the guaranteed market provided by the alcohol monopoly, and year after year in the sweat of their brow grow expensive products which nobody wants in order to hand them over for destruction by the state, are partners in a tremendous looting enterprise the annual cost of which to the French national economy is estimated at 400,000 million francs. (Incidentally the destruction of all this alcohol is the best thing that can happen to it; the alternatives are to dilute petrol with it, which means dearer and poorer petrol, or, worse still, to use it for the systematic poisoning of the people of France and the colonies. The latter have for some years been drowned in alcohol. The increase in exports of wine to French West and Central Africa from 352,000 to 1,584,000 gallons between 1938 and 1951 and of spirits from about 19,140 to 204,000 gallons marks the murderous progress of this kind of civilisation, just as the overcrowding of mental homes with alcoholics marks its progress at home.) But all these people have sufficient solidarity with all its large-scale beneficiaries to make sacrosanct this crazy system of state-promoted destruction of the state finances and the national health; and all the diminutive farms on which antediluvian methods are used on broken-up fields to produce unsuitable products at grossly excessive costs, and which are able to keep their owners' heads just above the water-line thanks to state subsidies and guarantees—one million, *i.e.*, 40 per cent. of French farms, yield a gross income of less than 300,000 francs each—contribute their share to making France an unprofitable enterprise incapable of competition, which has to struggle with its own agricultural "over-production" while simultaneously importing more agricultural produce than it is able to export. It is here that this economy of stagnation combined with guaranteed established privileges reaches its full absurdity. Its assumed beneficiaries have become its victims.

But even most of those who do "business" do very bad business. Nine-tenths of "independent businesses" are small family shops which employ no staff, and in 1951 three-quarters of them had an average yearly turnover of less than a million francs, which, even with a big profit margin, can yield only a pitiful livelihood. These figures are not based on tax returns, according to which practically the whole of the French commercial world would be starving, but is the consistent result of all serious investigations.

One grotesque result of the system of guaranteed established privileges is that the number of sub-let business premises increases yearly by about 8,000. Every business lease since 1926 has legally become a practically irredeemable "trade property", a possession acquired without investment by the leaseholder of the time by the mere fact of being in possession. The lease is a piece of property which can be bought or sold; alternatively the premises can be sub-let at ten times the rent paid by the leaseholder. Thus, at any rate theoretically, one little shop may be supporting three families: that of the owner; that of the leaseholder; and that of the man running the shop. The man who makes a living by selling a few pounds of vegetables or two pairs of shoes—two pairs of shoes is the average daily turnover of a shoe-shop—desires to make a meagre living and rightly complains about the hardness of his lot, but his living, poor as it is, is nevertheless parasitic, a part of the huge incrustation which has formed between production and consumption and makes illusory all efforts to reduce costs in the consumption industries, because every reduction in the cost of production is immediately absorbed by the middlemen and retailers.

French agriculture went through this bitter experience after the end of black market conditions, when the price of foodstuffs began to drop behind those of industrial products in 1948. Even positive collapses in prices in the markets were absorbed in the innumerable intermediary stages betwen the market and the consumer, in the bedlam of the Paris Halles and in the hands of individual middlemen. The price of cattle at a provincial market might fall to a half or a third, and in the towns consumers might be buying in grammes instead of in pounds, but the cattle-dealers, the wholesalers, the concessionaires at the Halles, the slaughterers, and the butchers held firm. The Halles might be filled to bursting with meat which was going bad, but the retail price remained unchanged. During the 1952 crisis the French textile and shoe industries—the latter, having been legally protected against all new competition since 1936, is technically one of the most backward—tried to combat the drop in demand by reducing prices. But the dealers simply pocketed the difference to compensate themselves for their reduced turnover, and instead of selling two pairs of shoes a day to live, sold one, and survived. Reductions in prices by the producers reached the market either not at all or after practically a year's delay, and only enabled the middlemen to survive the crisis.

The French consumer is far too used to this state of affairs to put up any resistance. He may stop buying, or be unable to buy, but it seems just as natural to him that prices should go up as that trees should go on growing. An experiment conducted under Government auspices may suffice to characterise the psychology that has developed in thirty years of now creeping, now galloping inflation. In a number of "test" shops cheeses were cut in halves, and one half was labelled at a lower and the other at a higher price. The more expensive half invariably sold more quickly. Higher prices have become a natural tendency which can be restrained and sometimes even stopped, but can apparently never be reversed.

The stagnation of the French building industry is the most striking, the most extreme, and the most disastrous example of all the vicious circles in this economic structure. Here the thicket of legally protected vested interests is so dense and intricate that eight years after the war a way out is barely even in sight. Under the Third Republic a short-sighted and demagogic "social policy" kept rents stable in the midst of a general depreciation of the currency for so long that the discrepancy between building costs and the yield from rents made building totally uneconomic. The rents from a house let off in flats ceased even to cover the costs of maintenance. For a quarter of a century practically no building has been done in France, except at state expense. The result of the "protection" given to tenants is complete chaos. Young families in France can find no adequate accommodation unless they can afford to pay two or three million francs "for the fixtures and fittings" to old tenants prepared to move out. Working-class quarters slowly degenerate into slums and roofs fall in over the tenants' heads while close at hand large numbers of spacious flats are empty, or are occupied for a few weeks in the year by a widow who lives on the Riviera and finds it inexpensive to keep on her superfluous dwelling, or draws a livelihood from sub-letting it at fantastic prices for a few months in the summer.

This monopoly income enjoyed by the sitting tenant has become an essential element in the budget of hundreds of thousands of Frenchmen, who because of the housing shortage are able to meet the rent of a whole apartment, sometimes many times over, by sub-letting an attic. The maintenance of the building, however, remains legally the responsibility of the landlord, who in reality has been expropriated; in practice it is nobody's business at all. This situation provides, however, one of the many fragmentary answers to the insoluble problem of what the inhabitants of this country really live on. The impossibility of eviction, the right "to stay where one is", has been extended step by step from the sitting tenant to all members of his household, and at the end of a parliamentary debate, the report of which in the *Journal Officiel* would yield ample material for a dozen comedies of manners, was extended even to a man's *bona fide* mistress. More than half the time of the French courts is taken up with questions of tenant's rights, and a dozen legal journals specialise in the subject; so that to the innumerable beneficiaries of this chaos, apart from all the middlemen of what has become a completely "confidential" housing market, there must be added a whole army of legal middlemen—advocates, counsel, legal advisers to the tenants' and landlords' associations, who exact payment for making legally unassailable the innumerable doubtful operations involved in getting rid of tenants or in refusing to move oneself.

The political effects of this state of affairs are just as vicious as the moral. When all voluntary forces fail, when *entrepreneurs* no longer show enterprise, when capitalists refrain from investment and the most urgent national tasks remain undone, the idea of compulsion and dictatorship loses its terrors in the eyes of millions of people. For no professor of national economy would be able to convince the French of the existence of some unalterable economic law which prevents France from building; poorer countries in which the war wrought more havoc than in France have been able to complete their reconstruction. But what is the role of capitalists and employers if all the forces and mechanisms of the liberal economy have been eliminated by law? And who is to take their place?

The Fourth Republic made a magnificent gesture in the first few weeks of its existence, solemnly pledging itself to make good all war damage. It undertook to pay the full costs of reconstructing and restoring all private property the destruction of which could be attributed to the war; in other words it assumed an obligation which in the course of more than ten years was to devour millions and millions of francs. But Parliament never troubled its head with the question of where the revenue to meet this expenditure was to come from. The Fourth Republic has inherited from the Third the tradition of imposing on the state the task of national capital formation and at the same time refusing it the means to carry out the task. During the first eight post-war years it was possible by more or less inflationary means to restore 350,000 dwellings—fewer than one-third of these destroyed in the war, and, in view of the technical and financial difficulties, that is no doubt an impressive performance. But meanwhile private building remained at the level at which it had been for a quarter of a century, namely zero.

The necessity of bringing the legal level of rents once more into harmony with building costs is so self-evident that it has not been disputed for years, and in the end the legislators of the Fourth Republic set timorously about the task. It was not only the unpopularity of the necessary steps that caused them continually to shrink back. The fact of the matter is that the French wage-level is so low that the French worker simply cannot be charged an economic rent. The whole French wages-and-costs structure had for decades been based on the calculation that the average Frenchman spent less than 3 per cent. of his income on accommodation—less than would be required for its bare maintenance. French building costs are so high that this would have to be increased to nearly 100 per cent. to cover interest on and amortisation of the invested capital; and on the costs side the way was blocked too. M. Claudius Petit, one of the most active Reconstruction Ministers of the post-war period, barely exaggerated when he said that the French building industry worked as in the time of the Merovingians. Calculated in man-hours worked by a trained workman, the building of a four-room house of the usual French type takes 25,000 man-hours—*i.e.*, a man's pay for twelve-and-a-half years—compared with 9,000 in England and 4,500 in America. Reduction of costs is not merely a question of technical resources. In France today there are cranes and tractors in plenty, but they generally serve only to increase costs. Experiments have shown that costs could be cut by more than half without any technical revolution, by rationalisation of methods alone. But rationalisation is incompatible with the guild organisation of the French building industry, which causes the smallest contract to be divided up among a dozen small firms, each one of whom sends his workmen to the site in his own good time, one in February and the other in September.

The building industry is not an industry, but a craft; 200,000 small firms with an average labour force of three, including the employer, divide up a minimal amount of building among themselves, and the real function of the *entrepreneur*, the organisation and co-ordination of the employed labour, is under existing regulations reserved for the architect, who draws up the plan, works out and agrees on the cost with client and builders, hands out the contracts, and supervises their execution. But the great majority of architects do not fulfil this function, and are technically not equipped to do so.

In December, 1940, the architects' association was turned into a guild in the best mediaeval style by Vichy legislation which is still valid, and the *ordre des architectes*, after the pattern of the great *corps d'état*, is a self-administered, and self-recruiting "estate" whose members are almost without exception products of the École des Beaux Arts. They are steeped in the cult of the traditional, and have completely preserved the tradition by which the architect is an artist; that is how he is described in the statute of the "order". He provides drawings of the plan and elevation, preferably including a turret, cornices, and bull's-eye, but not an exact technical work-plan or a binding calculation of the cost; constructional details can be decided from day to day on the spot, and adjustments can be made as necessary, and what the final cost will be will be known when the work is finished.

Under this system of construction proper planning of the work is practically impossible, and proper calculation of costs is replaced by resorting to a series of heavy handbooks which lay down how much should be charged for transporting a beam or a dozen tiles or installing a pipe or a window-pane, and how much time should be allowed for those things according to guild practice. Allowance has obviously to be made for the time taken by the single artisan who has to go and fetch a window-pane.

Again, the architect's fee is officially laid down by law and statute as a simple percentage of the building costs, the result of which, in the judicious words of Barberot's *Aide-mémoire de l'architecte*, the guild handbook in universal use, is a conflict in the architect's conscience arising from the fact that the more work, trouble, and care he devotes to looking after his client's interest, the less is his remuneration. In any case the subject of building costs is a well-preserved secret, sealed with seven seals from the profane. The established price catalogues which take the place of proper cost calculation are still those of 1913, revised, or rather enriched, with additional supplements, the last of which was added in 1934. Subsequently all that has been done has been to add overall percentage increases—the sliding scale of the building industry—as if there had been no change in building technique and methods since the first world war.

There has, indeed, been none. The first characteristic of a building site remains idyllic chaos. Workmen may turn up today or perhaps tomorrow, but they will probably have to go away again without being able to do anything because the wall in which they were going to lay a pipe, for instance, is not yet ready. The second characteristic, resulting from this, is the slowness with which building proceeds. Of 220,000 dwellings the construction of which had been begun at the end of 1951 two-thirds were still unfinished at the beginning of 1953. Moreover France, where there is no building without state subsidy, still builds as she did in 1900. Of the new buildings projected under the auspices of the Crédit Foncier in 1951 one-half were without bathrooms and one-tenth without lavatories and without running water. On the other hand, two-thirds were in masonry and only one-third in concrete or brick. In other words they were expensive, old-fashioned, uncomfortable, but built to last for ever. In present conditions none of those involved, from the architect to the plumber, has the slightest interest in modern methods or more rational organisation. In thirty years of minimal activity the French building industry has so thoroughly adapted itself to the principle of the biggest profit from the smallest turnover that this principle has become instinctive, and every building firm or architect's office has so to calculate its charges that it will be able to make a satisfactory living from building two gutters, repairing one roof, giving advice on one or two insurance cases, or acting as go-between in one or two war-damage cases. In a country whose housing shortage shrieks to high heaven the building industry suffers from chronic unemployment, with the result that the trade unions are part of the conspiracy and veto the immigration of Italian building workers or the training of Algerians. The vicious circle of stagnation is complete. The less building is done, the dearer it is, and the dearer it is the less building is done; and the abyss between production costs and practical financial possibilities now yawns so wide that all efforts to adapt the two to each other are hopelessly inadequate so long as they do not lead to a complete revolutionising of the structure of the building industry.

After thirty years of stagnation this congealment of established practice is hardly surprising, and it extends to the public itself, which remains faithful to the style of 1900 and knows nothing, and wishes to know nothing, of technical innovation. It is true that examples of most of these guild features are to be found in the building practice of other countries. The distinguishing feature of the French building industry is only that in decades of stagnation all these tendencies have been pressed to their ultimate logical conclusion.

Perhaps the only surprising thing is that the French state, which for ten years was practically the only patron of building and had contracts to hand out for the reconstruction of whole towns, was not in a position to dictate its terms and to demand proper building plans, rationalisation, and proper estimates. But the omnipresence of the French state is cancelled out by its impotence. The history of the French Ministry of Reconstruction is to a large extent the history of a long and hopeless struggle with the "order" of architects, which is sovereign in its sphere. No planning and building can be done without it, but it comes, not under the Ministry of Reconstruction, but, significantly, under the Ministry of Fine Arts, and in its Higher Council the order possesses an unassailable stronghold with legal authority of its own. The Ministry of Reconstruction possesses thousands of files about unreliable architects who neglected their contracts, falsified costs, testified to nonexistent war-damage or work which had not been carried out, went fifty-fifty with landlords and builders, and, according to the official report of an inquiry conducted by the Cour des Comptes, betrayed the professional principles to which they had taken an oath. But they all went scot-free.

Under the traditional method of inviting tenders for big construction jobs, contractors merely submit estimates for carrying out a job in a way which has been laid down in advance; they are not at liberty to suggest alternative ways of doing it. This, even if it does not make competition illusory by encouraging competitors to get together, provides no stimulus to any improvement in methods; and the disorder of the French budget, which for year after year was not passed by Parliament until July, *i.e.*, just at the moment when French industry begins its big summer sleep, meant in practice that the credits granted for the current year did not become effective until September, *i.e.*, not long before the beginning of winter and the end of the building season. Thus the state, the employer, was not so much the organiser as the disorganiser of reconstruction. Here, as in nearly every other field of the state economy, wastage of working time and materials went on for year after year, and the work that was done, being financed only from hand to mouth and subject to continual interruption because of the inevitable cheeseparing and postponement of expenditure, became the biggest factor in the wastage of public funds. The Ministry of Reconstruction never had an opportunity of tackling this tremendous task on the scale that it demanded, or with anything approaching adequate resources.

The building industry is an extreme example, but this brief examination of it will spare us an examination of other sectors of the national economy of M. Gingembre. Everywhere, from the production of vegetables to the administration of the colonial empire, one would be confronted with the same vicious circle of stagnation from which no way out is permitted. From top to bottom this national economy has got into such a state of congealment, and has grown so used to it, that, though everyone complains about it in general, in every concrete instance the phalanx of those involved immediately closes its ranks to protect its *situations acquises* from the slightest disturbing innovation. It has indeed so nearly approached a situation in which all existing situations have been transformed into permanent rights, privileges, and sources of revenue that all risks have been practically eliminated and bankruptcies practically never occur.

But all progress has also been eliminated. Prices have everywhere been equipped with the motor of a uniform coefficient of increase, but with a powerful brake which prevents them from ever falling; and they remain at a level which enables the most antiquated, inefficient, and unprofitable undertaking to survive. There is an uncommon amount of human solidarity about this caravan, in which the pace of the frailest and weakest determines the pace of all. The

French taxation system systematically grants privileges to the "economically weak", the craftsman, the petty trader, the small peasant, the small family business, by legal exemption from taxation, and this is supplemented by large-scale illegal tax evasion which is tolerated as completely normal. According to official calculations the latter amounts to 30 per cent. of the legal tax due in trade and the legal professions and to 70 per cent in agriculture. This amounts in practice to a regular system of bans and penalties on progress. The burden of direct taxation is borne exclusively by the big, modern, efficient concerns, whose large-scale organisation makes tax evasion much more difficult than it is for the little shops, which often get along without stocktaking or balance sheets and often without keeping proper books; and the yield of these taxes goes in subsidies and government purchases of unwanted goods, and finances the deficits which are the crutches which keep the "economically weak" on their feet.

The chaos and the fantastic injustice of direct taxation is such that indirect taxation, the taxation of consumption and distribution, which everywhere else is regarded as anti-social, but at least impartially affects the whole population, has become not only the only effective form of taxation in France, but also the fairest. In any case all French taxes without exception, including wage-earner's taxes, the burden of which is passed on to the employer, as well as the taxes on production and profits which are evaded, are automatically incorporated into prices. Every French employer and merchant has become a tax-farmer in the style of the *ancien régime*; he collects taxes from his employees and customers and gives a more or less honest account of them to the exchequer. This system of taxation works in the same direction as the vast army of middlemen; it acts as a systematic disincentive to any productive effort. It causes all efforts to reduce costs to appear to be a waste of time, as the results would only be swallowed up in taxation and middlemen's profits and lead neither to a reduction in prices to the consumer nor to an expansion of the market. The whole market mechanism has been successfully frozen in the *status quo*.

This national economy of self-contrived stagnation can equally well be regarded either as a caricature of capitalism or a caricature of socialism; in reality it is more or less equally remote from both, though it is certainly nearer to being a planned economy than it is to free competition—a negative kind of planned economy, the only law of which is sclerosis. The secretary-general of the Commission des Comptes et des Budgets Économiques set up by the Faure Government in 1952 under the chairmanship of M. Mendès-France, summed up the results of its investigations into the French economic structure as follows: "France, by refusing the discipline either of planning or of free competition, has chosen a controlled economy based on the protection of *situations acquises*. . . . After a long period of this kind of protection a sudden restoration of internal and external competition would have a more revolutionary effect on the French structure than a five-year plan." Such is the labyrinth in which dogmatic argument about Socialism v. Liberalism has gone astray, and completely lost touch with reality. In his observations on what has become the insoluble "prices and wages" question, published in his party newspaper on March 29th, 1950, the day before his death, M. Blum, the last original mind in the French Socialist movement, delivered himself of what was at bottom a liberal confession of faith in spite of its author's Socialist vocabulary.

"Wages in present-day France are and remain inadequate," he wrote. "They fail to ensure a normal, decent, human life to a large proportion of wage-earners. . . . Even when the various supplements and allowances are added to wages proper, workers' pay in France is below the average of the capitalist world. I shall not expose myself to the absurdity of comparing the living standards of the French worker with those of the American. But, keeping to the western European countries with which comparison is least open to criticism, the French worker earns less than the British or Swiss worker, less than the Belgian worker, and—though this is denied— less than even the Italian worker. . . . Why is it that France, if she paid the same wages as Great Britain, Switzerland, Belgium, or Italy, would risk pricing herself out of the international market? That is the real question that confronts the employers and the Government. . . . While the law of American capitalism, for instance, is to permit the birth of new enterprises, the law of French capitalism seems to be to prevent the death of antiquated enterprises. But French capitalism is unable to achieve this unnatural result without the toleration and even the intervention of the state. It is this that must be altered. To preserve economically weak producers wages have to be set too low and selling prices too high . . . [and] one can imagine the profits reaped in these circumstances by firms with modern organisation and equipment, working in conditions comparable with those of international big industry. These immoderate profits could be threatened only by international competition, but here again our monopoly capitalism can count on the tolerance and intervention of the state, and hitherto the state has never left it in the lurch. . . . Does the Government realise that the problem of wages, the solution of which cannot be deferred, is bound up with, I might almost say is subordinate to, the problems of the organisation of production? I believe so, because I hope so."

This last testament of Léon Blum throws a light on the dead end in which French Socialism has landed itself. All the mechanisms of competition, costing and price formation have been artificially eliminated from this stagnating guild economy, internally by price agreements and a Malthusianism which has grown instinctive and externally by tariffs and quotas. One way out might be *via* a totally planned economy. The other, which would be more revolutionary, would be *via* capitalism. The choice facing the building industry, for instance, is between forced labour and modern methods. But this alternative is so masked and concealed behind all the traditional slogans, ideas, and doctrines as to be inconceivable even in thought. The French workers—and the whole of the left intelligentsia in France which claims to instruct and guide them, and whose ignorance of economics is paralleled only by their doctrinal orthodoxy—take what they see before their eyes to be capitalism, and, as the great mass of its beneficiaries claim that it is a liberal economy, they naturally want the opposite; a by-product of this guild economy is five million Communist votes. The France of M. Monnet has sought a revolutionary way out in European economic union; but that has hitherto remained a conspiracy of statesmen and technocrats. The *pays réel*, the France of M. Gingembre, has successfully evaded the choice, and again and again it has succeeded in postponing the crisis which has shaken its structure and in unloading the growing deficit on to the shoulders of others; and the process which both made this unloading possible and simultaneously concealed it from sight is to be explained by that ambiguous term "inflation", which requires closer examination.

"The 'plan', like any undertaking of any duration, is thinkable only in conditions at any rate approaching equilibrium and relative stability of currency and prices. Otherwise the French will neither save nor invest," M. Monnet said in November, 1946, when he laid the first four-year plan of his "technical revolution" before the unanimous representatives of all groups of the national economy and politics. But inflation was already in full swing.

§3

ROCK OF SISYPHUS

THE fundamental decision was made in the first months of the liberation, and the way in which it was made, while everyone was talking of revolution, innovation, and regeneration, was characteristic of the climate of the time. What happened was simply that France failed to take the measure which was taken in all the other liberated countries of western Europe, including those with conservative governments. In these countries the measure was taken because its economic, technical, and moral necessity was recognised as self-evident, and because in its absence any reform was building on shifting sand; it was simply the reform of a currency which had been undermined by the war and the occupation. As a consequence of the Vichy régime's printing of bank notes to meet the German war levies and current state expenses, the note circulation had practically sextupled as compared with 1938—570,000 million francs as against 100,000 millions—but inflation had hitherto remained latent; business activity, production, and the circulation of goods were near zero point, and even the black market was a mere marginal phenomenon in an economy that had reverted to individual self-supply. The decline in the circulation of currency more than compensated for the increase in the actual amount of currency, and the notes put in circulation by the occupation régime, after being used for making essential purchases, disappeared, for lack of anything else to which they could be put, into the stockings and cupboards of the war, occupation, and black market profiteers. A stroke of the pen could have put all this currency out of action before it could have done any harm.

It is hardly possible today to reproduce the arguments used by the de Gaulle Government in rejecting the measures proposed by M. Mendès-France, its Economics Minister; similar measures were being carried out at the time in Belgium and were carried out in Holland immediately after the liberation. To a large extent M. Mendès-France was supported by the Socialists only. He proposed to declare all the inflationary currency in circulation invalid. Accounts would be blocked, there would be a sliding scale of exchange into the new currency, and the war profits thus laid bare would be heavily taxed. The strange coalition which rejected this measure extended from the Finance Minister and the old Radicals—M. Mendès-France's own party—to the Communists. The latter preferred rabid denunciation and the arbitrary acts of confiscation, blackmail, and revenge of their own "purge justice", an atmosphere of corruption, terror, and fear, to a real cleansing of the situation; the existing situation was likely to be much more fertile soil for the production of a "people's democracy". The coalition of the occupation and liberation profiteers with that of the ignorant and easy-going played straight into their hands. Instead of the measures proposed by M. Mendès-France, a "liberation loan" was arranged in the best classical style. So far from drying up the inflationary swamp, it sanctioned it, was equivalent to a general amnesty; the exchange of notes was unavoidable all the same, and was carried out after a year's delay, without any blocking of accounts, without any investigation into their origin, which had long since become impossible, and practically without checking or affecting the currency situation; and the Government, having missed the opportunity of taking the necessary deflationary steps, straight away set out on the popular path of a general nominal increase in wages, which opened wide the floodgates of the hitherto latent inflation and let loose swarms of purchasers armed with useless notes upon the glaringly empty markets and shops. It was the signal for the beginning of the year-long, hopeless race between prices and wages.

With that, every kind and category of beneficiary of war and inflation—worthy peasants and small traders, improvised middlemen and black market manufacturers, profiteers and outright rogues, petty hoarders and the millionaire Joanovici —were spared the necessity of opening their books to inspection, coming out into the light of day, having to calculate in real values and change over to legal methods and more productive activity.

It was never possible to reverse this decision, which was taken almost in the dark. All consumption goods, everything connected with the French people's food, clothing, housing, and daily needs, disappeared into the twilight of semi-legality and illegality. Wealth remained underground and goods remained under the counter, and the reviving circulation of money and goods took place, not through the normal market channels, but along the "parallel channels" of inflation. In the years that followed the whole of the economic, political, and social life of France was based on this unstable quagmire, which continually gave off the poisonous stench of corruption and public scandals. In this morass the Ministers of Economics and Supply were reduced to figures of public scorn, and every butchers' association and every wholesaler could cock a snook at them with impunity. All that these Ministers could do in reply was to indulge in the absurd Jacobin gesture of threatening them with the guillotine—the celebrated "death penalty for black marketeers and speculators" of M. Yves Farge. The history of the attempts to direct the French economy is one of capitulation all along the line; and the consequences were all the more serious for the fact that the capitulation took place piecemeal, bit by bit, in spite of endless attempts to check the process. This turned legality into a farce, and for every Frenchman contempt for the law became a sheer necessity. It ended by being taken completely for granted.

After this the French state finances were a domain of black magic, using the ancient magic formulas of "confidence" and "treasury intervention" to contend with a currency which was completely uncontrollable, either through the banking or the fiscal system. This country, whose whole credit system is state-controlled and through whose budget nearly half the national income circulates, is so to speak the only civilised country in the world in which, as in the time of Louis XVI, the treasury at the end of every two or three months does not know how it is going to be able to meet its current expenditure. The money which the state pumps into the national economy in its capacity as paymaster passes through no normal circulatory system at the end of which it reappears again, but unaccountably seeps away into underground bogs. It reappears again equally unforeseeably and unaccountably when some collective panic, a war rumour, a crisis, the first signs of a new bout of rising prices, or even some political operation, brings it into excited movement. All normal processes and reactions are eliminated or act in an unpredictable manner. The inflation of prices has long since ceased to be a technical financial question, but has become, so to speak, a natural law of the French economy; since 1946 it has been nourished, not by the printing press, but by the accelerated circulation of a "bad currency" which burned the fingers of those who held it and periodically made necessary an increase in the note issue which invariably turned out to be inadequate.

The impulse once having been given in 1944–45, the note issue always lagged behind increasing prices, and the combination of an increasing supply of goods with a relative contraction in the means of paying for them meant that the increase in prices persisted. It persisted even when the Central Bank and the Finance Ministry strained credit restriction to breaking-point and everyone complained of a shortage of money, and through long periods of stagnation and sales crises it always maintained itself at the level reached until there was no alternative to an increase in wages, which pumped new purchasing power into the market and set the spiral in motion again. A similar lack of connection has arisen between the note circulation and the budgetary and treasury deficit. During all the years in which, thanks to a rigorous budgetary policy, the state was able to dispense with the aid of the printing press, the note circulation regularly increased by from 200,000 million to 300,000 million francs. However, in the first half of 1953, in which the treasury was living from hand to mouth and had to apply to the Central Bank every few weeks for advances to meet current expenses, the note circulation achieved stability for the first time. The French state, with tremendous levers at its disposal, with a huge sector of the national economy under its control, with a direct financial share in the national economy such as is possessed by no other state outside the Soviet *bloc*, is exposed in utter helplessness to all the moods and crazes of the "market"; and the French economy as a whole resembles an antiquated workshop in which all the transmission belts have either grown slack or have been dismantled and power is transmitted either intermittently and unpredictably or not at all. Only the loosest and most doubtful connection exists between the budget and the financial position, between monetary circulation and the state of trade, between supply and demand, between production and consumption, between efficiency and profits, between costs and prices, between prices and output.

The fact of the matter is that black magic is not at work at all. Half a century of deliberate and systematic action by Parliament and the trade associations has served to eliminate all these normal connections and mechanisms, though the full extent and implications of what was being done was never examined. The apparent chaos is the result of the organisation of the most complete conceivable defence against any risk, disturbance, or necessity for adaptation. Inflation has ceased to be a mere monetary phenomenon; it has become structural. The France of M. Gingembre brings forth higher prices just as naturally as an animal breathes; only higher prices keep it alive. If about half the farms in a country and three-quarters of the business enterprises on their own showing carry on below the minimum level necessary to provide a livelihood for their owners, it means that the deficit in the national economy has become structural, that with all the protective measures—government purchases, guarantees, and subsidies—undertaken on its behalf—this economy is only just able to survive, and that it is vegetating at the expense of a state to the finances of which it has ceased to be able to contribute. This half of France, with the enormous weight thrown into the political scales by the villages and small towns that belong to it, has long since been unable to meet the costs even of reproducing itself, and is only able to survive thanks to continual outside subsidies. But it is powerful enough to insist on these subsidies. It produces no more capital, but uses it up, its own and that of the national economy as a whole. Moreover, this process is intensified by another, no less disastrous in its consequences—the sterile hoarding of gold and the flight of capital, two habits which have become ingrained after a generation of war and inflation.

In the last half-century less and less of the capital withdrawn from the French economy has been reinvested in it. It has been sent or smuggled abroad, or hoarded in the form of gold, and the most varied ways and means were found of putting it in "places of safety", out of reach of war, revolution, and the tax-collector. The French national economy became something to loot, a tub from which one took pickings with no thought of how it was ever to be refilled. In the last ten years before the war it was in full decline; its external deficit was covered only by the yield of pre-1914 foreign investments, and eventually only by the surrender of gold reserves, the steady diminution of which was masked by the temporary solidity of private investment capital and creeping inflation. The loss of capital in the second world war laid bare the whole extent of the damage that had been done, and at the same time intensified the tendency to withdraw from the economy what could be withdrawn from it. The whole wisdom that the average Frenchman had acquired from the experience of two world wars was that prudence demanded that he should lay up a nest-egg in America or Africa, or at any rate hoard gold and bury it in the garden. An investigation into that proportion of flight capital transactions of which statistical information could be obtained in the second half of 1951 showed that in all their manifold semi-legal forms they took from the country in six months just as much as was brought in by a whole year's American aid. Both the steep rise in the deficit in the balance of payments and the steady upward trend of prices are to a large extent to be explained by the mentality behind this flow of money abroad, which ended by forcing France to withdraw from the European trade liberalisation programme.

The double deficit resulting from the consumption and the withdrawal of capital, continually shifted to the shoulders of others in the form of the deficit imposed on the efficient section of the French national economy which is overburdened with taxation, in the form of higher prices and indirect taxes paid by consumers, in the "discrepancy between wages and prices" which keeps down the wage earners' standard of living and exercises now latent and now acute, but never absent, inflationary pressure, appears finally in the form of the deficit in the external balance of payments; and the most absurd feature of this deficit is that France, an agricultural country with one farm to every sixteen inhabitants, which yearly destroys at enormous expense its unsaleable surplus agricultural products, could, if its soil were worked more rationally—to say nothing of the potential wealth of its colonial empire—meet the whole of the western European food deficit. Yet it yearly imports 200,000 million francs worth of foodstuffs more than it is able to export. It is only thanks to its permanent external deficit that the French national economy is able to maintain its unstable internal equilibrium.

This deficit was for some years covered by Marshall aid, and since the end of Marshall aid ever more acrobatic measures, more and more short-term in their effect, have been required to finance it. This has been achieved partly by deflecting American military aid funds from their true purpose, partly by keeping the French deficit with the European Payments Union below the point of catastrophe with the aid of special loans and American emergency aid. But unloading the deficit on the "western solidarity" causes increasing displeasure among France's partners; a higher and higher price will have to be paid for it, and not only in prestige. It must in the long run lead to loss of independence and self-respect. It has brought the problem of the French structural crisis no nearer to a solution; on the contrary, it has served only to mask the problem and postpone its solution; and it has not stopped the inflationary process, but has helped to regulate and moderate it in such a fashion that the country has slowly adapted itself to it and combined it with the artificial maintenance of all its parasitic structures.

If the French social structure has thus maintained itself outwardly, it has nevertheless not remained unchanged. The path of inflation, like a social and economic battlefield, is sown with dead and wounded, and the worst-hit victims are not always to be found where the complaints are loudest. Loud and vocal complaints generally betray the presence of the well organised, who are able to look after themselves. Behind the façade of an unchanged society and the persistent protection given to all *situation acquises* there has taken place a whole series of partial or complete expropriations. Property owners have lost their rights to sitting tenants, and small shareholders to boards of directors, but above all there has been a complete extermination of that class of Frenchmen which placed its confidence in the state and the currency, *i.e.*, the *rentier* class. A whole petty bourgeoisie, which, with its virtues and vices, its industry, its frugality, its patriotism, its narrow-mindedness, and its political credulity, used to form a fundamental element in the French social structure, is dead, and from its ranks there have been largely recruited the mass of poverty-stricken old people, helpless and ashamed of their poverty, who cling frantically, though hungry and freezing, to the outward signs of respectability and are shamefully classified by a new statistical terminology as "economically weak".

But this extermination did not take place abruptly, at one blow; it did not act quickly, like the inflation in central Europe after the first world war. It was a slow, remorseless process, with periods of apparent stability and long, slow periods of decline; in the course of forty years the franc gradually lost $99\frac{1}{2}$ per cent. of its purchasing power. The process was slow enough to allow the most adaptable, if not necessarily the most honourable, time to switch from fixed interest securities to securities which would increase in value. The *rentier* as a fundamental element in the French social structure has not died out, but he has changed his character. The savers who counted on the stability of the currency and used to buy state securities have turned into gold-hoarders and owners of flight capital who speculate on a depreciation of the currency, and an industrious and frugal petty bourgeoisie has turned into a bourgeoisie of *situations acquises*, who exploit all the resources of their political and economic power, individually and collectively, to extract from their well or ill-acquired positions in the economy a more or less parasitic living based on monopoly and dear living, and levy tribute on producers and consumers alike.

The old-style *rentier* of a healthy society has turned into a new-style *rentier* of a sick society, a bourgeoisie of *débrouillards* to which French popular terminology has given the symbolic name of "B.O.F."—*beurre, œufs, fromages*; and the share of the social product that accrues to this new kind of *rentier* is certainly no smaller than was that of the old. This transformation took the form of a tremendous negative selection; the French social structure and the distribution of income between the various classes of the population have changed much less than the human content and quality of those classes.

In the midst of her stagnation and sclerosis, poverty and social decay, France is the only modern country in which the numbers, influence, and share in the national income of an independent middle-class based on one-man or two-men businesses and its share in the national income have increased, both absolutely and relatively—a remarkable achievement in the self-defence of a remarkably individualistic social and economic type in defiance of all the tendencies of the time. But this self-preservation was attained by the most ruthless methods. This was not the arising of a healthy bourgeoisie, but of an unhealthy, cancerous growth. These people are devoid of social or political scruples, thoroughly "class-conscious", pugnacious, and ready for the "class-struggle", and full of solidarity, because fully aware of the threatened nature of their position, which is justified by the performance of no social function. True liberalism, real competition, public morality, and honest facing up to questions would represent a deadly danger to them; and the most important thing in the world to them is the maintenance of their control of the key positions in Parliament and the state, the distributing centre of favours, privileges, and immunities. *Non olet?* Public life smells only too much. The degeneration of French domestic politics into an orgy of economic pressure groups is a reflection of this "transformation in stagnation".

The French working-class regards itself as the victim of the inflationary process, and often as its only victim, and it tends to take this for granted, as a proposition no longer requiring proof. But here too the inflationary process has confused and falsified all standards of measurement and comparison, and has led to innumerable incommensurable individual situations, some privileged, some handicapped. The difference between having a flat and not having a flat can mean the difference between prosperity and poverty. Some categories have been able to keep up, or even gain ground, in the year-long race between wages and prices, while others have been left hopelessly behind; and with the latter there must be included what was once a quite high level of officials in the government service. The fate of small groups of provincial workers employed in more or less stagnant local industries was entirely different from that of those in the big industrial centres. Nationalisation at first gave a positive position of privilege to the workers in the state key industries as compared with those in private industry, but two years later the wages paid by private industry, which kept afloat on the tide of inflation, began to compete with those in the state-owned enterprises, which were always unprofitable, had to struggle with inflation, and for political reasons had to sell below cost.

One of the most remarkable features of the French "class struggle" is that the capitalist role remained unfilled. The "struggle" was almost exclusively confined to the arena of the civil service, the nationalised industries, and that of state wages policy; and private industry looked on with malicious satisfaction while strikes and agitation for higher pay again and again shattered all efforts at stabilisation made by successive Governments.

Up to 1950 the legal wage "freeze", which was always held with difficulty just below explosion point, was continually circumvented by industrialists, as well as by Government offices. Innumerable methods of "black" and "grey" wages were devised. What with bonuses and special bonuses, allowances and special allowances, overtime pay, and the device of the thirteen- and fourteen-month year, a worker's pay-sheet sometimes extended over sixty columns or more, and his "real" pay vanished in the mass of his extra allowances. Anyone who has ever immersed himself in French wage statistics knows how hopeless it has become to try and find out what an "average" wage is. In particular the French social insurance scheme has caused a man's real wage—the pay he gets for the work he does—to become merely a proportion of his "social" pay, which varies according to his personal and family situation. But, whether the "social" pay is counted in with wages or not, the total paid out has sunk to little more than half what it was in 1938—or, put in another way, in view of the greater number working and the longer hours worked, has remained practically the same. The French wage structure too has undergone a radical "transformation in stagnation"; the emphasis has shifted from pay for work done to social dividend. The social insurance scheme has itself become part of the tremendous mechanism by which the state takes one half of the French national income out of the pockets of the productive sections of the population and redistributes it on principles which are partly reputable, partly disreputable, but are always in conflict with the productive principle.

This social insurance scheme, the great social achievement of the Fourth Republic, was brought into being "dictatorially", over the heads of those who were to benefit from it and of those who were to pay for it, by decree of the Provisional Government a few days before the restoration of the parliamentary régime. This, to judge by the oppressive atmosphere of virulent controversy and flourishing abuse in which the scheme has since inevitably become involved, was probably the only possible way of introducing it; little reliance could have been placed on public solidarity and social conscience. The whole scheme still has all the defects of a gigantic structure which has remained stunted because it was planned on too large a scale. The original idea was to make the scheme universal, embracing all sections of the population, on the British pattern. But this broke down on the united opposition of all the existing private or group schemes organised for the benefit of civil servants, employees, and workers. The result of year-long doctors' strikes, and the guerrilla warfare, amounting to positive sabotage, waged by the medical profession against "regimentation"—*i.e.*, above all against the inland revenue's gaining access to the amount of their incomes—was that the part of the scheme relating to illness and accident insurance emerged in a mean and crippled form; while the insured themselves demonstrated only too clearly the attitude of the French citizen to any state institution, which is that no opportunity of milking it must by any chance be missed.

The institution itself became a football in a bitter struggle between the Communist trade union apparatus and the Socialists and M.R.P. As soon as it was founded it was handed over lock, stock, and barrel to the Communists by M. Croizat, the Minister of Labour. The Communists filled its administrative offices to bursting-point with party and trade union officials; it was an opportunity simultaneously of gaining influential new positions of power and of shifting the costs of the party apparatus on to the social budget. In 1947 the Socialists and M.R.P. enforced the first free elections of the scheme's administrative councils by the insured, and the resulting blow to the Communists opened the big trade union crisis of that year; and finally the employers, the middle classes, and the parties of the right united in a bitter campaign against the "social extravagance", the huge burden, and the abuses of the scheme. It was obviously a most unfavourable climate for this great experiment to prosper in, and the innumerable petty feuds and controversies that arose caused it to be nearly forgotten that the introduction of such a scheme had been an urgent and inescapable necessity. At least a pittance—the old age pensions are no more than that —had to be granted to meet the appalling poverty of the aged who had been robbed of all their savings by war and inflation, and something had to be done by granting family allowances to arrest the continual decline in the birth-rate.

Both materially and morally the family allowances have become the most important part of the scheme. This is another field in which France is faced with the task of making good the catastrophic loss of human and material substance which took place under the "gay and happy" Third Republic. The result of the decline in the birth-rate in the inter-war period means that the number of French adults of working age will have declined from twenty-three millions in 1945 to twenty-one millions in 1965, while the number of the aged will simultaneously have increased from seven to nine millions. A continuation of the pre-war population trend would result in a further decline of the active population to seventeen-and-a-half millions in 1985, while the number of those beyond working age would remain stable at about nine millions; in short a picture of a superannuated, increasingly impoverished, and barely viable nation.

In the long view the most promising element in the French post-war situation is the improvement in the birth-rate which has been maintained since the end of the war, and the simultaneous decline in infant mortality from 10 to 4 per cent. The excess of births over deaths came to an end in 1934 and gave place in the last pre-war years to an absolute decline in population. But, after the steep rise in births in the immediate post-war period, an excess of births over deaths became stabilised at around three hundred thousand, and the French population has increased by three millions since 1939. The French people is starting to grow and rejuvenate itself again. But here too the breach in continuity acts as a terrible burden in the initial stages of the regenerative process. While the active population—the meagre years of the war and inter-war period—will continue to decline to a minimum in 1965, the number of aged and children at both ends of the scale will grow, and the burden of maintaining them will fall on this weakened inter-war generation. It is a real rock of Sisyphus which has to be pushed uphill in year after year of ever-increasing effort—and the effort falls in practice upon the shoulders of the wage-earners alone. The social insurance scheme has undertaken a redistribution of the same sum-total of wages in favour of the aged, the sick, mothers, families with many children, and those who earn the lowest wage; and the burden falls on the young, the unmarried, the childless, and the best-qualified workers. All other sections of the population have on the whole just as successfully refused to make any contribution to the restoration of the population as they have refused to contribute to its material reconstruction.

Thus the final balance sheet is full of contradictions. The achievements in economic and physical reconstruction were all the more impressive in view of the almost superhuman difficulty of the conditions in which they took place. The Monnet plan and the Marshall plan, the tremendous effort of the post-war period, and the immense expansion in industrial potential, created the conditions for a revival, but failed to set the engine of this national economy in motion. Certainly "in the long run" all this must eventually have its effect in daily tiny corrections and molecular movements. The equipment of the consumer industry has also been renewed, and, in spite of tremendous resistance and deep-rooted habits, the modernisation of French agriculture is slowly spreading from the old model areas of the northern and eastern part of the country and the Île-de-France. Here too we are confronted with the phenomenon of what seems to have amounted to nothing but a useless increase in productive capacity, which failed to exercise any effect on a sheltered, stagnating market.

In recent years the real nature of the problem has grown clear to an increasing number of Frenchmen, and the liberal experiment of the "Pinay year" rendered France the invaluable service of laying bare for all eyes to see the brakes and structural defects which hamper the French national economy, and at any rate put an end to some of the pseudo-liberal slogans with which the France of M. Gingembre used to furnish its mind. The French national economy, with all its inflationary distortions, has stabilised itself, and since 1952 the inflationary process has itself come to a standstill, since practically every section of the population has equipped itself with its own sliding scale—sliding scale of wages, sliding scale of agricultural prices, sliding scale of state and industrial loans based on the price of gold and goods—and, if it is possible to maintain this long enough, a general clean-up will become inevitable. And "in the long run", namely about 1965, the activation of the French population movement will have irresistible effects on the national economic structure and the nation's whole attitude to life. Here we have an organic process going on, which cannot be accelerated by any artificial means; it requires patience, patience with France, patience till the rock is hauled over the crest, and peace—for, if the rock once more rolls down into the abyss, it will be difficult indeed for anyone to move it again.

The threat of external catastrophe is not the only threat. "In the long run" is a terribly long time, 1965 is still distant, and the rock would be heavy enough on the shoulders of the weakened generation that has to carry it even if it did not have to carry the tremendous additional burden of a parasitic economic structure, and if at every step it did not threaten to sink into the morass of ever-latent inflation. True, the population's return to a normal age structure will perhaps automatically overcome the present sclerosis, "and then," as a report of the French economic council of 1953 says, "the decisions which appear so hard to us to make today will probably be made by a stream of young life, which will burst the existing structures asunder and throw the leaden weight of *situations acquises* off the shoulders of national politics. But in the decade which separates us from this new expansion we have time left to descend yet a rung lower on the ladder of the nations."

It is a dramatic decade in French history, even if the drama is barely conscious. The new life that is stirring beneath the unalterability of the old France is like the butterfly in the chrysalis. Will it succeed in time in bursting out of its cover, the stifling incrustation that has ceased to offer it protection? What can be done in the form of foreign aid has been done. The curious result of American aid, from which France benefited more than any other country, was that it produced, not gratitude, but a genuine sense of resentment against America. There are many and conflicting reasons for this, with which we shall deal elsewhere, but one of the strangest and most fundamental is a dim awareness that the Americans, though they perhaps saved France from upheaval and collapse, perhaps also saved her from the purifying crisis without which the stagnating areas and the parasitic structures in her economy cannot be got rid of. To the extent that this aid is not merely to help France over a single crisis and to restore her destroyed productive capacity, but serves to help artificially to bolster up a false equilibrium, it is charity, or worse; its effect is no longer healing, but corrupting, in the moral, legal, and etymological senses of the word; and that point has been reached in France, if it has not been passed already.

The Marshall plan did not fulfil for France the promise held out by the Monnet plan in the "revolutionary days" of the Fourth Republic, and it was impossible that it should do so; outside aid cannot refuse life into a shattered and ossified economic structure. The words which Mr. Eugene Black, the president of the International Bank of Reconstruction, once addressed to the "backward" countries apply almost without alteration to France. Economic development, he said, was not an article of export which advanced countries were either in a position or under an obligation to pass on to backward countries. It was a result which each country must attain by itself, out of its own sense of responsibility, hard work, and sacrifice. It would be a dangerous illusion to believe that an improvement in the standard of living could be brought about without any alteration in an economic structure which permitted a minority to keep the lion's share of the national income for itself. These words of Mr. Black's need to be qualified in the case of France by adding that this "minority" in her case is big enough to rule the country by democratic methods and to lend an almost unshakeable stability to the *status quo*; and that it is able to do this in the full conviction that it constitutes France herself, the genuine, true, and unique *pays réel*. And is it wrong?

This ossification of French structures is only an extreme, morbid example of a phenomenon that occurs in every country which has a history: namely the defence of a once attained social equilibrium, and its character, and individuality. "Pure capitalism" is an idea as grotesque and inhuman as is that of a totally planned economy, in which human beings are moved about as if they were quantities of labour power which must be applied to produce the greatest possible economic effect; and as grotesque and inhuman as its exact mirror image, that of continual, pitiless competition in which nothing would ever come to rest or reach final form. No society worthy of the name, no society which was not an amorphous horde, could exist in a state of economic Darwinism, in which everything was in a continual state of flux, with no respect for any situation or tradition, and "progress" was blindly and unselectively pursued by an unrelenting "elimination of the unfit". Every civilisation represents a damping down of the struggle for existence, the crystallising out of an enduring structure, and an order measured by values other than those of sheer profitability. Measured by material standards, the standards of material productivity, civilisation is parasitic.

The instinctive resistance with which France opposes technical progress, modern hygiene, rational nutrition, industrial organisation, statistics, and the discipline of the welfare state is *also* the resistance of a people with an ancient civilisation which at bottom has right on its side as against the whole of the "modern world". The involvement of blind selfishness and parochial interests in the battle against modernisation and rationalisation is obvious enough, but these are not the only factors. In unconscious alliance with them is the whole of that love of the old way and style of life, the French way of life, which finds expression, for instance, in the manner in which every Frenchman uses the word *petit*, even when he speaks of a *petit voleur* or *petit fraudeur*; in that love of individual skill and craftsmanship which, if it could have its way, would result in turning the whole of the national economy into a branch of the arts; and in the individual's complete and absolute independence of the state and of his environment which in the last resort can be secured only by the possession of *rentes, i.e.,* an independent income; a whole tradition, in short, which is opposed to all technical "efficiency" and yet creates an atmosphere of human civilisation for the sake of which a stream of tourists flows to France every year from all over the world, even if they are fleeced, held up to ransom, and treated with deliberate indifference or discourtesy. If Europe did not possess this centre of resistance to modern technique and the mechanisation of life, she would be poor indeed and ready for colonisation.

"Efficiency" is not the highest aim of humanity. But a modicum of efficiency has become a condition for survival, and if a society falls short of it, that society ceases to be productive, not only economically productive, but in the long run mentally productive too. Every civilised society has its privileged members. But if the privileges exhaust its substance, and stand in the way of effort, and on top of that are the perquisite, not of a cultured class, but of a mob of "B.O.F.s" and middlemen—including dealers and commercial travellers in the fine arts, who are engaged in the piecemeal sale of an ancient cultural heritage; if literature exhausts itself on the one hand in pamphleteering and polemics and on the other in reminiscences of *la belle époque*, civilisation itself is being sacrificed to these privileges.

Let us once more revert to something symbolic to which

we have referred before. A country that has ceased to be able to build is threatened, not just economically and socially, but at the heart of its civilisation; it is degenerating into a museum, and a badly kept museum. Look at the cathedral of Beauvais, that monument, tremendous and amazing even as a torso, of an architecture that defied the laws of space and gravity for the purpose of storming heaven; and then look at what has been set beside it by the mediaevalism of the builders' guilds and the "order of architects" of 1950. . . . Stability at the cost of life and security at the cost of substance is merely slow suicide; the tragedy of the classic French comic figure of Harpagon, who starved to death on a mattress stuffed full of his savings.

In the last resort it is something absurdly trivial which stands between France and her own health, between France and the fulfilment of the mission and the role which she refuses to relinquish, and for the world's sake and her own she must not relinquish; which stands between France and Europe, and in the last resort between France and herself. At its crudest and most prosaic level, it is simply her costs of production; not the technical productive costs of her industry, but those of her economic and social structure, the production costs of a guaranteed *douceur de vivre* which for the great majority of her people has long become illusory, leaving only a bitter after-taste of discouragement, impoverishment, and sclerosis.

There was wisdom perhaps in her wish to preserve her traditional peasantry, her petty industry, her craftsmen, and her small traders against the "big" men, and the basing of her statesmanship on the confidence of the *rentiers*. But this wisdom has turned to folly when her peasantry, bound to the productive methods of their fathers, are condemned to producing in the sweat of their brow wine and wheat that nobody wants and fruit which nobody can afford; when petty industry, craftsmen, and traders languish and decay in a nation that is growing poorer and poorer while the assured profit margins intended for their benefit serve only to provide an easy living for the "big men" against whom they are supposed to be protected; when the first victims of this "confidence" and statesmanship are the *rentiers* themselves; and the revolt of all against all quietly smoulders everywhere.

In her striving after the shadow of "petty happiness" France has wound herself into a cocoon, entrenched herself in an autarky which after half-a-century no longer provides self-protection but constitutes a self-blockade, and has become a *cul-de-sac* which itself generates all the chimeras and terrors by which she believes herself to be surrounded. France has everything needed to be a country of unlimited possibilities: a soil of great variety and fertility, an African hinterland the opening up of which has barely begun, an industry which is technically among the best-equipped in Europe, a working-class which in skill and adaptability need fear comparison with none. Nothing but anxiety for the *peau de chagrin* of an illusory security, which condemns all this to sterility or mediocrity, prevents France from becoming a country in full expansion, able to feed more than her own children, a European California able to welcome all willing to work, for all are needed to strengthen her thinned ranks, resurrect her decaying cities, and cultivate her neglected fields. Just as stagnation breeds stagnation, so does activity breed activity and expansion breed expansion. It is not true that a return to movement and expansion, a return to the world, would threaten France's soul. What threatens it is ossification. For how can stagnation overcome itself?

§ 4
WAY TO EUROPE—AND BACK

Two forces of different origin, both of which sought a way out of the French *cul-de-sac*, combined to produce the great new phase in French foreign policy of which the first concrete outcome was the European Coal and Steel Community. The first was based on realism and an idea, the political determination to free the remnants of Europe from old feuds and hostilities and build a new home for humanity on the battlefield of centuries. The second was a technocratic determination to smash the suffocating incrustation which stifles the French national economy; and both ideas were embodied in two real statesmen, M. Robert Schuman and M. Jean Monnet.

The new phase marked the end of a long road characterised by illusions and false moves. But when one considers the lies and illusions which prevailed in Europe in 1945, and the crop of hatred and, what was worse than hatred, revulsion and disillusionment left behind by the thousand-year Reich of the triumphant beer-house politician Adolf Hitler, the road was astonishingly short. Judged from the standpoint of necessity, it was long, perhaps too long, but from the viewpoint of that always troublesome factor, lack of psychological preparedness, it was short, perhaps too short. For in foreign policy France started by attempting a restoration that harked back into the remotest past, and after all that had happened she could scarcely do otherwise.

POWER POLITICS IN A FALSE EQUILIBRIUM

"FRANCE has gone for today and for many a day." That remark, made almost casually by General Smuts in one of his war speeches, as if regretfully noting an incontrovertible fact, remained for a long time like a thorn in the French mind. French politicians and controversialists never really took note of, and indeed hardly became aware of, the context in which the aged South African statesman made the remark—he was announcing "the end of the old Europe" and the transfer of the centres of gravity of world politics to non-European capitals as the consequence of the second attempt at European collective suicide; and the unlucky phrase provoked more indignation than hard thinking. The first, simplest, most fundamental, and most obvious aim of "free France" was at all costs "again to be present in the front rank of the powers" when the allies were victorious, to have a voice in the councils of the "great" in the settlement of post-war policy and in the setting up of international institutions. There could have been no better champion in this struggle for rehabilitation and prestige than General de Gaulle. In his mouth the word "France" summed up a whole legend and tradition, and in his eyes it was France, even if it was only her symbolic presence in the allied camp, which was the decisive factor in winning the war—in a far deeper and, in spite of the sceptics, far truer sense than that put out by the propagandists of his own headquarters who, to the world's irritation and embarrassment, ascribed all the allied victories to the *coups* carried out by the resistance, and mentioned also that Britain, Russia, and America had incidentally contributed a few soldiers, ships, and aircraft. General de Gaulle was speaking of a reality far deeper than that of the military strategists when, in the darkest days after the *débâcle* of Mers-el-Kébir, he said: "Thinking Englishmen cannot ignore that no victory would be possible for them if the soul of France ever went over to the enemy!"

Mystical truths of this nature are hard to use as political bargaining points, as General de Gaulle discovered for himself. Nevertheless they carry great weight and importance, as was plainly demonstrated by the fact that at the end of this pitiless war of material two myths, or powers living on credit, if one prefers to put it that way, were given seats side by side with the three world powers of the victorious alliance in the Security Council, and given the right of veto like them. These powers were France and China; moreover they were the France of de Gaulle and the China of Chiang Kai-shek. (Should the Britain of Churchill perhaps be added to them?)

Our age is far from being so cold and realistic as it maintains itself to be. The heritage of values and the power of suggestion summed up in the word "prestige", which is so often misused and worked to death; the fact that France as a "personality", as an incarnation of humanity and of the west, means for millions of people in all parts of the world something much more than and something quite different from the sum-total of her power or lack of it at any particular moment, an indispensable warming light in the intellectual and moral economy of the world; the almost inexhaustible credit of the French nation; all these things are no *clichés* which can be exploited with impunity for propaganda purposes. They entail an almost oppressive obligation, which can take a terrible revenge on a generation and a state which fails to fulfil it.

How many severe and profoundly unjust judgments on France, both today and yesterday, have been based on the high expectations which were had of the legendary France, and were only too often nourished by her own ill-considered propaganda? The France of Vichy had discarded this prestige like a burden which had grown intolerable; let the world cease to expect wonders from France, for France owed it nothing! The France of the resistance took up the burden again, lifted it higher than ever, both as a claim and as an obligation. The discrepancy between the claim and the reality could have no dangers for the "fighting French" in exile, or the bleeding France of the liberation, which was living on credit and on its heritage, and pathetically bridged the gap between the *grande nation* of history and a future France, about whose greatness it had and permitted no doubt.

General de Gaulle fulfilled this role with all his pride and all his stubbornness; he carried it to bursting-point, to the point of arrogance and quixotic exaggeration. His protest against the "absence of France" from Yalta, as from all the conferences of the allied chiefs of state, culminated in his haughty refusal to go to Algiers to meet the dying President Roosevelt on his way home from the Crimea. Practically the whole of General de Gaulle's war policy consisted of insisting with indomitable will on the "presence of France" in the councils of the great, on the maintenance of the French place in the world, and all the blows and disappointments and triumphs that turned to bitterness in his long and hard path through the intrigues and humiliations of politics in exile in hotel rooms and ante-chambers, as well as his success, must be judged by that standard. France, as General de Gaulle had said at the time of the collapse on June 18th, 1940, had lost a battle, but she won the war. But what war? De Gaulle's mistake, and very soon the French mistake, was to believe that it was a French war, an old-style, European local war. This kind of war had ended, and ended irretrievably, in 1940. Four years which changed the world had been repressed in the French consciousness, and were as if they had never been.

But in 1944 millions of people whose motherland was Europe waited for the voice of France; a voice of human dimensions in the midst of the steel colossi, an old traditional voice in the midst of the new world, the map of which had been so radically simplified that it was unrecognisable; a voice speaking for the old Europe in the midst of the continental *blocs*. In a strange and extraordinary way, which in France herself was only too easily misunderstood, with the approaching end of the war French prestige grew in a fashion entirely out of relation with her real strength. For France spoke for herself, but not for herself only. Hers was the only voice of the old continent which could make itself heard, and when she spoke she spoke on behalf of Europe.

In these four years Britain had been more and more driven to feel herself an island more distant than ever from the continent, the aircraft carrier of the English-speaking world, the centre of a Commonwealth scattered over five continents; and she has never returned. Germany had in the truest sense of the word disappeared, been wiped off the map; she was a no-man's-land, and not only in the political and military sense. Terrible as the final collapse of the Third Reich had been, it only set the seal on an intellectual and moral departure from the human community which had taken place twelve years earlier, and the collapse itself was the mere physical collapse of an accumulation of power which had been void of ideas and vanished without ever having possessed any civilised potentialities and possibilities for the future. Perhaps the worst crime of the Nazis against their own country was that they emptied it of everything that had any weight or value other than sheer material force, and allowed the idea that the world would be any poorer for the annihilation of Germany to die. The result was that even those who bore within themselves the German cultural heritage came to regard it as if it were a piece of archaeological knowledge, the memory of a vanished civilisation, like that of ancient Greece and Rome, having no relation to what was called Germany after 1933; and beyond Germany, right through Germany, though still concealed by the unity of the great alliance which was proclaimed for propaganda purposes, there had descended the iron curtain. All that was left was a Spain boycotted and excommunicated by the democracies, a devastated and silenced Italy, and a collection of western European petty states, restored curiosities for stamp collectors.

In the world's consciousness all that was left of the old Europe was France, and that gave added legitimacy to General de Gaulle's claim to a voice in all decisions about the post-war period. "It is impossible to settle the problems of Europe without Europe," he said. Something, indeed, of the "European" mentality which developed so astonishingly in the French resistance movement while it was still living under the terror of the Gestapo was perceptible as a barely conscious undertone in some of de Gaulle's speeches; when, for instance, in the midst of all the publicity given to the Vansittart and Morgenthau plans for reducing Germany to a purely agricultural state, he spoke of the Ruhr as the "great workshop and source of power for a human home"; or when, a few days before the end of the Third Reich, meditating on the suicidal obstinacy with which the Germans were holding out, he spoke of it as leading towards the destruction of a "great, and certainly a guilty, people, but nevertheless a people whose destruction the higher insight of Europe cannot permit." France demanded, and in the end was given, the right to speak in her own name and in that of Europe. And in that hour what was it that she had to say through the mouths of her new men?

At the end of the conference at which the United Nations was founded General Smuts said another terrible thing. "The voice of Europe was not to be heard at San Francisco," he said. Nevertheless M. Bidault spoke often and at length. He spoke to proclaim France's position as a great power by virtue of her history and her achievements, to demand recognition of France and her share in the victory, and to claim her share of committee chairmanships and priorities, but that was all. He made no contribution to the solution of any European question, produced no idea for the ordering of the convulsed continent, offered no constructive idea about policy towards the defeated; and what was the French answer to the "German question", which was then not a question put to Germany, but the question which Germany in ruins was putting to the victors: what do you now want of us?

De Gaulle and Bidault knew exactly what they wanted of Germany: the left bank of the Rhine, the Ruhr, and another Peace of Westphalia, which had once set the seal on the division of Germany into petty principalities and vassal states, and had so greatly contributed to anchor in the German mind the idea that freedom and national impotence were synonymous. In the unvarying formula that General de Gaulle repeated in every speech, this meant "the definite presence of French power from one end of the Rhine to the other, the separation of the left bank of the Rhine and the Ruhr basin from the future German state, or world of states . . . those are the conditions which France regards as fundamental."

The same thesis was proclaimed by General de Gaulle in June, 1948, on the 300th anniversary of the Peace of Westphalia, when he denounced the recommendations of the London conference on Germany which were to lead to the setting up of the Federal Republic. He said: "While France from June 18th, 1940, to January 23rd, 1946 (the day of his resignation as Prime Minister of the Provincial Government) developed her war effort from the zero point of the collapse until with victory she again entered the ranks of the great Powers, I unswervingly stated and defended the French position towards the German question. Its essential point is familiar to everyone; there must never again be a German empire . . . but individual German states, each having its own institutions, its own individuality, and its own sovereignty, which would be permitted to form alliances among themselves, and to enter a European grouping, in which they would find their own framework and potentialities for development."

Léon Blum, who for a long time was a voice in the wilderness, was one of the few who opposed this illusory policy of stubbornly adhering to the conceptions of a vanished age. In October, 1947, he very neatly summed up its consequences. "France was confronted with the fact that the Potsdam agreement, concluded without her participation, had amputated a large area of Germany for the benefit of Poland and Russia," he said, "and she demanded a corresponding amputation in the west as compensation, balance, guarantee, or pledge. . . . The French attitude in all fields was made subordinate to this unconditional demand. . . . We replied to its rejection by our great allies by systematic obstruction in all the interallied organisms charged with the control of occupied Germany, but this involved us in a second disadvantage, namely the prolongation of the anarchic state into which Germany had sunk. . . . This was really taking the shadow for the substance. I do not say that this policy was universally approved with complete conviction and a good conscience. Many people, even in Government circles, murmured, or repressed their indignation. But the great mass of public opinion was in agreement. Everyone followed the impulse which had been given, everyone except ourselves—and even within our own party there were those who found our disagreement and our 'independence' impolitic and imprudent. The Communists, as the champions of nationalism, marched body and soul behind General de Gaulle. . . . I am profoundly convinced that if France immediately after the victory had not gone astray into obstinately following the chimera of territorial amputations, it would have been possible and even easy to obtain the agreement of the great allies to the internationalisation of the Ruhr industries, to reparation deliveries in coal and manufactured goods, and to a federal organisation of the Reich. We ignored or spurned the possible in order to insist on the impossible, and what then would have been easy has become difficult or uncertain."

The essential complement of this *grand siècle* policy—doubly essential because France no longer even remotely possessed the strength necessary to carry out the policy of Richelieu in the twentieth century—was an old-fashioned pact with the devil. In earlier times this had taken the form of the Most Christian King's pact with the Turks; now it was the pact with Russia, concluded by that champion of the west, de Gaulle. The second great idea of de Gaulle's foreign policy was to base France's position as a great power, for which she was not qualified by her own strength, on holding the balance between east and west, with all the honours and advantages of an intermediary wooed by all parties.

Three months after their entry into liberated Paris, de Gaulle and Bidault departed for Moscow, declaring that history and geography alike inevitably made alliance with the Soviet Union the corner-stone of French policy; and an alliance which was to guarantee both the external security and the inner equilibrium of the Fourth Republic was signed in a spirit of overflowing good fellowship and rivers of vodka and champagne. "We are not presumptuous enough to believe that we are able to preserve the security of Europe entirely alone," General de Gaulle declared in his big foreign policy speech of February 5th, 1945. "For this purpose we need alliances. We have just concluded a fine alliance with the powerful and valiant Soviet Union. For the same purpose we also nourish the idea of one day concluding another alliance with brave old England, provided that she supports our requirements in relation to Germany, and provided that we manage to sweep away the relics of an antiquated rivalry in various parts of the world. . . ."

The difference in tone is noticeable. Léon Blum's assumption of the Foreign Ministry during the short period of office of his interim Government at the turn of the year 1946–47, and his personal initiative, taken over the heads of the officials of the Quai d'Orsay, in undertaking a swift journey to London, was required to break the ice between France and Britain and lead the way to the alliance of Dunkirk, which symbolically established the equilibrium of French foreign policy but in practice marked the collapse of that policy, the bankruptcy of which was demonstrated a few weeks later in the breakdown of the Moscow four-Power conference on Germany.

The tragic inadequacy of *grand siècle* policy had already been demonstrated in the post-war world of 1919. In the post-war world of 1945, which had undergone even more fundamental changes, it was tried again, and the foreign policy of the new France made its *début* in the old ruts. Such a policy was adequate for a Franco-German family squabble, in which world powers were called on in case of need to act as auxiliaries, only to disappear from the scene again as soon as their task had been completed. The tragic lack was neither of experience nor of judgment; judgment of the situation was, within local limits, correct; what was missing was any sense of the altered proportions of things in this mid-twentieth century. In 1648 the Europe whose diplomatists gathered at Münster in Westphalia after thirty years of chaos really was alone in the world, and any disturbance from outside was inconceivable. In 1918 Europe emerged from a war which was not just a European, but a world war. But the Russian revolution caused Russia to disappear for twenty years behind the *cordon sanitaire*, the United States withdrew into isolation, and, to her own and its misfortune, left Europe to itself. Consequently the statesmen of Europe were once more able to demonstrate their expertise unhampered. But in 1945 the armies of the Soviet Union and the United States met on the Elbe, at the centre of the European vacuum, and this time they remained, and the continent burst in two at the place where they met. The ruins of old Europe were haunted by the unteachable history professor, who knew his Bainville by heart and recited it to everyone who was willing to listen, proving irrefutably out of Caesar's *Gallic War* that the Rhine from all eternity had been the natural and God-ordained frontier between the Gauls and the Germans. True, France had the tremendous advantage over her allies, at any rate her western allies, of having a German policy. But it was a policy that was unacceptable to anyone else, and as France, unlike her Russian partner, lacked the power to carry out her policy on her own, it led her straight into a dead-end.

The "fine" alliance with the Soviet Union was a scrap of paper from the start. At the Yalta conference three months after its signature Stalin opposed the admission of French representatives to the allied occupation and control organisms, and even to the allied reparations commission, on the ground that the French contribution to the war effort had been negligible; eventually he agreed to the setting up of a French occupation zone in Germany only because its costs were to be borne by the English-speaking powers and because it was, so to speak, to be carved out of the American zone. The exclusive object of the Franco-Russian alliance had been Germany; but on no occasion did M. Bidault receive so much as the shadow of Russian support, either for the federalisation of Germany or for France's reparation demands, her Rhineland policy or its miniature substitute in the Saar. If it occasionally appeared that Russian and French wishes coincided—at any rate on international control of the Saar—it was only because the Soviet Union would have been only too glad to have extended its power from its own hermetically sealed zone to the industrial heart of Germany. But as soon as it came to concrete questions, such as the allotment of quotas for Ruhr coal, M. Bidault found himself in isolation with his pressing demands on behalf of the coal-hungry French industry; and, if the Kremlin tolerated noisy support of the French official case by the French Communist Party, which appeared to be a deviation from the Russian "line" and a proof of the independence of the French Communist movement, the object was not to give genuine support to the French case, but to drive wedges between the western allies; and for a long time it was successful in this.

The Soviet Union, with a lack of concern for its French allies which in Stalin's mouth often assumed a tone of open contempt, played its own game in Germany, which, in so far as it was not confined to the removal of all not irremovable assets as war booty and the making of insatiable demands for reparations from western Germany, consisted of a ruthless and brutal de-Germanisation of the annexed territories of east Germany, and the transformation of the Soviet zone in central Germany into a fortress, from which it proclaimed itself the champion of "German unity". It was a completely paradoxical policy, such as could be carried out only by a totalitarian state. For the western Powers it rapidly turned out to be impossible simultaneously to win Germany and to hold it down, to dismantle it and to democratise it. The turning-point came with the speech made at Stuttgart by Mr. Byrnes, the American Secretary of State, on September 5th, 1946, when he said that the American people wished to hand back the government of Germany to the Germans, and wished to help the Germans to regain an honourable place among the free and peaceful nations.

The French policy of equilibrium left them sitting between two stools. It was nevertheless pursued for a long time with remarkable obstinacy and at any rate negative successes. A lasting memorial to what Léon Blum called this "policy of systematic obstruction" was the French veto in October, 1945, repeated a year later, of the setting up of all-German economic authorities, which did so much to help the division of Germany into two parts which France herself was subsequently so vigorously to deplore. France helped herself to as much as she could. From her tiny occupation zone, which included a tenth of the western German population and industrial potential, she took as reparations what the Black Forest was able to provide in the way of timber and what south German industry was able to deliver in the way of machinery, building materials, textiles, and footwear; and, as a first instalment of the wider claims to which she unswervingly adhered, she carved the Saar territory out of her zone in order to create a miniature German republic on the pattern that she desired.

The setting up of this Saar state may seem in retrospect to have been planned and deliberate, but in reality it was nothing of the sort; it arose empirically at the point of intersection of two imperatives. In Paris the decisive factor in Saar policy was French industry's desperate need of coal, and moreover of coal the price of which did not, like Ruhr coal under inter-allied authority, have to be calculated in dollars; there was just an overriding need of coal, and that was what the French were after in the Saar. But with M. Gilbert Grandval, the French High Commissioner, there was established in the Saar an exceedingly independent political will, as happened with General Koenig in the French zone, as well as in other occupation zones, which were everywhere transformed into military exarchates under the practically sovereign rule of their commanders and their courts. M. Grandval was a *condottiere* who founded a state, and made the territory his own personal domain in the best and in the most dangerous sense of the word; and soon the Quai d'Orsay was left with very little say in the Saar.

An extremely original form of state arose on very solid economic, geographical, and historical foundations in this coalmining area, the development of which had been bound up with Lorraine since the beginning of heavy industry. From 1870 to 1919 the Saar, with Lorraine, was part of Germany, and from 1919 to 1935, with Lorraine, it was part of France; it now became "an area associated" with France, and its population, as the German politicians who demanded its return to Germany in 1952 were to discover to their astonishment, developed an independent political will of their own and did not feel either their German character or their welfare threatened by their political autonomy and their economic symbiosis with their French neighbour. This provisional state of affairs, which has become very enduring, has survived like a chance relic of the Versailles period and de Gaulle's Rhineland policy; decision on its final fate has continually been postponed to a still remote peace settlement. The Saar has gone its own way, and, so long as it fails to find a European home, it will remain a disturbing factor in all Franco-German relations of the old style. It is impossible to foresee whether it will work out in the end in a positive or a negative sense for Europe. It will be the former if the population of the Saar has its way, for it wishes at all costs to cease being an apple of discord between France and Germany; but the latter if it is left to the political jobbers on both sides of the Rhine, who believe they can kindle the destructive fires of nationalism whenever they make a loud appeal to the Saar question. Only harm is done by ignoring all the concrete problems involved and running noisily through an open door and proclaiming the Saar to be German—as if that were the question.

In view of many a hysterical outcry against "suppression" and the "French terror" in the Saar, and many a criminally stupid comparison between French policy in the Saar and Russian behaviour in east and central Germany, it is perhaps worth stating that the French in the Saar have no blood on their hands, that no inhabitants of the Saar have been deprived of their German language or civilisation or driven from their homes, that the autonomous Government of the Saar is neither a terroristic nor a "colonial" régime, and that it goes no further in the restriction of political liberties than most democratic states, which forbid parties which are opposed to the very foundations of the state itself.

The difference is that in the case of the Saar these foundations are less unassailable and are, by general consent, repeatedly confirmed by France herself, provisional, as provisional as the whole condition of Germany has been since the war's end; and, after all the criticism to which the French have been subjected, let it be added that France's Saar policy has never been totalitarian or barbarous, or based on terror and murder, that it envisaged no "de-Germanisation", no deportations or removals of population and no tyranny, and that after four years of German occupation of France, after the forcible deportation of hundreds of thousands to compulsory labour and concentration camps, after Oradour and Ascq, Auschwitz and Belsen, there was lacking neither moral justification for caution on the French side nor material need for compensation. If France only too gladly forgot that it was not she who won the war, Germany has only too soon forgotten that she lost far more than the war. The legitimate criticism of France's German policy is, not that it was immoral, but that it was non-contemporary and retrograde, and that in this ugly mid-twentieth century it was unspeakably old-fashioned and hopelessly romantic; and that it was inspired by historical antiquaries and well-intentioned students of Germany, who desired, in accordance with what they had learned at school, to take the uncouth Germans into the school of Latin civilisation and, in the words of Charles de Gaulle, "call them to the west, as Christendom and Charlemagne once did." There had been signs of this attitude in the inter-war period, and it was always at hand to proclaim its readiness to come to an understanding "with the Germany of Goethe and Kant", but not only left it unclear whether it meant Goethe or Kant or the problem-free eighteenth-century system of small German states, but also and above all failed to mention what was to be done with the much more problematic but real Germany of 1945. This policy of the idyllic miniature state reached the maximum of its potentialities in the Saar.

But, when the Saar territory was carved out of it, the French zone ceased to be profitable and lost its value as a pledge, and from the beginning of 1947 it became a deficitary undertaking—one more deficit added to the French economy. As late as the summer of 1948 General de Gaulle was reproaching his disloyal pupil M. Bidault for abandoning the attitude that France must not depart by one iota from the French claims sanctified by centuries, and for no longer insisting that, if the allies were not to be won over to them, the French must withdraw into their occupation zone and "orientate it politically and economically in the direction of France, as has already happened in the case of the Saar"; and in November, 1948, he again declared with heat and indignation: "This régime does not defend France. To defend France backbone is needed. . . . We have pledges in our hands, it was I myself who took them—the Saar, the left bank of the Rhine, Baden, a slice of Württemberg; it is only necessary to use them!" But this attitude of resentful self-isolation and purely negative insistence on titles, privileges, and pledges which had condemned French policy to disastrous sterility in the first decade after the first world war, had exhausted its possibilities, and it had simply become too expensive for France to be able to continue with it.

Even within her occupation zone there were strict limitations on her freedom of movement. She had been able to carry out the political detachment of the Saar on her own account and, to the extent that she could rely on her western allies, she was able to ignore Russian opposition to this. But she could use Saar coal, her primary and most urgent need, only with the consent of the allied distributive organisations, and the combination of demands for restitution, the validity of which was generally recognised, with territorial demands of which nobody approved did not improve the French bargaining position. The gradually conceded *quid pro quo* for allied consent to the use of Saar coal was French recognition of the *de facto* settlement in her absence of the Ruhr and reparations questions by Britain and the United States, and—this was half *quid pro quo*, half a declaration of bankruptcy—the fusion of the French with the British and American zones. These had already been merged with each other, and their fusion was the first step towards the foundation of the western German state. The result of the "policy of obstruction" of the first two post-war years was simply that France eliminated herself. While she was engaged in her own corner of Germany, isolated and ignored, trying to foster a brand of petty state particularism for which there was no possible future, the foundations of western German policy were laid without her.

Thus the four years in which M. Bidault embodied the continuity of the foreign policy the foundations of which he had laid jointly with General de Gaulle were a long, melancholy, and unwilling retreat from untenable positions. Before his departure for Moscow in December, 1944, M. Bidault declared: "Never again do we want to hear the phrase 'western bloc!'" The whole of the long path from the signature of the Russian treaty in that month to the signature of the Brussels pact in March, 1948, was punctuated by stereotyped assurances that nothing had altered, or could alter, the fundamental principles of French policy, which had been laid down once and for all. But the failure of the Moscow conference of 1947 involved the collapse of all the assumptions on which it had been based. All that it was possible to rescue from the ruins was a special agreement with the English-speaking Powers which assured her two most immediate necessities, coal and the Saar. But the Quai d'Orsay issued nothing but reiterated *démentis*, and French policy seemed to consist exclusively in firmly saying no to things today and asserting that they would not even be considered, knowing full well that they would have to be conceded on worse terms tomorrow.

True, neither public opinion nor Parliament desired any more detailed information. Both were completely absorbed in their domestic problems and conflicts, and were as devoid of understanding of or interest in everything beyond their immediate horizon as if a world war had never swept over France; they wished for nothing better than to shut their eyes to a world in which their domestic problems had lost all significance. The first Constituent Assembly devoted a single debate to foreign affairs, the second Constituent Assembly did not debate foreign affairs at all, and on the eve of the Moscow conference of 1947 the National Assembly devoted a single debate to foreign affairs which ended in dutiful unanimity on the "immutable foundations" of French foreign policy. Moreover, not a word of the debate came to the public ear, because a newspaper strike happened to be in progress.

Between this France which was so deeply immersed in herself and the divided, chaotic, faceless Germany of the early post-war years, in which nothing identifiable as domestic policies existed, but only a dangerous game of chess between the great powers, the occupation régime lay like a Great Wall of China, as insuperable as any iron curtain, and this was intensified by a complete lack of intellectual relations. The French Press—as, indeed for a long time the world's Press in general—showed only a retrograde interest in Germany, which at most awoke when some desperate, crackpot Hitler youth scrawled a swastika on a wall, a war criminal disappeared, or a smart journalist imagined he had discovered traces of the werewolves. The fact that the noise of arms beyond the Rhine was no longer the noise of German arms, and that the eternal "danger from the east" was now clothed in a very different uniform, did little to alter the feeling of discomfort. Germany stood for a point of the compass from which nothing but evil had ever come, and people were only too glad not to look in that direction.

This Great Wall of China was not based on hatred or resentment. It is significant that in this post-war period the cultivation of national hatred, and even the use of the word *boche*, were almost exclusively confined to the French Communists and their intellectual fellow-travellers; and even this was not a manifestation of spontaneous feeling, but was done to order. The real reason why Germany was ignored was an immense desire to be left in peace. But with the decisions of the London conference on Germany of the three western occupation Powers, though they were cautiously clothed as "recommendations", when it became clear that French diplomacy, purely to gain time, had surrendered practically all its "immutable foundations", and that all resistance to the re-establishment of a German state was at best a hopeless delaying action, if not a sham fight altogether, a storm of indignation arose in the French Press and Parliament. It was all the more violent because it was a rude awakening from illusions which had for a long time not really been believed in, but had been frantically clung to against people's better knowledge.

German politics were once more irretrievably on the move, and Germany herself slowly began assuming a countenance again. In that summer of 1948 events followed each other in rapid succession. Four-power control of Germany came officially to an end, the German currency reform was instituted, the Bank deutscher Länder was set up, the Russians replied by introducing an east German currency, the three western zones were unified, and the Russian blockade of Berlin for the first time caused the fact to dawn on a bewildered public opinion that the freedom and existence of western civilisation had to be defended no longer against Germany, but in Germany. In this collapse of the old stage setting M. Bidault, the Foreign Minister, quietly disappeared, and he remained in oblivion for a long time. He did not "fall"; there was no crisis over foreign affairs. The Schuman Government just disintegrated in the usual domestic political confusion. But, when the "long" Government of M. Queuille entered office after the endless crisis of the summer of 1948, M. Schuman had been seated in the Foreign Ministry for two months.

EUROPE MADE IN U.S.A.

A REVISED edition of the Richelieu policy had been possible only because of the fogs and mists of the early post-war period, but in the past year these had lifted sufficiently for it to be clear that what was at stake was no longer the hegemony of Europe, but the continued existence of the rump of Europe left east of the Elbe. This discovery was not made in Europe. Those who had a voice or a seat of power in the restored marginal states of Europe clung to their petty optimism of the moment, hoping to be able to continue, at any rate for the time being, in the old grooves. They would apparently have preferred death to the admission that the luxurious fittings and appointments of the former mansion in which they resided were inappropriate in the post-war workhouse. Cassandra spoke from America in the objective tones of a banker drawing a client's attention to the fact that he is heading straight for insolvency, from which no aid will save him unless he alters his ways. The article in which Mr. Walter Lippmann raised his sober cry of alarm on April 12th, 1947, was headed "Cassandra speaking", and it was the first public premonition of things to come.

"There is still some time left to prepare measures against the great post-war crisis, which is developing in Europe and will surely, if it is not checked and prevented, affect the whole world," he wrote. ". . . The crisis is developing because none of the leading nations of Europe—Great Britain, France, Italy, Germany—is recovering from the war, or has any reasonable prospect of recovery with the means at its disposal and on the plans and policies upon which it is now working. The nations of Europe are eking out a precarious existence. They are staving off the collapse of their currencies and of their present standards of life, not by successful production but only by using up their dwindling assets and the loans, the subsidies, and doles which come from Canada, the United States, and in small amounts from the few other solvent countries.

"The danger of a European economic collapse is the threat that hangs over us and all the world.

"I do not believe I am exaggerating. . . . The truth is that political and economic measures on a scale which no responsible statesman has yet ventured to hint at will be needed in the next year or so. To prevent the crisis which will otherwise engulf Europe and spread chaos throughout the world, the measures will have to be very large—in Europe no less than an economic union, and over here no less than the equivalent of a revival of lend-lease. To deal with the crisis, if it is not prevented, the measures will have to be infinitely larger and much more dangerous."

No word in this cry of alarm was exaggerated. Two months later General Marshall, the Secretary of State, made America's historic offer to help those willing to help themselves. He insisted that the initiative must come from Europe, and that the programme must be a joint programme, on which agreement must be reached by the largest possible number of nations, if not all. The statesmen of western Europe hastened to accept the offer; they did so with a speed seldom shown in diplomacy. General Marshall's famous Harvard speech was made on June 5th, 1948, and on June 7th Mr. Bevin and M. Bidault met in Paris and invited Mr. Molotov to a three-Power conference which met in Paris on June 27th. Its failure set a seal to the breach between the west and the Soviet *bloc*; the history of Europe for years ahead was settled within these weeks. Mr. Molotov walked out of the Paris conference and menacingly slammed the door behind him. He had vetoed, not just the Marshall plan, which had not yet been formulated, or any American conditions, or any particular methods or proposals of Mr. Bevin or M. Bidault, which he had not even begun to discuss; but the general principle of European co-operation, the idea of an organised Europe, and of any kind of contact between his own clients and the western world. Moreover he did this in the name of the antiquated principle of national sovereignty, while simultaneously demonstrating the deeper meaning that this "national sovereignty" had for Moscow by calling off, as if they were dogs which had gone astray, the Governments of Poland and Czechoslovakia, which had seemed ready to take part in the proposed conference. With this there began the tremendous post-war contest in which the United States backed the unification and reconstruction of western Europe while the

Soviet Union gambled on its disunity and collapse. Many partial successes have been gained in this contest, but no decision; and the struggle continues.

The sensational nature of this contest, in which the stakes were Europe, affected everything which could be called European. The first effect of the Marshall plan was to cause the statesmen of western Europe to sit down at the same table, and confrontation with each other's needs, wishes, and difficulties forced them to think in more constructive, more European terms; henceforth, even if they ignored their neighbours' plans, they acted in the knowledge of what they were; and a fair judgment of the results of these confrontations at the green table would be possible only if all the absurdities, mistakes, and errors which were prevented or were quietly buried because of them were taken into account.

True, dismantling went on in Germany for another two years with all the obstinacy of a process which had once been ceremonially agreed on, had been equipped with a bureaucracy to carry it out, was protected by powerful interests, supported by arguments which were regarded as sacrosanct, and carried along by the momentum peculiar to international routine; and deliveries of western German plant and installations to the Soviet Union went on for another two years as well. Nevertheless the absurdity of demolishing in Germany what was being laboriously constructed elsewhere was condemned to death on the day when reconstruction was endowed with the epithet "European" and included western Germany. But the peaceful aspect of the Marshall plan was more and more overshadowed by its warlike aspect. The struggle went on, and the grim threat of the appalling consequences of the division of Europe with which Mr. Molotov left the Paris conference was completely fulfilled. Western European reconstruction was inextricably identified with the cold war declared upon it by the Soviet Union, and though the Marshall plan led by many détours and devious paths in the general direction of an organised Europe, it led most immediately to the Atlantic pact.

The year 1948 was a year of growing panic. The *Gleichschaltung* of the "popular democracies" which was now completed, the tragedy of Czechoslovakia, the blockade of Berlin and the attempt to starve it out, the second wave of the Communist general assault in France and Italy, created an atmosphere of imminent war, and Europe started calling for military protection even more urgently than it called for dollars. As people in France are nowadays apt to talk as if the Atlantic pact had been forced by the United States on an unwilling Europe, it is worth bearing in mind how urgently and anxiously the French in particular appealed for military protection. He who made this appeal on their behalf was no hysteric, but M. Henri Queuille, the Prime Minister, that embodiment of the "average Frenchman", with the latter's small-town love of peace and quiet and optimistic wisdom in the art of living. On February 25th, 1949, M. Queuille addressed the following appeal to the United States through the United Press: "The United States can never permit France and western Europe to be invaded by Russia as they were by Germany. For the maintenance of the world's civilisation it is essential that such an invasion be averted, and the United States is the only power capable of preventing such a catastrophe. The world knows that Russia tried to gain control simultaneously of France and Italy by concentrating its efforts on political sabotage. It failed in this. But that does not mean that it has abandoned its purpose of gaining control of Europe. France, as an outpost of Europe, cannot hold out alone. Nor can she hold out only with the aid of the Benelux countries on the one hand and of Great Britain on the other. That is why western Europe must be in a position to count on the aid of the United States."

Moreover M. Queuille added that American aid must not be delayed until after a successful invasion. ". . . In the last resort we should be liberated again. But the consequences would be terrible. Next time you would probably liberate a corpse, and civilisation would probably be dead. No, the invasion . . . must be stopped before it begins. If, for instance, we could count on a force sufficient to prevent the Russian army from crossing the Elbe, Europe would be able to breathe again. . . . A fortnight after the invasion it would be too late."

That was the French prelude to the Atlantic pact, which was ceremonially signed in Washington on April 4th, 1949, and was ratified and put into force by the Governments and

Parliaments of all the nations concerned in less than five months; and in that prelude all the future misunderstandings were contained. If, in Paul Valéry's well-known phrase, good treaties are concluded between *arrière-pensées*, the Atlantic pact was no such treaty. The United States believed herself to be concluding an alliance, while Europe—the Europe of which M. Queuille was the mouthpiece, though in this matter he was not the mouthpiece of France alone—hoped to find protection against all threats, both from within and without, in a unilateral American guarantee. America regarded the pact as the starting-point of a European defence effort aimed at putting Europe on its own feet in the military respect, just as the Marshall plan was aimed at putting it on its feet in the economic respect. But Europe regarded it as a substitute for a superhuman, ruinous, and, so far as the visible future was concerned, hopeless effort on its own part. In European eyes the Atlantic pact, as a supplement to the Marshall plan, so to speak, was to provide that gratuitous security in the shelter of which reconstruction would first become possible.

That, in its crudest simplification, was the "misunderstanding of the *arrière-pensées*". But this misunderstanding had been indicated in advance on the map. Europe sought refuge from danger behind the broad shoulders of the United States, but geography put her in the opposite situation; it was not powerful America which lay in the danger zone, the front line, but war-shattered Europe. It was inevitable that the danger of another world war should call forth different reactions in Europe and America. In the eyes of the American citizen, war was a possibility which must be averted if possible; but, if it could not be averted, he was prepared to face up to it, and felt confident that he could do so. But for those who lived on the battlefield of Europe the thought of another war implied the end of all things, total and absolute catastrophe, and the words "victory" and "defeat" had been deprived of all meaning. War was a thing they were prevented from thinking about by that same instinct of self-preservation that prevents all living things from thinking about death; and the Atlantic pact was there to save them from having to think about death.

An American horror literature, circulated in commercial quantities, devoted to orgiastic portrayal of the horrors of atomic warfare and the end of the world, and appropriately adapted to different levels of intelligence, played its part in intensifying this fugue mentality; and, in a manner secretly welcome to its readers, it encouraged the idea that all national defence on traditional lines was hopeless, futile, and out-of-date. It seemed that Europe, having ceased to take part in the technical competition, would be just as helpless in a future war as a tribe of cave-dwellers armed with bows and arrows would have been in the wars of the first half of this century. But, apart from this secret and at bottom so comforting apocalyptic way of thinking, the discrepancy between needs and resources was so immense and the threat so urgent that "it did not seem worth while"; it seemed that any attempt to enter the armaments competition would be nothing but a childish challenge to disaster.

In France, where this defeatism became the prevalent way of thinking, there was the additional factor that the "American version" of the Atlantic pact, foreseeing an effective European self-defence, implied from the outset the rearmament of Germany, all the more inevitably because France, so long as she was spending half her military budget and using her best troops 7,500 miles away in eastern Asia, could exercise little military weight on the continent of Europe. There was a silent agreement to deny the irresistible logic of this, until a year later the outbreak of the Korean war overturned this table of the law too. The misunderstanding of *arrière-pensées* dragged on unsolved from Atlantic conference to Atlantic conference. It caused a certain discomfort, but could be kept out of sight so long as the partners limited themselves to discussion of the immediate tasks ahead and refrained from touching on the fundamental question of what they really meant by the pact. When the Communist invasion of South Korea began in June, 1950, Europe discovered that east of the Elbe there were 175 divisions and west of it only ten —two American, two British, and three French divisions in Germany, and three divisions in France; and M. Reynaud was able to declare in the French Assembly: "Where is the army of the west? It is an army of ghosts. . . . There is no army of the west. . . . Today we know for certain that if the Soviet Union in an attack of madness decided to march to Brest, it would march to Brest, without meeting the slightest obstacle on the way."

The Atlantic pact, reduced to its simplest psychological reality, meant the placing of Europe under the protection of the American atomic bomb. The protection was effective, but it was nearly as terrifying as the danger which it averted. A security the levers of which are not in one's own control is an uncomfortable kind of security, and Europe did not find in it the rest for which it had hoped. Depending whether the waves of panic were breaking over or receding from the continent, the Atlantic pact was taken alternately as submission to an intolerable American hegemony and as a hopelessly inadequate paper guarantee which provided no answer to the real problem, which was not how to win a war, but how to banish the danger and even the thought of war. Alternating moods of panic and reassurance similarly gave the word "Europe" the most contradictory meanings. It was used to imply at one moment a call by America to the nations of Europe, at another European revolt against American hegemony; sometimes it implied the "western *bloc*", sometimes the "third force", and sometimes "neutralism". The most disparate, illusory, and contradictory ideas found refuge under the infinitely extensible conception of "Europe", until it finally burst.

The reason why an equilibrium between the United States and her European partners within this alliance was never achieved was not American power and European peril; it was above all the fact that the Europe that might have been able to create such an equilibrium never came into existence. The Atlantic pact was to have been the emergency roof under cover of which European unification and reconstruction were to have been completed. The American emergency roof was provided, but the European house was never built; and "Europe" became the ring for a shadow-boxing match between national politicians who would rather have seen their countries separately become American protectorates than unitedly become an equal partner of the United States. They found in the Atlantic pact a not very dignified but infinitely more comfortable alternative to Europe; "Atlantic integration" was preferred to European integration.

The Atlantic pact was a military reinforcement of the Marshall plan—for a long time on paper only—but it simultaneously destroyed it. Before the Organisation for European Co-operation had completed the first year of its work, the scenery on the European stage was changed again, and the transformation of economic aid into the military aid programme of the mutual security pact began. Henceforward this was the fate of all European undertakings; they were never able to mature, but were always overtaken by a hurried new beginning in a totally different direction or using different methods; the result was that they were obscured or pushed to the sidelines, with the result that "Europe" ended by resembling a chaotic building site on which a dozen half or quarter-finished buildings lay higgledy-piggledy, making the whole look astonishingly like a heap of ruins. But, however much these conflicting or incongruous "integrations" overlaid, overlapped, complicated, and hampered each other in those years, some of the underlying principles of this tower of Babel can now be noted down, as the smoke of European week-end speeches is beginning to disperse, and what it was all about is beginning to become unmistakably clear—perhaps too late.

L'EUROPE CORDIALE

THIS is not the place for an account of the economic effects of the Marshall plan, which would involve drawing up a separate balance-sheet for each European country, showing in each case the yield of the American dollars and deliveries with which each was supplied. That statement, however, is sufficient in itself to show that, in spite of the tremendous successes achieved in the reconstruction and consolidation of the national economies of western Europe, the original conception underlying the Marshall plan did not come to fruition, or rather that it disappeared without trace on the way.

The politicians of Europe, and the local economic groupings which watch over their every step, while unremittingly proclaiming that the hour to create Europe had come, succeeded marvellously in pouring the new wine of this truly revolutionary idea—and with it the thousands of millions of dollars supplied by the American taxpayer—back into the old bottles of separate economic sovereignties. The United States, with a far-seeing self-interest, with a generosity and on a scale without parallel in history, sank millions of dollars in providing initial capital to enable European reconstruction to be set in motion without great crises and convulsions, on a reasoned and orderly all-European basis instead of in the form of a dog-fight between competing autarkies; and Europe used this capital to create anew a dozen fractional national economies, all disconnected and engaged in mutual currency and customs warfare, partly entrenched in economic stagnation, partly suffocating in unused productive capacity. In that sense the story of the Marshall plan is that of a misappropriation of funds on a world-historical scale.

The first year of the story was dominated by a long, tragicomic duel between Mr. Bevin and M. Bidault, which even on the surface was a dialogue of misunderstandings between two of the most opposite temperaments and types that it is possible to imagine; between the sober lack of imagination of a massive English ex-trade union secretary and the florid, word-intoxicated eloquence of a slender French ex-schoolmaster. Everything was lacking to enable the two to establish a contact of minds, or to even understand each other. Mr. Bevin was in M. Bidault's eyes an embodiment of the national characteristics which the French find intolerable in the "typical Englishman", and *vice versa*. The British Foreign Secretary never succeeded in taking "this dear little man", as he called him, really seriously, and M. Bidault, in spite of his utmost efforts, never succeeded in shaking Mr. Bevin's broad-shouldered contempt for abstract arguments about western civilisation, national sovereignty, and the like.

When M. Bidault spoke of the European economic organisation which was being set up as a permanent institution with clearly defined jurisdiction and of a "European statute" for economic co-ordination under the Marshall plan, adherence to which would imply strict obligations and not just provide "an opportunity for the utterance of pious wishes to quieten our consciences and put off the long patience of the peoples with dreams", Mr. Bevin spoke indulgently about a loose and informal "club" in which the Governments of Europe would discuss their wishes and plans and in the long run "acquire the habit of practical co-operation". Between the "legalistic" French approach and the "practical" English approach—descriptions which were used to conceal the very real difference between a binding obligation and "good will" which was revocable at any time—there was not even room for the beginning of understanding, even though the "European ideal" was spoken of by everyone from time to time. Mr. Bevin was never able to see anything in the French pressure for a real, institutional, European union but an underhand attempt to displace Britain in the competition for American favour, and he replied to it with such a growl that he occasionally found himself dangerously isolated between the American and continental "idealists".

True, the penetrating melancholy which M. Bidault made the fundamental note of French foreign policy, the vague, tragic gestures, and the agonised bitterness with which he spoke of the necessity of uniting "what remains of Europe", did not make his idealism very inspiring. He spoke over the grave of an unsuccessful mission, the failure of the supreme aim of acting as intermediary between east and west, to achieve which he had once set out to Moscow with General de Gaulle; a mission on which, as he gloomily stated, he had wasted an immense amount of good will and "sacrifices, compromises, and intellectual contortions"; and "Europe" was a second-best, which might, perhaps, one day make it possible for a "third force" to exercise the mediating, balancing role which France had not been able to exercise by herself. But more immediate than any such long-range possibilities was a more tangible idea which M. Bidault associated with the word "Europe"; that of an Anglo-French union, the unification of the two great western European democracies and empires, the idea which that brilliant player with ideas Churchill had tried to throw out as a life-belt to France in the darkest days of 1940; an Anglo-French Europe with which the three smaller partners in the Brussels pact—Belgium, Holland, and Luxembourg—could be closely associated, surrounded by a wider circle of countries belonging to the "relics" of Europe; and the whole would be big enough, strong enough, and based on sufficiently strong traditions to be able to "digest" western Germany.

This new turn was radical enough in comparison with the Russian pact policy of 1944; nevertheless it was a reversion to a familiar pattern, that of the *entente cordiale*; it meant going back to the other and more reliable ally of two world wars. This "Europe", the way to which lay along familiar paths, was the only one that ever became really popular in France—perhaps it is only granted to illusions ever to become popular. With astonishing obstinacy French politicians and publicists again and again recalled as one of the great missed opportunities of history Churchill's Anglo-French fusion proposal of June, 1940, which had long since been forgotten in England, and is noted by Churchill himself only as a historical curiosity in his eventful career. It was the failure of this idea which settled the fate of the "European economic coordination" of the Marshall plan.

The Britain which was the object of this wooing was an imaginary, aristocratic, old-fashioned, somewhat reserved and crotchety country, with a traditional veneer of French civilisation dating from the Norman conquest. This country did not exist, and at bottom had never existed. It would have been sufficient to cross the Channel for purposes other than attending official or social receptions (but unfortunately foreign exchange for this was lacking on both sides) to discover that this stretch of water separates two different civilisations and attitudes to life, and that it marks a far deeper cleavage than any frontier on the continent of Europe, whether the Rhine, the Alps, or the Pyrenees; the experience would have been sufficient to throw light on the abyss of non-understanding which arose. In current speech on the continent England belongs to Europe; in current English speech she does not; the Englishman travels "to Europe" as to an exotic land. The Britain of Bevin and the Labour Party was intellectually, politically, and economically farther from Europe than conservative Britain had ever been. But it would have been a grave mistake to suppose that, just because Churchill, in his spare time as leader of the Opposition, when he was not writing his memoirs or painting landscapes, preached "Europe" in order to annoy Mr. Bevin, Britain under his leadership would have given any other answer, though perhaps the "no" would have been couched in somewhat politer terms.

The British economy had been directed more and more away from Europe towards the Empire and America; it was only as the nerve-centre of the Commonwealth and the sterling area, and only in close dependence on America, that Britain could maintain her international position; the only hope of restoring her independence was a Puritanical austerity, which shunned infection from the decadent, shattered, and undisciplined continent. Britain's economic foundations were far more severely shaken than were those of France, and she carried on from day to day just as hopelessly and just as much in need of aid as any European client of America's. But her political structure and façade were intact, her self-confidence undiminished, and her natural national discipline had not been shattered by the collapse which had swept over every country in Europe from the Baltic to the Pyrenees; and she looked down with all the Puritan's contempt for Mediterranean man on the beggarly pack of continental good-for-nothings who desired to cling to her skirts. The fundamental idea of all British politicians, Churchill's even more than Bevin's, was not a European, but an English-speaking community, a family alliance of the great sea Powers Britain and America, on which the integrity of the Commonwealth itself depended; and no family squabble could do anything to shake the iron determination to place this solidarity over any other. The idea of Britain's giving up her special relationship with America and joining the queue of European suitors, of inserting a European economic directory between London and Washington, which, moreover, would have a voice in British and Commonwealth economic affairs, necessarily appeared to all responsible British statesmen as an attack on the very foundations of British policy. Even if M. Bidault had succeeded in winning Mr. Bevin over to an exchange of philosophical ideas, the wall to which he was addressing himself was built of harder stuff than Mr. Bevin's eardrum; and, significantly enough, this year of fruitless wooing was a year of bitter Anglo-French currency warfare, carried out, particularly on the London side, with complete ruthlessness and disregard of all co-operation organisms.

Thus from the outset the "Europe" that was set up was subject to vital limitations; it was provisional, non-binding, an arena of mere good will, which is no will at all. The participation of Britain in European economic co-operation, and her final agreement under strong American pressure to the setting up of a permanent European economic council, the Organisation for European Economic Co-operation, was finally achieved on the condition on which she successfully insisted: that such agencies should be mere book-keeping and clearing houses. This unyielding resistance, seconded by the Scandinavian countries, to all efforts to give political and economic authority to a European economic council, and combine the threads of Marshall aid in a European authority instead of allowing them to run direct to Washington, wrecked the basic idea of the Marshall plan. Economic aid, and subsequent military aid under the Atlantic pact, were forced back into the old channels of bilateral agreement between the United States and the individual countries at the receiving end, which engaged in autarkic investment and armament programmes, the promotion of parallel export drives which cancelled each other out, and a pitiful individual competition for American subsidies, credits, and orders; and America derived all the advantages, bordering on the exercise of tutelage, which inevitably accrue in such a situation to the party which has the power and dispenses the benefits. The price of British participation in the construction of Europe was the abandonment of a firm institutional basis because of the restriction of the project to the British method of "functional approach", which is a fine name for no method at all. Approaching the proclaimed goal of economic unity by infinitesimal steps, "percentage liberalisations", and advances of one millimetre at a time, means taking the whole problem out of politics and simultaneously painlessly disposing of it.

The Organisation for European Economic Co-operation and the European Payments Union, which were the crowning achievements of this process, have done a tremendous amount of work, enough to fill whole libraries, and produced an enormous amount of useful, laborious, and unglamorous results: the unification of customs nomenclature, the cataloguing and classification of the innumerable forms of discriminatory practices, and even a piecemeal assimilation of statistical methods, which for the first time made the performances, needs, and potentialities of national economies technically comparable and capable of being added up. All this was little adapted to inflaming the imagination of European public opinion, and for the man in the street it remained a book sealed with seven seals, but it was indispensable pioneering work in investigating the maze of the European economy. But, while the European calculating bureaux tirelessly drew up balance sheets of the individual European economies, these economies, in accordance with the law which causes every organised national economy to pursue an illusory autarky, drew farther and farther apart. All the efforts of co-ordination have enabled intra-European trade to keep only just alive, and at the first sign of crisis in each country a stroke of a pen was sufficient to render null and void all that had been laboriously achieved in the way of liberalisation in years of negotiation, and the whole labour of Sisyphus had to begin all over again.

France, paradoxically enough, whose Ministers were the most earnest advocates of European integration and were continually producing out of their hats revolutionary proposals for customs and currency unions and investment pools, acted as the brake on all efforts at European reconstruction and at achieving a balance and a liberalisation of European trade. This was because of her instability, her chronic deficit, and her always latent inflation. She was the bottomless pit into which more than half of direct and indirect American aid was poured without visible result; the "sick man of Europe", and the weakest link in the western alliance. This paradox caused her to be accused of hypocrisy or of empty phrase-making, and roused suspicion that her appeals to high ideals concealed a desire merely to shift her deficit on to the shoulders of others, or, more simply still, to pay for good American dollars with fine phrases.

The paradox, however, was only apparent. France was unable to overcome her national stagnation from within, or to set in motion the rusty mechanisms of her national economy by her own efforts. The combined defensive power of an organised anarchy, a bureaucracy that had become supreme, and a parliamentary system that had become negative, successfully prevented even the most obviously necessary reforms from being carried out. This was the very reason why French statesmen and economic politicians tried again and again to burst out of this national framework in which all development was blocked; but the British veto condemned it, with all the other national economies of Europe, to continue revolving in the same vicious circle.

The apparently so reasonable argument, used by all realists against the suspect "idealism" of the French proposals, namely that the individual European national economies must each be inwardly adjusted before unification was possible, that they must harmonise their currencies, taxation systems, costs, and investment programmes before the institutions for the implementation of a common economic, currency, and investment policy could be created—in short, that each country must start behaving as a part of a European whole before the latter had begun to exist—was in reality either an argument in a circle or an excuse—Munchausen pulling himself out of a bog by his own hair. No power on earth can cause French agriculture to produce for the requirements of the European market instead of for the deficit of the national alcohol administration so long as the European market does not exist; and foreign trade, particularly the arbitrarily manipulated foreign trade of our time, is no substitute for that reasonably assured and stable market without which agricultural production is a gamble of a kind with which the French peasant, after the experience of half-a-century of permanent and devastating crisis, simply refuses to have anything to do. British food purchases in France, for instance, varied unpredictably from year to year, all the way from mass imports to a complete import embargo, depending on the state of British dollar reserves.

Let us recall the conclusion of a French government commission which we have already quoted, namely that in France a Soviet five-year plan would be a lesser revolution than a return to a competitive economy. No government can introduce free competition by decree into a hermetically sealed area if free competition in that area has died out and it is not reintroduced by a free market from outside. Anything can be introduced by governmental decree, but not that. The self-defensive arrangements of this national economy, so powerfully organised both economically and in Parliament, have always closed as quickly as the organism of a mollusc over the pinpricks patiently made in its autarky by the "liberalisation percentages" of European agreements.

The vicious circle of "functionable integration" and the limitations of what is attainable by inter-state negotiation were best demonstrated by the classic example of France. The official representatives of national economic interests are unable to jump over their own shadows; the best that can be expected of their consultations is a catalogue of compromises along the line of least resistance; their efforts can lead to the establishment of no overriding authority or supra-national point of view. Even the relatively innocuous aim of doing away with customs and quotas was unattainable by the method of international bargaining about individual tariffs, to the accompaniment of protests and cries of alarm by all the sectional interests and parties in all the countries involved; even from the technical point of view of the negotiator, the apparently easier path of gradual adaptation and advancing step by step without touching on the question of sovereignty turned out to be the most intractable. All attempts at achieving a thoroughgoing co-ordination of distinct national economies by the method of negotiation turned out to be mere shadow-boxing. Alliances can be negotiated between Ministers, customs agreements can be worked out from case to case between civil servants, but the unification of two or a dozen national economies which have developed behind protective fences, whether in competition with each other or not, presents problems which far exceed what is attainable by inter-state economic diplomacy. The Anglo-French "greater Europe" remained a paper agitation in the void. The more the tons, the mountains, of paper accumulated, the greater became the resulting nightmare. Finally the whole thing turned into a yawning superfluity.

When M. Bidault was succeeded at the Quai d'Orsay by M.

Schuman nothing was altered in this respect. True, the sober, dry, laconic Lorrainer succeeded in doing something which M. Bidault had never managed to do, namely in talking to Mr. Bevin, and even in talking to him about Europe; he did so in the cool, objective tones in which he spoke of the necessity of balancing the budget or achieving a balance of international payments. Patiently and cautiously he cleared away accumulated differences and misunderstandings, in particular the protracted differences which had existed on German policy, the German occupation statute, the political organisation of western Germany, dismantling, and restrictions on German production; as well as the Ruhr problem, over which British and French politicians had for four years been engaged in bitter controversy. Since 1947 France had advocated the "internationalisation" policy which the British Labour Party had favoured at the end of the war. But in the meantime the Labour Government had abandoned this policy with the "selling out" of the insolvent British zone to America, and, with the American decision to hand back the Ruhr industry to German control, this ceased to be a subject of controversy between Britain and France. All this was a long and complicated process of liquidation prior to a new start; and the Washington agreement of 1949 between the three occupation Powers brought four years of confusion to an end. The first triumph of the new policy, however, was the British Government's entirely unexpected agreement in April, 1949, to the project for a European Assembly, the presentation of which to the five Powers of the Brussels pact had been the last move undertaken by M. Bidault. Mr. Bevin at the time had rejected it with both hands as an abstruse figment of the imagination.

The two things in reality belonged together. The imminence of the re-emergence of a German state out of the political vacuum in central Europe now set a dramatic term to the comfortable jog-trot of "European integration"; it was now or never, or at any rate so it seemed to be, though once again the outcome was to be neither a now nor a never. The "European ideal" had by this time grown very tired and been nearly talked to death, but the prospective resurrection of Germany provided it with a political motive force and lent it an urgency of which public opinion had been previously unaware. It was discovered that, if a German revival were not again to result in disaster for Europe, Germany must be integrated into a European unity. But that would be possible only if, when a German state came into being again, a European union were already in existence into which she could be received. But the necessary renunciation of German sovereignty could in the long run be purchased only by a similar renunciation by her European partners. A race began between "laying the political foundation-stone of Europe" and the restoration of a German state, and, for those who still believed in the possibility of a settlement with Russia, there was a third party in the race. The establishment of the German Federal Republic in Bonn simultaneously set the seal on German re-entry into the European system and on the division into two both of Germany and of Europe itself. The European Assembly at Strasbourg provided a roof under which western Germany was to join the other states of western Europe after an appropriate period of probation; and meanwhile in Paris a "last attempt"—one of many future "last attempts"—was made either to prevent both these developments by coming to terms with the Soviet Union, or by failing to do so finally to convince European public opinion of the inevitability of both.

The drama of this race was to a large extent external and "meant for the gallery", but it served effectively to impress a broad area of public opinion in all the countries concerned with the issues at stake, and to burst the bounds of old habits of thought. Events followed each other rapidly. On May 5th the representatives of the ten Powers—the five Powers of the Brussels pact which issued the invitation and the five Powers which accepted it, Norway, Sweden, Denmark, Ireland, and Italy—approved the statute of the Council of Europe; on May 8th the constitution of the German Federal Republic was approved by the parliamentary council in Bonn; on May 9th the Russians lifted the blockade of Berlin; on May 23rd the German constitution came into effect, having been approved by the Allied Military Governors and all the western German *Länder* except Bavaria, and on the same day a four-Power conference met in Paris which, apart from liquidating the blockade of Berlin and the counter-blockade, led to nothing; on August 10th the Consultative Assembly and Council of Ministers of the Council of Europe met at Strasbourg for the first time; on August 14th the first Parliament of the German Federal Republic was elected, and on September 7th it met in Bonn, two days before the end of the first session of the Council of Europe at Strasbourg. Europe and Germany had arrived with symbolic simultaneity. But in Bonn a state was founded, while at Strasbourg there was only a ceremonial act.

Because of the non-binding nature of its decisions, the Strasbourg Assembly was condemned to the same activity in the void as the Organisation for European Economic Co-operation, and there is no need to relate its history here; it was a more eloquent, less esoteric, but at the same time more ineffective re-edition of O.E.E.C. The condition of British participation here too was that it should be condemned by its own statute to the "constitutional impotence" of a mere club. Its members were nominated by their Parliaments and Governments, and sacrificed their holidays between their own parliamentary sessions for the purpose. They ended, in the teeth of violent British and Scandinavian opposition and contrary to the organisation's own statute, by arrogating to themselves the right to discuss all European problems, but the fact nevertheless remained that "they had no say". When Mr. Bevin in the Council of Ministers caused all the recommendations and suggestions of the first session of the Strasbourg Assembly to be passed on to the "appropriate authorities"— economic matters to the O.E.E.C., cultural matters to Unesco, and political matters to the various national governments—it was a highly symbolical act. He thus succeeded in three-quarters-of-an-hour in committing to the wastepaper basket the whole results of a four-week session.

But even with better will the outcome could scarcely have been different. The unbinding nature of this "Europe" was inherent in it. The "Europe" which met at Strasbourg and that which met in the O.E.E.C. in Paris—with two exceptions their membership was identical—was either too big or too small, but in either case was incapable of forming an organic whole. It was too small, because it was only half of Europe, the torso of a continent that had been split in two a hundred miles beyond Frankfurt-on-Main; Vienna was an eccentric frontier post and Berlin an "exclave" accessible only by air; and such internal equilibrium and capacity to form an economic whole as Europe possessed, or might have possessed, was wrecked because it had been crippled in this way. The "greater Europe" of Strasbourg, "the relics of Europe", to use M. Bidault's melancholy phrase, was a loose, far-flung chain of marginal states which spread in a huge semi-circle from the North Cape to the Bosphorus and hemmed in the Soviet *bloc*, which had advanced into the centre of the continent; and it was a collection of relics rather than a coherent whole. It had no centre of gravity and no equilibrium, and it lacked the capacity for self-completion; it was not even held together by a specially close network of reciprocal ties and common interests.

It was too big, or too scattered, to be able to grow together geographically, economically, and politically. True, the European assemblies in which the representatives of this vast extent of country, which ranged from Lapland by way of Ireland and Portugal to Kurdistan, did valuable pioneering work, irrespective of whether or not they really wanted unification or had it in their power to take practical steps towards it. They could be champions of European thought, symbols of moral solidarity, common ideals, and the promotion of a greater Europe, or "all Europe"; but in the last resort they could not be more than a debating society or devotees of a western mystery cult.

No doubt both these things corresponded to a need of the European situation. However, the common interests of all these threatened states on the western borders of the Soviet *bloc* were not specifically European, but were shared by the western world as a whole. The appropriate organisation in which they could all find a resting place—and in particular the only organisation which was big enough and elastic enough for Britain as the centre of an extra-European community of states and an island between the continents—could not be "Europe" in any form, but only the inter-continental organisation of the Atlantic pact.

It was in the North Atlantic Treaty Organisation that

decisions were made about the creation, command structure, armaments, "infrastructure", and financing of western defence, which, at any rate so far as the European partners were concerned, far exceeded their national potentialities and therewith burst the bounds of their national sovereignty; here there came into being an integratory process of tremendous proportions, but not a European one. The Atlantic pact has turned into something much more than an alliance and much less than a federation. The predominantly bilateral links that it forges between a single, predominant great Power and a number of allies, all smaller and some much smaller, make it much more like a hegemony in the ancient Greek sense of the word. The Strasbourg Assembly found itself in a vacuum between this great alliance and the independent national sovereignties of Europe. Integration into this peripheral activity in the void was offered to the German Federal Republic as if it were a high honour, but any idea that this was an adequate "integration of Germany into Europe" was patently absurd.

"Europe" henceforward followed many paths, but she got bogged down in them all. The Foreign Ministers of western Europe, like actors on a revolving stage which had got out of control, kept reappearing every few days against a different back-cloth, always playing a never-completed first act. True, their numbers, grouping, and function changed; they appeared as representative of the sixteen or eighteen Powers of O.E.E.C., or of the five Powers of the Brussels pact, or of the ten, twelve, and eventually fifteen Powers of the Council of Europe, or, with their American partners, as the select inner group of three Powers of N.A.T.O., or as the twelve Powers representing all the members of N.A.T.O. Each of these organisations set up its own permanent organisation, exchanged delegations and accredited representatives with the others, and co-ordinating committees were set up, the number of which grew in geometrical progression with the foundation of each new organisation. Their functions overlapped to such an extent that a special bureaucracy was set up for the sole purpose of exchanging and filing their statistics, plans, and resolutions; a sham world of supra-national organisations tirelessly organising their own activity in the void, grouped round the only solid reality, the Atlantic pact. Every month yet another "first step to the integration of Europe" was celebrated, but a hundred first steps were never followed by a second; the thing was a millepede which in spite of all its legs remained rooted to the spot. The fact that in spite of all the conferences and committees and after-dinner speeches the word "Europe" was not talked completely to death was miraculous; or proved that it contained a reality which could not be talked to death.

In spite of all this frittering away of effort, the movement survived. The "Europe" which continually came up against the same insuperable obstacle in its Anglo-French or "greater European" forms felt its own way forward in fields where progress was possible, in special agreements or fragmentary customs union projects, ranging from Benelux, the oldest example, to the hesitant paper plans for "Francital" and "Fritalux". But what was tried on too large a scale in Paris and Strasbourg was tried on too small a scale at The Hague and Turin. The Benelux project, that apparently so obvious plan for a reunification of the Low Countries, had been proclaimed before the war's end, but was stifled by its own limitations, and dragged on laboriously for years without coming to fruition; the project for a French-Italian customs union, which M. Bidault and Count Sforza after the first European meeting on Marshall aid indicated was going to be the first positive, practical step towards European integration, turned out to be a totally impracticable attempt to bring into being a useful exchange of goods between two countries suffering from nearly identical surpluses and deficiencies. But both attempts—as well as the total failure of the effort to combine the two in the form which became known to the world as "Fritalux"—taught at any rate a negative lesson, namely, that all these partial combinations lacked the partner who would have given them substance and driving force.

France had no need of and had little to offer a Mediterranean partner. North Africa, orientated by the French colonists exclusively towards France, since the first world war had unquestionably captured for itself the whole of the traditional place of Italy and Spain in French foreign trade, and it was this that condemned to failure, not only the "Francital" project, but all attempts at expanding Franco-Italian and Franco-Spanish trade. The components of "Latin Europe" grouped round the western Mediterranean are far too similar in structure for their integration to be able to set anything in motion, and the inner disequilibrium of each would be reproduced unaltered in the whole; for "Latin Europe" is itself a component of a larger unity characterised by a notable economic-geographical harmony; that of the western European chain of countries which stretches from Scandinavia or the North Sea to the Sahara and constitutes an integral whole, with mining, industrial, and agricultural areas which work in smoothly with one another. France, if she did not prefer to act as a barrier, could be the axis and natural intermediary between the fruits and the raw materials, the sun and the indolence of the south and the steel, the machinery, the technique, and organisation of the north, for she has feet in both camps. But the missing partner in this "Latin Europe", whom the Latin countries could not replace (for they required her too) was Germany. "Fritalux", which was still-born, was the crippled antecedent of the "little Europe" of M. Schuman.

Thus all attempts, both political and economic, ended at the same point, and all the "European" roads that had hitherto been followed turned out to be merely détours which finally led back to the great, the terrifying, the unavoidable root problem which France could neither get rid of nor evade; that of relations with Germany. That French politicians should prefer to deal with the German question, not alone, but in association with the victors, was intelligible enough. The underlying conception of the Moscow pact had been to do so with all the victors, and, failing that, they must tackle the question at any rate in "European solidarity" with their old British ally; that had been the "Europe" of Strasbourg. All these détours, however, were not in vain. In 1950 France took up the German question again in a spirit which would have been inconceivable without the new prospects opened up by the Marshall plan and the European movement, and was very different from the impotence and disgust with which she had dropped it in 1948. Another striking contrast with 1948 was that she was now confronted with a western Germany which was no longer a chaotic vacuum over which there hung a huge question mark, but had turned into a still unfamiliar but already recognisable personality. The German question, from being a monologue directed into the void, turned into a dialogue.

"LITTLE EUROPE"

It was a fortunate historical accident that the Franco-German dialogue which began tentatively at the end of 1949 was conducted by two men, M. Schuman and Dr. Adenauer, who were prepared to subordinate their whole policy, their careers, their political existence, and all the questions that tended to divide them, to the single aim of reaching an understanding between their two countries; and that there was sufficient in common between their political, intellectual, religious, and human backgrounds to make trust and mutual understanding possible, though from time to time the whole atmosphere about them was poisoned by misunderstanding and mistrust, which seemed to force them to assume outwardly the role of antagonists because of the offices they held. However big or small one may believe the influence of individuals on history to be, there is no doubt that these two exercised a great influence, not just by setting out on a policy of conciliation, but in creating an atmosphere which made such a policy possible. True, there existed in both countries a profound readiness—much profounder among ordinary people than among intellectuals and politicians—to turn over a new leaf in Franco-German relations and put an end to the old story of revenge and hatred. But recent history, still only too fresh in people's minds, had brought all the instincts of aversion and distrust to the surface again. However, it was the surface, not the depths, which was politically organised, and equipped with loudspeakers and all the power of custom and routine. "European" feelings were certainly stronger in post-war Germany than in post-war France. It was natural that in the total collapse of their national existence the Germans should have a lively desire to draw a line under the past and make a new beginning; and it was also natural that their neighbours thought they detected in German "European" aspirations a nasty after-taste of Hitler's "fortress of Europe", and the "common European fate" to which the Third Reich had condemned its subject peoples; for to its non-German inmates the "fortress of Europe" had been a prison.

The chain of misunderstandings has no beginning and no end. Perhaps the great mass of the German people has never understood the infamy which Hitler gave to the German name, or the shudder which the word *Kultur* aroused beyond the German frontiers after years of propagandistic misuse and demonstrations of violence. Perhaps they have never understood the irresistible, almost physical, defence reaction roused in the post-war world, not only among the French, but among practically all the non-German peoples of Europe, by the mere sound of a German guttural—though even stronger gutturals are to be heard elsewhere in Europe, in Holland, for instance, and even in German Switzerland. When the Germans looked at the physical and material suffering and destruction caused by the war, they might well conclude that as much had been done to them as to others, that the war had been conducted with equal brutality on both sides, and that the balance was equal. Quantitative calculations of physical and material damage are, however, beside the point. What was at stake was the name of humanity itself. The "biological philosophy" of the Third Reich, the perverse outpourings of a doss-house neurotic which were elevated into the official philosophy of a civilised country and led to the death factories of Auschwitz and Maidanek and the files of the S.S. race office, marked an absolute low-point in human history, with which no Stone Age, no burnings of witches, no war atrocities, or even the slave camps of Siberia, were even remotely to be compared.

Allied "re-education" efforts, collective guilt propaganda, and "victors' justice", however, did nothing to promote awareness of this among the Germans. The allies demanded remorse as if it were a debt due to them, clothed the right to booty in moral terms, spoke of Coventry, but not of Dresden, of Lidice, but not of Katyn, and spoke in the name of a civilised and united "democratic world", which was a lie, for the edifice was already crashing about their ears; and, in accordance with the law by which propaganda perverts even the truth with which it deals, causing every lie to produce its counter-lie, guilt was buried in collective guilt, collective guilt was buried in collective innocence, and everything was forgotten and nothing learnt.

On the other hand, what did the French people know of what was happening to and in Germany? And what did they care? On the western side of the morally and materially insuperable wall which for four years had surrounded a Germany that had become unrecognisable, there survived only traditional commonplaces, memories of the last senseless acts of terror committed by the German occupation régime, Ascq, Oradour, the shootings of hostages and the deportations, and a profoundly mistrustful uncertainty about what had become of Germany. Moreover a huge propaganda machine, that of the Communists, had been built up on the sole basis of exploiting these commonplaces, these memories, and this uncertainty. The Communists put socialism, internationalism, and social criticism in the lumber-room, and their propaganda machine played with obsessional exclusiveness upon all the emotions and sensibilities of the French people. In the name of the resistance and of patriotism it laid down a barrage against any understanding or reconciliation with the neighbouring country, which it invariably called "Hitler Germany", and denounced the "Nazi Adenauer", the "Nazi Schumacher", and the "Nazi Reuter"; and this barrage was sufficiently intimidating and sufficiently well aimed at all the weaknesses and contradictions in French official policy to prevent it for a long time from retreating from positions which had become untenable. The Communists and their fellow-travellers spoke deafeningly and triumphantly about Germany, and for long they were answered only by assiduous assent or embarrassed silence.

But all these things by which the two countries were divided did not constitute the real difficulty. They were all familiar to the point of satiety. They had almost ceased to be a problem; they were the waste-paper of history, and all that was needed to get rid of them was the will to do so, which was waiting to be activated on both sides of the Rhine. The difficulty was, and still is, that this will was never expressed simultaneously or with the same intensity or with the same objectives on both sides of the Rhine, and, in view of the total difference in psychological situations, even the words in which it was expressed appeared to be not understood, or misunderstood. France and Germany might have been living in different historical periods.

Even the point of departure was different to the point of mutual unintelligibility. From the German point of view the French had played only an ephemeral and peripheral role in the war, which had ended with the Russians and Americans meeting on the Elbe and submerging their country in the process. In the German mind, both in war and in defeat, France remained in the background, and she carried little weight, either as an enemy or an occupying Power, until in the inter-allied controversies over Germany's future, she appeared, not in the imperious role of a victor, but in that of a Shylock, railing at the world and insisting on her pound of German soil. But the French mind had at bottom remained where it was in 1940. It skipped the four years of war that followed and picked up the thread again with the allied victory. To the French the war was just a continuation of 1870 and 1914, *i.e.*, a direct Franco-German affair. For Germany the war ended with the total collapse of her national existence, and it left her with an almost unlimited preparedness for supra-national experiments; for France the end of the war meant the beginning of national restoration. By the time that France broke out of the *cul-de-sac* into which this led her and developed a certain "European-mindedness", the restoration of Germany had begun; and by the time that French public opinion had begun to get used to the idea of an equal partnership with a western Germany which had at any rate some of the characteristics of the Rhenish particularism that had once been hoped for, the chief preoccupation in Germany had become that of how to achieve reunification with her amputated eastern territories. The fashion in which the two countries marched out of step and the dissimilarity of their reactions can be followed in their attitude towards the cold war, which for France was an ending of illusions, and for Germany was perhaps the beginning of the rebirth of illusions; and it can be followed even in the ebb and flow of debate on the German defence contribution. A good many Frenchmen accused the Germans of being unwilling to play their part, though later they accused them of relapsing into militarism.

M. Schuman paid his first visit as Foreign Minister to Bonn and Berlin in January, 1949, to an accompaniment which was henceforth typical of the "Franco-German dialogue". The French Press was full of recollections that more than ten years had passed after the end of the first world war before a French Foreign Minister had visited Berlin; the Federal Republic was only four months old, and M. Schuman was the first representative of a foreign country to pay it a visit. This was greeted as a sign that there was to be no repetition of the disastrous policy of "too little and too late", which had refused to Brüning what it had later conceded to von Papen, and had refused to von Papen what Hitler had later helped himself to. It was not without misgivings that the Quai d'Orsay watched its independent Minister undertaking, alone and on his own responsibility, a "sentimental journey" to the scene of his youthful studies at Bonn and Berlin universities. The visit, as a semi-official Press note stated reassuringly, was "motivated by no urgent problems", but was taking place "at a favourable moment", "as the Foreign Minister's meeting with the Federal Chancellor is overshadowed by no political differences."

But no sooner had M. Schuman crossed the German frontier than the Saar question was suddenly raised out of a clear sky by the German Press, by deputies of the Bundestag, by Dr. Schumacher, the leader of the Opposition, followed in frantic competition by junior members of the Federal Government itself; and, to add a particular warm note to M. Schuman's reception, the Federal Minister of Justice made a speech about allied war guilt and all the wrongs that had been done to Germany in the course of centuries. The fact that Ministers publicly repudiated what they had said, and that the Press attaché of the Federal Parliament resigned in disgust at this folly, did nothing to improve matters; M. Schuman's visit of reconciliation ended in a cold douche. What the German politicians really expected of M. Schuman remained unclear; he could hardly have done more than repeat the assurances that he had given a dozen times already, namely, that the international statute governing the Saar territory was as provisional as that governing the Federal Republic itself, and that the "German character" of the Saar was not disputed by anybody. Apart from the attempt to mobilise world opinion against France, which remained illusory, all that was left was a domestic political exercise and a lot of broken crockery.

The French reaction was astonishment rather than indignation; they felt rather as if their Foreign Minister had been lured into an ambush and murderously assaulted. The basic tone of French comments was set by the organ of the Popular Republicans, M. Schuman's own party, which produced the headline: "They are starting again!" For a fortnight the world was treated to some "Franco-German tension" in the best classical style. The croaking that started up in the political frog-ponds on both sides of the Rhine, and the accusations and incriminations that started flying to and fro, were the result, not so much of ill will, as of sheer limitation of outlook and lack of vision. It would be an exaggeration to say that the waves of nationalism ran high—they merely splashed. But, though the Federal Chancellor pursued his aims head and shoulders over the heads of his colleagues and members of his coalition, though M. Schuman, following his path in equal isolation, quietly pushed aside the routine and the routine merchants of the Quai d'Orsay, at every step there arose a deafening chorus of domestic partisanship and opposition; and tremendous patience and strength of will were required of both men to avoid being forced by their own followers into a position of mutual antagonism.

They set themselves to assuaging passions, and persisted regardless of all obstacles. Above all they sought to avoid being dragged into the sterile game of mutual pinpricks, which was so alluring from the point of view of daily politics, but might one day have to be paid for in blood and tears. True, concessions for the sake of keeping together their respective parliamentary coalitions could not altogether be avoided, and a bone had to be thrown occasionally to satisfy those in either country whose national pride had been excited, or to avoid putting the other partner to the dialogue on the opposite side of the Rhine into too difficult a position. A double-tracked policy thus came into existence of which the Saar problem became the symbol; and ever and again the two statesmen, both of whom were convinced of the secondary nature of the Saar question and were in agreement about the prospects of eventually solving, or rather overcoming it, were forced to engage in a conversation as profitable as one between two deaf men. "The Saar is German." "I entirely agree, *mein Herr*, the Saar is German." "No, no, a thousand times no, *monsieur*, the Saar is German!"

All this excitement was in reality no more than the stifling smoke of a fire that had long since ceased blazing. An examination of the French Press of the spring of 1950, when the Franco-German dialogue was beginning to the accompaniment of a thousand difficulties, gives one a strong impression of the extent to which thinking Frenchmen of all shades of opinion had had enough, and more than enough, of the traditional anti-German feeling, which had become practically the exclusive monopoly of Communist propaganda, and of how unwilling they were to be discouraged by any discordant notes or echoes. When Dr. Adenauer attended a mass meeting in the Titania Palace in Berlin and was for the first time greeted publicly with the singing of *Deutschland über alles*, the French reaction was characteristic of the new attitude. The incident roused considerable indignation in the Press of the English-speaking world, and many commentators deplored in particular the effect that it would be likely to have on French public opinion, but in Paris indignation was scarcely discernible. Naturally after two world wars *Deutschland über alles* struck a somewhat discordant note in the ears of Germany's neighbours, but all the French newspapers, from *Le Monde* and *Figaro* to the left-wing Socialist *Franc-Tireur*, called on their German specialists to explain learnedly to their readers that *Deutschland über alles* had been composed by a German democrat of the 1848 period, and that it did not mean what it sounded as if it meant; and they even gently pointed out that the *Marseillaise* was after all not exactly a children's lullaby.

The pendulum had swung right over, and the time was

ripe for a move extending far beyond the scope of ordinary diplomacy. On March 8th, 1950, Dr. Adenauer in the course of an interview abruptly dropped the suggestion of a complete Franco-German union, and at first caused all the greater embarrassment because in the same breath he demanded the Saar back. But it was no other than General de Gaulle who, with characteristic breadth of vision, gave the Chancellor's idea his personal blessing. In the light of the historical perspective thus opened up, the "pledges" hitherto so dear to him seemed nothing but old junk, and he evoked the thousand-year-old memory of the battle of the Catalaunian plains, "in which Franks, Gallo-Romans, and Teutons jointly routed the hordes of Attila." "It is time for the Rhine to become a meeting-place and not a barrier, for there is no reason why these two nations should not unite," he said. "If one did not force oneself to look coolly at things, one would be almost dazzled at the prospect of what German qualities and French qualities (the general used the word *valeur*, which includes the military virtues), extended to Africa, might jointly yield. That is a field of common development which might transform Europe even beyond the iron curtain. . . . In the light of such prospects, what does the Saar dispute matter?"

De Gaulle, once more a visionary individualist standing head and shoulders over his astonished followers, combined with this declaration a sharp attack on the distribution of roles under the Atlantic pact, on the subjection of France and western Europe to the command and strategy of a non-European power which shared neither the threat to which Europe was exposed nor Europe's essential needs, and on the "servility of the régime" to American hegemony. The two attitudes belonged together and were complementary. De Gaulle was not the only one in whose eyes an integration of the European continent, to which Franco-German integration must be the key, was the only alternative to satellitehood. The belief that a divided Europe must inevitably decline to a state of dependence on the American protecting power was a deep but seldom expressed motive of much of the new "European spirit".

The Schuman plan, which was the concrete expression of

that spirit, was born of this state of mind. The stiffening of the Atlantic pact, which by now had completely displaced "European reconstruction" under the Marshall plan, was on the allied agenda. M. Bidault, then Prime Minister of a rump Cabinet which was creaking in all its joints, made a speech at the Lyons fair in April which was generally interpreted as a funeral oration over the grave of the European idea; he proposed that "Atlantic integration" should be not only military, but also economic. When M. Schuman, on the eve of his departure for the Atlantic conference in London on May 9th, surprised his own staff at the Quai d'Orsay by announcing to the world's Press, which was expecting anything but that, his plan for pooling French and German heavy industry, he supplied, not only the long-awaited European impetus, but also a counter-blast to complete "Atlanticisation" and incorporation in the American-led alliance— "rather with Germany than that!" At bottom he was inspired by the same idea as General de Gaulle. But M. Schuman was thinking, not of Attila and the Catalaunian plains, but of a process of peaceful construction in which France and Germany could work together.

The new and revolutionary feature of the Schuman plan was not the proposal of a western European industrial combination. Such proposals had been in the air since the end of the war, and had been made at innumerable Socialist or all-European conferences, and they reappeared whenever the Ruhr or the Saar questions ran into a dead-end. But they had never led to anything, and they were no longer taken seriously. What was important about the new move was that it shifted the European centre of gravity to Franco-German union as the indispensable and practically self-sufficient condition of any real Europeanisation. It was here that the obstacles lay, and here that they must be overcome, and everything else was subsidiary. M. Schuman's invitation, though it was of course directed to all the states which had taken part in the Marshall plan and were represented at Strasbourg, said specifically that "the French Government proposes to place Franco-German production of steel as a whole under a common higher authority, within a framework open to the participation of the other countries of Europe," the specific aim being that this should be "the first concrete foundation of . . . European federation." "The solidarity in production thus established," the invitation stated, "will make it plain that any war between France and Germany becomes, not merely unthinkable, but actually impossible."

Out of the European fog of Strasbourg there had crystallised the European heartland which alone could be a real starting-point for European unification. If this is to become a political reality, the Strasbourg Assembly will have played a role in relation to it similar to that played in the formation of the German state by the Frankfurt parliament of 1848, which undertook in a similar fashion to give a constitution to a Germany which existed only as an object of lyricism, a Germany whose terrestrial shape and frontiers it was unable to define. The wish-dream of an "Anglo-French Europe" was followed by a sober step towards the reality of continental Europe, which must be "Franco-German" or nothing.

The brief Anglo-French exchange of Notes which followed the invitation to Britain to take part in the proposed coal and steel community was a summary repetition, for the benefit of the hard-of-hearing, of the "European dialogue" of the Bidault-Bevin period. Britain was, of course, ready to join in any club, membership of which signified good will, but was not ready to enter into any binding commitments, and was not prepared to consider any renunciation of economic sovereignty; in other words, she was ready to take part in the Schuman plan provided that all its proposed institutions and aims were abandoned, and that it became an office for the exchange of information on the pattern of O.E.E.C. If France, Germany, and perhaps other European countries as well, were willing to advance further along the road to unification, they were assured of the British Government's best wishes and support, but they must follow the road alone. The position was stated clearly and unequivocally; and after this, if the "yes, but . . ." Europeans on the continent persisted in using British abstention as an excuse to oppose the project, the British Government was not to be blamed; it had done nothing whatever to encourage such a way out. The fact that it gave its approval to the idea of continental unification, and did not seek to thwart it, implied a revolution in British policy nearly as great as that which had taken place in French policy. The old and deep-rooted British tradition of the balance of power would have required Britain to thwart it. It would have been easy for the British to accept all the pressing invitations to sit down at the same table as the participants and water the plan down until it reached that degree of non-bindingness on which they would have insisted as the condition of their joining. But instead they offered their support. This clearly defined attitude was Britain's positive contribution to European integration, and one to be valued highly.

Thus the Schuman plan was a complete new beginning, outside and apart from all the existing European committees and organisations. It was new alike in its spatial setting and the method by which it was to be set up. Like everything long overdue which everyone has ceased believing in but then suddenly happens, M. Schuman's move came as a surprise. It was so cunningly aimed at the weakest spot in the restored "economic sovereignties" of Europe, and it was so quickly and enthusiastically driven forward by the enthusiastic team of planners round M. Monnet, its technical father, that the plan was already under way by the time its opponents had started organising themselves and looking for arguments.

An unspeakably absurd and malicious amount of nonsense was talked and written about the Schuman plan. It was called the "Europe of the trusts" and the "Europe of the Vatican". In France it was called a "Europe under German hegemony" and in Germany a "Europe under French hegemony". Dr. Schumacher called it a "petty European, I mean pan-French conception", and M. Daladier called it a "pan-German Europe". An anthology of this chronicle of folly would reveal, not very surprisingly, that the opposition on both sides of the frontier produced similar arguments, though in inverted form; both were fearful of the dangers involved in the indissoluble ties incurred in entering into this relationship. The German Social Democrats were not followed in their opposition by the trade unions, and many of their leading members followed them only reluctantly and against their better conscience. Nevertheless there was tragedy in the fact that, out of doctrinaire stubbornness or factional opposition, the German Social Democrats were able to produce no alternative to the only constructive idea of the post-war period other than that of "national socialism", a phrase with disagreeable associations which the Social Democrats unfortunately did not allow to be forgotten. Dr. Schumacher, in his opposition to the European idea, which he felt to be a betrayal of Germany, when he called Dr. Adenauer the "Chancellor of the allies" or said in the Bundestag debate on the treaty which brought the coal and steel pool into force that "he who signs this treaty ceases to be a German", came terribly close to the language used by the Nazis in an earlier post-war period, without having even the excuse of the treaty of Versailles.

The French Socialists had neither the voting strength nor the unanimity of the German Socialists. In France the monopoly of chauvinism had been seized by the Communists, and a number of French Socialists were in the front rank of the European movement. But M. Guy Mollet, the secretary-general of the Socialist Party, insisted with all the weight behind him of his office as Minister for European affairs which he occupied in the second half of 1950, that Europe could be created "with Britain or not at all", which necessarily meant not at all; and he produced strangely feeble and poor-spirited arguments to exclude partnership with France's continental neighbours. "Nobody," he said, "could advocate in the French Parliament a European union which consisted essentially of a union with our former enemies, Germany and Italy." This simply meant that he himself and the election strategists of the party committee did not dare do so, for others did; similarly M. Jules Moch, the Socialist Defence Minister, preached irreconcilability with Germany, which he considered unworthy of admission even to the Strasbourg "club". All this weighed all the more heavily because the parliamentary backing of French Government policy, between the Communists on the one hand and the Gaullists on the other, was incomparably weaker and more vacillating than that of the Federal German Government; and there was more than a paradox in the fact that General de Gaulle's Rally of the French People, which had been dazzled by the vision of Franco-German federation in the spring of 1950, was two years later united by one thing only, an obstinate hostility to the foreign policy of M. Schuman, and celebrated its last triumph in enforcing his departure from office and his displacement at the Quai d'Orsay by M. Bidault before it collapsed itself. That is the destiny of nationalism in Europe nowadays. It is still capable of doing untold harm, but is no longer capable of creating anything, and all its triumphs are so many acts of suicide.

However, there was something in all these phrases about "French", "German", or "Vatican Europe". As was pointed out by M. Joseph Hours, a French historian who with unusual consistency and single-mindedness has opposed the "European myth" in all its forms, Europe is indeed older than all the countries of which it consists, no matter what one may think of his conclusion that the separate countries represent progress while "Europe" represents reaction. Like many others, M. Hours had opened his atlas, and discovered that the "little Europe" of M. Schuman corresponded astonishingly closely—even to the Elbe frontier of amputated Germany—with the frontiers of the Carolingian empire before its division into France and Germany; and, indeed, the grouping that has arisen about the Franco-German core of the European Coal and Steel Community is no mere accident of diplomacy.

The Carolingian empire was the first form of Europe organised in the form of a state that arose after the barbarian invasions; it was the real birth—not rebirth—of European history at a time when the Moors had reached the Pyrenees and the Slavs the Elbe, though the clerics who wrote history regarded it as the restoration of the Christian Roman empire, the work of the Roman Church, the sole guardian of a buried tradition. This was the heartland which served as point of departure for the whole of the subsequent history of the west. For a long time that unity was manifested in an inextricable tangle of hatred and hereditary hostility, the dreadfully unified history of a Europe engaged in self-destruction. Nevertheless, appealing to it is no idle conjuring up of ghosts; the outline of the thousand-year-old "Carolingian Europe" is today once more palpably the outline of the countries west of the iron curtain, the continental battlefield of the last war, which involved for every single one of the countries within its borders the total collapse of its army, its state institutions, its national unity, and its self-confidence, either in the earlier stages of the war or the later. All of them have been through years of foreign occupation and chaos. They know that in the event of another catastrophe they would not be spared, and their confidence in the possibility of a national future in the old isolation, in spite of the re-erection of all the old signs of sovereignty, has been irrevocably shattered. The "greater European" conception was doomed because of the hopelessness of expecting the co-operation of countries which had survived the war with their foundations and traditions intact; for nobody gives up what he has not already lost, and even giving up the shadow is unspeakably difficult.

Fortunately none of the founders of the European Coal and Steel Community had the bad taste to propose that Charlemagne should be. its patron saint. The Coal and Steel Community is not a religious organisation, it is certain that clerics have never assembled in the Railway Palace in Luxembourg, and M. Monnet is the most unclerical type of French radical and "lay" citizen of the world. Yet it is more than a diplomatic accident that one of the small group of statesmen who set about building up "little Europe", in the teeth of blind and furious opposition and against mountains of inertia, came from Lorraine. Lorraine had lain exposed between east and west, incapable either of living or of dying, and for a thousand years it was continually fought over, crushed, and partitioned. The other two statesmen concerned also came from border provinces, the Rhineland and South Tyrol respectively, both of which had for generation after generation been bones of contention, dragged this way and back between German and non-German. All three came from the same kind of homeless European home as the people of the Saar, the Rhineland separatists, and the S.S. men of Oradour, whose trial first made plain to French public opinion the absurdity of the theory of national guilt, and of the absurdity of supposing it to be possible to separate right from wrong, good from evil, on the basis of national frontiers. It was also no accident that so many western progressives of yesterday were irritated by the fact that this first concrete step towards Europe was the work of a few men, a handful of elderly Catholic and conservative statesmen, whose outlook on the world dated from the time of Franz Josef and Wilhelm II, who were the only ones in the chaos of the post-war period to possess a common ethos, a common tradition, and a common language—in contrast with the Socialists, who set the tone in practically every European Government from Stockholm to Rome and from London to Prague in the immediate post-war years, but whose internationalism in this hour of destiny provided them with no rule of behaviour other than that their shirts were closer to them than their suits.

M. Schuman, Dr. Adenauer, and Signor De Gasperi were certainly no visionaries, and their social philosophy was perhaps deficient. What distinguished them from the ideologists was perhaps only the fact that they felt the European tragedy to be a European tragedy, and not a national or party political dog-fight, and that as genuine conservatives they possessed the real courage that is required to abandon much in order to preserve what is vital. For the European idea, the idea of the preservation of this spatially so small and threatened home of all the values of an ancient individualistic civilisation, which has already followed nearly to the end the path of self-destruction once followed by ancient Greece, has for a long time ceased to be revolutionary. It is in the truest sense of the word a conservative idea, but of a grandiose and radical nature that puts it poles apart both from the parochial conservatism of possessions and caste, to which it is utterly detestable, and from the wordy "revolutionism" which nearly destroyed the idea of Europe during those years. The abuse which was harvested by M. Schuman and Dr. Adenauer because of their European policy, while hundreds of others were earning bouquets and cheap applause with fine speeches about Europe, was perhaps the distinguishing mark of those who do not cry "forward!" but go forward. They brought Europe down from the rosy mists of idealism into the ungratifying and unpopular world of reality; for the whole of European history points to the fact that, whatever the ideal size of Europe may be, its core must be Franco-German unity, and that the first and decisive step towards Europe must be a closing of the breach between the two nations which have been the principal protagonists in the European tragedy; everything else is secondary to that.

If "little Europe" lacks the mythical greatness of the "whole of the west", a compensatory factor is that it forms a real, organic whole. The fact that the Coal and Steel Community was sited in an industrial landscape which obviously formed a unit gave it strength—the strength inherent in any attempt to re-establish an arbitrarily destroyed natural order. Moreover, this "little Europe" was by no means destined to be so small and poor as the disappointed "greater Europeans" supposed. The area has, after all, the second greatest industrial potential in the world. The biggest surviving world empire is available to it as a potential sphere for its activities; and the original announcement of the Schuman plan held out the tremendous prospect of the opening up of Africa—perhaps only for the space of a short reprieve which it may be engaged in wasting.

The driving force of the Coal and Steel Community came from the association of a sober, objective, concrete proposal with an overriding idea which even its critics opposed with a bad conscience. The subtlety of the plan lay in the fact that it hit on the weak spot through which a way could be driven into the front of national interests, and that it made a start with the European organisation of one of the most powerful of those groups of national interests; the industries concerned were important enough economically, politically, and militarily to represent a decisive breach in national economic sovereignties, and at the same time, because of their national political significance, were dependent enough on national intervention to be amenable to political decision.

European heavy industry had in fact never been a realm of "free economy", but a realm of privileges, state concessions, monopolies, cartels, centralised selling and distributive organisations, production quotas, and marketing agreements. These giants, susceptible to every fluctuation in the economic and political situation and the demand for arms, had always been dependent on state protection and state crutches, and their often disastrous role in politics was only the counterpart of that dependence. Thus the after-effects upon them of the war and its convulsions had been more severe and more lasting than they had been elsewhere; here the European lava had not yet had time to harden. The Schuman plan originated in the aim of preventing the return of German heavy industry to exclusive German control; and German heavy industry now secured its release from allied controls and restrictions by entering the Coal and Steel Community. It has remained in a complicated state of suspension between private ownership, socialisation, and internationalisation. The French coal industry has been nationalised, the French steel industry has been lifted out of the stagnation of the French national economy by the Monnet plan and national and Marshall aid funds, revolutionised, and made capable of competition. The heavy industry of the Saar—pivot of the balance, apple of discord, or connecting link—is partly under trusteeship, partly under joint French-Saar control. The Dutch and Belgian industries, the only industries involved that are truly under "private capitalist" control, are completely dependent on state protection; and the outlying Italian industry is a completely artificial, state-fostered product.

Thus the controversy between liberalism and economic controls, the dust of which inevitably obscures every economic question, arose here no more than it had done in the case of the Monnet plan. There was no question of making a decision on an economic programme, but only of the creation of an authority which should lay down and carry out a programme. Reduced to its simplest terms, the Coal and Steel Community is no more than an amalgamation and coalescence of the authority which had hitherto been exercised by six national Ministries over the separate fragments of this industrial complex; in other words, the fusion of six *raisons d'état* into one.

Its fundamental aim was only too evident, and was as easy and uncontroversial to state as it was hard, slow, and laborious to attain; it was to bring into being by means of a systematic investment policy and systematic abolition of economic restrictions the economic structure which would have arisen naturally in the industrial landscape between Westphalia and Flanders if the latter had formed a single, uniform, unrestricted economic unit, and had not been crippled, or bloated, or distorted to the point of monstrosity, by the barriers of national frontiers, national rivalries, national tariffs, and armament races. No more than this was necessary to make economic frontiers totally superfluous and to create a free field for expansion and competition. But years of piecemeal corrective steps, respites, reprieves, transitional and compensatory measures were necessary before this could be attained; and on top of this there was need of a reactivisation of the European economy extending far beyond the confines of these industries in order to make possible the re-adaptation of undertakings which were incapable of survival without state protection and a redeployment of their labour force; otherwise the impact upon them of the establishment of a common market would be that of a blind, destructive force, or the respite granted them would have to last for ever. The practical problem overstepped the usual boundaries, making the worn-out controversy between free enterprise and controls void of content in the light of the practical problem to be solved.

The point of departure in this experiment was not a "natural structure", but a historical malformation, and in dealing with it the orthodox liberal panacea of the "free play of forces", constantly preached from academic chairs but never put into practice, was as irrelevant, and fundamentally as frivolous, as the chorus of warnings against all change which came from the left. The left defended the existing malformation, with all its tangles and absurdities, as the last word in historical reasonableness. In the actual situation of Europe liberals, if they are to establish the conditions for a free market economy, are condemned to engage in long-term planning, while the aim of the economic planners is a rational economic structure identical with the rational division of labour of a free market—and therefore in the last resort capable of functioning without the planners' intervention; in other words, the economic structure postulated by classical liberalism which the national, opportunist liberalism of sectional interests has always shunned and avoided. In the face of the real alternative, which is decisive for the future of Europe—that between development or ossification, expansion or stagnation—the controversy between the planners and the liberals is mere verbiage.

The Coal and Steel Community came into existence after two years of uphill work and effort, and showed the genuine co-operation that is possible when Europeans of different nationalities engage with good will in a joint task. Dutchmen, Belgians, Italians, Frenchmen of Vichy and Frenchmen of the resistance, German democrats and former Nazis, were fused into a team as single-minded as the French planning commission had been under the impulse of the "inspirator" —the nickname said to have been given to M. Monnet by General de Gaulle after his declaration of war upon that pioneer's "integration policy". Anyone who has followed the work of this small group of technicians and observed the slow beginnings of co-operation among the "interest groups" of all the participating countries can discern some of the potentialities that would still be open to this ruined continent if its people were able to look forward instead of back, and ceased to be separated by mutually checking and crippling national institutions, but instead faced their joint problems jointly and thereby at last became aware of what they had in common.

But even this initiative is doomed to be stunted and bogged down unless its impulse is extended to still wider areas of the economy of western Europe. The gradual disappearance of customs and quotas within the Coal and Steel Community can result in no common market so long as currency restrictions, the chief obstacle to intra-European trade, are not overcome at any rate by free convertibility, and there can be no convertibility for countries lacking sufficient gold and currency reserves; and above all there can be no customs union without a common financial and foreign trade policy.

The Coal and Steel Community is still saddled with the "respite" granted to all the threatened malformations, and it has scarcely even begun to tackle its real social and economic tasks; and it is hard to see how they can be tackled effectively in the limited field of manœuvre left by six closed economic, fiscal, and currency systems, between the meshes of which only a limited flow of goods is possible. The Schuman plan has shown a way, but does not offer a recipe repeatable at will. Further sectors of the European economy cannot go on indefinitely being cut out and "integrated" under purely technical European officials if the result is not to be disintegration of individual national economies instead of European integration; and in the long run it is impossible to set up European economic officials in an extra-territorial, "supranational" no-man's-land without subordinating them to the control of a common political authority, however restricted the latter might be, and a European parliament. Without the combination of both postulates, a common market without currency restrictions, and a democratically controlled political authority, the "Europeanisation of the Saar", the prospect of which was opened up by the Schuman plan, remains an empty slogan. And if a new expansion of the European economy, without which the Coal and Steel Community will sooner or later have to stray back into the old path of quotas and production restrictions, is to become a reality, it will be necessary to go back again to the original basic idea of the Schuman plan, the joint opening up of Africa, over which a veil of silence has been dropped as if it had been premature and indiscreet ever to have mentioned it. "The consequences of what one wills have to be willed too." As in all creative developments, there can be no standing still; the only choice is between going forward or eventual failure, with all the unforeseeable consequences of a political and moral bankruptcy. Only conferences and sham parliaments can mark time for year after year.

Thus the Coal and Steel Community, even before it came into being, became the locomotive to which all the European initiatives, both old and new, were hitched. Innumerable plans were produced for the "integration" or "pooling" of transport, agriculture, pharmaceuticals, and electricity, and it became an alarmingly heavy load. It included the Saar problem, and all the plans and projects produced by the Strasbourg Assembly. Finally, in the euphoric "European high season" of September, 1952, after the community had come officially into force and the European Defence Community treaty was signed, the political federation of Europe itself was added to the load; a draft European constitution was to be worked out by the expanded parliament of the Coal and

Steel Community. But the heaviest and the most ill-fated burden under which this locomotive panted was that of the European army.

HESITATION ON THE BRINK

THE fate that overtook the Marshall plan was repeated at another level in the case of the Coal and Steel Community; no sooner had its peaceful work of construction begun than it was overshadowed by the cold war. Less than two months after M. Schuman had published his plan, the outbreak of the Korean war sent a wave of panic through the western world; and just a month after its outbreak, on July 25th, 1950, the American High Commissioner officially announced the policy of the American strategists. He said that the Germans must be given the means to defend themselves in the event of aggression; and M. Jules Moch, who was soon afterwards to become the French Minister of Defence, replied in a speech at Sète: "We should be mad if we were to agree to such a thing." But events could no longer be held up.

In the eyes of American public opinion the cold war had become something very like a "hot" war, and what counted now was no longer economic and social consolidation, but numbers of troops and quantities of arms. An end must be put to the game of toy soldiers in which the "European general staff" at Fontainebleau was indulging with cardboard tanks and "theoretical" troops; western Europe, with fewer than a dozen divisions, which were not even fully equipped or up to establishment, was an only too inviting field for a military walk-over; and there could be no more talk now of more American troops being sent to cover western Europe's defence deficit, for all the American troops that could be spared had to be sent to Korea. When the Atlantic Council met in New York in September the American proposal that western Europe should set about building up sixty divisions and that western Germany should supply ten of them was agreed to, except by the Germans, who were not represented, and the French, whose veto on the raising of German troops broke the unity of the allied front. The conference ended without result, though, according to the official statement issued at its conclusion, the council agreed that Germany must be put in a position to make a contribution to western European defence. The substitution of the term "German defence contribution" for "German rearmament" was the only concession that the French succeeded in obtaining, and henceforward French policy clung to this nuance like a drowning man to a straw.

Since the agitated summer of 1950 year after year has passed without the first western German soldier's having practised the most elementary arms drill—and that alone is sufficient to condemn the panic haste with which "German rearmament" was driven through under the pressure of an alarmed public opinion, regardless of the fact that in Europe its effect was bound to be rather like that of a bull in a china-shop. The subject was approached as if it were a matter of setting up recruiting offices overnight for a *levée en masse* of German troops, and warnings of the dangers involved in this sensational and over-simplified approach were overborne with arguments of the type of "now is no time for hair-splitting" and "soldiers must be taken where they can be found".

There was no dispute of principle behind the resulting controversy, which was conducted with the greatest noise and excitement and enriched the European ghost army with the ghost of a German army, and there was no argument about the immediate establishment of a German army, which was impossible in any case. The only question at issue was the time and the fashion in which German rearmament should take place. The "revival of the Wehrmacht" agitated all the nations east and west of the demarcation line, but hardly the politicians in the Kremlin. So long as the rearmament of her western European allies existed only on paper, and so long as American arms production had barely begun and deliveries under the military aid programme were confined to symbolic shipments of American army surpluses—nobody dared suggest that German heavy industry in the Ruhr, within range of the Soviet army, should go over to armament production—the demand for the arming of German contingents was nothing but paper sabre-rattling; the over-hasty propaganda change-over from the just concluded demilitarisation of Germany to its remilitarisation was a pure product of "psychological warfare"—the most unpsychological warfare that could be imagined, resulting in a maximum of noise and confusion and a minimum of useful effect.

Those hectic days brought to light the whole problem inherent in an alliance whose object was the defence of Europe, but whose weapons, power, and leadership lay in Washington. The American decision to oppose the Communist aggression in Korea and not to submit to "another Munich" served as an unmistakable warning against any further aggression, came to the rescue of the undermined self-confidence of the western democracies, and, in spite of subsequent disappointments, was perhaps the decisive turning-point in the post-war period. But the disparity between American and the European reactions, both in intensity and "morale", to the events in Korea was perhaps unbridgeable; the more the centre of gravity of American policy shifted to east Asia, the greater the disparity grew, until it reached a point of mutual unintelligibility. From the American point of view it was impossible to understand that in France the first reaction to the summons to rearm was one of obstinate obstruction, while in Germany it was met with an *ohne mich* ("leave me out of it!") campaign, a mixture of defeatism, defiance, and a spirit of calculated bargaining. Did Europe wish simply to hide its head in the sand and allow itself to be swallowed up without resistance?

From the European point of view, however, the American policy of strength, distorted to the point of caricature by the irresponsibilities of responsible politicians, seemed to be an alarming game with the fate of Europe; and this "openly conducted diplomacy" gave the sound of an ultimatum to every political difference which at a round-table discussion conducted in a more reasonable and moderate mood would have turned out to be based on mere misunderstanding.

Indeed, the idea of German rearmament became a bone of public contention before its consequences and implications had even started to be considered. It was proposed, for the purpose of strengthening the Atlantic alliance, to rearm a country which neither was a member of that alliance nor possessed a definable international status, a country which was crippled, had been divided in two, and enjoyed only provisional status. Its frontiers were not recognised by international law, and nobody took seriously as a defence line the absurd demarcation line which runs half way between Frankfurt and Berlin and right across the Potsdamerplatz. A German army, if it were to be raised at the speed desired by the American strategists, would necessarily be recruited chiefly of refugees from areas under Communist control and would inevitably turn into a "liberation army" for the purpose of regaining the lost east German territories, whether by the method of Tannenberg or of Tauroggen, and whether this ambition was spoken or unspoken—and German politicians tended not to leave it unspoken. The question of German rearmament inevitably raised the whole endless chain of questions which had overlain Europe like a nightmare since the uneasy peace of Yalta and Potsdam, and were bound sooner or later to come up again, though it would be better to deal with them as European rather than as German questions; moreover, tackling them after carefully weighing up their implications and what possible solutions there might be would be preferable to doing so under the influence of emotion and panic.

The proposal that Germany should be enabled to defend herself looked simple enough on the surface, but in fact involved squaring the circle. However, the excitement of those weeks was as ill-adapted to the mentioning of "legalistic scruples" such as those indicated above as it was, in view of the sensitiveness of the European situation, to stopping and considering the charge of dynamite that had been built into the new-born policy of Franco-German solidarity. The trouble here was not so much that there were objective differences of opinion as that an abyss of non-understanding surrounded those who wished to prevent the dreadful old game from starting all over again. When this was expressed on the French side, it was summarily, sorrowfully, or resignedly dismissed as "anti-German feeling", intelligible, of course, but outdated. When it was no less vigorously expressed on the German side, the only explanation found was blindness or disloyalty. This abyss of non-understanding appeared in shattering form in a number of British expressions of opinion, for instance in an article in the London *Observer* on the problems of German rearmament.

If Germany were really again to become a threat in five or ten years time, it suggested, would not the first effect be to re-create a common interest between Russia and the west, and would it not mean a re-establishment of some of the conditions which had so often made Russia and Britain allies in the past? Would not the reawakening of a certain amount of common fear of Germany be the key to better relations between Russia and the west? An American gave the answer in a letter to the *Observer*. Was not this the very way of thinking, he asked, which had led to the second world war? The world had had more than enough of this kind of *Realpolitik*.

But mere stubbornness was no longer possible. The French Government, if it were to oppose the German rearmament within the framework of the Atlantic pact of which all its allies approved, must offer an alternative, and this, the "integrated European army", presented itself with a kind of inevitability; France had already set out upon a path that led in that direction. The idea had been in the air. The eventual prospect of such an army in a European federation was obvious enough; but now it was brought somewhat prematurely into the immediate field of vision. At a memorable sitting at Strasbourg in August, 1950, a few weeks after the outbreak of the Korean war, Sir Winston Churchill had called for the immediate creation of a European army and a European defence ministry. His idea met with practically unanimous acceptance, and an enthusiastic Assembly greeted him as the future European War Minister. It was a tremendous scene, in which Sir Winston Churchill once again demonstrated his gift for seizing the historical moment; but it became a rather painful memory for the British Conservative leader when he became head of the British Government barely a year later and refused British participation in a European defence union as steadfastly as the Labour Government had ever done.

Thus the Pleven plan, the military version of the Schuman plan, was improvised; at first it could have meant anything from a Foreign Legion recruited in Germany to a complete fusion of European armies and armaments; and the only immediate result was a sceptical shaking of heads, and doubts whether this were really a revolutionary event in European history or a mere pretext to gain time. M. Pleven, the Prime Minister, when he laid the project before the National Assembly, said that the French Government had hoped that before the delicate question of common defence arose the existence of the European Coal and Steel Community would have accustomed the nations to the idea of a European community. But international developments had not allowed them time.

The European Defence Community was intended to prevent the return of the future German armed forces to German control, just as the Coal and Steel Community had been intended to prevent the return of German heavy industry to German control. However, the French Government was able to secure the assent of the French Parliament only to the negative part of this proposition; it said no to a German army, but would not say yes to a European army. The resolution by which the Assembly, after a confused and depressing debate, gave the Government a free hand to put forward its project in Washington provided a model for future debates on the European Defence Community. "The National Assembly, approving the Government's statement," it said, "and in particular its desire to permit no restoration of a German army or a German general staff, rejecting any addition to that, passes to the order of the day." It would have been useless to say no, and it was impossible to say yes, so the French parliamentarians said yes and no, and that is what they went on saying. French diplomacy was able to convince all France's allies of the utility and necessity of the European Defence Community, but it was unable to convince the French themselves of the seriousness of its intentions.

The over-hasty new stage in European unification certainly had a stimulating effect on those who were still lagging over the completion of the previous stage. The Socialists, who in the meantime had returned to the French Government, quietly gave a reluctant consent to the Schuman plan when this became inevitable if the French counter-proposal to prevent autonomous German rearmament were to go forward; and the fact that M. Schuman himself agreed to this unfortunate complication was largely because it was only by so doing that Cabinet agreement to the Coal and Steel Community project could be obtained.

But now the cart had been put before the horse. The Europe into which German armed forces were to be integrated did not exist. It was possible to put an industrial complex under the authority of a non-political, supra-national civil service, but it was impossible, absurd, and dangerous to create an army in a vacuum between the nations not subordinate to any political authority, a common army without a common policy and a common diplomacy behind it. It was therefore concluded that the political unification of Europe must be driven forward with redoubled speed, and the federalists welcomed the European army project as a means of attaining the political federation which it presupposed. Thus the step after next would help the one before, and the cart would act as the horse's legs. But the idea of political integration, having degenerated from a clear aim into a subsequently discovered implication of a reluctantly given decision, became hopelessly involved in the "yes-and-no" attitude with which the idea of the European army had been received, and eventually became a pretext to take back the implication together with the decision, and to upset the whole house of cards.

But, worst of all, the idea of Franco-German integration, which could have been made to appeal to a deep and real longing for peace on the part of both peoples as marking the end of the long and disastrous dissension between them, was now stamped as being a military necessity in the new world conflict. It was driven forward, not under the banner of confidence and trust, but in an atmosphere of mistrust and doubt, and all the vague and conflicting fears of a Europe that fell between all stools: fear of Russia, which made the raising of German forces desirable; fear of the Russian reaction if German forces were raised; fear of the enemy, and fear of the protecting power; fear of the rebirth of German military might; fear of the unforeseeable and incalculable developments and transformation of a provisional German state, which in its present form might last ten days or ten years, but could not possibly be final.

In Germany warnings were uttered by Dr. Schumacher against entering into an indissoluble tie with the west, which was indifferent to the fate of the German eastern provinces and at bottom would be only too glad to see the present Germany permanently reduced to her present size. A counterpart to this was provided by all the warnings given by the French "neutralists" against entering into an indissoluble tie with this rump Germany, which, in order to regain her lost eastern territories, might lead her into some adventure, or might desert to the east, but in any case was in a position to play a blackmailing role between east and west—playing off each against the other. These fears and dangers could be eradicated only by the closest conceivable form of tie, and thus the aspiration for closer and closer ties became itself the expression of a mistrust which only grew with the number of precautionary measures and reinsurances that were introduced and in turn engendered more mistrust; and the atmosphere of this new form of Franco-German dialogue was not improved by the fact that the advocates of integration used reassuring half-truths, leaving it to their opponents to state the consequences which must flow from complete political, military, and moral solidarity between the two countries. It should have been the object of a bold, far-sighted policy to create awareness of the solidarity that indeed existed between them, and a single election to a European assembly, no matter whether it were only half or quarter sovereign, would have done more to achieve this than a whole pile of diplomatic instruments. But it was a real gamble with the future of Europe to assume awareness of this solidarity, and to expect it at the first attempt to be sufficient to make possible a renunciation, not just of a tangible, measurable part of a country's sovereignty, but of the most ancient and sensitive symbol of that sovereignty, a symbol surrounded by the most superstitious myths, associated even with such things as the tassels on a uniform.

The difficulty was not of a technical nature. For the states of the European continent the old military symbol of sovereignty has, to an extent which has by no means penetrated the public consciousness, become an empty shell. No one of these countries still possesses the industrial, technical, and financial resources required for independent national defence; not one of them has any freedom of choice left in making military decisions or alliances. They are utterly lacking in the capacity out of their own resources to build up an army, a navy, and an air force of present-day standards and equipped with the whole range of modern weapons. On mobilisation in 1939 the old-style French army was able without difficulty to put a hundred divisions in the field; fifteen years later the setting up of a dozen divisions had become a task which France felt to be an intolerable and superhuman burden. But in the popular mind the army is still a body of men armed with guns and rifles and commanded by officers, and military mythology still lingers in the world of ideas of clanking swords and Homeric battlefields. European armies have long since become totally inadequate for national defence in the full meaning of the word, though they are still suitable for "tactical" or guerilla operations, or for purposes of occupation, police actions, or at best for colonial expeditions. In that sense it is true that they have remained national. In the wider sense they are a glittering façade, capable of putting on impressive parades, but they have nothing behind them. But in the public mind the whole discussion turned about these inadequate and fragmentary "police armies", and France was excluded in advance from "European integration" because of her military responsibilities in her colonies.

The military defence of western Europe about the integration of which the experts negotiated was something totally different; it was a huge industrial undertaking in which the armed troops were only the end of a long chain of production and transport arrangements, an undertaking entirely outside the scope and range of the pocket-handkerchief states of Europe. In the vast undertaking of "Atlantic integration", in the huge international system of military bases and "infrastructures", in their dependence for weapons, supply, and finance on the American "arsenal of the west", in the international division of labour in regard to armaments and forms of armed service, and in their renunciation of the decisive, strategic, "heavy weapon" of our time, the nations of Europe have long since lost all real independence in armaments and defence. When the unified supreme command was initiated with General Eisenhower's tour of inspection in January, 1951, they lost even the appearance of independence.

The countries of continental Europe were the area of deployment of the Atlantic organisation and lay in the immediate danger zone, protected by no ocean and no channel. It was obviously desirable to restore to them as a whole within this huge organisation some part of that autonomy and specific gravity which as individuals they had lost. It was, indeed, the only alternative to a state of hopeless satellitehood; and, in the midst of all the storms and controversies about the shadow of former national pride, the working out of contractual obligations between the military specialists of France, Germany, Italy, Belgium, Holland, and Luxembourg went forward with an astonishing lack of friction. Public discussions and the objective work of defence planning went forward on two completely different levels of consciousness, and never has the hopeless backwardness of current thought in relation to the technical revolution of the twentieth century been more grotesquely visible. In the eyes of public opinion everything seemed to hinge on the symbolic question of the level at which the various European contingents were to be integrated or amalgamated; but what was integrated was not so much armies as the whole edifice on which they were based—training, promotion, supply, logistics, finance, etc.; and, above all, the whole armaments economy (for which the Coal and Steel Community in fact supplied the pattern and the basis); in short, the whole "infrastructure" of defence without which an individual military unit is unable to move a step. Article 106 of the European Defence Community treaty, which proposed to withdraw from individual countries and hand over to a joint board the production of war material of all kinds, the purchase and sale of arms, research and experimentation in armaments, the procurement of prototypes, the distribution of contracts and authority over the armament industries—and the exception from these provisions of the French overseas territories—should have sufficed to dissipate fear of the secession of any one partner; and in fact nearly all the attacks that were made on the treaty were based either on ignorance or on misinformation, and were aimed at a public that was neither aware of the precision and detail of the huge mass of technical work done by the negotiators, nor able to understand the mechanism of "integration".

It was certainly not surprising that such a complex mechanism made no appeal to the public imagination. What might have been capable of making such an appeal was not this technical integration at the base of the pyramid, but a striking and easily visible symbol of unification at its summit— *e.g.*, the European defence ministry which Sir Winston Churchill with his sure psychological instinct conjured out of the Strasbourg sky in August, 1950. But this political symbol was beyond the competence of the committees of experts. In the absence of a common political authority the European defence commission was another "non-political" technical authority entrusted with the setting up and organisation of European defence, from the leadership of which it was specifically excluded. In other words, everything was provided except the roof. In its absence the "European army" was subordinated to N.A.T.O. command, with the result that the sole purpose of the whole complicated structure seemed to be to secure the participation of German forces in Atlantic defence without accepting Germany into N.A.T.O.

It was on this point that real criticism fastened. General de Gaulle, in remarkable superficial agreement with Dr. Schumacher, though his approach was in reality quite different, made a violent onslaught on the "satellite" status of Europe in relation to America, and came out for an open Franco-German alliance in the classical style, though he relapsed from the only too classical clarity of this proposal into the most dreadful confusion of ideas. In his project, which was laid before the National Assembly, he added to the system of European alliances that he recommended a common parliamentary assembly to be elected by the participating nations, though there would be no point to a federal appendix to such a structure. Dr. Schumacher's and General de Gaulle's criticisms were put forward seriously and in good faith, but were as little understood by their followers as was the work of the E.D.C. negotiators itself. The political influence that both men exercised in this matter rested almost exclusively on complete and systematic misunderstanding of what they had to say, in fact on pure negation. The *ohne mich* wave in Germany was just as grotesque a misunderstanding of Dr. Schumacher's opposition as was the parochial patriotism of many of the followers of General de Gaulle. The only effect of their attitude of opposition at all costs was complete confusion of the issue and sterile obstructionism.

Meanwhile at the diplomatic and technical level the "revolution at the green table" went irresistibly forward. On May 26th, 1952, the allied conventions with the German Federal Republic were solemnly signed in Bonn, and a day later the European Defence Community treaty was solemnly signed in Paris. A vast collection of documents were involved, including two dozen agreements, protocols, supplementary protocols, and declarations. The Foreign Ministers of the west, in innumerable groups and constellations of four, six, three, seven, and fifteen, had to put about five hundred separate signatures to them. The ordinary citizen was bound to feel the same blank astonishment at this mountain of diplomatic agreements as at the sight of a millepede in motion. How could it possibly move without its feet getting in each other's way?

Perhaps the most acrobatic achievement of these diplomatic agreements, and a primary reason of their complication, was the transformation of western Germany from an occupied country into an ally while preserving the letter of the German unconditional surrender. In the course of its breakneck career the diplomatic millepede had constantly to stop and look back over its shoulder for fear that it might inadvertently have achieved unification with the Soviet Union, or some other miracle. A year earlier the representatives of the "big four" powers had spent three-and-a-half months at the Palais Rose in Paris arguing about the agenda for negotiations on Germany without being able to agree even on the first point; but now, in May, 1952, something happened which no one except those directly involved had expected to happen: the "little European" millepede had succeeded, not only in starting to move, but in reaching its goal. Diplomacy had done all that it was able to do, and between the signature and the reality there lay nothing but ratification by the six Parliaments concerned; or rather by two of them, for however great resistance there might be among the other states concerned, the decision lay with France and with Germany, and with them alone.

But this also meant that the time had passed when the Cabinet policies of a few persistent politicians and the quiet work of a group of "technocrats" were sufficient to promote the grand design over the heads of parliaments and people who were partly hostile, partly indifferent. A kind of diplomatic automatism had developed in the joint labours of this handful of statesmen, impelling every question that was insoluble on a purely national basis in the direction of a European solution. The average politicians in each country reacted towards every controversy with the usual outbursts of nationalism, and, whatever the problem might be, the Cabinets in Bonn, Paris, and Rome responded by talking of its "Europeanisation". The Schuman plan provided the answer to the struggle for industrial hegemony which had centred about the future of the Ruhr; and the European army was intended to be the answer to the insoluble and emotionally charged problem of German rearmament. Dr. Adenauer and M. Schuman sought the answer to the embittered Saar dispute in "Europeanisation". But "Europeanisation" was bound to remain nothing but a slogan unless the political unification of "little Europe" was achieved.

The automatism was driven forward more quickly and more anxiously; time was running out, the unique situation in which the key positions in foreign affairs in Bonn, Paris, and Rome were occupied by Christian Democratic "Europeans", firmly supported by a Democratic Administration in the United States, was drawing to a close, and any delay threatened to be fatal. Under the E.D.C. treaty the assembly of the proposed community was entrusted with the task of preparing a draft European constitution and preparing for European elections. When it became clear that there was going to be delay in ratification of the treaty by the six parliaments involved, the Assembly of the Coal and Steel Community at its first euphoric session in Strasbourg in September, 1952, took the bit between its teeth, appointed itself an *ad hoc* preparatory constituent assembly for "little Europe", and in the record time of six months presented to the six

Governments the finished draft of a European constitution and a European electoral law. The whole European structure of signed treaties and projects, defying all the laws of gravity and preserved from collapse only by keeping constantly in motion, now rested on the slender and terribly untried reality of the European Coal and Steel Community. The structure had not been built up from below, but hung like an avalanche over the nations, who were busy going about their daily lives and had hardly begun to suspect what was impending.

The revolt, however, did not come from the depths of roused national feeling. The great mass of the French people looked on with incredible indifference at the progress of the diplomatic game being played with the future of their economic sovereignty, which had become a caricature, with the future of their state, which no longer worked, and the future of their army, in which they no longer had confidence. It was an indifference in which two different kinds of discouragement held the balance even. The first was a bitter feeling that henceforward the fate of France would be decided between America and Russia, and that even the military unification of Europe was an American invention, against which a Russian party in France conducted agitation; the other was an obscure longing for a new beginning, away from the old tramlines on which everything had been running hopelessly in circles for years and on which all enthusiasms ran themselves to death.

But the technical monstrosities of "European integration" failed to satisfy the aspirations for a new beginning; between these aspirations and the European policy of the diplomatists there stood like a wall the inertia of the old party routines and autarkic ideologies, which were not critical of or hostile to the new problems, but were completely out of contact with them. The usual parochial squabbles of yesterday and the day before, about lay schools, taxes, and wine and wheat prices, played their role in the general election of 1951, but there was no word of the European union which was being busily planned by the diplomatists and had been declared to be the official aim of French foreign policy. The opponents of E.D.C. complained just as much as its supporters about the impossibility of raising any public interest in this vital question. No one has better described this state of stolid indifference than a thorough-going opponent of E.D.C., M. Louis Salleron, who in April, 1953, wrote of this "abdication into equivocation" in *Le Monde*:

"Does the country jib at this? No. It even seems secretly to desire this unheard-of change, which consists in dissolving its own political form into the totally unknown. It knows that for decades it has not been governed. It prefers a total risk to the slow death which it regards as certain. It has never been able to modify its institutions, or the sacred dogmas on which they rely. And now that which neither victory nor defeat, nor intelligence, nor rioting, nor the right nor the left, could shake or amend, is thrown away for a mess of pottage in the centre. National sovereignty and its parliamentary representation are going up in smoke. The country consents to this. It knows its soldiers, its men of learning, its engineers, its workmen, its peasants. It knows itself and its history. It has enough confidence in itself for the future to do without something which no longer counts, and to tempt fate, which has often been kind to it. Why should it cling to a constitution which, its most learned jurists assure it, is authorised to carry out its own contradiction and decree its own disappearance? . . . These odds against politics are manifestly absurd. They are contrary to universal experience and to the nature of things. But how can one help excusing them when politics have ceased to be anything but degrading? Perhaps in the last resort such a surrender might be analysed as an act of faith. . . . It is possible that, just as there is a 'dark night' for the soul of mystics, there is a 'dark night' for the soul of nations. But in that case it is in the lucidity of absolute clarity that France must make up her mind to enter the night. . . ."

The "revolt against Europe" came neither with such clarity nor from such depths. The results of a carefully conducted poll carried out in May, 1953, by the French Institute of Public Opinion, publication of which just before the big parliamentary debate of the following November led to violent controversy, surprisingly showed that only 22 per cent. of those asked were opposed to E.D.C., that 46 per cent. favoured it, and—perhaps most surprising of all—that only one-third "didn't know", though replies to supplementary questions showed how slight was the degree of factual knowledge of what was involved. The farther one went from the political and intellectual circles of the capital, the greater was the equanimity with which the E.D.C. proposals were almost instinctively accepted, though the feeling was too inarticulate and too remote from the political platforms and microphones of Paris to be perceptible in the political debate. It was not the country as a whole, but the political personnel of the organised Republic, the mandated incumbents of a sovereignty to which they clung the more firmly the less capable they were of exercising it, who rose in alarm against a development which in the last resort undeniably threatened "the institutions"—that sum-total of all *situations acquises*, well protected inertia, comfortable routine, big and little incomes derived from ossified ideologies, artificial shortages, and stagnation; all the little feudal privileges of an ancient state apparatus for which "national sovereignty" is far too big a word, though it constitutes its most concrete, solid, and today almost its only content; and the European policy of the Cabinet floated so loosely on the surface that the "revolt of those in possession" sufficed to sweep it away. The fate of this policy was decided, or rather frittered away, from day to day in small parliamentary or party manœuvres, horse deals, and points of procedure. E.D.C. had never been explicitly approved by Parliament, even in principle, though it had been the official policy of all French Governments for two years. Not one of the governing parties had taken up an unambiguous position to the "little European" conception, even the M.R.P., which was the most committed to it, and was the party of M. Schuman, but also that of M. Bidault. All the parties had drifted on without finally committing themselves, and each one of them was more or less equally divided between supporters of E.D.C., opponents, and those who could not make up their mind. Nobody had said no, and everybody had said "yes, but . . ." and all that was necessary was to shift the accent from the "yes" to the "but".

The flag of resistance was raised, symbolically enough, at the annual congress of the Radical Party at Bordeaux in October, 1952, by M. Daladier; a M. Daladier who had learned since 1938, when, trusting in the peaceable and innocuous intentions of the Third Reich of Adolf Hitler, he had handed over Europe to the knife. Having learned by experience, this time he recognised the danger threatening from the warlike Federal Republic of Dr. Adenauer. "When they say Europe, they mean Germany, and when they say Germany they mean greater Germany," he said, exactly reversing the words of Dr. Schumacher, who had talked of Europe as meaning "greater France". Having discovered the "German danger" fifteen years late, the new "peace in our time" which he offered as an alternative to M. Schuman's "suicidal" policy was to be concluded with the Soviet Union, whose innocuousness he proved with ample statistics about the superiority of western industrial potential very similar to those with which he had once proved the innocuousness of Hitler's Germany. Everyone learns from history what he can, and the ex-*lycée* masters who play such a prominent part in French politics have a very special way of confusing a knowledge of history with an understanding of the present; and for the first time a Radical congress saw its two "grand old men", M. Herriot and M. Daladier, who for thirty years had disputed the role of principal tenor to the party, agreeing in uttering a warning against the "European adventure". They were united against the Ministers of their own party, and also united in advocating an alternative policy: reconciliation, not with Germany, but with Russia.

This was the signal for the resurrection of all the ghosts of the past which had been withdrawn from circulation since the liberation; all Munich and all Vichy rose in the interests of national defence. A dinner of the "Democratic Alliance", at which M. Flandin, the living embodiment of the capitulation policy of 1938, condemned this "European federation which meant the suicide of France" and declared that it would be madness to think of concluding a treaty with Germany, was attended, not only by a few Gaullists who had deserted the cause, but the whole of the capitulation and the whole of the collaboration: MM. Georges Bonnet, Francois Piétri, Léon Bérard, Paul Faure, Maître Isorni (Marshal Pétain's counsel), MM. Baréty and Taittinger. The "gravediggers" of yesterday returned to the front of inexorable nationalism, gallantly waving the tricolour. The "European army" was the signal upon which shields were raised against any kind of European integration. What Marc Bloch had called "small-town France", the France of patriarchal little factories, small shops, and local notables, awoke from its slumbers, and saw that its doors and windows were no longer securely bolted. In its name M. Gingembre, of the Association of Small and Medium Businesses, declared war upon the "Europe of trusts, international business, and high finance"; and in the same spirit M. Paul Ramadier, the Socialist veteran, advised his comrades to close the door on Europe and instead devote themselves to the cultivation of their little gardens. "Every country has its own greatness", he wrote. "Our industry develops more slowly than German industry, but our agriculture, however inadequate, nearly suffices for our needs." Greatness is another thing that everyone measures by his own standards. General de Gaulle withdrew his Carolingian vision of 1950 and now spoke with lofty contempt of "this so-called European army, this band of countryless men into which France is supposed to fling her soldiers, her weapons, and her money higgledy-piggledy with those of defeated Germany and defeated Italy." The Communist Party was naturally opposed to any constructive policy or to any diversion of history from its predestined road to catastrophe; and the small but noisy group of "neutralist" and "progressive" intellectuals also added to the uproar. All this created the impression of a mighty groundswell of opposition, though it was based on the most confused, inconsistent, and contradictory motives and amounted to nothing but pure negation. General de Gaulle and M. Gingembre, M. Flandin and M. Thorez, M. Moch and M. Daladier, added up to no alternative policy or outlook, but merely to an exceedingly powerful brake-block.

Thus with 1952 the "Schuman period" in French foreign policy came to an end, and with it the triumvirate which had been predominant in European politics for several years was broken up, and the machinery of "Europeanisation" was blocked at its vital spot. The history of the first seven years of the Fourth Republic seemed to end where it had begun; with M. Bidault. This bold idealist, who has totally unjustifiably acquired the reputation of being a small-scale Machiavelli, had once more to assume the ungratifying role which he had filled for four years after the liberation and which it seemed to be his destiny, if not his vocation, to fill: namely with flowery formulas and deep melancholy to embody a policy which is no longer applicable, though it is impossible to admit the fact. Before it had been the Rhineland policy, and now it was European policy, at any rate that European policy which stood and fell with a certain diplomatic constellation.

Nothing was withdrawn and nothing altered, except the tone. "We all want to create Europe, but we do not want to disappear in it," M. Bidault said, and thus shifted the emphasis from partnership to the special position of France as a power which was not only European. Her overseas empire must remain outside the European community politically, militarily, and economically, and her prerogatives as a member of the Security Council with the privilege of the veto, as a member of the board of directors of N.A.T.O. and of the victors' club, the "big three", "four", or "five", must not be affected by her entry into the "little European" combination. In fact, the marriage contract must strictly preserve French property rights.

All this was not new. French Africa had, contrary to the original declaration of principles, been left out of the Coal and Steel Community, and the E.D.C. treaty specifically excluded the French colonial army and all that belonged to it from E.D.C. authority. What was new was chiefly the strong emphasis placed for domestic political reasons on all the inequalities which in any case arose out of the original situation and the existing international protocol. A comparison, exaggerated for controversial reasons, was made between the French Union and the British Commonwealth, and the conclusion was drawn that France had just as good reasons as Britain not to enter into European ties; and an almost captious legalistic concern was shown to build up the diplomatic hegemony of France as a counterweight to the feared economic hegemony of Germany.

The Rome conference of the six "little European" Foreign Ministers in the spring was the first to be held without M. Schuman. It received with a sense of acute discomfort the draft constitution for a European political community which had been drawn up six months previously, and laid it aside in embarrassment; and M. Bidault had the painful task of submitting a large number of supplementary protocols, conditions, and interpretations to the E.D.C. treaty which had been signed nearly a year before. The protocols sounded less like clarifications of the treaty than shovelfuls of earth over its coffin. The anniversary of the signature of the treaty came and went, and there was no more talk in France of its ratification. It looked as if it were never going to reach even the stage of preliminary examination by the appropriate parliamentary committees, and in the jargon of the Palais Bourbon it was known as the skeleton in the cupboard. In the summer there came the triumph of the right and left extremists in the Italian general election, and with it Signor De Gasperi's departure from the "European triumvirate". "Europe" went out of fashion, and the "European army" seemed to have been no more than a crafty device with which it had been possible to hold up the world for three years until the situation which had called for action had passed by. The archives of state chanceries are full of treaties which have never been ratified and put into force and have slowly faded into forgetfulness.

This calculation would no doubt have turned out to be correct if the diplomatic construction of Europe had been only a European ideal and not an answer to a very definite problem, which remained to be faced even if the all-too-clever calculators had in the meantime forgotten the fact. Irrespective of other motives and hopes which might have played their part, the real impetus had come from the necessity of finding a place for Germany on the map of Europe after the second world war. "Little Europe" was a direct answer to the German, and not to a French, Italian, or Dutch question, and if it were rejected an alternative had to be found. True, the question of the national future of Germany was not a matter of immediate concern to every single inhabitant of Beauce, Périgord, or Calabria, and it was only very occasionally and incidentally of immediate concern to the average politician at the Palais Bourbon; but it was inevitably a matter of immediate concern to the Germans, though their interest in it was often felt to be disturbing, if not actually indecent. The immediate reaction of the other partners to a discarding of

"European illusions" meant no more than a more or less regrettable return to the only too familiar. But for Germany there could be no such return; for her it was not the path of European union, but that of national restoration which led in the direction of adventure. The result was what the professional diplomatists and routine politicians had least expected. The partner for whom the whole European policy had been devised, the only one to whom it was not offered as a free choice, but upon whom it was imposed as a disciplinary measure, and for whom it was *a priori* not a diplomatic formula but a new form of national existence, took it seriously and accepted it. True, the fact that the German Bundestag elections of September 6th, 1953, which turned out in practice to be no more and no less than a plebiscite for Dr. Adenauer, were certainly not a demonstration of faith in the European ideal only. They were in the first place a success brought by success itself, a vote of confidence in the policy which had brought German economic revival, political rehabilitation, and international credit. But the very success of this policy was a fruit of its moderation, single-mindedness, and directness, and the vote of confidence it was given was also a repudiation of defeatism and of all desperadoes who still thought in terms of *revanche*. Germany, which had been the passive object of European policy, had turned into its driving force.

But for a good many French politicians the triumph of this most western, most francophile, statesman was a surprise more unpleasant than a wave of German nationalism would have been. The very size of Dr. Adenauer's vote was alarming —"these Germans are immoderate in everything, even in their moderation!"—and the authority with which the Federal Government was henceforward able to speak for western Germany—and morally for the whole of Germany after the "plebiscite-in-reverse" of the east German rising in June—provided as striking a contrast to French political decadence as the "German economic miracle" did to French economic stagnation. It was this unambiguous German acceptance of European integration on almost any scale and on almost any terms that caused "Europe" to be doubly suspicious in French eyes. The advantages that Germany expected from European union must obviously be very great indeed—political and moral "liquidation of guilt", an opening of the doors of the world to German industry and technique, and the opening up, if not the conquest, of the European and even of the Eurafrican market. If the whole thing could not be cancelled out, could not at least the price of French consent be raised so long as French diplomacy still held the keys in her hand?

The fact that the roles had been reversed, and that it now seemed that France must be won over to German European policy and not *vice versa*, was, at any rate from the point of view of the little grocer's shop, an advantage, and in great affairs petty craftiness seldom pays. Henceforward it was uncomfortably clear that the success or failure of European unification depended only on Paris, and that no alibi could be found in Bonn, Rome, The Hague, or Brussels. Government and Parliament were forced to take the skeleton out of the cupboard, and after eighteen months of vacillation it was no pleasing sight.

France—or rather a group of clever politicians who had seen in advance that in spite of the blow of 1945 Germany would grow strong again, and that it would not be possible in the long run to treat her purely as an object of politics, and that she would have to be treated either as a partner or as an enemy—had put "Europeanisation" on the order of the day; and at the moment when France had emerged from her resentful isolation and assumed the leadership of a constructive European policy, all Europe had felt relief, and had unquestioningly acknowledged her leadership, for which it had long waited in vain, after the second as after the first world war. The impetus could have come only from France, not only because France was the only surviving continental power which possessed a seat and a voice in the council of the victors, but above all because it was hardest for France to give that impetus; and when that impetus was given, Europe had seemed transformed. But a France that had become leaderless had been unable to maintain her position, and she had descended more and more into the role of an unwilling straggler; and now, when the German Federal Republic specifically proclaimed a loyalty to the grand design which

France no longer proclaimed, the diplomatic victory which the French had gained by their initiative threatened, in spite of all diplomatic etiquette and polite reserve, to turn into an immeasurable diplomatic and moral French defeat, associated with all the odium of double-talk and dishonesty which attaches itself to a policy which claims to be permanent and lasting while in reality it is nothing of the sort.

The whole parliamentary history of France had been exclusively filled with domestic matters, but now for the first time a foreign affairs problem resulted in a severe crisis, overshadowing everything else; though Europe was no longer just a foreign affairs problem; the traditional cleavage between home and foreign affairs had become as illusory in France as elsewhere. The "European question" split the Government, whose Ministers openly disavowed each other; after a dramatic and confused foreign affairs debate the Prime Minister secured a few weeks' respite for it only by abandoning any explicit policy and dissociating himself from his own Foreign Minister. It divided the Government majority, divided the opposition, and it divided every single party, from the Socialists to the conservatives, into "European" and "anti-European" factions engaged in violent mutual hostilities. It entangled itself in domestic political questions on which the demarcation of political line was entirely different; and in the resulting confusion the formation of any parliamentary majority was utterly impossible; though perhaps it may have set in motion the painful and long-overdue process of political regrouping which will not only overthrow the ossified, ideological party structure, but lead to a revitalisation of French political life.

Only two groups were unitedly opposed to the "Carolingian" policy—the extreme left and the extreme right, the Communists on the one hand, and on the other the variegated sediment left behind in Parliament by the receding of the Gaullist wave. A strange phalanx of men who had assumed false beards and borrowed historical costumes claimed to represent the revolt of the national consciousness in this crisis: the Communist fifth column, the "separatists", as General de Gaulle had once called them, and the group of ex-Gaullists who had deserted de Gaulle and had been contemptuously repudiated by him when they fell greedily on the "manger of the régime", and now justified their participation in the Government and the Government majority by obstructing every conceivable foreign policy in the name of the General's theories.

The connecting link and spokesman of the two wings of this phalanx was M. Daladier, the last survivor of Munich, who had once been pelted with rotten eggs by both. The fact that this outwardly so variegated "national front" was the only one to develop at any rate the suggestion of an alternative policy to that of European integration was paradoxical only in appearance. This alternative, at first put forward very tentatively and then more and more outspokenly, was nothing but a revival of the old pact with the devil, a resuscitation of the "Moscow-Paris axis". The idea was to play off the Soviet Union against America, or walk the tightrope between the Russians and N.A.T.O., and it demonstrated the diplomatic wisdom characteristic of Balkan Machiavellis, the virtuosity of dwarfs who believe themselves able to use the continents as cards in their local feuds. In the Thorez-Daladier-de Gaulle galaxy the Communists or their taskmasters were undoubtedly the only ones who knew what they were doing; they exploited with virtuosity the inner logic of the nationalism in the limitations of which the others ensnared themselves out of habit, lack of imagination, and blindness.

Outside this "national front", in the parties of the democratic centre, minds were divided by different criteria; reduced to the simplest terms, by the breadth of their vision. No national hatred, no passionate emotion, and no evil memories were invoked. The advocates of a European policy spoke of a Franco-German future, and their opponents spoke of France, and of France only. The fact that the German future was also at stake, and that at this parting of the ways no French politican could escape responsibility for what might become of Germany in five or ten years' time, did not seem to concern the latter, and it was this that gave the debate its unreal flavour. If a note of nationalism was sounded in the speeches and arguments against a European community, it was not a confident, proud, or resentful nationalism, but the petty, frightened nationalism of the *petite nation*. It was alarm at the prospect of the German bull breaking into the china-shop of petty French happiness; and behind it all was a very likeable dislike of all "efficiency", whether German or American, and at the same time an almost morbid and totally unjustified belief that in open competition France would always and in all fields inevitably be worsted. M. Robert Lacoste, a Socialist opponent of European union, an old trade unionist, and a Minister of Production in the early post-war period, described this attitude as nothing but hydrophobia. "There are pessimists", he said, "who do not believe in the possibility of getting the French people voluntarily to make the persistent effort required to free our nation from sterility. . . . The Coal and Steel Community, liberalisation, the economic integration of Europe would, it is believed, throw France violently into the hard struggle of competition, force her to adapt herself and take up the struggle in order not to go under. In short, it is a matter of taking a puppy by the scruff of its neck and throwing it in the water to make it learn to swim." He added that these pessimists were frivolously optimistic. It was better, he said, to paddle cautiously in the water for a bit, to test the depth, or first to learn the strokes on dry land. But, after six years of cautious splashing about in the water of European economic co-operation, the French economy is more frightened of the water, more autarkic and protectionist than ever. Paddling and swimming are two totally different things, and no one has ever learned to swim from paddling alone.

Perhaps only fear of the deluge would have been a sufficient reason to justify a plunge into the water—though in that case it would have been too late to learn to swim. But the deluge, the threat of which accompanied "the European community's" every step from the outset, did not take place, and the feeling of urgency died away. More by luck than by judgment, western Europe survived the Stalin era, and the first cracks that appeared in the apparently so flawless granite of the Soviet empire, its ideology, its economy, and its system of satellites, served as a justification, or at any rate a welcome excuse, for no longer believing in the wolf whose coming had so often been announced but had never come. At the opposite pole of world politics, in the United States, tension, in spite of much loud talking, dropped too. The end of the Democratic era was also the end of the "European" era in American policy, though no alterations were made in the mechanisms of the Atlantic pact or the postulates of western unity. But the trend that first became perceptible as a mental and moral estrangement in the relations between Europe and America must lead sooner or later to a crisis of the Atlantic system, which has not found its inner equilibrium, and at conference after conference has evaded the fundamental differences between the respective points of departure without having ever overcome them. The whole dynamic of the international situation, in which fear and ineluctable necessity provided the driving force for European integration, is beginning to break up, the impulses are fading away, and the centres of will of the cold war, the tension of which, however, did not diminish, seem to be decaying from within. A chapter of the post-war period has ended, and the shape of the next is not yet discernible. But the Europe whose creation began under the aegis of the approaching apocalypse has lost its driving force.

Will the drop in temperature and the diminution of alarm set free forces more positive than were those mobilised by agonised awareness of danger and impotence? The Europe of the cold war, of Russian pressure and American aid, advanced to within a pace of fulfilment—and one pace from the goal is as distant as a hundred if the will to make it is absent. There remains the will-power of Europe itself, the Europe of which M. Monnet said that it will be "a fruit, not of fear, but of self-confidence"; but what is present is less will-power than good will, which is not will at all. There also remains—or rather there is on the way—a younger generation which has learned to take Europe seriously and to look at Franco-German history with new eyes; and those who have noticed where French university students of the present day spend their holidays are able to believe that a European generation is growing up in France, entirely without diplomatic aid, which will tomorrow take the place of the gerontocracy of Clochemerle. But the first ten years after the first world war also produced such a generation, and the fruit of new ideals which ended up in the old ruts, and of European enthusiasms which led nowhere, was bitter. And finally there remains all that has been actually achieved in the way of European integration and its half-completed "supra-national" institutions, the whole momentum of a political and institutional process which has been set in motion and battles against obstinate adherence to old ways. The High Authority in Luxembourg, at the risk of being charged with exceeding its powers and abusing its position, has not hesitated to use the Coal and Steel Community as the lever of European policy; it did not restrict itself to coal and steel, but set itself to widening the European breach. But the contact between the diffuse good will on the one hand and the technical set-ups that have come into being as the result of European policy on the other, the contact that would have given life to both, has not been found. Between them there lies like a thick, isolating layer the barely shaken routine of traditional day-to-day politics with its ossified ideologies; and the disintegration of the European national states has proceeded much faster than the integration of Europe.

When something that is going to happen finds the straight way blocked, it starts happening fragmentarily, chaotically, by devious, indirect routes. The apparently intact framework of national sovereignties to which the parochial politicians still cling has in reality long since broken down on all sides. Economically, financially, and militarily no single European country is still able to stand on its own feet. In the process of "Atlantic integration", in the division of sovereignty between Germany and the former occupying Powers, in all the supra-national councils, committees, and organisations on which all Europe is represented, even in the Coal and Steel Community (which as an isolated relic of a development which, stopped in its tracks, has turned into an extra-territorial technocracy instead of into a western European federal ministry for heavy industry), what has taken place has been not so much an overcoming of national sovereignties as a decay of national sovereignties; it has been the disorganisation of an old order rather than the creation of a higher order. Ever greater and more important sectors of public life have burst out of a national framework which has become too narrow for them without a new framework's having been put in its place, and thus tend more and more to escape from the existing forms of public control and state organisation. Examples of this are western European heavy industry, the European commands under N.A.T.O., the international finance, armaments, and investment planning committees which carry on by means of conferences and committees, but are subject to no overriding political authority, above all to no politically responsible authority. In the last resort they are dependent on the United States Congress, which grants or withholds appropriations, and the American Administration which spends them. "Europe is obviously tending towards being ruled by an American commission," Valéry wrote in 1951. "Its whole policy tends in that direction." Europe is perhaps not striving towards that end, but its whole policy—or rather its whole incapacity to form a policy of its own, tends in that direction, *i.e.*, towards becoming ripe for colonisation.

In this apparent pause for breath in European post-war history it may seem inviting to stop and return to "normality", to the old political game. But what would that be returning to? To "her own little garden" in the case of France and to *Realpolitik* in the case of Germany? It is an inviting prospect, but it is no longer possible. The fragmentation of Europe into sovereign particles has ceased for half a century to be normality, and it can never be normality again, even if it persists as an abnormality. Within this cracked framework democracy becomes an agitation in the void, and hole-and-corner dictatorships lack greatness; the only content of political life becomes defence of sectional interests. The restoration of the old sovereignties which exist only as a façade and are only shadows is no longer a return to "one's own affairs", which in reality are one's own affairs no longer. Such a return would be possible only in the form of a chauvinistic and chaotic revolt against history itself, similar to the dreadfully pointless revolts in the late history of Greece against the consequences of centuries of self-destruction—that late Greece which, in its decline into the provincial, in its colonial administration, and in its pathetic arrogance over a departed greatness in the midst of a Hellenised world whose brilliant motherland it once had been, is so alarmingly reminiscent of the age in which we live. For history will one day speak of

Europe as a unit, whether it achieves unity or not, just as it spoke subsequently of Greece as a unit, though Greece was never unified, but went down in hereditary hostilities and local feuds. Thus the first steps to the concrete achievement of Europe also became the crisis of European consciousness, and the crisis of national consciousness as well. The crisis was bound to come, and it did not come too soon. Not only has the age of European cabinet politics and routine diplomatic manœuvring come to an end, but also that of irresponsible proclamations of the European ideal in week-end political speeches. Europe is no longer a distant ideal, but an almost tangible new shape emerging from behind the tottering old ones; and politicians must accept or reject it, for the responsibility of choosing between achievement and bankruptcy cannot be shifted from their shoulders. True, from a short-range point of view the consequence of a declaration of bankruptcy would be that sense of relief that is always felt when one can turn aside from a creative task and go back into the apparently still usable old grooves. But during all these years Europe has been there, if not as a movement with driving force behind it, as an almost fatalistically accepted aim of development; if not as active faith, as a myth; the vision of a European future which nobody dared openly to oppose because there was and is no alternative. If the myth is shrugged off with the contemptuous scepticism of progressive intellectuals for romantic wish-dreams, or with the disheartening double-dealing of the "yes, but" politicians, all that remains is to wait for the spectres and perversities which will fill the void.

During the debate on the ratification of the European Coal and Steel Community treaty General Aumeran, a deputy of the classic French right, declared that the dead of two world wars had not fallen so that France might be handed over to economic conquest by Germany; and M. Pleven, the Prime Minister, replied that the dead of two world wars had not fallen so that everything might begin all over again. That is the tragic dialogue that runs like a thread through the whole of the European debate. But who can ask the dead what they died for? And when will the living begin to think about the living?

§ 5

LA FRANCE, LA FRANCE SEULE...

"IN 1928, when the French heard Aristide Briand talking of a European union, the idea at first gave them the impression of astonishing novelty. But on further reflection they recalled that they had heard talk of something of the kind before. That was at the time of the Romantics, the time of abundant emotions, fine phrases, and long beards, in short, the time of the illusions of 1848." Those are the words with which M. Joseph Hours began his far-reaching historical survey of "The European idea and the idea of the Holy Roman Empire" in the *Année politique et économique* for the first quarter of 1953. Its editor, M. Bernard Lavergne, supplied an introductory note calling urgent attention to its profound topical significance. "There never was an idea that conflicted more violently with every French tradition," he said. "It is in vain that M. Robert Schuman, who is thoroughly imbued with Teutonic culture, assures us that it is a French initiative. Henceforward no educated Frenchman will be able to accept an unabashed falsehood of this kind." It was no wonder that all the "anti-Europeans" fell with enthusiasm on this long-awaited treasure-store of historical arguments which finally revealed that the European idea was not progressive, but reactionary, and that nationalism was not reactionary, but progressive, and thus relieved the consciences of all the left wing, progressive, revolutionary, and so international-minded ideologues who have now discovered the autarkic national state to be the last word in history.

"Europe began in unity. It is older than the nations of which it consists," M. Hours says, and goes on to claim that the European idea is no more than a cunning attempt to restore the (German) Holy Roman Empire. The history of France, on the other hand, is that of national resistance to the "Empire", the revolt of the national idea against unity, the unity of the Church as well as that of the Empire, which in M. Hours' eyes fuse into one. The struggle of Philip the Handsome against the temporal power of the Pope and that of Francis I against the universal empire of Charles V, the Gallican national church of the *ancien régime* and the anticlericalism of the republic, were all phases of the same, never-ending struggle against the "supra-nation" which must now be taken up against its latest form, that of German-Catholic "Europe". "The past is not dead, but survives in the German cultural world of Adenauer, Schuman, and De Gasperi. The imperial tradition, which had survived in Germany, has no roots in France, and the current European idea has therefore a better prospect of turning to the advantage of those who live in it than it has of benefiting those to whom it means nothing. . . . To the extent that (French) Catholicism is liable to the temptation of becoming political, it is also liable to the temptation of becoming anti-French, and the European union which seems to be leading it astray today still presents itself in the guise of the Roman Empire of Charles V."

In another survey, similarly delving far back into history, M. Hours had already traced the ancestry of the M.R.P., the youngest French political party, which emerged after the end of the war, and the only really "European" one, to the most ancient "anti-French and anti-Gallican" tendencies in French history, to the earliest resistance of the religious orders to the absolute royal power, to the "Burgundian party" of the Hundred Years War, to the Ultramontane League of the wars of religion, to the Fronde, the Vendée, and the anti-republican congregations—it appeared that M. Schuman's party was the same as that which had sent Joan of Arc to the stake and murdered Henry IV. It also amounted more or less to a party of ill-assimilated half-Frenchmen, whose historical points of departure and strongholds, significantly enough, were Alsace, Lorraine, and Celtic Brittany, "as if the use of the French tongue were a particularly strong obstacle to the progress of Christian Democracy among the electorate." M. Hours' historical analysis of the anti-national European movement ends with these indignant words: "The truth is the existence of the various countries. May those who desire to put an end to the life of France say so openly in the light of day instead of trying to reach that aim by tortuous paths."

The first reaction to this effusion, as to all historical travesty, can only be sheer astonishment. M. Hours stands Bainville on his head. In French patriotic history books the privilege of having "revolted against the west", which he claims for France, had always been unswervingly attributed to the Germany of Luther, and even in her most anti-clerical moments it would never have occurred to the "eldest daughter of the Church" to identify the Catholic spirit and holy Rome with "German-ness". But whether Bainville is stood on his head or his feet is of little consequence; historical argument to prove a nationalist thesis can change its ground at will, but it cannot transcend the limitations which the ancient Greeks called idiocy, and it is always exactly the same, whether the language is French or German. Perhaps the most shattering feature of M. Hours' analysis is how reminiscent it is of the outpourings of German nationalism; one might almost be reading Ludendorff in reverse. There is the same woolly accumulation of loose and inexact comparisons between incongruous ideas belonging to different periods, the same indiscriminate jumbling together of the undivided Christianity of the period of the Crusades and the Roman Church of the post-Reformation period, of the Church and the Carolingian empire, of the Carolingian empire and the German Holy Roman Empire, of Teutons and Hapsburgs, of the Hapsburg empire and that of Bismarck, its mortal enemy. It is a playing with words, myths, and shadows, in which some truth may lurk, but not much.

France never revolted against the (German) Holy Roman Empire because she never belonged to it; indeed, the whole birth and development of the French nation took place outside and independently of the Holy Roman Empire. The Hundred Years War was fought, not against "the Empire", but against England, and in the Wars of Religion and the Fronde the enemy was Spain, which was a contemporary western national state of the same type as France, not a myth belonging to a previous age which never became a reality at all. If myth is taken instead of reality, M. Hours is entitled to feel at home everywhere in Europe. The Germany of Bismarck can also be regarded as a revolt against the German Holy Roman Empire which started out from the colonial territory of Prussia, and a whole tradition of German nationalism—that in the name of which Dr. Schumacher accused Dr. Adenauer of treachery—has always regarded the German Holy Empire as the enemy of the German nation, as the betrayer of the work of national colonisation in the east, as an ultramontane and profoundly un-German idea; and even the national state of Italy arose as part of a revolution against papal Rome. In this sense the history of every European nation is that of a revolt against Europe.

But if all the historical distortions and writing to prove a thesis are deleted from M. Hours' essay, a grain of truth nevertheless remains, the truth that is contained in every caricature. Nowhere else in the world is the national state so deeply rooted as in France, and nowhere else has the root system of the national state so completely invaded the whole of the nation's mental and material life. France is the nation *par excellence*, *la nation* which at bottom refuses to accept the idea of *la nation* in the plural; it is the only one which in a deliberate revolutionary act rejected all the pre-national symbols of cross, crown, and people, and set itself up as *la nation* while all around there were still nothing but peoples, and made of the word *nation*, which had hitherto signified only "origin", a supreme political idea; not as one particularism among many, but as a supreme and unconditional "one and indivisible" unity, which tolerated no others by its side.

The French national idea was no nationalistic idea. It was the opposite of exclusive; it was all-embracing. Belonging to *la patrie* meant the opposite of being one of a band of subjects. The *Marseillaise*, with its appeal to *les enfants de la patrie*, became an international revolutionary song, and it was the supporters of France in Germany, Italy, and Switzerland, *i.e.*, according to modern ideas, agents of a foreign power, who were the first to call themselves patriots; and no nation has found such complete fulfilment in itself—least of all the Germans, who have never been able to find fulfilment as a nation and have achieved an identification of the kind only in a descent to the lowest level, the biological level of an obscene blood-cult. Nowhere else has a nation in the "state of innocence" of the moment of its birth made such a universal claim to speak on behalf of the whole of humanity. Nowhere else has a nation so completely equated itself with civilisation, and nowhere else have the rights of man been equated with the rights of the citizen. The French language was equated with the language of civilisation, French intellect with the universal intellect, and French customs with human customs. When France spoke she believed herself to be speaking in the name of humanity, and she did so with a self-assurance which was without arrogance or obscurantism, because there was no one else to compare her with; and she did so without exclusiveness, because every human achievement was given honorary French citizenship, and "everyone had two countries, his own and France." What from outside, from the subsequently awakened self-consciousness of other nations, may appear to be *hubris* or madness must, if its greatness is to be appreciated, be looked at from within, as it was at the moment of *la nation's* first emergence from the stifling atmosphere of dynastic prehistory, intoxicatingly aware of itself as a unit with the power to will and the power to act, in the great dream of liberty, equality, and fraternity.

But this history of *la nation* came to an end, and fundamentally it came to an end at the very hour of its revolutionary self-constitution, though the French consciousness still draws nourishment from that tremendous act, the promise of which took away the breath of the contemporary world and still takes away the breath of later generations. The state of innocence, however, did not survive the moment of birth. The proclamation of *la nation* which had grown conscious of herself marked the beginning of the nations, of "national awakenings" and national conflicts; and with the tremendous impetus given to the process by the Napoleonic empire, which was simultaneously an attempt to put into practice the universal claim of *la nation* and a terrible disclosure of its contradictions, the most fundamental of the changes introduced by the great revolution turned out to be the imposition upon the free citizen of the liability to conscription—which was the first obligation that accompanied his newly-gained liberty—and the change to national warfare from dynastic warfare waged by professional soldiers and mercenaries. At the end of a quarter of a century of revolutionary wars which proved the impotence of dynastic armies in the face of citizen armies, the cry of *"Aux armes, citoyens!"* was answered by the same cry of "Citizens, to arms!" elsewhere, and Herder's dream that "Cabinets may quarrel with one another, state machines may make war on one another, but not nations" was over. The idea of *la nation* underwent the steep decline into nationalism, which is its perversion and betrayal.

France found a degree of fulfilment in this idea which was not equalled elsewhere. Nevertheless the fulfilment was never complete. The self-constituted nation was never the whole nation, and its claim to totality, its refusal to accept the validity of any loyalty higher or lower than itself or outside itself, bore within itself the germ of self-mutilation from the beginning. The anti-clericalism which the republicans inherited from the Jacobins was another aspect of the pitiless extinction, not only of the dynasty and the aristocracy, but also of federalism and regionalism and all local autonomies, in short of all ties of a non-national, pre-national, or supra-national nature, which threatened to come between the isolated individual and the "one and indivisible" nation. The struggle against the Church was both the point of departure and the motor of the revolution. The fire which fused France into a nation destroyed the community's roots, just as it destroyed the symbols to which it looked up. It turned the state into a soulless, universally present and impotent abstraction having nothing but police functions in relation to a society simultaneously total and anarchic, which it dissolved into nothing but individuals; and the cinders that it left behind were the "internal *émigré*" groups and organisations, of which the Church is the biggest, which have populated France since that time.

In spite of its claim to totality, the nation has also failed, as we have seen, to absorb the "post-national" elements which have entered its sphere since the revolution: namely big industry and the working-class employed by it. No place has been found for either of these in the "social contract" of a society which consists of innumerable petty bourgeois and small peasants. It was not without reason that republican France mistrusted modern economic organisation and protected the small, individualistic economic units against the big. But the necessities of the social and economic organisation of big industry have burst her inner structure before bursting her national framework. One line of this development has led to the Europeanisation of heavy industry, and the other to the dissidence of the working-class, which constitutes a new "inner *émigré*" class; one leads in the direction of European integration, and the other in the direction of national disintegration.

Thus a truth is contained in M. Hours' caricature, but only a half-truth. "Europe" is no clerical idea, and if it is true that pre-national forces and an old spirit of supra-nationalism, which republican ideology long fought but never succeeded in completely eradicating, survive in the Popular Republican Movement—a tradition not represented by the Church or the ecclesiastical hierarchy, but kept alive by a series of writers extending from Lamennais by way of Péguy to Bernanos—it is also true that the true spirit of liberal capitalism has inspired the direct and logical development from the Monnet plan to the Schuman plan, which was nothing but a second Monnet plan.

"European France" includes both the oldest and the newest France, neither of which has ever found a place in the total demands of *la nation*. Hence the split that runs through all the traditional parties and all the traditional political philosophies in France, which has for long been incapable of forming a political will, but only loose and non-binding groupings, based on personal affinities and origins, each of which contains within itself all the contradictions characteristic of France as a whole, and the sum of which have turned the party political activity of the republic into an empty game with meaningless labels, which lies like an obscuring veil between the nation and the vital questions affecting it. In the face of any great national decision these political groupings—now as at the time of Munich—burst asunder. Besides the "Christian Democrats" gathered round M. Schuman and the "technocrats" gathered round M. Monnet, nearly every party has its "European fraction" consisting of its best and most honest minds: M. André Philip, for instance, among the Socialists, M. René Courtin among the Liberals, and M. Paul Reynaud on the traditional right. These men too could claim to be France, its strongest and most vital elements, and to represent the element of forward-looking self-confidence in a nation of backward-looking doubters and sceptics.

But these "Europeans" are individuals, representatives of a deep and diffuse feeling perhaps, but not of an organised movement with a clear-cut aim; and they too are liable to be affected from time to time by the parochial domestic political atmosphere. The constituted nation is still that of M. Gingembre, the France of the sheltered sleepy small town, of closed doors and shop-windows and limited horizons, and the whole domestic political mechanism of the republic, the whole structure of the established parties and ideologies, and of French democracy itself, the place of which has been usurped by mere parliamentarianism, is cut to the measure of this little France, to which the budget deficit and the lay schools question seem adequate preoccupations for a great nation which prides itself on its universality. The political life of the *pays légal* is organised round such problems and round them alone, and they are perfectly adequate for the requirements of the citizens of Clochemerle and Chénérailles. They are not adequate, however, for the requirements of the French role as a great Power, the requirements of a world empire that was destined to be absorbed in the *grande nation,* but can never be absorbed into the *petite nation,* or for the requirements of modern France herself. And finally another *bloc* that lives outside the self-constituted nation is the working-class, which as an "inner *émigré*" class gives its half-hearted loyalty to the Communist Party because neither the party system nor the social structure of the petty bourgeois republic offers it any future. The secession of the working-class has long since outgrown any mere conflict of social interests.

The French Communist movement has become the most acute symptom of the crisis of the French national consciousness, and it deliberately exploits the nationalism arising from that crisis. Dismissing Communist nationalism as a sham is taking the task of opposing it too lightly. At first it may have been a sham and a tactical manœuvre, but in the course of the party's progress *via* the resistance movement and participation in the government of the country it has long since become the party's real face, to such an extent that the most characteristic feature of the Communist style is nowadays its wholesale use of chauvinist terminology. The French Communist Party has taken over everything associated with French nationalism. It has of course adopted the Jacobin tradition of "revolutionary patriotism" directed against an "inner enemy" as in the Terror, a type of patriotism so appropriate to the Communist Party; and it has adopted Robespierre, the tyranny of virtue, and the guillotine of the Committee of Public Safety. It has also adopted the optimistic rationalism of the enlightenment movement, and, not content with that, it has taken under its wing Joan of Arc and Richelieu, and Maurras as well as Marat. The Communist movement claims that it alone is truly French, that there is no patriotism other than Communist patriotism, and that the only true *patrie* is the promised "people's democracy" in which the great French revolution will be completed. The notes once characteristic of the *Action Française* are now to be heard in the Communist Press. It was the Communists who talked of "Schuman *le boche*", and it was the veteran Communist trade unionist and internationalist Monmousseau who shouted at Léon Blum: "Blum, in Yiddish that means a flower!" A provincial Communist newspaper once remarked that "Blum, Schuman, Moch, Mayer do not smell of good French soil", and it was *l'Humanité* which printed a caricature showing the "men of the American party", Schuman, Moch, and Mayer, drawn with crooked noses worthy of the *Stürmer*, saying to each other in embarrassment while the Marseillaise was being sung on the Communist benches: "Do you know that tune?" "No, it must be one of those French songs!" And it should not be forgotten that the party bard and agitator Louis Aragon, who ten years before had been pouring scorn and contempt on his country and its army, produced at the end of the war the following monument of chauvinism, than which there could hardly be a more complete repudiation of the spirit of French civilisation. In a manifesto in *Les lettres françaises* he wrote:

"We can, we shall, demand from this guilty people a terrible and lasting tribute; we shall forge for the German people the heaviest and most crushing yoke that history has ever known.... But what shall we exact from them for what we have lost that can never be repaid? For the intellectual life-blood of France? ... Territories certainly. And we call for silence from the timorous, the scrupulous, who fear to see France as great as the picture that we have of her.... I herewith propose that not a single French book, not a single French picture, not a single French sculpture be left in German hands; that a clause in the peace treaty lay down that all French works of art, of whatever kind they may be, be handed back.... Berlin, Munich, Vienna, and Dresden must not remain in possession of this life-blood of France.... French art is by rights the property of France...."

This style is no longer used by anyone except the Communists; they alone play on the whole rabble-rousing keyboard of chauvinism. But it is not just a question of vocabulary and unscrupulous propaganda. Nationalism is the disease of a nation which is in search of—or has already lost—herself, and Communism has identified itself with this disease all over the world. It is useless to argue with Marx or Lenin when we are confronted with the Communism of the Stalin period and after, and completely absurd to try to combat it with the nationalistic arguments which the Communists themselves have collected from the rubbish heaps of history and turned into their principal weapon.

Communism, in its course through the colonial countries and the "backward areas" of Asia and the South America, in which it has found a following that was denied it in the industrially advanced countries, has changed its face, and, as Lenin once prophesied that it would, it has indeed returned to Paris by way of Asia, but in a form different from that in which it set out; in the form of a nationalistic counter-revolution of pre-capitalist countries against the industrialised west; and in this new form it has derived new strength from its old roots in the France which fights against the advance of history. Nationalism is today the reactionary doctrine *par excellence*, the mobilisation of all atavistic instincts against progress to supra-national organisation. It is a revolt against history, and in the last resort against the demands of life itself; and it has become the most natural instrument of a Communist strategy which with obsessive energy and cold logic systematically erects barricades everywhere against all constructive developments in order not to be cheated of the final catastrophe which it expects to lead to its own triumph. This weapon is so natural to it that Communist nationalism has long since become as real and honest as any Communist dialectic can be.

It is not in the least surprising that this nationalism in all countries should be centrally organised and directed, and this is far from being so paradoxical as it is believed to be by those who still confuse patriotism with nationalism. We have already seen a Fascist international in existence, in a more amateurish but deeply related form; and the slogan: "Chauvinists of all countries, unite!" has a deep significance. While national feuds and frontier quarrels continue, the principle of frontiers and national feuds is safe. So long as the chauvinists of all Europe are engaged in vilification of each other, they are united in opposition to the powerful fundamental tendency of our time to do away with national boundaries, and blind to the ineluctable conclusion that in the labyrinth of a dozen competing autarkies, parochial imperialisms, and pocket-handkerchief sovereignties, Europe is doomed to paralysis and death. Even the fusion of a revolutionary mystique with reactionary practice is as old as the hills, an ever-recurring symptom of decaying societies, which are invariably privilege economies, in which innumerable people live in increasing hopelessness, clinging to their pitiful privileges as to an anchor-sheet, in the midst of a general stagnation, characterised by continually increasing prices and a continually increasing shortage of goods. Another thing that the Communist movement has discovered in the course of its excursions into colonial nationalism is the usefulness of entering into alliances with local mandarins and potentates in order to oppose "foreign influence", *i.e.*, the explosive incursion into archaic societies of technique, rationalisation, and new forms of civilisation.

True, the French working-class is no half-starved, fanatical, excitable mob which allows itself to be driven on to the streets by cynical politicians or dancing dervishes like those of Cairo or Teheran, even though that is how "progressive" intellectuals like Jean-Paul Śartre like to regard them. In its efforts at "direct action" the French Communists have been increasingly compelled to rely on the North African sub-proletariat with which the French colonial mercantilist system populates the poor quarters of French industrial cities —a sub-proletariat which owes allegiance less to Communism than to its own Prophet; and it is here that nationalism of the "backward area" type has found the human material that it requires. The Communist Party itself has long since ceased to be a "proletarian party", which is a relic of the past; and, if it does all in its power to prevent its strategic reserve, the trade unions, on which its strength still rests, from being torn from its hands, it has long since swarmed out of its starting position into innumerable branch organisations with a view to the conquest of the petty bourgeois nation itself. It systematically plants amid the latter all the reflexes with which the rebellious "colonial peoples" react to the technological pressure of the surrounding world; it encourages the view that France is the "proletarianised nation" up against "foreign plutocracy". True, the French petty bourgeoisie are no fellaheen; but nationalism of that kind is thoroughly adequate for small peasants and artisans, vegetating on the poverty line and with limited horizons, who have learned to fear like the plague the slightest incursion of true liberalism or fresh air into the artificially preserved, archaic system in which they live.

In this connection a new type of "backward area Communists" has developed which has been scarcely noticed by the sociologists, who cling to the old *clichés* about the nature of the proletariat; but it has been avidly seized on by the Communist recruiting agents. A notorious murder case, in which a whole family of British tourists fell victim in August, 1952, in the most archaic part of Provence, the investigation of which produced no results for a whole year because of family and local loyalties, throws light on this new type of Communist, who is unintelligible to western theorists, but has become important in all "backward areas", including the south of Italy and the south of France. The old peasant Dominici was rolling in wealth, but used the methods and lived in the comforts of the Stone Age. He was the patriarchal ruler over his large family, his grown-up sons trembled in his presence, his wife and daughters-in-law were not allowed to eat at the master's table, but had their meals in the kitchen. He was the tyrant of the village, lord of life and death over his fields, the whole area of which he nightly paced with dog and gun; and, while patrolling his fields one night, he shot down like game three strangers, man, wife, and child, who had erected their tent on his land. Here was this absolute owner and paterfamilias in the ancient Roman sense of the word, a phenomenon from ancient antiquity—a militant Communist, over whom the party held its protecting hand throughout the police investigations. We are concerned here, not with the crime, but with the man. What did "Communism" and "the party" mean to this prehistoric patriarch? The answer is that it meant what the *mafia* meant to the peasants of Calabria and Sicily, and what the xenophobic secret societies of east Africa and Asia mean to their adherents. Features similar to those which loom darkly through this criminal case were to be found among the partisans in the resistance movement and subsequent post-war developments.

If one is to give credit to Satan for driving out sin, credit can be given to the French Communists for having anticipated and exhausted the possibilities of any real Fascist movement in France—if one can still use the word "Fascist", which has degenerated into a mere term of abuse, in the meaning that it once had for its adherents, to whom it meant a nationalistic "revolution" against national degeneration, a terroristic "racial community" organised as a reply to anarchy, a general mobilisation of the economy as a reply to economic decay, and a general mobilisation of the people "as at the front" as a reply to the class struggle. In the inter-war period France had numerous more or less intellectual Fascist groups which populated the *salons* and the Latin quarter, but she never had a real Fascist movement. Even the embryonic forms of such a movement were second-hand and pseudo-Fascist; significantly enough, the most important of them, Doriot's

"French Social Party", was a break-away from the Communists; and its present-day successors are death-cults devoted to the victims of the "purge" and of the persecution of collaborationists.

The starting-point of any new, post-war Fascist movement —and not only in France, but elsewhere too—would obviously be the resistance movement, and not the old, pre-war, forms of Fascism, and obviously it would have to have a different name. If its basis is called "anti-Fascism"; the word "Fascism" is obviously unusable. But a state of disorder in which the energies of innumerable people can find no useful outlet and the impulses of liberty themselves fail can always be the starting-point of a march towards a new, totalitarian "order". In Italy and Germany after the first world war it was experience of the trenches which provided the emotional starting-point for Fascism. The experience of "the great comradeship of the united nation" was exalted in contrast to the degradation and frittering away of national energies involved in economic crisis, in the Marxist class struggle, and in the individual struggle for existence implicit in a free economy. War-time experience in the trenches also provided the mystique for Colonel de la Roque's "Croix de Feu" movement in the inter-war period. But the French did not have this experience in the second world war. The real resistance was the opposite kind of experience; it involved individual refusal to submit, responsible personal decision, and personal adventure. The bases that might have been present here for a "national revolution" were seized by the Communists.

When the war ended there were innumerable young "activists" of the real and the false resistance movements for whose energies there was no outlet, innumerable young intellectuals in revolt against "bourgeois society", whose origins and whole mentality fifteen years earlier would obviously have impelled them towards the patriotic leagues or the *Action Française*. But now they were just as naturally impelled towards the Communists.

Apart from the technique of organisation and propaganda which was always common both to Communism and Fascism, the Communists have long since taken over practically all the slogans and subject matter of the former Fascist movements, including the systematic exploitation of national hatred, economic nationalism and protection of the middle class, and chauvinism and conservatism in the arts. The Communists condemn atonal music, abstract painting, and experimental or unedifying literature as "alien", or "degenerate", or "American" or "Fascist" (the Nazi word for it was *Kulturbolschewismus*); and they exalt trashy literature and painting as "socialist realism".

General de Gaulle's gravest mistake was to believe it possible two years after the end of the war to use the forces of the resistance for the "mobilisation of the national energies" and the formation of the Rally of the French People. In France, as elsewhere, nationalism can now be used only for destructive purposes. The social structure of petty bourgeois France liberates no energies, but absorbs them, directs them into the old ruts, and, after permitting them a short *Sturm und Drang* period, ends almost invariably by fitting them into the traditional *douceur de vivre*. The Gaullist troops marched in the direction opposite to that of their leader, defended no national greatness, but "petty good fortune", and after six years of painful misunderstanding the movement ended like a masquerade, marching into the parliamentary morass at the point where it was deepest. Not General de Gaulle but M. Gingembre was the true embodiment of the *pays réel*.

If the French parliamentary routine and the party system of stagnation by mutual consent is no more able to offer an alternative to Communism than is the French social and economic system, and has no prospects other than discouragement to hold out, the stigma of being a "foreign party" still adheres to the Communist Party and suffices to hold it in check. But what does that stigma amount to in a country whose society is decaying and whose problems burst national boundaries? When the French Communists are accused of being the "Russian party", they reply pointedly enough that their opponents are the "American party", and draw attention to the "satellite" status of a nation dependent on foreign subsidies, whose budget has to be balanced in Washington and whose defence is organised in America. "American colonisation" has become the first and last word of Communist propaganda, in France as in the Far East, in South America as in the Levant; that is the level at which the Communist world organisation now rates France. In the uproars in the National Assembly which have now become traditional the words "traitor!" and "foreign party!" fly backwards and forwards like boomerangs, the "agents of Moscow" denounce the "agents of Wall Street" and *vice versa,* "dollars" are answered with "roubles", and "Munich" is answered with the "Hitler-Stalin pact", as if there were nothing but fifth columns in this country, and no more French parties. On these occasions it is scarcely possible to avoid the impression that the national idea has returned to its birthplace after its triumphant progress round the world only to end in a conjuring up of nationalistic spectres.

The France of M. Gingembre, however, is also the France of M. Jean-Paul Sartre, who is, if not the greatest, at any rate the most typical representative of the "left wing intelligentsia" which still enjoys the reputation in the world of being the truest expression of the French spirit, even if it is only the spirit of greater Paris. Perhaps the most obvious symptom of the crisis of the French intellect is that for ten years it has been expressing itself in a quasi-profound jargon borrowed from Hegel, Marx, Heidegger, and Nietzsche, full of the most unassimilable Germanisms. It accepts Marx's prophetic utterances of 1848 as the last word about the human situation, Zarathustra's "God is dead!" as the last word in enlightenment, and *Beyond Good and Evil* as the last word in ethics; and it proclaims these things to a nation in every hole and corner of which they have long been discovered and discussed. As a bold and revolutionary counter to the petty bourgeois nostalgia for the French *fin-de-siècle* it has discovered the German *fin-de-siècle*; and the most original post-war achievement in the literary life of Saint-Germain-des-Prés has been imitation, even in details of pose and accent, of the "great nausea" of the previous post-war period in Germany. The spectacle has become too strange and bewildering even to be profitable to the tourist trade; it has reached a pitch such that it is legitimate to hope that it may be the prelude to a new beginning.

The first and most obvious reason for the confusion is that artistic, like political circles, are "left wing" and "revolutionary", and the whole vocabulary of revolt still points in a direction to which apparent movement is taking place, while the truth is that the social structure of this old country has become almost motionless, and its ideology has become ossified in the historical drama of the great revolution; it represents no vision of the future, but a tradition, *i.e.*, the past. The smile of Voltaire, the *audace* of Danton, the gestures of Robespierre, have been repeated and imitated innumerable times before coming down to Sartre, Duclos, and Guy Mollet; it is movement at most within a closed system of reference, like that which takes place in the semi-circle of Parliament, where the deputies sit arranged from left to right, and take up a "right" or "left" position towards every question instead of facing each other like Government and Opposition in the British Parliament and taking up a position to the subject at issue.

The problem of *littérature engagée*, which appeared on the political-literary scene with the resistance and at first monopolised it, and that of combining an active voice in the actual building up of the republic with the tradition of revolt against all existing or conceivable forms of terrestrial order which was so deeply ingrained in all left-wing intellectuals, were at bottom identical with that which had baffled and reduced to ineffectiveness the whole non-Communist left in France. The problem was how to bring the traditional ideology into harmony with responsible democratic practice without admitting that in the past they had been reconcilable only on a level of mystification, and that now, with a Communist mass organisation in the country and the Soviet army on the Elbe, they were not reconcilable even on that level. The predestined "final aim of history", which held all the French left-wing intellectuals in its grip, made their political evolutions resemble a fascinated and alarmed buzzing of flies round the dazzling Communist flame; that was the logical outcome of the French national legend. In their controversy with Rousset about compulsory labour in the Soviet Union M. Sartre and M. Merleau-Ponty confessed that Marxist ideas were unfaithfully followed in the Communism of the present day, to which they served as decoration rather than a motive force. Nevertheless those ideas remained. "We have the same values as a Communist. . . . He has values in spite of himself. We may think that he compromises them in the Communism of the present day. Nevertheless they are ours." The circle is thus closed, and there seems to be no escape from it, save in a vertical flight into metaphysics; to these intellectuals a return to reality from their revolutionary millenarianism would be apostasy.

How to take a creative part in social practice and at the same time to sit on the heights of ideological postulates and despise everything that has been or could be done presents an insoluble problem. The lack of relation between thought and action, even the action of a political pamphleteer, which was tolerable in the old radical routine and in the quietism of the verbally revolutionary Third Republic, has developed into a crisis in the face of the problems of the post-war world, which cry out to be dealt with, for the pointing of an accusing finger is no longer sufficient. The tragi-comedy of an ideological system of references which has become unserviceable but remains sacrosanct can be followed through the whole of the "activist" literature which fills France with its controversies more vigorously than ever, though in a nightmarish confusion. The French left, which combines complete self-sufficiency in all theoretical matters with an infinite ignorance of economics, has never known Karl Marx, the difficult author of *Das Kapital*, but only Karl Marx, the revolutionary journalist; it knew only the Marxian eschatology—that on which the state church of the Soviet Union has been built up —but not the Marxian method of social and historical criticism. The result is thinking in terms of slogans, and the use, not of carefully differentiated sociological conceptions, but of such simple and absolute categories as "masters and slaves", "rich and poor", "oppressors and oppressed". Fundamentally all that the French left-wing intelligentsia has taken over of Marxism is misunderstanding of *The Class-Struggle in France*, which fitted in well enough with its own understanding of its own revolutionary myth; and with this ideological baggage it plunged with a moving alacrity into the cold war, to fight it out on the basis of a number of assumptions which it had taken over unexamined and with a system of co-ordinates on which Russia lay on the "left" and America on the "right", and France, the real France of the small town and the small man, lay not at all.

Jean-Paul Sartre, master and preceptor of a whole intelligentsia, can, in view of the disconnection between his philosophical background and his political conclusions, be described as the founder of a high school of Orwellian doublethinking. In his simultaneous roles as philosopher, pamphleteer, playwright, literary eschatologist, and political "activist" he has continued to perform his balancing act with existentialism and popular Marxism, and in endless torrents of words has refused to answer the question of how he reconciles the two; whether he regards as true and real "the self choosing" man of his philosophy as a total product of his own self, or the man postulated by his sociology as a total product of society. All that is certain is that each of these and its opposite are total and absolute. The synthesis of the sensational "existentialist" thesis and its remorseless sociological antithesis would be far too banal and old-fashioned for such a brilliant mind to be inclined to make it; for it would be the old-fashioned morality of all the western moralists since Hesiod and Montaigne, who have reconciled in the human state freedom and determinism, individualism and responsibility, mastery of fate and submission to it, man's grandeur and his insignificance. But it is so much more effective, like M. Sartre, to deal separately with each aspect of this polarity and drive it to its most abstract absurdity, and to leave poor, banal man, who is neither his own creator nor a mere bundle of reflexes, to smaller thinkers; and thus this scintillating dialectic remains no more than a double game with two conflicting postulates.

But the individual's total lack of relations postulated by Sartre the existentialist philosopher, and the same individual's total absorption in the collective postulated by Sartre the Marxist, have something fundamental in common; *i.e.*, the abolition of all personal responsibility, and with it the abolition of all foundation for any human order. In this the "Sartre case" is truly symptomatic of the crisis of the French intellectuals. When confronted with the so immediate, practical, and by no means insoluble problems of France, an acrobatic leap from the most radical individualism into the total "socialisation" of man is the only thing that makes it possible to go on undisturbedly pontificating about the myth of the great revolution without accepting the humiliation of descending to the despised level of a "reformist" on the one hand, or on the other abandoning the claim to be a politician and withdrawing into *belles lettres*.

The yield of all this in terms of political philosophy is pitifully small. The existentialist Sartre has emptied Marxism of all content and turned it into a rotating system of messianic assumptions. As Marx postulated as the final aim of history the elevation of mankind by the world revolution and the elevation of the proletariat into a universal class, this prophecy must be fulfilled, even if it has to be by way of forced labour and the police state, for otherwise history would have no meaning; it is true that this would fit in perfectly with the assumptions of Sartre's existentialism. Moreover the Marxist Sartre has turned existentialism into an empty, rotating system of psychological reflexes. His proletarian is a product of bourgeois prejudices. His complicated psychological mechanism works like this: "For the bourgeoisie . . . the worker becomes an objectivisation of unfathomable violence. The worker knows it . . . and by a new assertion of the projected personality attributed to him he proudly acknowledges and proclaims the violence with which he is reproached." In Sartre's view the Jew is the creation of antisemitic prejudice which the Jew himself is forced to acknowledge. Woman, as has been shown by Simone de Beauvoir in two thick volumes, is the product of male prejudice. Jean Genêt, pornographer, thief, and pederast, to whose works Sartre has written a voluminous introduction, in which he demonstrates all the admiring perplexity of a profoundly good man when confronted with the "problem of evil", is obviously the product of moral prejudices. "What after all is a thief?" he asks. "Nothing but a man whom honest people consider to be such. . . . *Genêt est un excrément*, and it is as such that he vindicates himself." And thus our moralist, assuming the prejudices which he lends to others and which in turn are nothing but a projection of his own, always lands on his feet, like a cat. There is an admirably acrobatic quality about his thinking, which has enabled him to practise with great fluency the art of replacing the other party to any controversy he engages in by a caricatured projection of the prejudices attributed to him. But too much rotating in circles in his case seems to be resulting in exhaustion; and one might say of Sartre's "message" what he himself says about evil: "It is a 'marginal hallucination'; it is never within one's direct field of vision; one can only see it out of the corner of one's eye."

After the end of the war "Sartre and Camus" were spoken of as a pair, joined, like Goethe and Schiller, by one of those "ands" against which even the gods fight in vain. They were the twin stars in the firmament of the new France, both bathed in the aura of the period—nihilism, sombre despair, the senselessness of life, and revolt against God and the world. In spite of all the differences between them, both were spokesmen of the same ruinous condition of modern man. But Camus went the opposite way to Sartre. As editor of *Combat*, on the day of the liberation he proclaimed that his immediate aim was revolution, promising to define what he meant by this in the days to come, and he accompanied this declaration with an accumulation of tautologies characteristic of those days, such as the "immediate setting up of a real people's and workers' democracy". But Camus started with a frank confession of the incompatibility of his philosophy of total "absurdity" with his search for a constructive political ethic. This led him away from the revolution which he proclaimed as editor of *Combat*—to the total revolt of man against the senselessness of his existence, against morality, against the silence of the universe, "against God". It was from this position of total and absolute rebellion, from which he derived morality and fraternity, that Camus arrived at his condemnation of revolutionary terror as a "betrayal of the human revolt"; and not until he attained his position of totally repudiating a universe in which this life was absurd and any other devoid of meaning was he able to dismiss the revolutionary myth according to which the mere seizure of power by one particular party would fulfil the whole purpose of history, or rather give history a meaning. In other words, only Prometheus could unseat the Politburo, and a total myth could be supplanted only by a still more total one; and the anointed high priesthood with whom this intellectual conflict was conducted in the name of the whole of suffering humanity seemed to be unchangeable.

In his violent controversy with Sartre, which signified the end of a whole period of post-war French literary history, Camus disputed the right of Sartre and his colleagues of *Les Temps Modernes*, "who have never moved anything but their editorial chairs in the direction of the movement of history", to talk continually "in the name of the workers and the oppressed"; only a few lines later to threaten himself "to talk a different kind of language" in the name of "this poverty, which finds thousands of advocates but never a brother, this justice, which has its Pharisees too, this people cynically misused for purposes of war and power, these victims who are exchanged and doubly betrayed by their executioners, and finally in the name of all those for whom history is a cross and not the subject for an essay!" The controversy continues in increasing bitterness. The rest of it, because of its specifically French complexities and confusions, is scarcely intelligible beyond the Channel or the Rhine, for it is related solely to the situation of French intellectuals caught up in the myth of the great Revolution.

In this dispute Sartre has on his side all the advantages of the unscrupulous controversialist who never allows himself to be tied down in any position, but always keeps open a dialectical way of escape. But Camus has the advantage of the humility of a genuine seeker after truth. He is the supreme witness to the incredible difficulties that beset the path of one who has apostasised from an ideology which claims apostasy as being exclusive to itself. All the work of Camus tends to be a search for a new basis for fraternity and human dignity, but it is doubtful whether *l'Homme révolté* provides it, unless it is to be found once more in the affirmation of the "absurd" and unmotivated solidarity of which Camus makes a much bigger and plainer parable in *La Peste*. The consummation of all the revolt in the exaltation of the "Mediterranean spirit" with which *L'Homme révolté* ends, is, like Nietzsche's "high midday", an escape into lyricism. But this provides a clue. For Camus the only true and creative·revolt is the work of art, and only art or nature calls from him that note which is to be detected in his first book *Les Noces*, when he exclaims at the sight of Florence "that at the heart of my revolt acceptance slept."

His is the same lonely and absolute revolt in which that great adventurer Malraux, after far wider and more extensive détours by way of all the civil wars of the present age—Communism, the resistance, and Gaullism—found the sum of all the tragedy and heroism of man which he failed to find in revolutionary activity—"for if battle does not displace the absolute, it makes it possible to forget it"; the tragedy about which he is no longer able to speak except in transcendental terms, for "the religious vocabulary is irritating here, but there exists no other" (*Les Voix du Silence*).

In all this much more than politics or sociology is at stake, even if these are seen to be implicit. Does it imply a flight from "activism" into art or metaphysics? Even if it were so, it would be well worth while. In the midst of her material sclerosis France has preserved an intellectual liveliness which technically and commercially more successful countries can only envy. But deeper sources of the French crisis are at work than those of her state or social structure. The French spirit, which for a century-and-a-half lived without transcendentalism, with lopped roots, so to speak, in the self-fulfilment of a completely rational and intelligible history, has grown restless. The word "fate" which was so characteristic of the Germany of yesterday, but in France, which believed, not in fate, but in reason, was an almost alien conception, has with Camus and Malraux made a powerful irruption into the French self-communion. With all its dark and tragic implications it has dangers which are only too obvious, as is illustrated by recent German history, but, if the challenge is faced and accepted, the results may perhaps be fruitful.

What has happened to *la personne France* has never been more plainly and profoundly expressed than by Albert Camus in his *Letters to a German Friend*, written in 1944 when the war was still in progress. "To present ourselves before you," he wrote, "we had to return from afar. . . . We had to conquer our pleasure in mankind, the idea we had formed of a peaceful fate, and our profound belief that no victory was worth while, while every mutilation of man was irremediable. . . .

But now it is accomplished. We had to make a long détour, and we are very late. . . . But you did what was necessary, and we entered history. And for five years it was no longer possible to enjoy the song of the birds in the cool of evening. . . . Yes, we had to follow you. But our difficult achievement was to follow you into war without forgetting happiness. . . ."

It was indignation at finding themselves flung back into the barbarous stream of history after attaining the fulfilment of the seventh day of creation that was the purest, most fundamental, and most profoundly unpolitical motive of a resistance which Camus felt, not as a national, but—"in spite of you"—as a European cause; as the cause of a Europe which already here he equates with the idea of man and his revolt "against the world, against the gods, and against himself". But the embodiment of this Europe was France, which alone held out against the blind stream of history. "That was why we remained backward in relation to all Europe, which always succumbed to the lie of the moment, while we undertook to search for the truth."

France indeed completed and rounded off her history, and brought in a rich harvest; and all she wanted was to remain as she was. But two German invasions broke into her self-centred tranquillity. The first left her severely wounded, and the second, like a robot which spoke no articulate speech and possessed no recognisable human countenance, ran amok over her and tossed her into the midst of a European tragedy in which she had wished to have no part and for which she felt no responsibility. She found herself engaged in a historical process in which the categories of her national myth, by which she measured the world, no longer applied. This national myth was that of the great Revolution; the nation was the absolute and supreme unity, and the sovereign individual the final and ultimate measure of all things. But this national ideal always drew sustenance from its expansion into the supranational and universally valid, and in the form of nationalism it can only negate and destroy itself. The French intelligentsia, which discovered the European cause in the resistance, has to an alarming extent forgotten again that France cannot live alone, and that, so long as she remains France, cannot be responsible only for herself. To step out of the circle of a history that is over and done with is a difficult, a tremendous, a truly revolutionary act. But the personality of France is threatened by nothing except a tragic retreat into herself. Lot's wife looked back and became a pillar of salt. No nation is less in danger of losing herself and her rich heritage in a wider community than this ancient civilisation, whose crystal clarity extends even into the forms and patterns of everyday life; her idea of human civilisation would possess a conquering force greater than all the imperialisms and ideologies if she still could only believe in it herself; and no nation is in greater danger of ossification by repeating the tragic and finally pathetic refusal of the Attic *polis* to grow into something greater than itself. For the power of assimilation on which France used so confidently to rely, looking forward to drawing the whole of mankind into her *civitas,* has come to an end only to the extent that her receptivity to alien things, which was its condition and its deepest essence, dries up and turns into mistrustfully defensive self-sufficiency. France cannot find herself again in such a retreat. *La France seule* has grown too small even for France herself.

No one has any claim to make upon her. France owes the world nothing, neither revival nor greatness, nor that European leadership which history imposed upon her. Whether she owes it to herself is a matter that she alone must decide. Yet how will France, and how will Europe, continue to exist when those who still have hopes of her have given them up? Nothing more shatteringly expresses the fatal temptation of resignation to which France is subject than the words of Edouard Herriot which President Auriol quoted at Donzère and again at Tignes in the face of a critical, unjust, and impatient world:

"France had the right to withdraw into her own grief."

EPILOGUE

THIS picture of France dates from the spring and summer of 1953. The last touches were added during the "Laniel period". It is thus a picture taken at a stationary moment, almost a dead point, in post-war history, when refusal to make decisions seemed to have been erected into a principle of government. Was not the essential preliminary to the installation of any new Government that it must commit itself to not committing itself on any of the fundamental questions with which France was faced? It was one of those periods of profound confusion in which the observer's mind is filled with contradictory emotions: on the one hand resignation and discouragement, the feeling that things are like that, and will never change; on the other an uneasy feeling that such a state of affairs cannot possibly last, and that something is bound to happen. However, the reasons why it could not last did not lie in France. Now as ever, the requirements of the world position which France claimed so passionately were in conflict with the imperturbable wisdom of Vimoutiers-en-Auge. The loss of French international prestige manifested at Bermuda became flagrant with the protracted presidential election at Versailles. The first reaction to this of a frustrated and exasperated national pride was that which always precedes a return to health—an outbreak of impatience with all the people who crowded solicitously round the bedside of "the sick man of Europe" and all the doctors who proffered well-meant but more or less inopportune advice. In December, 1953, when Mr. Dulles urged France at last to ratify E.D.C., failing which America would be obliged to undertake an "agonising reappraisal" of her policy, M. Claude Bourdet, a journalist who in certain respects was representative of the Parisian, if not of the national mood, came out in his weekly newspaper *l'Observateur* with the headline *C'EST CAM-BRONNE QU'IL NOUS FAUT*. No phrase could better have summed up the state of mind of the Laniel period.

Since then there has been a great change—mental even more than physical. Within a few months France passed from complete discouragement to abounding confidence, not, it is true, without danger of relapse. So great was the change that what seemed true yesterday is no longer true today, though perhaps it may be true again tomorrow. That is another reason for not retouching a picture drawn before the pendulum started swinging. Caution alone imposes such restraint, for it is difficult to paint a portrait of a body in motion. Since the summer of 1953, under two successive Governments armed with full economic powers, there have been avalanches of reform decrees, and innovations which had been waiting for years in the files of the economic and financial Ministries have been produced in bulk. All this has resulted, not in a coherent system of reform, but in a thousand detailed retouches, including such diverse fields as administrative formalities, the taxation system, the national alcohol administration, superannuation funds, architects' fees, and the administration of the Halles. Not only would it be difficult to draw up an inventory of all these fragmentary reforms and to measure their impact; but who would dare at this stage to prophesy which of all these innumerable items will be put into practice, and which will share the fate of so many others which have been solemnly voted, decreed, and publicly proclaimed during the last half-century and have remained a dead letter? In all this bustle, however, the basic social and economic structures have been scarcely affected; and, to the extent that they have been affected, it has been the result, not of decrees, but of the new sap which during the last ten years has been rising in the old French tree.

It was actually the contrast between the surface immobility and a deep sense of renewed vigour which made the Laniel Government appear in the eyes of public opinion to be the very incarnation of impotence, and caused even its most indisputable merits to be unrecognised. In the political field, and above all in foreign affairs, the Laniel period was one of indecision and almost of abdication, but in the economic field it lacked neither effectiveness nor luck, and it left its successors a better and healthier situation than had been enjoyed by any Government since the liberation. The long crises which preceded M. Laniel's accession to office resembled all the other Government crises from which France had suffered for so many years, except that it was worse. The Treasury was bare and incapable of meeting its obligations, the Prime Minister was appealing to Washington, to the European Payments Union, and to the Bank of France for aid, credits, and moratoriums, desperately stopping one gap while opening another, the pilot of a ship which seemed to be leaking everywhere. The brief crisis caused by the fall of the Laniel Government was accompanied by none of these anxieties. The Treasury was solvent, gold and foreign exchange reserves were adequate, the Bourse confident; in fact all the financial questions which yesterday had been insoluble had vanished as if by magic, and Parliament at long last found time to turn its attention to other and graver matters which were falling due.

Was it a miracle? Economics hardly lend themselves to miracles, though in France more than elsewhere they are subject to the influence of psychological factors about which there is always a touch of magic. In fact, however, the influence of long-term developments was beginning to make itself felt. The big re-equipment and modernisation drive of the post-war years was beginning to bear fruit, and the spirit of modernisation was beginning to spread from the reconstructed key industries to the more somnolent consumer-goods industries. Also, as the foreseeable future always forms part of the present, the French post-war "demographic revolution" has made itself felt well in advance. The prospect of the new and more numerous generations who have not yet left, or even reached, their school desks has already put a question mark against the permanence of structures which have been immobile for so long and were so well adapted to a country whose population was shrinking and whose needs were static; and the "school crisis"—not the quarrel about "lay" v. "clerical" schools, but the grave inadequacy of school accommodation—is a premonitory sign of this crisis of growth. These are the forces of a slow, organic regeneration which, in spite of all the vicissitudes of the post-war period, have been at work beneath the stagnant surface.

For the first time a favourable environment exists for these factors of growth and regeneration. The "Pinay stabilisation" was paid for by a year of stagnation which was also, at any rate in part, a year of reorganisation. But it created the conditions for the first healthy, *i.e.*, non-inflationary, expansion which France has known since the last war, and perhaps since the one before last. It would probably have been too fragile to stand up to the slightest panic, the slightest shock in the international situation. But all over the world the temperature had dropped. While world prices fell, French prices, though they refused to decline from the heights reached during the last inflationary wave, at any rate ceased to climb. Speculation on the next war and the apocalypse came to an end, not only in France. But in France, where prospects of war had not stimulated effort, but discouraged or corrupted it, relaxation of the cold war did not, as elsewhere, mark the end of a boom, but the end of a paralysis. In France, as elsewhere, people resumed calculating in real values and for the long term, and many things returned to order because of that alone. Productive work and healthy investment returned to favour wherever the law, corporate regulations and customs, and the state, with its misguided redistributive system, did not stand in the way.

The most striking outward sign of this change was the drop in the price of gold. This had begun on the world market since 1951, but on the highly speculative French market it did not exercise its full effect until the autumn of 1953. In 1952, when the Pinay Government floated a loan guaranteed against "all risks", not only against depreciation of the franc, but against depreciation of gold in relation to the franc, the French public hardly took the latter eventuality seriously. But now for the first time buried gold and the sterile possession of foreign exchange turned out to be bad business; and for the first time it was clear that it would have been more advantageous to invest one's money in almost any other way. To the French saver, whose whole outlook had been distorted by forty years of inflation, this meant no less than a revolution. The sole explanation of the new solvency of the

Treasury is the return of monetary circulation to the surface of the banking system, into which the state can dip with an ease which in turn is not without its dangers. There no longer seems to be anything threatening about the deficit, which goes on increasing, and the public, without wishing to look further, merely notices with relief that the period of alarm is over, and that the barometer has returned to set fair.

The degree of responsibility for this favourable turn of events to be attributed to the economic policy of the Laniel-Edgar Faure Government is hard to estimate. It was no less eclectic and no less at the mercy of converging or conflicting sectional interests than its predecessors, and these various pressures were more unconcealed than ever. But it had the good fortune of being able to swim with the stream instead of having to fight against it, and it succeeded in energetically and consistently utilising and encouraging the trend. It set out on a policy of systematic expansion, and, thanks to the change of tide, it was able to make a number of bold steps which would have been impossible or fatal to its predecessors. Budgetary orthodoxy had ceased to be the great preoccupation. Healthy and non-inflationary expansion is a very relative term. The French economy, stabilised in its inflationary distortions, is on a basis as artificial as ever. All the structural causes of inflation, from the hypertrophy of the commercial sectors and the multiplication of profit margins over and above production costs to the deficit of nearly a billion francs accumulated by the state, persist in hardly attenuated form; but such stimulus has become a normal and permanent necessity to this hothouse economy.

The economic policy of the Laniel Government was, however, by no means confined to the preservation of existing structures. Its fundamental aim and ambition could be summed up as the desire to turn France into a capitalist country in the western sense of the word. In particular, by a fiscal policy systematically favouring both the concentration of enterprises and their modernisation and specialisation, it accentuated a trend already evident in the industrial sectors of the economy, not without simultaneously aggravating the disequilibrium between "advanced" and "backward" France, the demarcation line between which can be approximately shown on the map by drawing a line from Brest to Geneva. There is no doubt that this policy has tended, and tended successfully, in the direction of putting France "on the map" of the modern world. But there is something strangely contradictory in the effort to turn France into a competitive industrial society by manipulation of the fiscal system and reconversion supervised and partly financed by the state while at the same time carefully refraining from exposing it to competition. The great prospect of the "integration" period, the prospect of freeing the European exchanges and progressively establishing a great common market, could no longer be envisaged, either as an attainable aim or as a method of revitalising the French economy. The experiment has been conducted in a sealed chamber, sheltered by exchange control and artificial exchange rates, by extreme protectionism under which quotas are replaced by entry dues superimposed upon customs duties which have turned the cautious and always revocable increases in the percentages of trade liberalisation into nothing but a conjuring trick; and these dues, killing two birds with one stone, are used to pay export subsidies, thus simultaneously making possible the maintenance of high prices on the protected home market while selling at lower prices abroad at the expense of the French consumer; and the whole of this precarious equilibrium continues to depend partly on American aid which, maintained under various headings at a level of a thousand million dollars a year, stops the gap in the balance of payments; and partly on the tolerance of France's European partners, who open their markets to French exports without reciprocity.

It would be imprudent to try to prejudge either the duration or the outcome of this experiment, the results of which are obvious, but limited; and even assuming that France could lastingly dissociate her fate from that of a Europe ground between the great economic *blocs*, it is doubtful whether, relying on her own resources alone, it is possible for her to extricate herself from the vicious circles of her protectionist economy and resolve her fundamental problems: those of restoring life and movement to her anaemic south, providing her agriculture with a healthy market outlet, and putting her African empire to good use while there is still time.

These autarkic reforms are like an ingenious effort to improve the atmosphere of a close room by all the refinements and resources of air-conditioning—doing everything, in fact, except opening the windows; and if the official attitude is that it is the intention to open the windows wide on the day when the temperature, composition, and movement of the atmosphere are exactly the same inside and out, there is no reason to suppose that this happy result will ever be attained. Apart from the successful resistance of vested interests and protectionist habits, there is in all this an ingrained mistrust of the natural play of forces of a free economy, and a profound conviction that it is better to produce synthetically, as in a laboratory, the theoretical conditions of a competitive market than to risk the shocks and hazards of real competition; in short, that the "blind" choice of a free market is necessarily always inferior to the more perspicacious choice of the Ministry of Finance. If at the base there is the enormous force of resistance of *situations acquises*, at the summit there is a lively mathematical intelligence nurtured on Keynesian theories, looking a little lost and out of place in the France of 1954, which is so unlike Britain of the slump years. In the last resort, however, this synthetic capitalism with which it is desired to endow France is completely in the tradition of the French mercantilism which was inherited from the *ancien régime* and consists of protectionism and enlightened state intervention.

However, it was not in the economic or domestic field that the crisis was brewing; the trouble came from outside France. What came to grief in the spring of 1954 was a foreign policy of power and prestige for which any real basis was lacking, a policy based on borrowed resources and a juridical scaffolding that was more ingenious than solid. The principle of the policy represented by M. Bidault was that France was a world Power with important European, Atlantic, African, and Asian interests and prerogatives on all of which she insisted, preferring to risk losing them all rather than abandon any single one. Perhaps more than in Europe or in Africa this policy showed what it was capable of in relation to the Government of Viet Nam, with whom the Quai d'Orsay, after the French débâcle, was still haggling over the grant of those attributes of sovereignty which, had they been granted in time, might have permitted it to face Viet-minh nationalism on equal terms instead of being branded as a "colonial puppet Government"; and it was perfectly in harmony with the logic of such a policy that France, having never known how to make the necessary concessions to her chosen partners, was finally forced to grant them to the enemy whom she was fighting. In every field and in every latitude it was the policy which in the case of Germany Léon Blum had once called that of taking the shadow for the substance.

In France this policy was most unfairly criticised as being one of subservience to America. It could just as well have been argued that it was an audacious attempt to conduct at American expense a system of power politics which was beyond French strength and resources. To an extent that went generally unperceived, because it seemed so natural, American foreign policy, and with it that of the whole Atlantic alliance, were taken in tow by French diplomacy, not only in Europe, where practically nothing was done except at French initiative, but also in North Africa, in connection with which the United States sacrificed to true or false French interests its Arab policy and its traditional "anti-colonialism", as well as in Indo-China, where it paid the expenses of a war neither the political conduct nor the military strategy of which suited it; and the recompense for which the United States vainly and impatiently waited was, paradoxically enough, that France should at last consent to ratify the European solution to the German problem which she had herself proposed and forced upon her hesitant partners.

"Europe" still occurred in official programmes and speeches, but, after M. Bidault's return to the Quai d'Orsay, "Europe" was reduced to the military integration proposals of the European Defence Community, the almost absurd surviving fragment of a policy the wider aspects of which had been tacitly abandoned; now that the consequences that flowed from them were unacceptable and no longer even contemplated, this surviving fragment was merely a number of integrated army corps lacking either political basis or leadership. It was for the sake of the consequences rather than for the sake of the project itself, in order to use it as a lever of unification, and to prevent it from dragging down in its fall all that survived of the policy of European integration, that the French "Europeans" were condemned to support E.D.C., which was so well conceived to rally round itself every conceivable type of opposition; opposition which was of the most contradictory nature, ranging from technical criticism to ideological hostility, from doctrinaire "anti-Europeanism" to simple dislike of the revival of German armed forces, however integrated they might be. E.D.C. attracted the violent hostility of the Communists and "neutralists" to "Atlantic" policy in any form; it simultaneously attracted the opposition of the doctrinaire supporters of an all-out Atlantic policy. A simple, vague "no" to E.D.C. had the virtue of rallying impenitent pacifists, traditional militarists, French nationalists, and "Soviet nationalists", Machiavellians who sought a "reinsurance in the east", and simple, parochial conservatives; and the whole was dominated by a deafening campaign against the "rearmament of Nazi Germany" which seemed to revive all the old "popular", anti-Fascist and resistance fronts on the benches on which Communists, Gaullists, nationalists of right and left, sat as neighbours.

In the two years since this dialogue between deaf men began, the reasons for, and the very conception of, the defence community had receded into oblivion, so much so that its supporters and opponents had got to the point of making play with the same bogies and brandishing almost identical arguments for or against it. The fact of the presence of·Russian armies in the centre of Europe was forgotten, while supporters and opponents of E.D.C. competed with each other in drawing attention to the "German danger". Everyone, or nearly everyone, was "for Europe, but against the *Wehrmacht*". Some opposed E.D.C. because in their view it would revive the German army, others advocated E.D.C. because it avoided the creation of a German army. But, if the conclusion differed, the premise—that the rebirth of a German national army and German entry into N.A.T.O. must at all costs be prevented —seemed to be universally accepted, at any rate in public. On the day when the National Assembly, having rejected E.D.C., implicitly gave its approval to the acceptance of a German national army into N.A.T.O., and made it clear that it had rejected Europe but accepted a German army, those who had listened to so many speeches at public meetings must have wondered whether they had not had their legs pulled.

But in reality it was not against German but against French entry into a supra-national organisation that the upholders of French sovereignty revolted; and all the preliminary conditions, protocols, and interpretations of the Quai d'Orsay were aimed at making integration as binding as possible on Germany, while leaving France, which was to participate in it without participating, the maximum possible amount of liberty.

As the controversy dragged on it degenerated into a war of religion in which the conflicting parties opposed each in the name of the most exalted myths, those of "Europe" and "the nation". This holy warfare never succeeded in rousing the great mass of public opinion, the multitude of ordinary people, who perhaps discerned better than the doctors of international law how artificial the debate was. To the end by-elections and public opinion polls showed no hostility or even excitement at the prospect of an integrated European community, even a military community. No sign one way or the other came from the prosperous and discontented country. Supporters and opponents of E.D.C. held each other in check in Parliament, where all parties were paralysed by the question, as well as in the Government, which had lost even the appearance of ministerial solidarity or a consistent policy. The decisive shock had to come from elsewhere.

France was engaged in the most acrobatic diplomacy, involving numerous acts of dangerous tightrope walking, and the shock came from the most exposed point, where the danger was greatest: Indo-China. An armistice in Indo-China had become inevitable, and between the Bermuda and Berlin conferences M. Bidault strained every nerve to gather into his hands all the cards which would enable him to negotiate it from a "position of strength", not face to face with the enemy, but in a conference of the great Powers in which France would have behind her all the weight of the western alliance; a conference in which negotiations would take place, not on the basis of the local military situation, which was hopeless, but on that of the international balance of power. This was the supreme test of a system of power politics based on the resources of others. But in the face of the tragedy of Dien Bien Phu the great western alliance subsided into confusion; a policy based on reciprocal illusions ended in disillusion. America, disappointed in a military and political situation in Indo-China the gravity of which the French had always concealed from her, though they had presented her with the bill, withdrew from an engagement which was assuming unforeseen dimensions, and chose the comfortable path of the righteous man who has been disillusioned. Sheltering behind the British veto on direct intervention and virtuously disapproving of all negotiation with the Communists while failing to envisage any alternative to doing so, she ungraciously withdrew from the conference, leaving M. Bidault to face the eastern *bloc* alone. Never was the difference between the verbal intransigence and the practical prudence of the new Republican team in Washington more disastrously demonstrated than during these feverish weeks, when threats in Washington of a preventive war against China alternated with assurances to the electorate that the United States would in no circumstances engage in "another Korean war". Never did the so-called strategy of "massive reprisals", that lame compromise between the crusading spirit and the spirit of budgetary economy, more strikingly demonstrate its incapacity to respond to the limited reversals, the local conflicts and pin-pricks which constitute the daily fare of international politics. Reduced to the sole device of threatening apocalyptic war on every occasion, it sowed terror among America's allies and protégés without making much impression on her enemies, and finally ended in resounding inaction. The "moral crisis" of the Atlantic alliance, which had been foreseeable for some time, had begun. But, in spite of everything, the power of the United States remained the backbone of the west, and it was it alone which made possible the more elastic and flexible British diplomacy which now became France's last hope. However, in the eyes of public opinion all this meant the end of a huge bluff which might have set the world alight.

Under this shock the Laniel Government, which was at the

end of its tether and was torn between "defeatists" and "bitter-enders" so far as the Indo-China war was concerned, just as earlier it had been torn between supporters and opponents of E.D.C., disintegrated in an atmosphere of public contempt, aggravating its weaknesses by gratuitous acts of authority. The tragi-comedy of the Russian ballet, the widely advertised insubordination of Marshal Juin, the incidents at the Etoile, all created an atmosphere of crisis. With a disintegrating Government and an Assembly which granted it shorter and shorter respites behind him, M. Bidault, faced with a Geneva conference which threatened to disperse without results, went on struggling with the courage of despair, and the armistice which was to be signed a month later was well on the way. But to the combined opposition of right and left, which was joined by all the disappointed, the anxious, and the indignant from the Government camp, this was an irresistible opportunity to get rid at one blow, not only of this Cabinet, but of a whole gerontocracy, and to put an end to seven years of centre government and ten years of M.R.P. control of foreign and imperial affairs. M. Mendès-France's political criticisms had previously always been on a technical level, but on the day after a violent speech by Mr. Molotov, in which the Russian Foreign Minister clearly indicated his desire for a change of interlocutor, M. Mendès-France, the virtual leader of the opposition, entered the fray to deliver the *coup-de-grâce*. This was the end; and if the combined opposition which brought it about, with its double centre of gravity—Communist and Gaullist—was too anomalous to devise an alternative policy, it was adequate for the appointment of the committee of liquidators which it had refused to appoint a year before. The "continuity of French policy" had tied itself into a Gordian knot which it had become necessary to cut.

It was much less than a revolution, but much more than a government crisis of the usual type. A moment of complete confusion, characterised almost by *coup d'état* conditions, enabled a *fronde* of technicians and "realist" journalists to rely on all the Government's opponents at once to shake the phalanx of irremovable personalities, to break up sacrosanct routines, and to carry their leader into power, to the accompaniment of a wave of almost messianic publicity. This Government's chief characteristic was that—leaving aside the brief, interim Cabinet of Léon Blum—for the first time since General de Gaulle's resignation it was not a parliamentary Government, but the Government of one man, aided by his personal "brains trust"; it lacked a clearly defined parliamentary opposition, and made its way with varying majorities depending on the questions at issue, and with a permanently provisional Cabinet depending on the fluctuations of that majority. Its second characteristic, which was in harmony, not only with the character of its leader and his team, but with the conditions in which his power was exercised, was rapidity of action. It was only by continually advancing, vaulting over obstacles, using speed to outwit the ponderous machinery of the parties, which was always preparing an assault upon a point which had already been left behind, and by concentrating attention on one question at a time in order to dispose of it immediately—in official language opening one file at a time in order to dispose of it immediately—that it was possible to prevent its opponents, who differed on every question just as its supporters did, from combining. In short, it was only by frantic speed that this Government could maintain itself and prolong its career from one hazard to the next.

But perhaps its most striking feature was the novel and very American style of its propaganda, even the details of which were inspired by President Roosevelt's New Deal. France, the most centralised state in the west, puts at the disposal of its Governments powerful instruments for influencing public opinion, from the wireless to the Government-controlled Alliance France Presse, which is the sole source of information for the majority of newspapers. The effective use of these, however, as of the enormous state apparatus of the "old monarchy", is normally held in check by the mutual jealousy of parties and groups. Now, however, these instruments were given full scope, providing the Government with extra-parliamentary support more dependable than that of the parties, associating public opinion with Government decisions, amplifying successes with an assurance and an optimism which made a clean break with the melancholy silence of its predecessors, and gave the country the feeling that at last it had a Government, and that at last "something was being done".

All the various groups opposed to *immobilisme* had gathered round M. Mendès-France because he was, properly speaking, not a politician, and because his own opposition had always been on the technical and financial level. In the eyes of a public opinion which had belatedly discovered the consequences of the mistakes in monetary policy committed immediately after the liberation, he had become the man who in 1945 had been right, and, to the universal misfortune, had not been listened to; and a whole myth had grown up round that now remote decision, the details of which have incidentally never been cleared up. Since that time the criticisms of Government policy made by the man who came to be known as the "French Stafford Cripps" had always, so to speak, been those of an accountant. What does it cost? he asked. Can we afford it? His perpetual criticism of the policy of strength in Indo-China and Africa, his opposition to a policy of *grandeur* on credit, to inherently unproductive military expenditure, had never been on other lines. As a potential Prime Minister he fulfilled in one definite and important respect an essential condition that had also been fulfilled by M. Laniel: during the two years in which E.D.C. had been the centre of controversy he had never taken up a definite position towards it. It was a subject which did not interest him; the idea and the ideology behind it were alien to his realistic mind.

He came forward in the first place as the promoter of domestic economic and social reform, a French "New Deal", and it was in that capacity that he was greeted upon his accession to power by French and international public opinion. Also his close analysis of the distortions and scleroses of the French economy after decades of inflation and protectionism was fundamentally the same as that of the French liberals and "Europeans". It was with his practical conclusions—which were far less precise and concrete than his criticisms—that they differed. Where the latter saw salvation in a market enlarged to the size of Europe, M. Mendès-France and his group of national reformers insisted that this economy must be put in order within its established framework before it could face a free market. This was clearly not a matter of irreconcilable opposition between two mutually exclusive views, but rather a matter of preferences and priorities. But in practice, and particularly in the existing political context, the "question of method" was decisive, and it explains, at any rate in part, the benevolent neutrality, which at first sight seems surprising, of the groups of economic interests in regard to the "national economic revolution" of which M. Mendès-France made himself the standard-bearer and which invited them to convert, and even to reconvert, themselves, but at the same time reassured them by preserving their protectionist shield intact.

Moreover, in this sense the "New Deal" had already been in force under M. Laniel, and the economic policy which had been the most acceptable aspect of the last Government's period of office has continued without any notable change, with the same incumbent, M. Edgar Faure, at the Finance Ministry. M. Mendès-France, plunged into the midst of immediate political and international necessities, scarcely had time "to open the economic file", and the general trend remained unaltered, even if the Prime Minister was responsible for inspiring certain improvements in the publicity given to economic policy, and for the greater emphasis now put on its social and human side, including the campaign against alcoholism and the free distribution of milk to school children. The doctor, called in late, found the patient in good economic health, but suffering from grave juridical anxieties, and without hesitation he transformed himself into a legal adviser. Vital decisions were pending concerning Indo-China, North Africa, and Europe, and M. Mendès-France installed himself, not in the Finance Ministry, but at the Quai d'Orsay, to attack in a new and realistic spirit problems which had been steeped in a false continuity.

It would be idle to recall the dazzling succession of lightning conferences and throws in which M. Mendès-France indulged. He won his first audacious gamble, that he would secure peace in Indo-China within a month, thus ensuring the survival of his Government and assuring himself of immense popularity. At that moment nobody, not even the chagrined "old men" who had been displaced, desired to look too closely at the conditions of this liquidation, which had been delayed too long. Only the Viet Nam Government, abandoned by everybody, raised an impotent protest against agreements which left it more or less in the position of the Czechoslovak Government on the day after Munich. There had been only too much delay in Asia; within a few weeks the old trading stations in India, the last remnants of the empire of Dupleix, were evacuated in turn.

Before the world had recovered its breath the second stroke followed: the Prime Minister's lightning visit to Tunis, solemnly resuming the Franco-Tunisian dialogue which had been interrupted for more than two years and proclaiming anew, and practically in the terms once used by M. Schuman, the French intention to grant "internal sovereignty" to Tunis, in short resuming after three wasted years the experiment of 1950. The masterly feature of the psychological shock tactics on this occasion was that M. Mendès-France took Marshal Juin with him to Tunis. The marshal's views on colonial policy had probably not changed since the days of his proconsulate in Morocco and his patronage of the feudal plot against its Sultan, but not long before he had rallied violently, if late, to the anti-E.D.C. camp, and he had accounts to settle with M. Laniel and M. Bidault. This unexpected combination was perhaps the most outstanding example of a brilliantly acrobatic policy which made the utmost use of a given situation and gained striking immediate successes at the risk of infinite future complications.

The next task was to open the third file and to emerge somehow or another unscathed from the European imbroglio. It is still too early for a proper description of this great drama of many plots, which transformed the Palais Bourbon and the chanceries of Europe into agitated ant-heaps. If it is true to say that the attitude of the French Government and its leader was, so to speak, equivocal without equivocation, it was by that very fact a reflection of the National Assembly and of the parties. True, M. Mendès-France buried E.D.C. with an indifference which was shocking enough to the five European states which had subscribed to this French project; four of them had ratified it after long and violent internal debates, and one or two of them had actually had to alter their constitutions in order to conform with it. But it was not M. Mendès-France who killed it, and the grave-digger's function is a function of public health. Some way out had to be found, and the situation was one from which it was probably impossible to extricate oneself with elegance. But the Assembly, in purely and simply removing E.D.C. from its order of the day in order to go on holiday next day without even suggesting an alternative,' made no political decision. It simply abdicated. The negative majority which did this was provided by a hundred Communists who stood for no French cause, and by almost the same number of ex-Gaullists; nobody knew what cause they stood for. This majority suggested no alternative to the project which it had voted to destroy. Instead a kind of *carte blanche* to repair the damage was left to the Prime Minister and to the allied Governments.

But at any rate France, and with her the west, had emerged from the *impasse,* even if it was in a retrograde manner, and an open check was preferable to a state of indecision which threatened to last for ever. In view of the double bankruptcy, both French and American, Sir Anthony Eden assumed the initiative, as he had done in the darkest days of the Geneva conference, and the abandoned French solution was replaced by a British solution, to which Britain held the key. In two months, after another astonishing sequence of diplomatic journeys and conferences, plans were laid for a new European and Atlantic edifice. The new plan showed evidence of hasty improvisation; false windows and blanks were left in it, but the structure as a whole was sound, and, after the dismay and confusion which followed the rejection of E.D.C., there was good reason to proclaim the rapid successes of London and Paris as a miracle. The new arrangements provided in essence for the entry into N.A.T.O. of Germany with an autonomous army, which was precisely what the French Parliament had vetoed for four whole years. What remained of the powers of integration which the E.D.C. treaty had reserved to the European defence commission now devolved upon the American general commanding the Atlantic forces in Europe—which was the logical outcome of the maintenance of European sovereignties. The remnants of the repudiated European community were represented by the "regional grouping" of the resuscitated Brussels pact. This had been originally intended to be an alliance against Germany, but it was transformed into an alliance including Germany and Italy; and it was the British decision to give an undertaking, more formal than it had given in relation to E.D.C., to put its forces stationed on the continent at the disposal of this regional grouping which finally made the whole agreement possible. By this fact the "little Europe" of six nations was turned into a "big Europe" of seven nations, with the British participation on which the "anti-Carolingians" had always insisted; and the price of British participation was what it had always been for all the *Europes cordiales* which had been still-born before 1950. As the agreement on this point has not been concluded, it is still too early to foresee what the organisms of the Brussels pact, which is being turned into Western European Union, will acquire in the way of real authority, but it is clear that this authority will be strictly limited to the continental field, *i.e.*, to the six nations of the former E.D.C. It is already evident that Britain is only reluctantly accepting participation in the exercise of simple powers of inspection and checking, but not in submitting to them.

If this "Europe" of seven nations were to develop and outgrow the framework of a simple alliance between sovereign states, it is clear that it would once more first have to contract into the "little Europe" of six nations, with the additional complication of a seventh honorary member keeping an eye on the others, but without assuming their obligations. That is not to say that British participation is without significance. For British diplomacy it creates a situation in which it is a mediator both between Europe and America and between the European nations themselves; and, in the eyes of many politicians in Europe, this tutelary presence, though one day perhaps it may irritate them, for the time being calms apprehensions about any "exaggerated" European adventure. But this implies that the continental "little Europe" is, after all, not a gratuitous invention of Carolingian ideologists, but is and remains the kernel of a possible Europe which will be re-formed when European unification returns to the order of the day. For the time being it is well and truly buried; even its definite achievements, such as the Coal and Steel Community, are compromised, and it is more than doubtful whether they are still capable of serving as springboards for a new start. But the factors which led in the direction of European integration have not disappeared; they may change in form and intensity with the fluctuations of the cold war and the cold peace, they may be disputed or neglected, but in no circumstances can a fragmented Europe regain equilibrium or acquire a future. The gravest eventuality would be that France, in making a definite return to the traditional concept of national *Realpolitik,* would by so doing cause Germany to do the same; and a return by Germany to a purely nationalist outlook would involve the reconquest of the national framework which has been destroyed. For Germany the idea of the national state is now either chimerical or irredentist, and in renewing the links with her history which she wished to outgrow she would find herself once more faced with all the temptations and dangers to which a "nation between the fronts" is exposed. The European problem is still posed by Germany. The "liquidation of Franco-German contention" to which M. Mendès-France and Herr Adenauer addressed themselves on the margin of the Paris conference, apart from an ambiguous and provisional settlement of the Saar question, half way between "Europeanisation" and a return to the statute of Versailles, resulted only in some ideas as general as they were generous, and it must be hoped that they will bear better fruit than their predecessors of the interwar period.

The armistice in Indo-China, the resumption of the Tunisian conversations, the London and Paris agreements, the Saar compromise, constitute a rich harvest, and "the Mendès-France experiment" will mark a date, if not a turning-point, in French post-war history. After this demonstration of dynamism it will be difficult to return to certain habits of procrastination and *immobilisme*. But there can be no government by surprise without a certain element of illusion; and illusion is bound sooner or later to involve disillusion, often unfair, but nevertheless inevitable. In politics "there are no solutions"; problems and conflicts do not wait for the file concerning them to be opened, and do not disappear when the file is put away. Four months after the armistice in Indo-China the Prime Minister was negotiating in Washington the amount and the conditions of American aid for Viet Nam. Three months after the psychological shock in Tunis the deterioration in the situation in the North African protectorates became accentuated, and troubles reached Algeria for the first time. After the vacation the parliamentary régime resumed its rights all the more freely by reason of the fact that the necessary liquidations had been carried out, the European community had been discarded, the Atlantic alliance reaffirmed, and the obstructions removed. A breach had to be made in a continuity which no longer consisted in anything but clinging without enthusiasm and even without conviction to outworn formulas in order to avoid having to make a choice; and the danger is, not that the breach was too violent, but that it was not violent enough, and that it was not a breach implying boldness or the birth of a new spirit. But the series of resounding acts, and above all the exasperated "no" of August 30th, 1954, perhaps served to free France from a strange impotence complex, from an obsessive feeling of humiliation, which caused her to believe that she was invariably the sacrificed ally, the junior partner, that she had been betrayed, sold, subjected to tutelage, and delivered over to the sinister plans of Washington, Bonn, and the Vatican. What value would there have been in a "yes" which expressed nothing but resignation at no longer having the power to say no? Perhaps there are situations in the life of nations as there are in the life of individuals when accumulated disappointment and frustration must burst out before it is possible to overcome them and make a new start. *C'est Cambronne qu'il nous faut!* There was something of this in the gesture of August 30th, 1954, that triumph of General Aumeran won in an atmosphere of bravado and defiance of the world and of the century. In that sense it was an act of liberation, and it seems that since that time the climate has miraculously become healthier, that argument has become less heated, that the prevailing co-existentialism has been transformed into Atlantic realism. . . . But for how long? And who would have foreseen such a thing in the tumult of the certainly historic but extremely unedifying session in which E.D.C. was buried? But also who would have foreseen nearly a century and a half ago that the unprintable *mot de Cambronne* would reconcile France to the memory of Waterloo, to the extent of making it a popular and almost likeable episode?

December, 1954.

INDEX

Académie Française, 18, 38, 48, 68–70, 269
Action Française, 35–7, 437
Adenauer, Dr., 375, 381–2, 386, 389, 407, 411, 415, 425, 427, 467
Administration, development of, 6–27
Africa, French North, 235–54; and v. Algeria, Morocco and Tunisia
Africa, French West, 215; and v. Madagascar
Agriculture, 329, 366
Algeria, 56, 99–101, 203, 206, 213, 215, 220–4, 235–9, 243–54
"Algerian Manifesto", 243–5, 248, 250, 254
Anouilh, Jean, 71
Arab League, 266
Aragon, Louis, 88, 432–3
Atlantic Alliance, 134, 397, 468; and v. N.A.T.O.
Atlantic Charter, 226
Atlantic Council, 395
Atlantic Pact, 355–7, 359, 372, 383, 420
Aumeran, General, 423, 468
Auriol, Vincent, 163–4, 297, 448

Baillis, 10
Bainville, Jacques, 10, 420
Balzac, 65, 73
Bank of France, 25, 188, 295, 319, 451
Bao-Dai, Emperor, 208, 232–3
Beaumanoir, 8
Benelux, 355, 361, 373
Bérard, Léon, 411
Berlin blockade, 351, 355
Bernanos, Georges, 81, 430

Bevin, E., 353, 360–3, 368, 370, 384
Bidault, Georges, 111, 113, 121, 124, 133, 181, 184, 340, 342, 344, 348–349, 351, 353, 360–1, 363, 367–8, 370, 383–4, 387, 410, 412–14, 456, 458, 460, 464
Bismarck, 426–7
Black, Eugene, 330–1
Black Market, 316–18
Bloch, Marc, 90–4, 412
Blum, Léon, 82, 89, 117, 123, 132, 140–3, 246, 293, 313–14, 341–2, 345, 432, 456, 461
Boissy d'Anglas, 219–20
Bonnet, Georges, 86, 411
Bonte, M., 84
Bourbons, 4, 35
Bourdet, Claude, 449
Brazza, 213
Brazzaville Conference, 218
Britain, 84, 175, 204, 219, 226, 230, 245, 279, 286, 313, 326, 337–8, 349, 352, 355, 362–3, 368, 370, 373, 384, 413, 455, 465–6
Brüning, 379
Building industry, 304–11, 314, 333
Byrnes, J. F., 345

Cachin, Marcel, 31, 88
Caillaux, Joseph, 48
Caillé, René, 211
Cambon, Paul, 279
Camus, Albert, 444–7
Canada, 352
Capets, 4, 6, 10, 16, 28
Carolingians, 11, 124
Centralisation, 39, 50
C.G.T., 87, 107, 121, 126–8, 138, 146–57

Charlemagne, 6, 28
Chiang Kai-shek, 231, 337
Chinese People's Republic, 233
Christian Social Movement, 34, 59, 113
Christian Social Party, 124
Church and Clergy, 5, 25, 33–5, 425–6, 429–30
Churchill, Sir Winston, 174, 293, 337, 361–3, 399, 405
Civil rights, 62
Civil Service, 18
Claudel, Paul, 89
Clemenceau, 31, 122
Clovis, 11, 28
Colbert, 16, 54, 209, 221, 252
Colonisation, 79, 209–16, 237–8, 244–5
Cominform, 134, 139, 146, 290
Communist Party, 31–2, 55, 80–8, 98–118, 120–1, 124–32, 134–62, 166, 170, 184, 190–1, 295, 297, 314, 317, 327, 344, 355, 377, 386, 396, 412, 417, 431–41, 460
Conseil d'État, 16, 19–20, 144
Constitutions, 43, 114–15, 119–23, 219
Coppet, M., 228
Corneille, 24
Coste-Floret, M., 208
Cot, Pierre, 220
Council of Europe, 370
Council of National Resistance, *v.* Provisional Government
Cour de cassation, 19
Courtin, René, 431
Croizat, M., 327
Crown, Powers of, 6–8
Crusades, 5, 426
Currency, 78–9, 316–19, 323, 393

Daladier, Édouard, 31, 86–7, 385, 410–12, 418
Darlan, Admiral, 101, 204
Darnand, M., 99
Daumier, 15
Déat, Marcel, 97–8
Delacroix, 29

Delfosse, M., 153
Depreux, Édouard, 222
Dien Bien Phu, 459
Doriot, M., 86, 98, 436
Dreyfus Case, 29, 38, 63, 229
Duclos, M., 129, 440
Duguet, M., 153
Dulles, John Foster, 449
Dupleix, 213, 464
Dupuy, M., 154

Eboué, Governor, 204, 217–18
Economic structure, 80–2, 286–334
E.D.C., 197, 394, 399, 404–10, 413–414, 449, 457–8, 460, 464–6
Eden, Sir A., 465
Eisenhower, General, 404
El Glaoui, 268–71
Empire, First, 19
Empire, Second, 14, 21
Épurations, 97, 107–8, 225, 317, 437
European Coal and Steel Community, 335, 387–8, 390–1, 393–5, 400–1, 404, 407–8, 413, 419, 421, 423, 427
European Payments Union, 188, 322, 364

Family structure, 50
Farge, Yves, 318
Fascism, 80–1, 106, 436–8
Faure, Edgar, 188, 453, 463
Faure, Paul, 411
Ferhat Abbas, 221, 245–6
Ferhat Hached, 278
Ferry, Jules, 207
Flandin, M., 86, 411–12
Fontaine, 8
Force Ouvrière, 150–1, 178
Foreign Legion, 216, 234
de Foucauld, Vicomte Charles, 211
Fouché, 65
Fourastié, Jean, 296
Frachon, Benoît, 145–6, 150
Francis I., 16, 425
Franco, General, 82, 86, 266
French Union, the, 203, 220, 231, 233, 250, 413
Freycinet Plan, 44

INDEX

Galtier-Boissière, M., 289
de Gasperi, Signor, 389, 414, 425
de Gaulle, General, 83, 86, 95–103, 106, 110–19, 122–3, 132, 135–9, 143, 162–8, 170–2, 176–7, 184, 191–2, 203–4, 218, 246, 291, 317, 336–42, 346, 348–9, 361, 382–3, 386, 393, 405–6, 412, 418, 438, 461
German Federal Republic, 369, 372, 379–80, 386, 406, 411, 414–15, 467
Germany, 10, 51, 82–6, 92–3, 111, 283–4, 288, 338–42, 344, 347, 351–2, 354, 376, 378
Gestapo, 37, 339
Gide, André, 71
Gingembre, M., 187, 301, 311, 315, 438
Giraud, General, 101, 204
Giraudoux, Jean, 71
Goebbels, 89, 136
Grandval, Gilbert, 346
Guillaume, General, 269
Guyot, Yves, 65

Habib Bourguiba, 244
Hapsburgs, 12, 93, 426
de Hautecloque, M., 274
de Hauteville, M., 208, 273
Héneff, M., 127
Henry IV, 28, 425
Herriot, Édouard, 84, 114, 140–1, 165–6, 411, 448
Hitler, 82–5, 89, 98, 128, 136, 335, 376, 379, 411
Hoarding of wealth, 321, 323
Ho Chi-minh, 231–3, 244
Hohenzollerns, 93
Holy Roman Empire, 10, 424–7
Hours, Joseph, 387, 424–7, 430
Hugo, Victor, 71

Individualism, 57, 59, 73–4, 324, 332
Inflation, 315–34
Indo-China, 197, 207, 211, 215–16, 225–6, 230–4, 455, 458–60, 463, 467–8

Industrial development, 25, 73–4, 77–8, 299
Industrial profits, 178
International Monetary Fund, 144
Islam, 239–43
Isorni, Maître, 411
Istiqlal, 244, 259, 262–3, 266, 268–270
Italy, 339, 352, 355, 414

Jaurès, 140
Jefferson, Thomas, 12
Joan of Arc, 28, 425
Jouhaux, Léon, 87, 145, 150
Judicature, 17–18
Juin, Marshal, 256, 268–9, 460, 464

Kemal Ataturk, 243, 250
de Kleist, Henri, 61
Koenig, General, 346
Koestler, Arthur, 130
Korea, 186, 230, 357, 395–6, 399, 459

Labonne, Eirik, 256, 262
Lacoste, Robert, 419
Lamennais, 430
Lamoricière, General, 238
Laniel, Joseph, 201–2, 272, 449–51, 453, 459, 462–4
Laval, Pierre, 99, 108
Lecœur, Auguste, 153, 156
Legal system, 7–9, 15, 18
Legion of Honour, 40
Lend-Lease, 353
Lenin, 433
Le Nôtre, 14
Letourneau, M., 208
Le Troquer, André, 101, 222
Liberation, the, 105 et seq.
Lippmann, Walter, 353
Literature, 72–3; and v. Académie Française
Louis XIII, 16
Louis XIV, 9, 11, 93, 205, 212
Louis XVI, 212, 318
Louis XVIII, 93
Lyautey, Governor, 213, 216, 256, 263–6, 279

474 INDEX

Madagascar, 225-30
Maginot Line, 46, 78
Malraux, André, 171, 446
Mangin, General, 216
Marivaux, 29
Marchand, 213
Marshall Plan, 133-4, 145, 168, 176, 181, 185, 195-6, 293, 295-6, 321-322, 328, 330, 353-4, 356, 359-60, 362, 364, 374, 383, 391, 420; and v. U.S. credits
Marx, 286-7, 439, 441
Mauriac, François, 36, 269
Maurras, Charles, 35-8, 432
Mayer, Daniel, 143
Mayer, René, 143-5, 161-2, 182, 189, 432
de Medici, Catherine, 28
Mendès-France, M., 109, 313, 317, 460, 462-7
Mers-el-Kébir, 204, 336
Messali Hadj, 244, 248, 251
Ministerial patronage, 39-40
Moch, Jules, 143-5, 152, 182-3, 386, 395, 412, 432
Mollet, Guy, 386, 440
Molotov, 84, 133, 353-4, 460
Monmousseau, M., 127, 432
Monnet, Jean, 185, 291-5, 301, 314-315, 335, 385, 393, 420, 431
Monnet Plan, 290-8, 328, 330-1, 430
Montesquieu, 53
Montherlant, H. de, 71
Morgenthau, Mr., 339
Morocco, 211, 215-16, 229, 235, 252, 255-73, 464
Moscow Conference, 343, 349-50, 374
M.R.P., 59, 113, 116, 120, 123, 128, 138, 160, 166, 178-9, 181, 194, 327, 410, 425, 460

Napoleon III, 19, 212
Napoleonic Code, 62
National Assembly, 16, 123, 163, 172, 187
National Debt, 195

National income, 21, 161, 318, 324
Nationalisation, 26, 56, 155, 325, 391
N.A.T.O., 156, 290, 372, 405, 413, 418, 422, 457, 465
Neo-Destour, 243-4, 274-5
Nizan, Paul, 88
North African landing, 204

O.E.E.C., 314, 364, 370, 372, 384
Oradour, 208, 388

Panama scandal, 80, 208
Paris, natural capital, 6
Paris, position and influence, 13, 20
Paris Commune, 29, 33, 171
Paris Conference, 354, 369, 467
Paris *Halles*, 21-4, 66, 110, 304
Parodi, M., 102
Pascal, 24
Paul, Marcel, 153
Péguy, Charles, 430
Périllier, M., 274
Pétain, Marshal, 38, 86, 89, 94, 96, 108, 128, 171, 191, 204, 289, 293, 411
Petit, Claudius, 307
Petsche, M., 180
Philip I, 5-7
Philip II, 7-8, 15
Philip, André, 431
Piétri, François, 411
Pigneau de Behaine, Bishop, 211-12
Pinay, Antoine, 165, 189-95, 200, 452
Pleven, René, 218, 400, 423
Pleven Plan, 399
Poincaré, Raymond, 33
Poland, 341
Police methods, 62-5, 68
Population, 21, 77, 300, 327-8
Popular Front, 26, 46, 81, 87, 166, 174, 181
Potsdam Agreement, 341, 398
Provisional Government of the French Republic, 95-103, 109, 111-12, 119, 326, 341

Queuille, Henri, 165–71, 177, 179, 182, 184, 351, 355–6

Racine, 24
Radical Party, 166, 194
Radical Socialist Party, 166
Ramadier, Paul, 130, 132, 138–41, 155, 412
Republic, Fourth, 17, 26, 30, 38, 59, 95, 119, 123–4, 137, 153, 159, 169, 177, 187, 192, 220, 301, 306–307, 326, 330
Republic, Second, 30
Republic, Third, 14–15, 17, 30, 38, 42, 45, 83, 96–7, 124, 165, 177, 214, 295, 305, 327, 441
Revolution, French, 12–13, 24, 30, 50, 60, 81
Reynaud, Paul, 140, 143, 172–7, 182–3, 188–9, 193, 357, 431
de Rhodes, Alexandre, 211
Ribbentrop, 84
Richelieu, 65, 93, 111, 209, 342, 352
Robespierre, 60, 432, 440
Rochefort, Henri, 207
Roches, Léon, 211
Roosevelt (F. D.), Mr., 338, 461
de la Roque, Colonel, 437
R.P.F., 135, 138, 172–3, 184, 187, 190, 386
Ruhr, 133, 296, 339–40, 342, 349, 383, 407

Saadane, Hadj Ahmed, 222–4, 245
Saar, 344–9, 379–80, 382–3, 388, 391, 467
Saint-Just, 174–5
Salleron, Louis, 409
San Francisco Charter, 226
Sartre, Jean-Paul, 71, 435, 439–46
Sauckel, 99
Schools question, 187
Schumacher, Dr., 379, 385–6, 402, 405–6, 411, 427
Schuman Plan, 185, 253, 382–5, 390–5, 399–400, 407, 430

Schuman, Robert, 134, 142–4, 161, 208, 253, 274, 280, 335, 351, 368, 374–5, 379–80, 383, 385, 387, 389, 395, 401, 407, 410–13, 424–5, 430, 432, 464
Senate, 18, 43
Sforza, Count, 373
Sidi Mohammed, Sultan, 256, 262–264, 266–72, 464
Siegfried, André, 200
Smuts, General, 336, 340
Social Insurance, 326
Social Organisation, 58, 326–8
Spain, 82, 339, 426
Stalin, 84–5, 98, 344, 419, 433
State loans, 193, 317, 329
States-General, 29, 112
Stavisky scandal, 80
Strikes, 131, 146–9, 152–3, 325–6, 350
Syria, 226

Taittinger, M., 411
Tax systems, 55
Taxes, exemptions and evasion, 44–45, 287, 312, 321
Taxes, Inspectorate of, 17
Tenants' protection, 45
Thierry d'Argenlieu, M., 231
"Third Force", 162
Thorez, Maurice, 31, 83, 86, 104, 112, 117, 132, 148, 153, 158, 167, 191, 412, 418
Trotsky, 128
Tunisia, 197, 207, 229, 235, 243–4, 255, 273–82, 464, 467
"Two Hundred Families, the", 43–44, 80

Union of Independents, 172–3, 177
United Nations, the, 105, 203, 208, 279
U.S. credits, 130, 195, 197, 322, 360, 365, 422, 454, 468; and *v.* Marshall Plan
U.S.S.R., 84, 99, 111, 114, 134, 158, 175, 226, 233, 245, 341–5, 354, 358

Valéry, Paul, 51–3, 76, 356, 422
Van Co, M., 208
Vansittart, Sir R., 339
Vergniaud, M., 142
Versailles Treaty, 78
Vichy, 37–8, 86–9, 94, 96, 98, 102, 107, 109, 113–14, 191–2, 288–90, 308, 316, 337, 393, 411
le Vidocq, 65
Violette, Maurice, 245–6
Viollet-le-Duc, 66
Voltaire, 4, 24, 33, 205, 440

Wages, 121, 178–9, 299–300, 313–314, 317, 319, 322, 325–6, 329
War, First World, 78
War, Second World, 90–1, 96–105, 282–3, 321
Washington Agreement, 368
Watteau, 29
West Indies, 221

Yalta Agreement, 105, 338, 344, 398